ACROSS THE PACIFIC

ACROSS THE PACIFIC

An Inner History of American–East Asian Relations

Revised Edition

Akira Iriye

Imprint Publications, Inc.
Chicago

TO THE MEMORY OF JOHN K. FAIRBANK

Published by Imprint Publications, Inc., Chicago, Illinois.

Printed in the United States of America.
96 96 94 93 92 5 4 3 2 1

Library of Congress Catalog Card Number: 92-073114
ISBN 1-879176-08-4 (Cloth)
ISBN 1-879176-07-6 (Paper)

Foreword to the Revised Edition

I am grateful for the opportunity provided by Imprint Publications to reissue *Across the Pacific* with two additional chapters. The book, first published by Harcourt, Brace & World in 1967, was an attempt to trace the often tortuous history of United States relations with the countries of East Asia by examining their mutual perceptions. Such an undertaking reflected my view that international relations could never be fully understood unless one delved into the intellectual, emotional, and psychological sources of people and their leaders in one country as they dealt with their counterparts elsewhere. Such an approach, a "cultural" perspective on international history, remains one of the ways in which I study the past.[1] I have been pleased to note that the approach has found increasing acceptance, and that *Across the Pacific* seems to have been read rather widely for a specialized book of its kind. Over the years, it has been my real personal privilege to encounter students, scholars,

[1] See my essay, "Culture," in Michael J. Hogan and Thomas G. Paterson, ed., *Explaining the History of American Foreign Relations* (New York, 1991).

officials, and others who have told me that the book has made an impact on their own thinking.

In considering the book, which has been out of print for several years, for republication, I have decided against rewriting it on the basis of recent scholarly works. These have been most impressive, both in quality and quantity, but to incorporate their findings and perspectives into this revision would have amounted to writing an entirely new book. Rather than attempting such a task, I have concluded that it would be better to keep the original 1967 version as it stood and to append to it a brief survey of developments since the 1960's. I hope the new edition will prove useful to the new generation of students and general readers in the United States, East Asia, and elsewhere.

I dedicate the new edition of this book to the memory of John K. Fairbank, my teacher and friend who graciously wrote the introduction to the first edition. Thanks to a great extent to his leadership and example, the field of U.S.–East Asian relations today is prospering not only in the United States but also in many countries of Asia, the Western Hemisphere, and Europe.

The writing of the additions to the book was carried out in London, where during the first six months of 1992 I was a Centennial Visitor at the London School of Economics. I would like to express my sincere appreciation to the School for providing me with a comfortable and stimulating environment in which to work. As always, my wife and daughters have been a constant source of encouragement as well as constructive criticism. Finally, the expeditious appearance of the new edition owes itself to the heroic efforts of Anthony Cheung of Imprint Publications, and I am deeply appreciative.

July 1992 *A. I.*

Introduction

This is an unusual book. It not only describes the major phases and incidents of American relations with China and Japan. It also analyzes the successive images that these three peoples have had of one another during the modern century of their relations. The episodes of international contact and the images or stereotypes of public opinion are marshaled in parallel. No other book has ever done this so well or so comprehensively. It is possible here only because the author is an unusually gifted historian, better prepared for this three-sided task than anyone else in the field.

The relations of the American people with China and Japan have developed in recent decades rather suddenly and certainly catastrophically. When we fought Japan in the Second World War, we had had contact with that country and people for less than a century. When we fought the Chinese in Korea a few years later, we had behind us a century of what we thought were peaceful and constructive relations. How could these two great powers across the Pacific so suddenly reverse their roles? How did the militaristic Japanese enemy of the 1940's become the firm ally of today, and the Chinese ally of the 1940's become the implacable communist enemy of today? It is surely an understatement to say that we lack perspective on our trans-Pacific relations. As the reports come in from still another war on the Asian mainland, we may well turn to a historian for guidance.

The strongest aspect of Dr. Iriye's book is his historical objectivity, his capacity to understand the views of the respective sides in international acrimony and crisis. But this perspective is a hard-won product of long effort coupled with unusual gifts and special circumstances.

Dr. Iriye was born in Japan in 1934 and his first preparation for the objective appraisal of international conflict was provided by the example of his father. Professor Keishiro Iriye had been trained in law at one of Japan's leading private institutions, Waseda University in Tokyo. He lectured and wrote on international law at a time when Japanese militarism made this a difficult, if not actually dangerous, profession. He combined this with experience as a journalist and spent three years in Geneva and Paris (1938–41). During the Japanese War in China he also spent two years in Nanking (1943–45). By that time he had already published books in Japanese on the Anglo-Russian rivalry in China (1935), the status of aliens in China (1937), and the failure of the Versailles treaty system (in three volumes, 1943–44).

Akira Iriye followed in his father's footsteps but in very different circumstances, in the new, postwar generation. He came to the United States and took his bachelor's degree at Haverford College in English history in 1957. He was by this time thoroughly bi-cultural in Japanese and English and had a grounding also in Chinese. He accepted the invitation of a Harvard History Department committee on American Far Eastern Policy Studies to take a scholarship and enter this new field. Under these auspices he spent the next four years concentrating mainly on modern Chinese history and writing a volume which was eventually published by the Harvard University Press in 1965 with the title *After Imperialism: The Search for a New Order in the Far East, 1921–1931*. This is a careful study of the various initiatives taken by the Americans in the Washington Conference, by the Soviet Union in its aid to Sun Yat-sen and the Chinese Communist Party, by the Chinese revolutionaries of both parties in the mid-1920's, and by the Japanese who subsequently seized Manchuria. This study led Dr. Iriye into a comparison of these four powers in their approaches to the Chinese scene and its problems. It also involved him in the study of Russian policy and materials. Securing his Harvard doctorate in 1961, he became a teaching fellow and tutor and then an instructor and a lecturer in the History Department, until he joined the staff of the University of California at Santa Cruz in 1966.

From the beginning of his academic career, Mr. Iriye took a special interest in the images and stereotypes lying behind the public policies in the countries on either side of the Pacific. He wrote and published studies dealing with the Sino-Japanese struggle over Manchuria, the growth of Japanese policy toward the United States, and the treatment of Japan in American writings and policies in both the nineteenth and the twentieth centuries. Confronted by the diametrically opposed attitudes and evaluations of the public in different countries at various historic times of crisis, he was inevitably struck by the incompleteness of the picture that each people tended to have of the others whom they faced. He found stereotype and ignorance substituting for knowledge and wisdom, quite as much in the United States as in China and Japan. Impressed with the need to explain American attitudes to his own countrymen, he first wrote a popular volume in Japanese, which has met a favorable response from the Japanese reading public. Now he has written this volume to give the American reader some appreciation of the fluctuating views and attitudes that have accompanied the last century of our trans-Pacific relations.

We can all agree that the Chinese Communist view of the United States today is distorted almost beyond recognition, but what can we say of the American image of China? How close has it come to reality at different times—for example, in 1942–1943 when we voted a half-billion dollars of aid to Chiang Kai-shek and when Madame Chiang addressed both houses of Congress? Or later in 1943 when articles by Pearl Buck and Hanson Baldwin began to question the vigor of the Chinese Nationalist war effort? One can go through the record from year to year during the last century and chart the fluctuations of American enthusiasm or disillusionment, admiration or distrust concerning "China." It is self-evident that not all of these American appraisals were correct.

Precisely here lies the value of Mr. Iriye's work. By charting these fluctuations of attitude and appraisal, both as to the facts and as to moral and other interests involved, he gives us a greater perspective on ourselves today. Of course, he sows seeds of doubt as to the infallibility of our judgment, but since he does this with equal clarity and convincingness for both Japan and China, we can only welcome it. We have only to follow the record as he traces it out and realize that a certain degree of unrealism about East Asia has had us in its grip at all times.

The aim of this book, however, is not to debunk our past or expose the human frailty and unrealism that have agitated leaders on both sides of the Pacific. The aim is a good deal more constructive, for the author is plainly a member of the new generation of international scholarship. This generation is composed of young researchers who are not culture-bound, who have a world view that encompasses the various cultures and uses the social sciences, and who are unafraid to put the interest of the human race above that of any particular nation as they look at the historical record. Approaching trans-Pacific relations in this spirit, Mr. Iriye is able to transcend the nationalistic and parochial concerns that have dominated much earlier historical writing. This is because he is writing the history not of any one country but of relations among several countries, using the records of all of them. He notes, for example, that the United States became an Asian power in the late nineteenth century when the whole world was becoming self-consciously concerned about the international scene. The new American imperialism of the 1890's was part of a world phenomenon. Its protagonists here had their counterparts, often unknown to them, in the other countries. Even when they came into conflict, they represented attitudes based on common assumptions such as those of national interest or Social Darwinism.

Similarly when this book takes note of the Chinese response to Western contact and the sending of Chinese students to the United States in the 1870's, it immediately contrasts this rather tardy Chinese action with the more vigorous and earlier efforts of Japanese to study the West *in situ* in the 1860's and 1870's. As in so much of their modernization, China and Japan followed somewhat similar paths, but the island kingdom did it so much more quickly while the continental empire lagged so far behind. In each case,

Mr. Iriye indicates the historical factors producing this remarkable contrast.

Quite aside from its comparison of national attitudes and experiences during this century of contact, this survey provides many new and critical estimates of famous statesmen and their policies. These are based on recent research, some of it by the author himself, and they often put their subjects in a new perspective. For example, from the American record Dr. Iriye argues that John Hay's Open Door policy, which has been usually viewed as the American way of keeping up with the imperialists, also had its domestic basis in the American scene. He suggests that Hay was on the defensive against the American expansionists of 1898, that he put forward a policy which won public support and thereby avoided a more concretely expansionist approach to the Far East. His ringing pronouncement in favor of China's territorial and administrative entity in 1900, in the second set of Open Door notes, was a warning and a form of pressure against the other powers, but even more, in this view, it was a veto against the American naval expansionists who favored seizing bases on the Chinese mainland.

Mr. Iriye dates our "moralistic diplomacy" back to the Taft administration. Instead of the "dollar diplomacy" usually ascribed to William Howard Taft and his secretary of state, Philander C. Knox, Mr. Iriye sees them resorting "to financial tactics to achieve ends that were basically moral. Most fundamental was the principle of 'fair play,' as Knox called it. The United States would expect the foreign powers as well as itself to adhere to the Open Door policy, which by this time had become synonymous with the principles of equal commercial opportunity and China's territorial and administrative integrity." In Manchuria in the early twentieth century, the effect of this American effort was merely to push Japan and Russia into their secret and overt division of spheres in the area. This failure notwithstanding, the United States had, for the first time, announced "its entrance into the Far Eastern world as a morally oriented nation. . . . Somehow it was felt to be America's mission" to help the victims of Japanese expansion, to side with some Asians against others.

To this was added, at the time of the Republican revolution of 1911–1912 in China, the idea of Chinese-American friendship.

Helping China against Japan thus became a general American attitude for the first half of the twentieth century. Wilsonian idealism could be invested in this effort across the Pacific, especially since it remained a unilateral American task separate from the international *Realpolitik* of the imperialist powers. Thus our heritage today has in it a background assumption that the American role across the Pacific is to champion the rights of deserving peoples against the evil tendencies of great powers who menace them.

To say this and nothing more would seem to support the reverse type of extreme idealism that favors leaving the Far East strictly alone because it is "none of our business." Of course, the problem cannot be so easily solved. Increasingly we have become a Pacific power. We have felt obliged to fight in East Asia three times in a generation. Dr. Iriye addresses himself not to the either-or question—should we or should we not be involved there?—but rather to the question of manner, with what moral ideas have we endowed our efforts in international relations?

In my own view, the main point to make concerning American policy in East Asia is simply that before 1922 it could afford to be divorced from naval power because the British fleet and, after 1902, the Anglo-Japanese alliance provided the basic underpinning of the international power structure. Increasingly from 1931, however, it was found in Washington that American policy, in its theoretical pronouncements, needed the practical support of naval power. Since 1945 the United States has had such power on its hands and has used it in East Asia. Today we are in midstream, still somewhat inclined to want a "moral diplomacy" based on principles good in themselves whether or not backed up by force. But we have learned that international stability must be undergirded by some structure of power relations—something we did not like to contemplate during most of our early history in Asia.

Mr. Iriye illumines the minuet-like shift of America's partners in East Asia. The rise of Chinese nationalism in the 1920's quickly turned toward anti-imperialism. While this could be specifically anti-Japanese during the 1930's and until 1945, it was capable of being diverted thereafter into the anti-Americanism of today—something that seemed hard to imagine in the early phases of American-Chinese friendship during their resistance to Japan's militaristic expansion.

In contrast with the growing incomprehension today between

Peking and Washington, this volume notes the growth of that earlier impasse in understanding between Washington and Tokyo. Mr. Iriye describes the fatalism with which some Japanese militarists viewed the future of their relations with us. The Americans on their part were grievously surprised by Japan's seizure of Manchuria in 1931. From the Japanese side at that time came "the emergence of pan-Asianism as an official ideology." Thus Japan's expansion against China thereafter could be justified not only in terms of national survival and security, but as an expression of Japan's duty toward less advanced Asian peoples who needed leadership against Western imperialism. Many Japanese liberals refused to believe that there must be an American-Japanese showdown and hoped until the last moment that it could be averted in 1941. But by its own inner necessities, the Japanese drive for empire eventually smothered these hopes. Mr. Iriye highlights the wishfulness with which Japanese military planners hoped that their seizure of Southeast Asian oil could make them independent of the American supply while, at the same time, seeing in American policy a readiness to accept this *fait accompli* and work out a "common-sense" compromise.

The many considerations, both practical and moral, that enter into the subsequent development of the triangle of American-Chinese-Japanese relations make a fascinating and complex study. As this survey comes down to recent decades, it enters the era of maximum controversy, when personal impressions vie with incomplete research and there is a multitude of views concerning might-have-beens. The author's focus throughout, however, is on the images and, as part of these national images, the moral considerations that enter into policy formation, both at the level of public opinion and in the decisions of the statesmen.

As he points out, the Pacific war greatly heightened each people's consciousness of the others. Wartime feeling further increased the hold of images that had been inherited. In their Great East Asian War, the Japanese generally felt all Asians should assist them in a struggle against Anglo-Saxon democracy and Soviet communism. Asians should help "restore Asia to the Asians." The wartime Japanese view of America, as Mr. Iriye can testify from first-hand contact, was full of clichés and stereotypes. These imputed to America a purely materialistic superiority not matched by spirituality. America's moral unworthiness, it was hoped, would prevent an effective war effort. In the end, the desperation of defeat eventually redounded to the benefit of the Occupation when the American program proved constructive rather than destructive. In the same years the American image in Chinese eyes was gradually shifting from that of wartime ally to the bifocal postwar image of a great power that inadequately aided and even betrayed the Nationalists and yet on the mainland was seen as the implacable enemy of the Communists.

By the time one approaches the end of Mr. Iriye's illuminating survey, one must feel, I think, that our American assumptions about East Asia and our instinctive responses to problems there have been and still are far less conscious and far more blind and culture-bound than we realize. Try as we will, we can seldom refrain from identifying ourselves emotionally with the cause of an underdog who is demanding freedom or justice, nor should we necessarily condemn such generous impulses in ourselves. The test comes in the degree of realism, the breadth of grasp of hard details, that accompanies our emotional involvement. Mr. Iriye's appraisal suggests that too often we have leapt before looking and become partisans in feeling before making a serious intellectual effort to see all sides, including particularly our own side.

This book raises far more questions than it settles. It is much needed today.

John K. Fairbank

Preface

"Lessons of history" have been generously cited to give an air of legitimacy to national policy. In his famous article commemorating the "victory of the people's war," Lin Piao, Chinese defense minister, has compared current United States policy to prewar Japanese imperialism; since the nature of the two imperialisms is the same, he argues, and since the Chinese people crushed one, they should employ similar tactics to destroy the other. To present-day Chinese, regardless of their domestic turmoil and struggle for power, the history of Sino-Western and Sino-Japanese relations provides countless lessons that should serve as guides to the formulation of policy. The American people, on their part, have often heard their leaders talk about the Vietnam war in relation to Munich or the Manchurian incident. The past record seems so self-evident that the mere mention of 1931 or 1938 tends to give policy an impression of respectability and authenticity.

It is ironic that Chinese and Americans, two of the most history-conscious peoples, should today confront each other through the medium of a most distorted picture of their mutual relations during the past century and a half. An image of historical relations tells a great deal about the present state of Sino-American relationship but not much about the past itself. Given the hostility between the two governments, there is a psychological need to believe that this situation was initially brought about by the opponent. For a Chinese it is reassuring to be reminded that throughout modern history the United States has done everything to exploit China, while an American, believing in a traditional friendship between the two peoples, would easily be convinced that there could have been just one answer to the rupture of that friendship. In an age of mass education, a simplistic picture of the past spreads like opium, numbing the mind and clouding considerations of national interest.

Yet the problem lies deeper, for United States–East Asian relations have always exhibited similar tendencies toward simplification, emotionalism, and dogmatism. The fanaticism of a Great Proletarian Cultural Revolution or the frustrations of a Vietnam war should not be allowed to obscure the fact that throughout modern history China, Japan, and the United States have met, collided, and reacted toward one another in a most violent fashion. Policies have been made on the basis of considerations tangential to the Pacific, mutual images have been formed with little basis in fact, and wars have been fought even though policies and images have not postulated wars.

To study this phenomenon in historical perspective is to apply an intellectual analysis to a situation hitherto almost devoid of it. Emotion, prejudice, and sentimental theorizing have colored the minds of China, Japan, and America as they confront one another. For this very reason an honest attempt must be made to penetrate the surface and study the crude reality of misunderstanding, misperception, and miscalculation. What follows, then, is not an outline of government-to-government relations. Nor is it a digest of well-known episodes and anecdotes. Rather, it focuses on mutual perception across the Pacific, on how policy makers and thinking people in America, China, and Japan have viewed each other, the world and their common problems—how, in short, they have tried to define their respective realities. How these realities are related to the three peoples' historical experiences and to the over-all international system provides a fascinating and meaningful subject of study. This, then, is an "inner" history of American–East Asian relations.

This book is an outgrowth of my research and teaching while at Harvard University. I am immensely indebted to the university's unsurpassed resources, both human and bibliographical. I was particularly fortunate to participate, for a number of years, in Harvard's special program in American–East Asian relations. For Chinese and Japanese materials, my research was helped by the facilities at Stanford University, the Academia Sinica, and Tōyō Bunko.

My greatest personal and professional debt is to Professor John K. Fairbank, who has done more than anyone else to promote the study of American–East Asian relations and to demonstrate the truth that historical knowledge is universal. Professor Ernest R. May has never failed to give me encouragement, guidance, and insights, when these were most needed. My good friend Professor Waldo Heinrichs, of the University of Tennessee, has spent countless hours going over the entire manuscript and has made valuable suggestions. It has also been read in part by Dr. Marilyn B. Young, to whom I am indebted for stimulating comments and stylistic revisions. The University of California at Berkeley and Santa Cruz has generously provided funds and secretarial help for the preparation of the final manuscript. Finally, for years my wife has shared with me the writing of books as well as the bringing up of children.

For permission to use certain manuscript materials I would like to express my thanks to the Harvard College Library and the John M. Olin Research Library of Cornell University.

A. I.

Spring 1967
Santa Cruz, California

Contents

Foreword to the Revised Edition v

Introduction by John K. Fairbank vii

Preface xv

I THE INITIAL ENCOUNTER, 1780–1880 1

1 East Asia in America 3

"Despotic Asia" 3
The Self-Contained Society 7
The Particularistic Society 10
"Peace, Commerce, Honest Friendship" 13
The Enlightenment of Asia 17
The Reception of Asians in America 28

2 The Asian Response to America 33

The Representative Americans 33
The Preservation of the Faith and the State 40
The Secrets of Power 45
American Liberty or American Power? 47

II IMPERIALISM, NATIONALISM, RACISM 51

3 *The End of the Century* 53

New Definitions of National Security 53
The Conflict of Civilizations 57
Japan Adopts Imperialism 64
Reform in China 68
The Waning of American Influence 71
Alarms over Asia 76

4 *Imperialism—Japanese and American* 83

Anti-Imperialism in China 84
Japan and America in China 86
Rehabilitation of China 90
Political Consciousness in China 93
Japan in an Imperialist War 97
The Menace of Japan 102
China as an Economic Interest 108

5 *The Genesis of American-Japanese Antagonism* 111

The Problems of an Asian Power 112
Championing the New China 117
Friendship Reciprocated 129
Japanese-American Enmity 131

6 *Chinese Nationalism and the United States* 138

Anti-Japanese Sentiment 139
The Washington Conference 143
Leninism in China 145
An Economic Friendship 150
China: Anti-Foreignism Among All Factions 153
The Tradition of Sino-American Friendship 156
The Prospect of Japanese-American Conflict 161

III SINO-AMERICAN CO-OPERATION AGAINST JAPAN 169

7 *America's Failure to Assist China* 171

The Triumph of Military Thinking in Japan 172
Morality in International Relations 178
Chinese Hopes for American Aid 188
Global Implications of a Crisis 194
The Resolution to Stand Alone 198

8 *Toward Pearl Harbor* 200

American Policy and Global Security 201
The New Order in Asia 207
China: The Expectation of American Aid 211
Toward War 216

9 *Images of the Pacific War* 227

The Overcoming of Modernity 229
A New Spokesman for Asia 232
War for a Democratic Asia 238
Which China? 243

10 *Chinese Communism and Postwar Sino-American Relations* 250

The Gap Between Power and Policy 251
The American Role in a Civil War 258
American Views of Asian Communism 264
Chinese Communists View America 271

IV THE SINO-AMERICAN CRISIS 279

11 *The Military Confrontation* 281

The Defense Perimeter 282
Redefining Asian Interests 285
American Policy and Attitudes in the 1950's 292
Chinese Interpretations of America 300
The Sino-Soviet Split 305
Friction in American-Japanese Relations 310
Peaceful Coexistence in American Policy 313

12 *Epilogue: Toward a More Peaceful Pacific* 321

V DEVELOPMENTS SINCE THE 1960'S 331

13 *The End of an Era* 333

Changes in the San Francisco System 333
The Vietnam War 337
The Cultural Revolution in China 339
A Cultural Revolution in America 341
Japan's Economic Success 346
A Geopolitical Revolution 349
The Nixon Shock in Japan 359
The Crisis of the Bretton Woods System 362

14 Toward a Post–Cold War Order 368

The 1970's and the 1930's 368
The Emergence of Cultural Diplomacy 372
The Asian Economic Miracle 378
America in Decline? 385
An Emerging Asian-Pacific Community? 390

The Literature of American–East Asian Relations: A Short Bibliography 393

Index 409

I
The Initial Encounter, 1780–1880

1
East Asia in America

The initial encounter was ideological. Asia was an idea in America, and Americans took the initiative in responding to that image. New England merchants, it is true, cared little for ideas as they sailed for the Eastern seas in search of goods and markets. In the 1780's several ships already were visiting Canton annually, but the trade was not unique. Merchants went there just as they had taken their ships to the West Indies, the Mediterranean, and the African coast. They respected native customs and institutions, disposed of their cargo, and obtained new items, with the sole aim of making money from the carrying trade. They brought back teas, silks, curios, and even live Chinese to be shown in America, but their direct role in cultural contact between the two peoples was limited.

"Despotic Asia"

It was not by the merchants but by those who stayed at home that the initial image of China was formed. Intellectuals and statesmen of the young republic had little time to study and think about Asia, but they often thought about themselves and their nation, and their self-image told a great deal about their world view, of which China would form a part. From the beginning, it is true, there were two distinct ideas about the nature of American society. One, a maritime view, perpetuated the prevalent British attitude that trade was the backbone of the state. The other, an agrarian idea, conceived of American development in terms of landed expansion. These two views were not mutually exclusive, and most Americans at this time shared both. But at the same time they implied different attitudes toward the outside world. The maritime view would, of course, picture the United States as a nation trading with other nations. Whether one looked eastward or, beyond the continent, westward, there was always Asia as a link in the network of trade routes. Even before the Opium War of 1839–1842 the countries of East Asia were considered to be commercially important enough to merit the sending of trade missions and stationing of consuls. In the eyes of Americans on the east coast, the Pacific coast was almost synonymous with the Oriental trade, and efforts were made to secure a good harbor in California and to prevent potential rivals from establishing a foothold on the west coast to the frustration of American opportunities in the Pacific. From such a point of view, East Asia was an essential part of the world commercial system in which the United States was an active participant.

The agrarian view, on the other hand, had little to do with Asia. It is true that some farm products, notably cotton, could and would eventually find their way to China. Before 1840, however, there was little interest in cultivating that market. The domestic market was expanding, and England and other European countries, in their initial stage of industrialization, could take care of American surpluses. The westward movement was a self-contained phenomenon, unrelated to Asia or the Pacific. What is notable is that the agrarian view of America, too, postulated a world view. The Jeffersonian image of American society made up of free, democratic, and land-tilling yeomen implied that this was the best possible kind of human society. There were certain values for which the nation stood, that would best be protected in an agrarian setting. These values would then be used as a yardstick with which to measure other societies.

Thus one's image of America produced an image of the world and, if indirectly, an idea of Asia. Quite apart from the immediate economic relevance of Asia to America, there was the view that the latter represented the new, and the former the old, world. The oft-mouthed phrase "God's American Israel" implied that here had been born a new nation, free from the shackles of the past and yet related to other preceding societies. The United States was the newest and therefore the most advanced country in the world. It stood at the apex of human history and embodied in itself the highest qualities of civilization. This image of "Young America" was an a-historical conception. America was at once young and most mature, at once new and most advanced, unrelated to the old world and yet springing from the past. The American nation was qualitatively different from other countries, and yet it was not unique since it could conceive of a mission to spread the benefits and values of its existence to others.

This ambiguity was inherent in the early American view of itself. When applied to the old world, it produced interesting corollaries. If Europe was older than America, Asia was much older than Europe. If Europe was behind America, Asia was further removed from modernity. True, "Asia was the seat of civilization when Europe was barbarous," as an author wrote in 1839. But this was precisely the point. Asia was the birthplace of humanity and civilization, but it had since decayed or remained stagnant, while the West had caught up and in time surpassed it. In fact, the East in the nineteenth century seemed exactly the same as it was two thousand years earlier. Nothing changed in the East: "Better fifty years of Europe than a cycle of Cathay." When one looked closely, one found in Asia habits and institutions which had long been overcome in Europe, and one missed in the East what had become prevalent features of Western life. "The political governments of the East," wrote *Knickerbocker*, "are Despotisms, subordinating the citizen's substance, liberty, and even life, to the arbitrary will of an individual inheriting the sceptre by right divine." Technology was at a primitive level, trade was discouraged, the masses suffered from disease and malnutrition, religion was artificial and crude, paintings and sculpture were grotesque, and the status of women was pitifully low. One found Asia, in other words, the opposite of one's image of America. One contrasted America's liberty to Asia's tyranny, commercial development to agrarian stagnation, Christianity to pagan cult, respect for women to polygamy, material advances to primitive conditions of life.

America, however, was not simply the opposite of Asia. They were related as two stages in the flow of human history. Asia was not merely a geographical term but represented a stage in human development. It symbolized the nature of man at this particular period of growth. This was the corollary of the view that America represented the newest stage in history. Thus considered, America and Asia were more than two opposite principles, for the one grew out of the other. As one writer put it, the "undefined something to which man has tended" was "none other than that whose reality is now ours;—ours because the human race has been struggling for it." In the writer's view, all events of the past, present, and future were interrelated as they revealed the steady march of man from barbarism to civilization. Such a conception of history always has two possible implications; it is possible to argue either that a particular human group's place in the march of civilization is determined by its specific traits and nothing can arbitrarily change it, or that in the grand panorama of human progress all artificial boundaries between nations and societies are insignificant and ultimately all will partake in the benefits of civilization, regardless of their past. There is no doubt that throughout much of the nineteenth century American thinking was inclined to the second, more rational than historicist, view. The *Democratic Review* was expressing a common idea when it wrote, in 1839, "Let it be understood that the same nature is common to all men, that they have equal and sacred claims, that they have high and holy faculties." The implication was that if only those elements in the East that had impeded its progress were removed and replaced by those that had contributed to Western civilization, the former would once again regain its ancient vigor and join the march of humanity. America stood at the highest stage of human advance, but this did not mean that only Americans were endowed with special faculties for that position. On the contrary, the American example merely revealed that if only others saw the light and made the same effort, they too could enjoy the benefits of freedom and civilization. It was just a step from here to the idea of mission; it was America's moral mission to stand as the symbol of progress and impart its blessings to others. "It depends upon us," said a writer in 1840, "whether our fellow men shall reach the elevation whereof they are capable, and . . . whether or not [we shall] confer on them the most inestimable of all earthly boons, the boon of Civilization."

The American people's view of themselves thus led to a picture of the world and of human history. It is to be noted that these ideas were found in the south as well as the north, the west as well as the east. Most Americans may never have seen an Asian, much less visited Asia, but they had an image of Asia because they had an image of America. Asians lagged far behind Americans, and they suffered from centuries of oppressive rule and degrading customs. But they were potentially as capable of awakening and progress as Westerners. "Let a free and well conducted press," wrote a visitor to Asia, "pour forth its fertilizing streams of knowledge upon the fallow mind of the vast multitude, and they will acquire that love of free agency which God has planted in the human heart." If only arbitrary restrictions were removed from the Asian masses and they were given an opportunity to embrace truth and reality, they would bestir themselves and re-enter the society of civilized nations.

Such exhortations had little practical result. Only a tiny handful urged the "opening" of China and Japan to international intercourse, and even a smaller number of men actually went to Asia with a sense of mission. They and the merchants, whose sole aim was profit, played a role in developing a Chinese or Japanese image of America. Back home, however, they did little more than confirm the existing image of Asia. For most Americans, Asia was still a mere idea which did not give them a sense of personal involvement. It was perhaps for this very reason that the perfectionist conception of man was so painlessly applied to Asians.

The Self-Contained Society

The Chinese had their own rational, perfectionist idea of man. Confucian man was the embodiment of the right principles, to be attained through education, regardless of race, age, or religion.

These principles were largely social principles, defining relations among men and among states. The Chinese state, ruled by the Confucian emperor with the help of Confucian bureaucrats, was itself the source of legitimacy. Other states related themselves to it as members of a family. If there were those who had not attained the principles of right conduct, they would just have to be treated accordingly; regulations and ordinances, instead of moral codes, would be applied to them. But they, too, could aspire to membership in the Confucian world order. Ultimately, there would be achieved a universal commonwealth, in which all shared the same principles and lived in peace and harmony.

It is beside the point that an agrarian economy sustained the Confucian orthodoxy. There could have been a plausible commercial empire under the same principles. What is striking is the absence of an economic content in the Confucian orthodoxy, which is fundamentally a political dogma. This is related to the more basic fact that Confucianism allows for no social change. What is postulated is an eternal political order, made up of a hierarchy of educated elites, where, though dynastic changes do occur whenever the ruling house loses touch with the right principles, its downfall will be followed by the establishment of another Confucian monarchy. No alternative social or governmental system is conceived. There is little incentive for technological innovations because these would not help in one's Confucian status, the only source of legitimacy, morality, and profit.

If the American view of history was a-historical, the Chinese idea was pseudo-historical. History was merely a record of dynastic changes, in which individual exploits were described in minutest detail. But there was neither a philosophy of history nor an attempt at analyzing human development in terms of stages. There was little interest in relating other societies to China except in the Confucian setting, transcending time. There was no contrast between old and new, much less East and West. The past was seen in the present, and distant lands became meaningful only insofar as they chose to relate themselves to China. Lacking an idea of progress, the Chinese mind, unlike the American mind, did not ponder the possibilities of awakening the unenlightened from their slumber of centuries. Mission was a concept alien to the land where one strove for self-realization through studying the orthodoxy, not through spreading the benefits of the social order to the uninitiated. While American society was aware of and interested in the outside world, Chinese society was not and remained self-contained.

The effects of this difference on the initial Sino-American encounter would have been tremendous under any circumstances, but the years 1780–1840, when that encounter took place, was no ordinary period. This was the time when modern Europe was born. The use of steam power and machines revolutionized the productive system; greater productivity led to emphasis on export trade, leading in time to the idea of free trade; Adam Smith evangelized the notion of the separation of state power from economic power; public opinion was becoming nationalized, and the enlightened public took avidly to the idea of a natural social order, based on the dignity of man, endowed with the faculty of reason; military institutions, reflecting the rational thinking of the time, were changing human organizations, with a new emphasis on national armies, the frontal attack, and power as an index of national greatness. In international relations, the Napoleonic Wars did not affect the notion of the balance of power among presumably equal states. Though in fact a handful of major nations maintained the peace after 1815, nobody quarreled with Metternich's formulation of international relations as those based on the principles of reciprocity, solidarity, and respect for acquired rights.

By necessity and by choice the United States was drawn into the European world as it went through these changes. Mutual borrowing of ideas and technology went on painlessly and almost unconsciously. American society, it has been suggested, was a "fragment," split off from the old world; it had no remnants of feudalism and no class conflict. The fragment's view of the totality would thus be different from the totality's view of itself. But this did not prevent Americans from importing European technology and pondering over the same problems that concerned Europeans. The United States, after all, was a full-fledged member of the "family of nations."

This was not the case in China. The Chinese mind remained insensitive to changes in Western society. During the height of the French Revolution, the Chinese emperor could write, to George III, that "our ceremonies and code of laws differ so completely from your own that, even if your Envoy were able to acquire the rudiments of our civilization, you could not possibly transplant our manners and customs to your alien soil." The occasion was the sending of Lord Macartney, whose refusal to perform the kowtow, against the precedent set by all earlier Western envoys, might have revealed something new about Europe at that time. The Chinese still had little need for foreign things and it never occurred to them that vast changes in distant lands might some day shatter the foundation of the Confucian orthodoxy.

China = isolated

Under the circumstances, there was no Chinese image of America, not even to the extent that one could talk of an American image of China. Those who did not share the Chinese world view were irrelevant to it. Foreign merchants in China would be tolerated so long as they conformed to established practices, but there was little incentive to know more about them and their lands. American merchants, to be sure, impressed the Chinese in Canton as more respectful of China than other Westerners; and certainly Chinese officials were well aware of America's geographical location and political independence. But the outside world had not yet become a problem. It seems appropriate that the only known account of Western countries written by a Chinese at this time was a record transmitted by a blind man. Hsieh Ch'ing-kao may have traveled in Europe and America before he became blind, but in his simple descriptions there was no attempt to find meaning.

The Particularistic Society

The Japanese were politically even more isolated than the Chinese but they were not necessarily blind to possibilities of change. By 1800 thinkers had already appeared who had become aware of discrepancies between the natural order and the existing political order, and were distinguishing between the two. State power seemed devoid of *a priori* moral authority, because the source of legitimacy was evidently artificial, going back only to 1600. Perhaps because of this very fact, there was a stronger sense of loyalty among the samurai and other classes in society. Loyalty, whether to one's feudal lord, family, or *han* (fief), gave meaning to life; though the samurai had lost his primary task of fighting for his lord, devotion to him and his *han* legitimized his status. Often this devotion took the form of learning. The knowledge of pragmatic sciences would enhance the power of one's *han,* and the pursuit of knowledge could give one the same sense of struggle for goal attainment that actual combat for one's lord would give in war. This particularism made Japan more receptive to foreign culture than China. The Japanese were ready to learn from the West, through Dutch merchants who were permitted to come once a year, because European sciences seemed to offer things of pragmatic value. Since natural moral value was not found in the existing political order, psychologically it took no painful reorientation to study Western physics, mathematics, anatomy, and astronomy. The principles these sciences exhibited in no way seemed to contradict or undermine the Japanese social order.

The same attitude underlay the Japanese view of the world. Unlike America or China, Japan had no universalistic notion of history. Japanese history was seen as continuous, either in terms of the imperial house or of the feudal institutions. Japan was unique, but by the same token all others were also unique. There was no pervasive philosophy of history or a comprehensive world view, but there was awareness of the world beyond. Actually, it was because of this very awareness that the country had been partially closed to foreign intercourse, since the 1630's, for fear that extensive foreign trade and communication would disrupt the social order. The Japanese had always paid attention to happenings outside of Japan, and they were keenly interested in such events as the American War of Independence and the Napoleonic Wars. Before 1800 they were already becoming uneasy about the attempt of Westerners once again to come to Japan and force resumption of open contact.

Thus it is not surprising that we find the Japanese engaged in a serious debate for over half a century before the Perry expedition —a debate on resumption of foreign contact. It is significant that the debate usually took the form of discussion on maritime security, a theme that would return again and again in the course of Japan's encounter with the West. From the first—at a time when even the notion of national security was alien to China—Japanese feudal lords debated whether the country's defense needs were adequately met, whether the resumption of foreign contact would enhance or diminish the threat to national existence, and whether foreign trade would add to or deplete national wealth. No decision was yet reached, except that the Japanese decided to postpone the decision as long as they could and meanwhile tend to the strengthening of maritime defense. Before 1840 these measures were considered sufficient, and Western countries did not seem powerful enough to necessitate a radical departure from the existing policy. American captains were turned away time and again as they sought to enter Japan.

It is obvious that an average Japanese intellectual or official knew more about America than his Chinese counterpart. If both were still isolationist, it was for different reasons. The Japanese were curious to find out facts about Western life and history, and long before Perry's visit they had studied American geography. On the whole, however, curiosity stopped short of inquiring after more than superficial events and facts. The Japanese showed greater interest in wars, technological advances, and political happenings than in the intellectual developments that might have lain beneath them. When, for instance, a Dutch biography of Napoleon was translated in 1837, it is said that there was a great difficulty finding the Japanese equivalent for the Dutch word "Vrijheid," freedom. The concept was not in the Japanese vocabulary, and no effort was made to find out more about Western political ideas. A few years later, Japanese found it extremely difficult to understand the word "republic." It may be said that the Japanese tried to absorb relevant Western knowledge piecemeal, without attempting to form an integrated picture of the world. There was no unity of knowledge in Japan.

The initial encounter was thus an indirect contact between the American mind on one hand and the Chinese and the Japanese minds on the other. What they thought of one another was conditioned more by what they thought of themselves than by what they actually saw of each other. In the 1840's, however, involvement suddenly deepened.

East and West met head on during the Opium War, and Chinese isolation crumbled as the victorious England, followed by several others, signed official treaties with the Ch'ing empire. A few years later Japan was walking along the same path toward direct Western contact. The industrializing, nationalistic, revolutionary West was forcing the reluctant and tardy East to enter the "family of nations." All of this fitted the preconceived notion that the Americans had of what should happen in Asia. Yet the Chinese and the American world views would be tested once the two countries established closer contact, and the Japanese would have to evolve their own system of response to new developments.

"Peace, Commerce, Honest Friendship"

The mid-nineteenth century was a period of momentous change for the United States. Territorially, Texas, New Mexico, California, and Alaska were added to the Union; economically, an agrarian economy developed into an industrial economy, experiencing the "take-off" stage in the 1840's and the 1850's; politically, the question of sectional influence on national policy was taken to the battlefield. Still, Americans continued to talk of Asia in much the same framework as earlier.

An industrializing America thought a great deal about trade with China and Japan in the 1840's and the 1850's. With the signing of commercial treaties with the Asian countries, the way seemed to have been opened for expansion of American trade in the Pacific. While Europe and Latin America were much more important than Asia in this connection, it seemed quite natural that American ships and goods would find their way across the Pacific to the shores of Japan and China, as an entrepôt of world trade. "Multiply your ships," exhorted Senator William Seward, "and send them forth to the East." This theme was reiterated with renewed vigor after the 1870's. Now the emphasis was on exporting the products of American industry. Americans never tired of pointing out the imperative necessity of selling surplus manufactures which saturated the domestic market. Price indexes were falling, and the expansion of overseas trade was a favorite and simple panacea on which everyone agreed. It was natural that as Americans looked at the globe they should note East Asia as a potential solution to these problems.

There was thus an image of China and Japan as markets for the manufactured goods that could not be consumed at home. There was no expectation that the Asian countries might themselves industrialize. The time for that, even if it should come, seemed to lie in the distant future. Before then, as these countries were more and more opened up to foreign contact and their people became acquainted with Western products, their demand for these goods would increase. Under the protection of treaty tariffs, American exports would easily find their way to the Eastern markets.

The disparity between image and reality, expectation and achievement, is striking. Perhaps it was for this very reason that Americans always exaggerated the promise of an Asian market. The longer it failed to materialize, the greater the need would be to overcome frustrations and paint a picture of what might have been and what might yet be. At any rate, American exports to China and Japan never grew in proportion to the growth rate of American export trade as a whole. Imports from these countries always surpassed exports to them, though in over-all American trade the reverse was almost always the case after 1875. Besides, China and Japan continuously bought natural products from the United States, such as cotton, wheat, and tobacco, and not manufactured goods as Americans hoped. For these the Asian purchasing power was excessively low, even without higher tariffs. Also there was competition from European exporters, which grew keen after the opening of the Suez Canal in 1869.

But the significance of the economic image of China and Japan lies deeper. By defining America's national interest in Asia as economic, the United States government could calmly follow the Jeffersonian dictum of "peace, commerce, and honest friendship with all nations." Ideally, no forceful measures should be employed to initiate trade, though actually naval power might have to be employed to protect it. From the beginning the official view was that relations with China and Japan were friendly because they were basically commercial. President John Tyler's letter to the Chinese emperor, on the occasion of the dispatch of Caleb Cushing in 1843, referred to the emissary as a "messenger of peace." He was to seek a treaty to regulate trade, "so that nothing may happen to disturb the peace between China and America." President Millard Fillmore's letter to the Japanese "emperor," entrusted to Commodore Matthew C. Perry, referred to the protection of shipwrecked Americans and the supply of coal and provisions, in addition to the opening of ports for commerce; trade was mentioned as a foundation of amity among nations.

The idea that commerce is by nature peaceful, and therefore that commercial relations will lead to peace among nations, goes back to eighteenth-century European thinking. American statesmen from the beginning subscribed to the notion and believed their country was more consistently carrying out this policy while European governments had to worry about dynastic considerations, territorial disputes, and revolutions. It is not surprising, then, that Americans attributed to their East Asian relations entirely peaceful intentions, free from any such ulterior ambitions as European powers might be entertaining in Asia. By the same token, it did not seem necessary to pay close attention to East Asian matters. Americans and Asians would engage in trade, which the United States government would encourage and protect with means at its disposal, but trade was a matter for private individuals to conduct. It was enough that American merchants be treated the same as European merchants—the "most-favored-nation" principle was always at the base of American thinking, but this was by no means a unique position. After all, no country would want anything less than a most-favored-nation treatment. Apart from this all-pervasive principle, the government in Washington was not overly concerned with Asian matters until the end of the century. At a time when it took nearly a year for messages to go back and forth between Washington and representatives in East Asia, the situation was perhaps inevitable. Even so, adherence of Washington to a strictly commercial policy is remarkable.

The passivity, if not lack of interest, on the part of the home government left American representatives in China and Japan to act on their own initiative. And they were often colorful figures—Commodore Perry, assuming a haughty air of determination toward the prevaricating Japanese officials; Townsend Harris, berating Japanese mendacity yet adopting the posture of a sincere friend of Japan; Peter Parker, a missionary diplomat, scheming to capture Formosa; Humphrey Marshall, determined to uphold China's integrity against what he believed to be European designs for partitioning the empire; and Anson Burlingame, heading the first Chinese mission abroad and preaching China's cause wherever he went. But historians have taken these men too seriously, and have exaggerated their importance in United States policy. Actually, there is little evidence that much of what they said was ever taken seriously by the State Department, which adhered to a passive and cautious policy. The importance of these emissaries lies in the impact of their action on Asia. Their role in the Asian setting was considerable, but this must not be confused with United States policy.

Both the State Department and its representatives, however, shared a belief in the uniqueness of American–East Asian relations. While at times the United States acted together with European powers in using force to protect nationals and in negotiating for more treaties, this did not diminish the belief that American interests and policies in Asia were distinct from those of other countries. It is interesting that almost every new emissary that went to China or Japan saw fit to enunciate what he believed to be America's role in Asia. Mostly such declarations were flooded with expressions of friendship for the Asian people and stressed differences between the American attitude and that of other foreigners. This fitted with the Washington government's image of peaceful, commerce-oriented relations with countries of Asia.

Here again, reality and image differed. The problem was that the allegedly peaceful policy of trade required force for implementation. If Chinese and Japanese were unwilling to trade amicably, if they were hostile to American merchants, or if they refused to entertain American commissioners at the capital, then naval force would have to be employed to ensure the desired objectives. To this extent the United States would not be different from other Western governments. If, on the contrary, the United States were to act unilaterally against the alleged ambitions of European powers in Asia, this, too, would require sufficient force. In fact, available means were pitiably small. In 1853, for instance, Perry and Marshall quarreled over how best to employ the fleet in Eastern waters—to protect American merchants in China, whose security was menaced by the Taiping rebellion, or to proceed to Japan to force the opening of that country. Lacking sufficient naval power, the United States could not in reality engage in independent action. The Perry expedition is the exception to this general rule. As a result, the United States had either to join forces with European navies or to wait until they had accomplished their aim and then participate in subsequent negotiations under the principle of most-favored-nation. Both these courses were pursued. It is, therefore, possible to say that the prevalent image of American policy in East Asia was evolved within the framework of military collaboration with Europe, especially Great Britain. Because the British lead was always taken for granted, it was possible for Americans to talk about their distinct attitude and unique relations with China and Japan. All this was logical enough, given the emphasis on commerce in a setting lacking in the tradition of international trade.

The Enlightenment of Asia

If trade had been the only factor, however, there would not have been the same amount of moralizing about American–East Asian relations. Americans did not simply look at Asia as a potential market; a desire for friendly relations was reinforced by a sense of mission, which was often related to an image of America's future as a Pacific nation. The sense of mission, of course, could sometimes be an *a posteriori* justification for accomplished fact. The desire for material benefits, for instance, could be cloaked by talk of bringing China and Japan into the community of nations. Ending Asian isolation was a frequent theme in public policy statements, calculated to appeal to popular imagination while the basic interest was in trade. At the same time, there is no denying the fact that Americans, even those without any direct involvement in Asian trade, welcomed the opening of China and Japan. The language they used in approving these steps was that of mission and of natural right. It seemed only natural that Asian countries be brought into contact with advanced countries of the West. Trade would serve as a harbinger of change, and through exchange of goods new ideas would be introduced and enlighten the hitherto dormant populations.

If for the majority of Americans these were comfortable thoughts that did not necessarily impel them to specific action, there were others who felt a strong enough sense of mission either to go to the East themselves or actively advocate such a cause. The idea of service to China and Japan, as they parted from the policy of seclusion, was appealing to many who groped for meaning in their own existence. It is always difficult to determine precisely what motivates a man to decide to devote his life to the service of another country. But it is easy to recognize the challenge for a nineteenth-century American. Whether he had already made good in America, or whether he had not achieved his ambitions in his own country, the satisfaction of going to a distant land in the capacity of an adviser, if not of a teacher, would seem to have been a fundamental factor. He did not have to renounce his American heritage. On the contrary, he was going to Americanize China or Japan. Few were so naïve as to believe that America was the embodiment of perfection and that all its ideas and institutions could be transplanted abroad. But all were convinced that American society was a step nearer to perfection than other societies, and that if these latter sought to reform themselves there was much that Americans could do to help. Looked at from this side of the Pacific, the nations of Asia seemed to be waiting for precisely such help. Americans could teach the Chinese and Japanese rudiments of technology and modern science; they could introduce Western ideas and customs; they could assist the Asian governments as they struggled to survive in a turbulent world; above all, Americans could bring Asians to a new and higher level of spirituality.

This last needs elaboration, for the type of Christianity that was transmitted to Asia by Americans was a particular product of the nineteenth century. American Protestantism in the first three quarters of the century stressed individual salvation through regeneration. It was often evangelical and doctrinally rigid, prescribing a strict pattern of behavior for believers. Perhaps because of the very simplicity of this religious system, it seemed plausible to talk of the "evangelization of the world in this generation." Nothing that Americans had read seemed to cast doubt on the belief that non-Christians remained in the state of darkness simply because they had not seen the light. If, as it was so often remarked, the same nature was common to all men, there could be nothing wrong with the assumption that Chinese and Japanese would embrace Christianity the moment their artificial restrictions were removed and they were confronted with true believers come from America.

There were, to be sure, skeptics. Some felt Asians could not be expected to embrace a religion uprooted from its environment. Institutional and metaphysical barriers would be tremendous. If Asians were to become truly Christian, that would be the time when Asians ceased to be Asians. This was precisely the premise on which the activists based their trust, but skeptics doubted if it could be achieved in one or two generations. There were others, notably Ralph Waldo Emerson, who found some value in Oriental religions. He felt the Occident had something to learn from the Orient even as it offered to help the latter. And a writer in *Christian Examiner* in 1859, anticipating twentieth-century thought, asserted that elements of Orient and Occident might all "coalesce and contribute to the nobility of man." "The Persians, the Arabians, the Hindus, the Chinese," he predicted, "while learning much from us, will also be our teachers, and help to form the great Asiatic races and nations and religions and civilizations that are to be." These, however, were voices submerged under the louder call for evangelization of China and Japan. Missionaries, of course, believed in the ultimate success of their mission. It was not they alone, but their home boards and the churchgoers who contributed to their work, who were convinced of the meaning and feasibility of foreign evangelization.

The sense of frustration and disappointment that invariably awaited missionaries is a good index of their initial hopes and expectations. Because of their simplistic version of Christianity as well as simplified notion of proselytization, they were bound to be disappointed at the meager result of their endeavor. To cite just one example, J. L. Atkinson of the Congregationalist American Board was full of hope when he first arrived in Japan in 1873. "Only let the Government restrictions be removed," he wrote, "and let it be known to all that there is the fullest liberty to hear and enquire concerning this new Religion, and to accept it and live it unmolested, and we all feel confident that audiences would be immense and believers many." Four years later, he was writing that "young Japan, school-going, railroad-building, newspaper making and reading, enterprising Japan," was thoroughly atheistic. After seven years of unceasing efforts he begged the home board to give him ten more years of their patience before he could show some fruits of his labor. "For it must be ever borne in mind in America," he wrote, "that the Japanese are a *heathen* people. They are polished, intelligent, suave, apt, enterprising, eye-taking, cheerful people, but they are none the less heathen from top to bottom." One would wonder why it took this missionary seven years to discover the fact. Such, nevertheless, was the case with many Americans who went to the East. Their image of China and Japan had been totalist in that they had pictured the Chinese and Japanese as standing at a particular stage of development and susceptible to wholesale transformation. Religion would naturally be part of the metamorphosis. What Americans found once they got to Asia was that Asians could change aspects of their institutions without necessarily changing their habits and thinking patterns. The discovery necessitated rethinking about the nature of non-Western societies.

Thus the writings of American missionaries, educators, and others who spent several years or more in China and Japan tell a great deal about the process of this rethinking as well as the gap between initial assumptions and subsequent discoveries. These writings all display skepticism about the possibilities of rapid and fundamental change in the East. But by the same token they make an honest attempt at understanding traditional Asian societies. Often these American writers develop genuine affection for East Asian culture, and sometimes they even assume the self-imposed function of speaking for China or Japan, to make these countries less misunderstood by Americans at home. Not infrequently Americans of long residence in China would compare the country favorably with Japan, just as those in Japan would champion the latter.

Most comprehensive accounts of Chinese society in nineteenth-century America were written by missionaries (like S. Wells Williams, John L. Nevius, and Justus Doolittle) after many years of work in the field. Thoughtful and detailed, their writings are amazingly free from moralizing and preaching. It is true that they on occasion resort to clichés; Williams talks of the "debasing effects of heathenism upon the intellect" of the Chinese people; and Doolittle refers to China's "perishing millions, who are hastening to idolatrous graves at the rate of thirty-two thousand [*sic*] every day." On the other hand, the descriptions of Chinese life given by these authors are so detailed, straightforward, and factual that they could have been written only by men who were in love with the people among whom they lived. Nevius points out that Chinese are as human as others, with vices as well as virtues, and they are inherently neither superior nor inferior to Westerners. They are possessors of an advanced civilization and are justly proud of it; their power of intellect is impressive, and their honesty is proverbial. Obviously unhappy about the praise heaped upon "progressive" Japan, he points out that "the Japanese, having been accustomed for ages to learn from the Chinese and the Dutch, naturally take the position of pupils, and are, for this reason, outstripping the Chinese in learning from Western nations a knowledge of the modern arts and sciences; while the Chinese have been too proud to learn." The author's preference for the latter is unmistakable.

These writers had ready answers to the charge that missionary work had produced meager fruit. As Doolittle writes, "If the Chinese were ignorant savages or barbarians, and numbered only a few thousands or hundreds of thousands, like the Sandwich Islanders fifty years ago, it might perhaps be expected that they would be influenced to embrace Christianity with comparative ease and speed." But the Chinese are in fact a civilized, literary, and cultured people, proud of their heritage. They cannot be expected to be converted to Christianity in a few years. This does not mean that missionary work is meaningless and futile. On the contrary, here lies the challenge. Given sufficient time, the Chinese will never fail to be attracted by the true religion. It is interesting that such hopes are usually added as if by an afterthought at the end of long treatises on Chinese customs and institutions, as though the writers themselves are not sure of the relevance of proselytization. There is a logic gap between the view of China's traditional culture so lovingly described and the sudden call to evangelization. The gap remained unfilled until a new conception of missionary work appeared on the horizon.

Writers based in Japan revealed similar traits. They readily recognized the difference between Japanese eagerness to adopt new ideas and China's "deadening conservatism." However, Americans of long residence in Japan, just as in China, were not satisfied with casual and simplistic observations. The more they came to know Japan, the less they were sure that the imposition of Western civilization was all to the good of the country. Townsend Harris, the first resident foreign official in Japan, and his Dutch-born interpreter, Henry Heusken, were constantly bothered by the feeling that they might be doing disservice to human civilization as a whole by forcing the acceptance of Western institutions upon the reluctant Japanese. William E. Griffis, whose *The Mikado's Empire,* published in 1876, remained the best American book on Japanese history for decades, noted in 1873, "they are one of the most polite, good-natured and happy nations in the world. By introducing foreign civilization into their beautiful land they may become richer; they need not expect to be happier." Another consistent friend of Japan, the American journalist E. H. House, stressed discontinuity in recent Japanese history; the outward ease with which the Westernization process was initiated and carried on concealed internal tribulations, since the past Japanese experience had not prepared the nation for such a radical transformation. Carrying this point further, Charles LeGendre, in the employ of the Japanese government in the 1870's, noted that the Japanese had not outgrown their feudal system and therefore were not ready for a Western form of government. Lacking a political tradition that in the West had led to the development of constitutionalism, it was doubtful if a Western form of political organization was best fitted for Japan. "A country is not necessarily free because it has a form of government similar to that of other nations whose people are free." Japan should have institutions best fitting its needs, not necessarily those of advanced countries.

•

Americans who stayed home or traveled in the East only briefly had naturally a simpler image of Asia. They, including officials in Washington, were inclined to view Chinese and Japanese as divided between forces of reaction and of progress, with the unquestioned certainty that the latter would in the end triumph. Official policy was to encourage this trend wherever possible, and the public response was to find in progressive Chinese and Japanese an image of progressive Americans. As before 1840, a particular view of civilization lay at the basis of American thought. Civilization, wrote Frederick Grimke in 1856, "is that state in which the higher part of our nature is made to predominate over the lower, and the qualities which fit men for society, obtain an ascendency over their selfish, and anti-social propensities." Similar statements could be multiplied, from American writings both before and after the Civil War. What Grimke and other writers took for granted was that the state of civilization thus defined was attainable by all men; there were no inherent ethnic, historical, and other factors that determined the degree to which a country was civilized. "The faculties, propensities, and passions of men, are on an average, the same which they always were." It followed that only "circumstances," such as despotic institutions and foreign conquests, impeded the cultural advance of a people. Let freedom of thought be exercised by all men, then they would show a greater impulse toward civilization. This was what America had done, and there was no reason why others, if placed under similar "circumstances," should not respond likewise.

It is not surprising that the American mind, delighting in such thoughts, should have been more favorably disposed to Japan than to any other Asian country during the second half of the nineteenth century. Everything, from Japan's response to the Perry expedition to the Meiji government's policy of Westernization, conformed to the preconceived notion of an arrested society resuming its march to civilization. At the time of the Perry expedition a writer wrote, "The thirty millions of Japan await the key of the western Democrat to open their prison to the sun-light of social interchange." The reports of the expedition were such as to prove the correctness of American assumptions. The Japanese people seemed friendly, intelligent, and eager for higher civilization. It was only their country's peculiar isolation and their leaders' despotic rule that prevented them from achieving it. "The Japanese is the most curious, inquiring person, next to a Yankee, in the world," wrote Bayard Taylor, who had accompanied Perry. "He would be an inventor were it not for the policy of his government, which fears nothing so much as a new idea." It is significant that American praise of the Japanese people often took the form of comparison with other Asians, especially Chinese. Because the two East Asian countries were "opened" at about the same time, their different responses to outside stimuli offered a favorite topic of discourse to Western men of learning. Already in 1856 the *North American Review* was warning its reader that the "popular idea that they [the Japanese] belong to the Chinese subdivision of the human species . . . is, probably, entirely unfounded. In language, in the method of writing, and in personal appearance, there is so great a diversity as to make it quite certain that the two nations belong to widely parted races." *Harper's Monthly* noted in 1860 that the Japanese were far in advance of other Asian peoples since they manifested "an aptitude for acquiring the civilization of the West to which no other Oriental race can lay claim." *Frank Leslie's Illustrated Newspaper* compared the "refined and enlightened" Japanese with their neighboring "birdsnest and puppy dog eaters," while the *Atlantic Monthly* contrasted China, "so palsied, so corrupt, so wretchedly degraded, and so enfeebled by misgovernment, as to be already more than half sunk in decay" with Japan, a nation of "vigor, thrift, and intelligence." The author of a pamphlet for the "Information for the Million" series went even so far as to consider the Japanese more closely related to Europeans than Asians in their bodily and mental faculties.

If by 1860 there was already this extent of contrast in the American perception of China and of Japan, it can easily be imagined that the gap continued to widen between the American images of these two countries. This was all the more the case as Americans soon found that Japan's leaders, not simply its people, were very receptive to outside influence. Initially, Japanese authorities had been pictured as oppressive and stifling the people's aspirations for greater communication with the outside, modern world. Many accounts contrasted the "good-tempered and industrious" common people with "haughty and outrageous" officials, indifferent to innovation. Soon, however, even the latter were seen as divided between a party of liberals, approving of greater foreign intercourse, and a party of conservatives, whom some called Know-nothings. The balance between the two, it was believed, would determine the policies of the Japanese government. A typical example of this view was the American report on the assassination of a high Japanese official, Ii Naosuke, in 1860. The New York *Times* called him "Prince Gotairo," which was a more or less accurate rendition of Ii's position as elder statesman. But the headline of this news article read, "Assassination of the Tycoon of Japan." There was even a subheadline reading, "Assassination of the Emperor of Japan." Whether the prince, tycoon, and emperor were really one and the same person was not questioned. What did seem significant was that the victim of assassination was at the head of the Japanese government that had adopted a forward policy toward outside contact. His death, therefore, seemed to mean the ascendance of the conservative opposition. Soon it was found out, to the relief of all, that the man involved was not the emperor or the tycoon but the "prime minister." Accordingly, it was expected that the liberal policy of foreign relations would continue to be pursued. There is irony in the prevailing ignorance of the fact that this "prime minister" had been the one person in Japan who had stood for commercial relations with the West and that his death unleashed all the anti-foreign forces of the country.

Japan's domestic instability and the civil war that this episode, among others, eventually ushered in were likewise fitted by Americans across the Pacific into their own scheme of progressivism versus reaction. It was in the interest both of the United States and of the cause of civilization that the party of progress, centering in the shogun's office in Yedo, triumph over the forces of reaction, which Americans were now aware predominated at the Mikado's court in Kyoto. The American government and people, if they paid any attention at all to developments in East Asia during the 1860's, all hoped for the success of "the Japanese government" in re-establishing order and stamping out anti-foreign diehards. It came as something of a shock, therefore, when the political change of 1867–1868 transferred power from the shogunate to a new government nominally headed by the Mikado. Believing the latter to be reactionary, the American press unanimously expressed concern. The New York *Times* wrote, "the process of civilizing Japan threatens to prove a very difficult one in consequence of a strong objection on the part of a majority of the Japanese Nobles to becoming civilized." The newspaper advocated vigorous support of the ex-tycoon by the American fleet, in the interest of civilization and commerce. The New York *Herald* deprecated the anachronistic action of the reactionary princes and predicted the successful regaining of power by the party "with enlightened ideas, sustained, as it is, by the moral support of all the Western nations." Soon Americans learned that the allegedly anti-foreign government of the Mikado was pledging itself to observe the existing treaties with foreign governments and to take every responsibility for protecting the lives and property of foreigners in Japan. The reaction of the American press was again instantaneous. In an editorial entitled "The New Era in Japan," the New York *Tribune* noted, "from the vigorous character of the people we have a right to expect that she will be the first among the East Asiatic Countries to rise to a level with the more civilized nations." The newspaper welcomed the prospect that the new government would further lead the people along the path of civilization.

As the new Meiji government in the new capital of Japan, Tokyo, showed promise of stability and took energetic steps to transform the country, the "awakening of Japan" became a favorite conversation piece in American society. Japan was awakening from a sleep of ages, wrote an author in 1872, and "throwing aside the cumbrous garments in which she has been wrapped . . . stripping for the race of mental and material improvement in which other and younger nations are striving." "The marvel is," echoed another, "that a people hitherto so averse to change should take to innovations with so much earnestness." Henry M. Field, whose *From Egypt to Japan* was one of the best-selling travelogues around this time, summed up the feeling shared by American admirers of Japan:

> This is one of the most remarkable events in history, which, in a few years, has changed a whole nation, so that from being the most isolated, the most exclusive, and the most rigidly conservative, even in Asia, it has become the most active and enterprising. . . . This has taken Japan out of the ranks of the non-progressive nations, to place it, if not in the van of modern improvement, at least not very far in the rear. It has taken it out of the stagnant life of Asia, to infuse into its veins the life of Europe and America. In a word, it has, as it were, unmoored Japan from the coast of Asia, and towed it across the Pacific, to place it alongside of the New World, to have the same course of life and progress.

Here in a nutshell were factors that made up American thinking on history, civilization, and world problems.

How did Americans explain such a magical change in Japan? The answer was found in the very premise on which these observations were founded. The Japanese, like any other people, were basically intelligent people, potentially capable of change. But their aspirations had been suppressed by their feudal leaders. This had been an unnatural state of things, which was bound to give way once the people were given an impetus either from outside or inside. Now, under foreign impact and the enlightened leadership of the new government, the right order of things within Japanese society had been restored and the popular aptitude for higher civilization given an outlet for expressing itself. Note that now praise was heaped upon the very group of men who had engineered the political change of 1868, who only a few years earlier had been looked upon as the enemy of progress. In the years after the Meiji Restoration it was the former government of the shogun, the symbol of forward-looking policy in earlier American writings, that was singled out as the culprit in Japan's retardation for centuries. As an article in *Potter's American Monthly* put it, "The continuation of . . . radical innovations under the administration of the reigning Mikado must inevitably place Japan and her people in that position among her sister nations of the world from which, by reason of the ruling despotism of the Tycoon, she has been for ages deprived." A logical extreme of this line of thought was to view the emperor as central to the political change in Japan. John Russell Young wrote, after he came back from a world tour with ex-President U. S. Grant, "At [the emperor's] bidding the Tycoon resigned an empire. When the Emperor commanded, the feudal princes . . . surrendered rank, honor, heritage, and emolument . . . Even the people . . . changed in a day, and never questioned a change, because it was the will of the Emperor." How such an image of Japan squared with that of progressive Japan was never questioned; it was sufficient to note that the potentially capable Japanese had rallied around the emperor, who had resolved to bring the nation up to the level of a higher civilization.

It will be noted that in describing Japanese progress Americans employed historical and geographical analogies; Japan was pictured as having leaped from the Middle Ages to modern times, and left Asia for the Western world. The frame of reference in either case was unmistakably Western. Japan, which in the 1840's had appeared to be in a state of life comparable to the European Dark Ages, was twenty years later alleged to have entered a modern era; a nation that had seemed to typify Oriental torpor and exclusiveness was now described as more Western than Asian. Until the 1880's, when new ideas of cultural relativism, historical determinism, and anthropology began to color American writing, Japan was pictured as the least Asian of Asian countries. The implication was that other Asians still remained dormant. Russians, considered half Asiatic and half European, seemed finally to be stirring themselves to discard their Asian heritage for Western development, as indicated by the emancipation of serfs. The Chinese and Indians, on the other hand, were on the point of "perishing" unless strong civilizing influences were brought upon them from outside. It is most probable that when Americans thought of Asia in the 1860's and 1870's they had China in mind. As the *Overland Monthly* once again reminded its readers in 1871, the Chinese were "cold, snaky, slow, cowardly, treacherous, suspicious, deceitful . . . will hear of nothing outside of the 'Middle Kingdom.' " The American image of China suffered in proportion as the image of Japan brightened.

Americans tended to view society as an integrated whole, and they could not condemn some aspects of another culture without passing judgment on its entirety. Nevertheless, Americans were not slow to admire Chinese culinary art, ancient civilization, or lacquerware. An interesting footnote is the respect some showed for the Chinese examination system. Emerson had thought the system revealed the Chinese concern for education, and many approved of it in theory as an expression of egalitarianism. Since this was in such marked contrast to the spoils system in the United States, it was natural that spokesmen for civil service reform should have advocated the introduction of a Chinese system. Opponents of the idea protested vehemently, saying such a plan was Chinese and therefore alien to America. For once there was a serious debate on the applicability of a Chinese institution to America, not vice versa. No civil service reform, however, was enacted until 1883, and it is doubtful if Chinese inspiration had much to do with its passage.

The Reception of Asians in America

One factor in the contrasting images of China and Japan was the actual contact with Chinese and Japanese in America. Throughout most of the nineteenth century Chinese and Japanese visitors to the United States represented different backgrounds and produced in American minds sharply distinct images. An American was likely to have met a Chinese domestic or laundryman, or a horde of coolie laborers working in the mines and on the railways in the west. Very few educated Chinese appeared in America; groups of students were sent by the Peking government in 1872 and several subsequent years, and some others came on their own. In 1868 a Chinese embassy, led by the former American minister, Anson

Burlingame, toured the United States, rousing enthusiastic responses wherever they went. These events served to reveal that China, too, was awakening. The American press generally considered the year of the Burlingame mission as the decisive turning point in Chinese policy; it seemed symbolic that the oldest empire, which had hitherto appeared immobile, should have called on a citizen of the newest nation to head its first official mission abroad. The government in Washington responded favorably, concluding the "Burlingame treaty," reiterating America's respect for Chinese sovereignty and opposition to interference in that country's internal affairs, mutually guaranteeing reciprocal "privileges and immunities" to their nationals, promising American supply of "suitable engineers" to work for the Chinese government, and expressing the two governments' recognition of "the inherent and inalienable right of man to change his home and allegiance." This last item was prompted by Secretary of State William Seward's interest in securing Chinese labor; he reasoned that obtaining cheap labor was the one sure way of promoting American industrialization and competing successfully in foreign markets. All in all, the events of 1868 served to draw American attention closer to China which, as an observer said, "has become our next neighbor on the West."

The warm reception given to the Chinese mission, however, seems primarily to have been directed at a fellow American, Burlingame. He captivated American audiences by his eloquence and passionate plea for understanding. His words exactly fitted American preconceptions and fired American imagination. He talked of the East now seeking the West. "China, emerging from the mists of time but yesterday suddenly entered your Western gates, and confronts you by its representatives." Burlingame exhorted Americans, "Let her [China] alone; let her have her independence; let her develop herself in her own time and in her own way. She has no hostility to you. Let her do this, and she will initiate a movement which will be felt in every workshop of the civilized world." There is no question that Americans, listening to Burlingame, now saw China as he saw it, just as he must have deliberately chosen words to produce this effect. His efforts, however, were not decisive enough to offset an image of Chinese that many Americans had already formed through their contact with coolie laborers. In fact, the very year of his visit saw a Democratic candidate for governor of California winning his election on the platform of Chinese exclusion. The Burlingame treaty, with its liberal immigration clause, proved a swan song of this phase of American-Chinese relations.

Most Americans were likely to form their view of the Chinese through their contact with coolie laborers or, what was probably more likely, through secondhand accounts of these workers in the western states. Because the Chinese came as "sojourners," to make money and return home, and many of them had not even come voluntarily, they reminded Americans of slavery and of the contract-labor system of the Colonial days. They seemed to pose a threat to America's free institutions. Their quaint manners and apparent lack of interest in Americanizing themselves struck the native population, many of them immigrants to the new western states, as subversive; conversely, should the Chinese decide to stay and make America their home, this was considered a grave threat to the health of American society. The alleged vices of the Chinese—opium smoking, prostitution, gambling, "tong wars"—would have a corrupting influence on the rest of the population. The image of the Chinese state as despotic and inhuman reinforced such arguments. The Peking government, it was asserted, would send "every malefactor in the prisons . . . here as contract laborers." Chinese workers, bringing with them the customs of the old land, were pictured as maintaining their close family and clan ties, thus forming an *imperium in imperio* within American society. Under the circumstances, it would be exceedingly difficult for individual Americans to live in harmony with them.

The obverse of the American sense of mission, the anti-Chinese sentiment, became one of the facts of political life in the United States. A characteristic response of a nineteenth-century American would, in theory, have been to welcome Chinese into the community of democratic and freedom-loving people. He would have tried to acculturate the Orientals, believing them to be as capable of absorbing truth and civilization as others. In fact only a handful of clergymen actively interested themselves in this task, while the majority of Americans, no matter how strongly they may have been stirred by a Burlingame mission, remained unconcerned. Talk of civilization and progress was not translatable into specific action with respect to coolie laborers. The prevailing image of China as inept and arrogantly traditional undoubtedly had much to do with such an attitude. The presence of a trickle of students from China does not seem to have significantly altered the picture. If anything, the view of China as helplessly conservative and that of Chinese laborers as unassimilable tended to color even the American attitude toward educated Chinese visiting the United States. An article in 1880 contrasted Japanese and Chinese students in America and described how slowly the latter seemed to shed their traditional ways of life.

Very different was the American reception of Japanese visitors. From the first governmental mission of 1860 to the influx of students later on, American reaction was friendly and good-natured. The 1860 embassy, coming in the middle of a tense political atmosphere in the United States, nevertheless aroused tremendous curiosity. The New York *Times* pronounced it an event "most momentous to the civilization and the commerce of the world for ages to come." Some recognized for the first time differences between Japanese and Chinese, others were impressed by the simplicity of manners displayed by the Japanese visitors, and still others observed the extreme inquisitiveness with which the Japanese surveyed the unfamiliar institutions of the United States. All of this served to confirm the image of Japan casting aside its policy of seclusion and eagerly turning to America for friendship and guidance. Subsequent visits by students and officials everywhere repeated the same pattern. Americans extended their cordial welcome to Japanese studying at Ann Arbor, Harvard, and Rutgers. Some, like T. L. Harris, invited Japanese youths to participate in their religious communities. Others, like Walt Whitman, wrote poems about their sight of Japanese visitors. Some of the most distinguished American educators responded to the request from the Japanese legation in Washington that they offer suggestions for educational reform in the new Japan. Japanese seemed to be intent on learning all they could from America. As a memorandum presented to the Congressional committees for foreign affairs and appropriations stated in 1872, "the fact seems now to be generally acknowledged that the Japanese people not only desire to follow, as far as possible, in all educational and political affairs, the example of the Americans, but that they look upon them as their best friends, among the nations of the globe." It was a pleasing thought that every

Japanese returning from America was becoming an active agent for Americanizing his native land.

•

Until the 1880's East Asia in America was an idea, an expression of America's own search for identity. Japan was, and China was not, becoming like America. Everything fitted neatly in an over-all pattern of cultural monism that made up American consciousness. This is another way of saying that Americans did not yet have to think seriously about Chinese and Japanese matters. There was as yet no deep American involvement in Asia, whether political or economic. The actual trade relations with China and Japan were minimal, and America's part in international politics in the East was such as to drive John A. Kasson, United States minister to Germany, to pour forth an expression of his "sorrow, bordering on a sense of shame, that the blindness, weakness, and timidity of a long continuing so-called American policy has made our flag on the Pacific Ocean insignificant." It was because of the very limited nature of American–East Asian relations that Americans could delight in an image of progressive Japan or of friendly policy toward China. But times were changing. The day was fast approaching when the United States would not view Asia with complacent detachment.

2
The Asian Response to America

Just as Asia evoked certain images in the American mind, America as an idea also grew in East Asia. During the first half century of direct contact, between the 1830's and the 1880's, Chinese and Japanese developed and responded to various ideas of America. The contrasting images the Chinese and the Japanese had of the United States were an index of their different traditions and responses to the West.

The Representative Americans

How did Asians form their view of America? Americans in China and Japan provided one kind of raw material. American diplomats, merchants, missionaries, and governmental advisers were not entirely distinct from those of other Western countries; diplomats of all "treaty powers" would co-operate together to protect their nationals or to negotiate new treaties, and American merchants and missionaries were not always acting as nationals. They were in Asia to make profit or save souls, and their being American made little difference in their endeavors. Nevertheless, contact with Americans was often the way Chinese and Japanese came to have some initial notion of America. To the extent that they looked at Americans as Americans, they were developing an image of the United States.

In China officials tended to generalize about the United States from their chance encounters with individual Americans. At the time of the Opium War, Lin Tse-hsü, the principal Chinese official at Canton, early saw differences between British and American merchants. He felt that the latter were more respectful of Chinese regulations and less aggressive than the former; American merchants were "good barbarians." Elijah Bridgman, the American missionary, confirmed this view of America when he openly denounced the opium trade. Lin saw the missionary in person and became convinced of the correctness of his initial impressions. Several years later another missionary, Peter Parker, gave precisely the opposite impression to a Chinese official. For Yeh Ming-ch'en, governor general at Canton, Parker was the worst and most outrageous of all foreigners, always threatening the use of force to obtain his ends. It followed that the United States was pursuing sinister policies. During the Taiping rebellion, high Chinese officials were impressed with the selfless services of Frederick Townsend Ward in organizing an army against the rebels. His successor after his death, Henry A. Burgevine, another American, was, however, thoroughly disliked by the Chinese. His unreliability and treasonous acts were such that the Ch'ing government put a price on his head. During the period of the "T'ung-chih restoration" that followed the suppression of the Taipings, Anson Burlingame, American minister, was the official most trusted by Prince Kung, who was in charge of foreign affairs. He had managed to convey the impression that of all the foreign envoys he best understood China's problems and therefore that the United States was most favorably disposed to China.

Examples can be multiplied. It is sufficient to note that the role of individual Americans was crucial in the formation of a Chinese view of the United States. Since permanent legations abroad were not established until late in the 1870's, contact with foreigners in China was often the only way through which the Chinese developed their perceptions of the world. Note, for instance, how Tseng

Kuo-fan, perhaps the most prominent official in mid-nineteenth-century China, characterized Americans in 1861:

> Of all western barbarians, the English are the most crafty, the French next; the Russians are stronger than either the English or the French and are always struggling with the English barbarians, who are afraid of them. The Americans are of pure-minded and honest disposition and long recognized as respectful and compliant toward China. In 1839 [Commodore Lawrence Kearny] reported to Assistant Military Governor Yang Fang that he was willing to act as mediator [between us and the English]. . . . In 1853 the rebels occupied Nanking and it was reported that the American chief proffered his good offices at the headquarters of Hsiang Jung. . . . When the English and French barbarians attacked the capital of Kwangtung, the American chief never assisted the rebels. . . . Thus, while the American barbarians have always been sincerely loyal to China, they have never been in close alliance with the English and French barbarians.[1]

Here is a rather big generalization based on scattered incidents covering over twenty years. No wonder some other Chinese officials, looking at different Americans and episodes, came to opposite conclusions. During the second Anglo-Chinese War (1856–1860), for instance, several key officials reported that Americans were no different from the British and French; they might act differently, but "their minds are all the same," as an official put it. Kuei-liang, a principal Chinese figure at Tientsin, memorialized to the throne his first impression of Americans: "Little did we expect that their language would be so insolent. They threatened us by identifying themselves with the British." Americans had stayed out of the war, but they were merely fishing in troubled waters.

Because individual Americans in China differed in temperament, philosophy, and tactics, it was natural that the Chinese views of America should also have fluctuated. The same thing may be said about the view the non-official Chinese had of Americans. American merchants and missionaries figured prominently in the treaty

[1] Cited in Earl Swisher, *China's Management of the American Barbarians, A Study of Sino-American Relations, 1841–1861, with Documents* (New Haven, 1953), pp. 690–91.

ports, and after 1860 Christian preachers were allowed to proselytize in the interior of China. For some Chinese, American merchants and missionaries were better than other foreigners; for some they were worse. There did not develop an intellectually coherent and differentiated image of America from these encounters.

The situation in Japan was somewhat different. There, though Americans came in touch with much wider circles of men than in China, these Americans were only one factor in the formation of a Japanese view of the United States. As in China, however, certain key American visitors made powerful impressions.

Commodore Perry, for one, produced an electrifying effect on Japanese officials. They had for some time been reading about the West and had been particularly impressed with the British victory over China, and so Perry's visit did not create an image of America as an aggressive naval power distinct from other countries. A select group of Japan's foreign affairs specialists were psychologically ready for a Perry visit. What the four "black ships" did for them was to confirm the image of a militarily superior West expanding steadily eastward. As Kawaji Toshiakira, a principal diplomatic figure at this time, wrote, Japan was now the only country still untouched by the West; it was being steadily encroached upon from all sides. That is to say, the Perry expedition was not considered an exclusively Japanese-American affair, but rather an opening page in Japanese-Western contact that had long been anticipated. Nevertheless, the fact that Japan submitted to Perry's pressure was of crucial significance for the Japanese, since it was from that moment that they resolved to strengthen the country to match Western power. In this sense the American commodore came to symbolize the coming of a new era for Japan.

It was, however, Townsend Harris rather than Perry who was instrumental in creating a distinct image of America in Japan. It was through Harris, the first resident foreign official, that the Japanese had a taste of modern diplomacy. His self-consciously devout demeanor and uncompromising attitude concerning treaty matters greatly impressed the Japanese. They were shocked by Harris' warning that Britain, France, and Russia were scheming to invade Japan. And at least some Japanese officials became convinced of the advantages of an open trade policy, largely as a result of Harris' "lectures." Above all, they were tremendously moved by the American's seeming unconcern with his own personal security, as he defied all warnings about attempts on his life. When he alone of foreign envoys refused to leave the capital of Japan after his secretary, Henry Heusken, was assassinated, the Japanese respect for him reached a new height. Bakufu (or shogunate) officials gladly and openly acknowledged their trust in and indebtedness to him. When he left Japan in 1862, the Tokugawa shogun sent a note to the United States president, expressing his gratification that the American envoy had brought about "happiness" between the two peoples.

The view of America that Harris evoked in the Japanese mind as a teacher and a symbol of stern justice and religious fervor was perpetuated through American missionaries and educators who followed him. They far outnumbered Europeans in Japan, and they seem to have found a rapport with Japan's educated class, primarily samurai (and, after 1871, ex-samurai). Many of these Americans were possessed of qualities, such as fearlessness, self-discipline, and the sense of superiority, that were understood and respected by the Japanese. It was chiefly from American missionaries that modern Japanese learned the ideas of God and salvation. The concept of monotheism attracted many for its forthright simplicity, and the idea of service to the Lord could be equated with the feudal precept of loyalty to one's lord. After the Meiji Restoration of 1868, many found in Christianity a new ethic to replace the feudal ethos, and those that had fought the civil war on the side of the Tokugawa shogunate were particularly attracted to the new religion, which seemed to offer solace and give life a new meaning. Even secular Americans, in Japan as teachers, were mostly devout Christians and combined religious and ethical teaching with more mundane subjects. Men like Captain L. L. Janes and William Clark, teaching at the two extreme ends of Kyushu and Hokkaido, equally excited the Japanese youths by their moral exhortations.

In contrast to China, where the influential scholar-gentry class was extremely slow to recognize the value of Western studies, in Japan there was an early awareness among the samurai class of the need to study modern science, technology, and other matters. As a result, there was greater willingness to seek foreign teachers and absorb what they could teach. This, together with the Meiji government's policy of "obtaining knowledge in the world," predisposed much wider groups of men than in China to study at foreign-established schools in Japan. As the majority of these schools were at first founded by Americans, the image of Americans as teachers became firmly implanted.

By their mere presence in China and Japan, Americans served to create impressions of the United States. But more directly, some of these American visitors talked and wrote about their country's history and institutions. Undoubtedly here was an important source from which the Chinese and Japanese derived an image of America. Probably the most crucial roles were played by two American missionaries who were early in China, Elijah Bridgman and David Abeel. Bridgman's history of the United States, written in 1838 in Chinese, was the first detailed account of the country in that language, and Chinese officials referred to it time and again as they talked about or wrote their own descriptions of America. The book soon found its way to Japan and there remained a standard reference work. The *Illustrated Gazetteer of the Maritime Nations,* ascribed to Lin Tse-hsü and published in 1844, drew on Bridgman's work when dealing with the United States. This book, in its several editions, was probably the most popular book on foreign countries in mid-nineteenth-century Japan. Thus Bridgman's description of America's geography and history directly contributed to the Chinese and Japanese knowledge about the United States. Another interesting example is the role of Abeel in Hsü Chi-yü's *Brief Gazetteer of the Oceans Round About,* written in 1850. This again was an influential volume, both in Japan and China. Hsü obtained many facts about American history from Abeel, and his writing is a good index of what he wanted to absorb from the American missionary. Among the facts recounted by Abeel, what seems to have struck the Chinese most was the personality of George Washington. Hsü was particularly impressed with Washington's refusal to establish a dynasty after the colonies won their independence. "Surely Washington was an extraordinary man," he wrote. "He refused to receive pecuniary recompense. He labored to rear an elective system of government. Patriotism like this is to be commended under the whole heaven. Truly it reminds us of our own three great ancient dynasties!" This passage, in various paraphrases, would be found in countless Chinese and Japanese writings on America.

•

Americans in China and Japan thus contributed to the formation of Chinese and Japanese views of America. Because contact with foreigners was more limited in China, a handful of Americans there made potent impressions on a small group of Chinese. In Japan there were also key American individuals who created a certain image of the United States. But the presence of Americans was not the only source from which an image of the United States could be derived. Many Chinese and Japanese came to the United States and saw it first hand from the 1860's on. In the case of China this kind of contact made little impression on the society itself. Partly this was because most of the Chinese who came to the United States were bonded servants. Even those who came on their own initiative seem to have been less instrumental than their Japanese counterparts in influencing their country's understanding of America. The difference seems to have been not in individuals but in how they and their new experiences were assimilated and put to use by their cultures when they returned home. It is illuminating to compare two of the first Chinese and Japanese students in this country, Yung Hung (Yung Wing) and Niijima Shimeta (Joseph Neeshima). Yung Wing did not come from a scholar-gentry family; his father was a comprador in Canton. Thus it was easy for the son to have access to foreign merchants and learn to speak English. It was primarily to obtain a humanistic education that he wanted to study abroad. As he wrote, he aspired to becoming a leader of men, and this could be achieved only if he became an educated man. An American education fulfilled these requirements. Yung Wing intended to use his Yale degree as a symbol of learning and influence, and sought to offer services to his country after his return. Characteristically, he found that the only avenues of advance that were immediately available were through foreign commercial houses or in the legal profession. His country was not in need of his special talents; years would elapse before he had a minor post with his government. The so-called Yung Wing mission, the sending of Chinese students to the United States lasted for only ten years, between 1872 and 1881. There were few career incentives for Chinese students abroad. In the end Yung would marry an American and settle in the United States.

The case of Niijima was in every way different from Yung's. Niijima belonged to the samurai class, and his linguistic ability was almost non-existent when, in 1864, he conceived of the idea of smuggling himself out of the country. He just wanted to get away from a stifling political atmosphere. He was eager to absorb whatever the West could offer him, so that he might better serve his country on his return. He chose the United States not only because the ship that took him away was American but also because, among all the countries of the world he had read about, the United States had impressed him most. His image of America before he left Japan was a country of a new, true religion where people were united in the worship of God and enjoyed immense opportunities, economic, political, and educational. His ten-year stay in New England did not disappoint him. He took his studies and religious experiences very seriously, and saw the hand of God in everything he did. He fell deeply in love with the United States, which seemed to have everything that was relevant to his native land. Upon his return to his own country, he became an influential figure in modern Japanese education.

The Preservation of the Faith and the State

The contrast between a Yung Wing and a Niijima was at once the contrast between China and Japan. Mid-nineteenth-century China was still largely untouched by a sense of crisis; though the Ch'ing dynasty was shaken by the decade-long Taiping rebellion and by countless other uprisings, there was as yet no intense questioning of the validity of established institutions. Almost every decade after the 1830's saw embroilment with foreign powers, and the proud aloofness of the Chinese empire was already a myth, as treaty port after treaty port was opened up, envoys exchanged, and Peking thrown open to foreign residence. Still, in the minds of the Chinese leaders all these could be comprehended as slight modifications in China's foreign relations. To be sure, Western governments could not be equated with traditional tributary states; international law, of Western origin and applicability thus far, had to be learned; Western military power and industrial development could no longer be shrugged off as irrelevant to China; and some institutional reforms were definitely needed if China were to cease to be continuously on the defensive. In order to withstand the pressure of the West, China was to strengthen its military defenses. Arsenals and shipyards were to be built, and military technology studied.

The Chinese world order as the sole frame of reference had disappeared. But China remained, and for its leaders the country was still the embodiment of wisdom and virtue. Just because the West was expanding it did not mean that China should give up its traditional culture and ways of life. It simply meant that China should improve its military capabilities so as not to remain an idle victim of Western expansion. The preservation of the faith (Confucianism), as they said, necessitated the preservation of the state. International relations were comprehended in power terms, and the world was viewed pluralistically. But China remained a unique state. If Chinese values and mores no longer seemed to be applicable universally, this was no reason to give them up. Thus the changes induced in China by the recognition of Western economic and military power were not nearly so great as those in Japan. Until the 1880's there was still a bifurcation between "barbarian" experts and the bulk of the scholar-gentry class. Foreign affairs were dealt with through a group of low-ranking specialists with no intimate ties to the main strata of society. A number of key offices were occupied by foreigners themselves, like the major positions in the Maritime Customs Administration. As for the top leadership in the Ch'ing state, the court circles and governors were aware of the problems the West was imposing on China. But even those who were most willing to innovate defined the country's task as "self-strengthening."

This background explains official Chinese views of the United States before the 1880's. As already noted, some Ch'ing officials early noted differences between Americans and other Westerners in China, and this sometimes became the basis of policy. Such an attitude probably represented what the Chinese wished to believe rather than what they really believed. However, Chinese history abounds in instances where the principle of "divide and rule" is applied to subjugate barbarians. Despite the collective term "barbarians," the Chinese had tried to distinguish between different types of barbarians. Thus it was natural that, being confronted by the power of British barbarians, some Ch'ing officials should have believed that they saw something different in Americans. Part of this was due to the fact that for them the United States was the "farthest west." The country seemed too far away to indulge in open territorial ambitions. The British, who epitomized Western power; the Russians, with whom the Chinese had had territorial and trade disputes across the long land border, and the French who supported Catholic missionary activities in the interior of China, appeared much more real. It must also be added that American officials did their best to encourage an impression of America's friendly attitude toward China.

The view of the United States as somehow different from other countries rationalized the policy of utilizing the former against the latter. During the second Anglo-Chinese War, for instance, some high officials were in favor of separating the United States from Britain and France. It was thought that in view of mutual jealousies among foreigners they could be treated separately, and that perhaps Americans might be persuaded to mediate between Chinese and British. This view did not last long, as seen above, and Chinese officials soon recognized the futility of using Americans against other barbarians. Still, the idea did not completely disappear. The Sino-American treaty of Tientsin (1858) had a clause stipulating, "if any other nation should act unjustly or oppressively, the United States will exert their good offices . . . to bring about an amicable arrangement of the question, thus showing their friendly feelings." The clause was placed there by Kuei-liang, the Chinese negotiator, who was inspired by the same desire to separate the United States.

From the beginning the United States was recognized as one of the three or four major nations of the West, together with Britain, France, and Russia. The Tsungli Yamen (Foreign Office), organized in 1861, had the English, French, Russian, and American divisions. This last, however, had charge of relations with Germany, Peru, Italy, Sweden, Norway, Belgium, Denmark, and Portugal in addition to the United States. The division was also to concern itself with Chinese laborers abroad. In contrast, the English division dealt only with Britain and Austria-Hungary, the French division with France, Holland, Spain, and Brazil, and the Russian division with Russia and Japan. The fact that so many countries were included within the American division was an indication that the United States was considered one, but the least important, of the four major foreign countries.

Even at this early stage, however, the importance of the immigration question in Sino-American relations was recognized by Ch'ing officials. Not only did the American division deal with the matter, but the minister to the United States, first appointed in 1875, was specifically instructed to take charge of protecting Chinese laborers in North and South America. In fact, for a number of years, the same official was appointed envoy simultaneously to the United States, Spain, and Peru. Spain seems to have been included because of the misconception that it was somehow connected with Latin American countries where there were many Chinese laborers. As Chinese were attacked and murdered in the western states only a few years after the 1868 Burlingame treaty regularizing Chinese immigration to America, officials in Peking were at first puzzled and then perturbed. From their point of view, it was Americans who had wanted to import Chinese labor to begin with; it was pure selfishness to turn against these laborers just because they were no longer needed. This view, that Chinese labor had played a role in America's economic development and yet was later subjected to persecution, was first enunciated by Ch'ing officials at this time and has stayed in Chinese consciousness ever since. The Chinese minister in Washington usually showed great alacrity in responding to anti-Chinese outbursts and succeeded in obtaining indemnity for the families of the men who had been molested and killed.

As the Chinese saw their "dwarfed" neighbors, the Japanese, adopt Western manners and institutions and launch upon an outgoing foreign policy, Sino-American relations became imperceptibly intertwined with Sino-Japanese relations. If the Chinese were uneasy about Japan's Formosan expedition of 1874, presumably to retaliate against the island's aborigines who had killed Liuchiu (or, as the Japanese called them, Ryukyu) fishermen, there was a greater cause for alarm in the fact that the expedition was joined by Charles LeGendre, an American military adventurer. Ex-President Grant, on a tour of the Far East in 1879, was asked by the Peking court to intercede on its behalf to settle the dispute with Japan about suzerainty over the Liuchiu islands. Here again the

Chinese were disappointed to note that Grant seemed to become decisively pro-Japanese as soon as he landed in Japan. But this issue was nothing compared with the more serious question of Korea. The Chinese early recognized a Japanese scheme to detach the peninsular kingdom from China, to which it was traditionally bound as a dependency. As a countermeasure, some officials, notably Li Hung-chang, toyed with the idea of using American influence to discourage Japanese aggression. This was probably the first appearance of the idea of Sino-American co-operation against Japan. But the Chinese grossly miscalculated, for the United States was no less interested than Japan in the opening of Korea to foreign trade and in encouraging Korea's diplomatic independence. Commodore Robert W. Shufeldt in fact first went to Japan, in 1880, to obtain Japanese assistance in his mission to negotiate a Korean-American treaty. After his efforts were frustrated he went to China and there so impressed Li Hung-chang that the latter sought to obtain the American's services in the reorganization of the Chinese navy. This, too, came to nothing due to opposition on the part of jealous foreigners. Undaunted, Li sought to procure a Korean treaty for Shufeldt, in which China's suzerainty over Korea would be recognized. The attempt again failed as Shufeldt was reluctant to enter into what appeared to be an alliance with China against Japan over the Korean question. In the end a Korean-American treaty was signed "upon a basis of equality" between the two countries, thus repudiating China's legal claim over the kingdom. Li Hung-chang acquiesced in it, feeling a gesture of friendship with the United States would reap its reward.

Thus there was no coherence in China's official attitude toward the United States. What shape it took was often a function of specific incidents as well as of China's relations with other countries. It is difficult to talk of the evolution of a Chinese policy toward the United States. The tactic of using America against others was advocated time and again and given up as often. No clear formulation of policy toward the United States was felt necessary. This is a significant fact. At no time was America considered a direct threat to China, its ruling house and established order. The path that China trod, from the Opium War and the opening of the treaty ports to the initiation of "self-strengthening," would not have been very different had the United States not sent its merchants, missionaries, and officials to China. Nevertheless, it must be noted that such adjectives as "respectful," "compliant," and "peaceful" were used by Chinese officials only with respect to the Americans they saw. At least for certain groups of Chinese the United States was different from other Western nations. Whether the difference lay in Americans simply lacking the aggressive nature of Europeans or in having more positive virtues, this notion was never to disappear completely from Chinese consciousness.

The Secrets of Power

Like their Chinese counterparts, Japan's leaders in the 1860's and subsequent decades clearly recognized the military superiority of the Western nations. Military strengthening was one of the objectives enunciated by the Meiji government as soon as it was organized. While the Ch'ing officials were generally satisfied with pursuing this goal, however, the Japanese were almost desperately interested in finding out what lay behind the West's superior power. Such a national concern reflects the fear of Western encroachment roused by the Perry expedition. It also reveals the fact that, unlike China, Japan had not developed a high level of cultural integration, so that one could learn from the West without raising serious moral and ethical questions about the preservation of Japanese cultural essence.

That concern with the source of Western power accounts for the enormous impression the United States made on Japan from the 1860's on. By 1873, between two and three hundred Japanese students in their teens were studying in the United States. American-educated Japanese youths returned home to make the history of early Meiji Japan, founding schools, publishing newspapers and books on world history and geography, introducing new techniques in farming and in industry, and becoming diplomats, generals, and admirals.

Even at the time Niijima Shimeta had made his trip to the United States (1864), a number of Japanese had already visited America. In 1860 an embassy of more than seventy samurai was sent to Washington by the shogunate to obtain ratification for the 1858 commercial treaty. The products of science and technology struck them all; they marveled at railroads, carefully observed arsenals, admired the gaslight, were amused by the flush toilet, and took copious notes on all the marks of American material progress. A milestone in the Japanese discovery of America was the Iwakura mission of 1871–1872, the first mission sent by the newly established Meiji government to observe Western countries and possibly discuss treaty revision. It included some of Japan's foremost political leaders, most of whom were in their early thirties. The sophistication of their observations is a measure of how much knowledge of the West they had absorbed in ten years' time. Detailed observations of every aspect of America's economic life were made, and politics were not ignored. Men like Ōkubo Toshimichi and Itō Hirobumi, who literally engineered Japanese modernization at this time, were tremendously impressed with the industrialization and political movements that they saw in the United States.

In fact, from the time of the Iwakura mission, economic development and the development of popular political consciousness became the key objectives of Meiji Japan. In these, the Japanese felt, was the secret of Western power for which they had been seeking. Power was derived from political and economic modernization; politically, an educated and enlightened populace must share national concerns with their leaders, and economically trade and industry must be expanded to increase national wealth. Only if these measures were carried out would military strengthening be of value, for military power was not equivalent to national power. Unlike the Chinese, who had not looked far beyond the bare fact of Western military supremacy, the Japanese had grasped two essential aspects of modernity. But they did not ask themselves whether the economic and political changes they desired could be separated from changes in social structure and ideological orientation—whether, to put it simply, modernization could be achieved without Westernization. The Japanese leaders wanted to appropriate Western methods, not Western values. They did not discuss the moral implications of Western political institutions. And internationally it seemed clear that the Western countries were powerful and aggressive, and bent on extending their might wherever possible.

For some Japanese officials the United States represented the ultimate in political and economic modernization. Although Britain was obviously more powerful militarily, America exemplified what the Japanese considered to be characteristics of the modern state. Japan, to be sure, could not follow the United States and establish a republican form of government. As Ōkube wrote, republicanism was suited to a new nation and a new people, but not to a people accustomed to tradition and bound by old practices. Education, however, was a different matter. American textbooks, teachers, and even the American school system seemed relevant to Japan as the nation began the task of inculcating in its people the idea of nationhood. In the economic realm, the history and geography textbooks issued in the 1870's by the Japanese Education Ministry all pointed admiringly to America's fabulous natural resources, productive activities, and magnificent buildings. A description of American history concluded by saying,

> In recent years this country has grown increasingly rich and strong. Its trade flourishes, steam boats navigate the Pacific Ocean, frequenting Japan and China at regular intervals, and transcontinental railroads connect the Pacific coast with the Atlantic coast. Truly it may be said that the United States occupies a commanding position in East Asian trade.

American Liberty or American Power?

The United States, of course, was not only the Japanese exemplar; it was also a Western power. And because that was so, it is far easier to say what Meiji Japanese adopted from the United States than it is to say how the Japanese felt about the United States.

The policy of the Japanese government was fairly steady; what was desired was treaty revision, and since that required the consent of all the powers, there was not much point in courting friendship with the United States to the detriment of relations with the others. However, the Japanese did think that the United States was more favorably inclined than others in considering treaty revision. This impression was probably derived from the experiences of the 1850's; as the country that opened Japan, the United States might also be expected to take a lead in altering the treaties. The Iwakura mission, discussing these matters in Washington in 1872, discovered that such was not necessarily the case; the State Department was then unwilling to consider treaty revision. But the feeling persisted that the United States was less tough than others and that Japan could count on its sympathetic attitude when the time came for negotiating treaty revision.

On one aspect of the treaty revision question the United States was sympathetic, and that was the Japanese drive for tariff autonomy. Protective tariffs to encourage the growth of native industry and reduce foreign imports were one of the things that most interested Itō as he studied American commercial practices in the early 1870's. Nevertheless, Japan was not overly solicitous of American good will, fearful of thereby arousing European suspicions.

It is more difficult to say how the educated Japanese, apart from the government, viewed the United States during the first years of the Meiji era. As the government charted a cautious course toward treaty revision and sought to effect modernization "from above," it inevitably created dissatisfaction among those who wanted more radical change. Concerning political and constitutional reform, both those in and out of the government drew inspiration from the West, but the latter were less cautious and more idealistic. During the 1870's and early 1880's, they avidly turned to European political writers, especially Bentham, J. S. Mill, and Rousseau, as well as lesser figures of nineteenth-century England. These authors, who were early translated into Japanese, gave the advocates of popular rights a vocabulary of protest and a framework for agitation. Benjamin Franklin seems to have been the only American whose life and thought made a deep impact on a number of Japanese. He was regarded as an epitome of the American idea of liberty. On the whole, the United States seems to have been associated in the minds of the early Japanese liberals with independence, freedom, and the struggle against tyranny. This, rather than individual American writers, was what fascinated the Japanese. "Give me liberty or give me death" was as widespread an expression as Confucian precepts, and the view of America as born free and abundant in opportunities was already a cliché.

This explains the exodus of a number of Japanese to the United States which began in the 1880's. Those opposed to the government and self-consciously aspiring to freedom had every reason to go to America. They found the atmosphere at home oppressive and stifling and felt they could freely express their ideas and associate among themselves more openly in America. The hero of an influential political novel, *Chance Meetings with Fair Women* (1885), goes to America in search of freedom; as he visits Independence Hall in Philadelphia and views the Liberty Bell, he is tremendously moved and driven to contemplation. He resolves to fight against tyranny in several countries. Despite its excessive sentimentality, there is no question that the portrayal of the United States as the land of the free was by then a widespread convention.

It is, of course, true that not everyone went to the United States in search of liberty. The popular rights enthusiasts were after all a politically conscious minority, mostly of samurai origin and with some means to support themselves. To a second, marginal group—those who were too indigent to indulge in the luxury of political agitation but also too restless and ambitious to remain satisfied with their lot—the United States meant educational opportunity. Unable to obtain formal schooling and enter government service in Japan, they could work and study in the United States and then return and do something constructive.

This image of America as a land of freedom and opportunities must be juxtaposed to an opposite view, that which emphasized the fact that the United States was a Western nation. Like the European nations it had sought the opening up of China and Japan for trade and residence; it was a treaty power, enjoying extraterritorial privileges and other rights under the "unequal treaties." The popular-rightists in Japan agitated not only for more political rights for themselves but also for greater autonomy for their nation. They accused the government of timidity in negotiating treaty revision and of making too many concessions in return for modification of the treaty system. When these nationalists talked of the injustice of the treaties, they inevitably had in mind the United States as well as the European governments. They felt that "Europe and America," the term used to describe the West, were employing their power to control Asia and keep Asian countries in a state of "semi-independence," to use an expression by Baba Tatsui, a British-educated publicist. No distinction was made between various Western countries. Nakae Chōmin, probably the most energetic publicist, wrote in 1881 that Japan was "constantly insulted by the nations of Europe and America"; national rights were steadily being encroached upon, and equality had long been lost. The only remedy lay in expanding the "inalienable rights of freedom" at home and co-operating with Asian countries to resist Western pressure. Nakae and his fellow agitators were well aware that the very ideas of freedom and independence were of Western origin; the awakening of Asia could not be accomplished without the infusion of Western ideas and technology. Moreover, it was believed that the people in the West, apart from their governments, were in sympathy with the Japanese struggle for equality. Before the 1880's only a tiny minority rejected the values of Western civilization and leaned toward anti-Westernism. In the minds of those who believed both in Western ideas and the fact of Western expansionism, there was no clear-cut connection between these two. It was enough that Japan should try to resist Western power by adopting Western ideas and institutions. Treaty revision symbolized this attempt. The tension between the two components of the Japanese idea of the West was nevertheless real. The United States, because its policy in Asia seemed less aggressive than that of a European power, presented a less serious intellectual problem than Britain or Russia. But the problem was there, and it remained to be seen how the Japanese would resolve the tension once the United States definitely became a dominant Asian power.

II
Imperialism, Nationalism, Racism

3
The End of the Century

Treatises abound on America's emergence as a power at the end of the nineteenth century, and on the increased role of East Asia in world politics. What one misses is an effort to transcend a parochial treatment of such subjects. Most writers have tended to view these phenomena from the perspective of a narrow geographical area. Few questions have been raised as to whether developments allegedly peculiar to Europe or America were not also discernible in Asia, or, conversely, whether the allegedly universal phenomena of capitalism and imperialism did not produce different responses from area to area.

New Definitions of National Security

Such preliminary remarks are especially pertinent in the discussion of United States–East Asian relations. There has been a tendency among specialists to look almost exclusively at internal factors to explain America's rise as a Pacific power. Quotation after quotation has been produced to show that Americans felt a sudden surge of interest in Asia in the last years of the century. Few have bothered to note that much of what Americans were saying at this time can be duplicated in Europe. For the problems faced by them were by no means unique; changes in the American perception of the world had their counterparts elsewhere. Moreover, Asians themselves were experiencing rapid institutional and ideological changes. These changes were not merely "responses to the West." Part of the West's changed attitude in the 1880's and the 1890's was itself a response to the developments in the East. Finally, one must note that while Americans now talked and thought about Asia more than ever before, Chinese and Japanese did not reciprocate. There was a decline in the role of America in Chinese and Japanese life. All in all, these years were of seminal importance for American–East Asian relations, and no simplistic and parochial approach is likely to help in the analysis of this complex period.

Technological development was the key factor transcending national boundaries. How the societies adapted or tried to adapt themselves to the new conditions of life brought about by these changes is the theme usually found in European and American history but no less relevant to Chinese and Japanese history.

The most obvious and probably easiest aspect of the response to technological change was also the most universal. This was reevaluation of the problems of national security. Europe still had its master thinkers; such names come to mind as Count Alfred von Schlieffen, who early noted the role of railroad transportation in modern warfare, and Louis Hubert Gonzalve Lyautey, who developed the idea of the modern military officer, well versed in national affairs and social problems. Scholars such as John R. Seeley, and statesmen such as Joseph Chamberlain joined the chorus, emphasizing anew the importance of colonies in the national defense system. What all these men were advocating was a new conception of security. On the one hand, the nation's foreign policy and military policy would have to be closely integrated, and together they would have to preserve and expand the economic life of the people. On the other hand, extra-European factors would have to be considered as a vital part of the European state system. It would not be enough to maintain a balance of power in Europe; true political stability would depend on a world-wide balance of power. In such a conception, the nation's security demanded state-encouraged industrialization and increased armament at home, and the acquisition of a new empire abroad. The empire may be termed militaristic; closely integrated into a national security system, overseas naval bases, colonies, and spheres of influence would add to national strength and prestige, and they would in turn promote industrial development at home. The new empire was thus essentially a product of the process of modernization.

Since technological advances transcended the confines of Europe, it is natural that echoes of the new thought were found in other lands as well. In the United States a new school of thought came into being, emphasizing the essential importance of sea power in the national defense system. Whereas, earlier, national security had been taken for granted as implicitly dependent upon a balance of power in Europe, the stirrings of new currents in Europe inevitably forced American attention to a re-examination of the problems of defense. British economic and military supremacy, which had been a guarantor of stability in the world, could no longer be taken for granted; technological advances were enabling the European navies to expand their spheres of operation, no longer making the American continent immune from their attack; and neo-colonialist thinking was driving the powers to a quest for overseas territories. Under the circumstances, it is not surprising that in the United States sea power seemed increasingly important, and that there should be many advocates for construction of a modern navy, completion of an Isthmian canal, and acquisition of overseas naval bases and coaling stations. As in Europe, there was also renewed emphasis on self-conscious patriotism and the assertion of national prestige. All these were elements that were supposed to make up the nation's strength and guarantee its security. Captain Alfred Thayer Mahan was the spokesman for the new school of thought, but it would be wrong to single out his writings, as many have done, and treat them in isolation from developments in contemporaneous European thinking.

Neither was Asia blind to the challenge of modern technology. In China influential provincial officials such as Chang Chih-tung and Hsüeh Fu-ch'eng were beginning to feel that something more than the program of "self-strengthening" was needed if the country was to cope with the problems of the new age. The realization grew that military strength was not merely a matter of ships and arsenals; industrialization must be promoted, the educational level of the people raised, and above all a greater degree of political cohesion must be achieved in order to guarantee the security of the dynasty and the state. The emphasis on education is especially noteworthy. Some Ch'ing officials were departing from the earlier view that though Western techniques might be borrowed, Chinese tradition was otherwise adequate. Now the view arose that aspects of China's political institutions and social ideas might also have to be transformed. The bulk of the scholar-official class, to be sure, still remained loyal to the Confucian principles of social and familial order. But even the conservatives were now extremely sensitive to the defense and security needs of the country. They were less against Western technology than against Western expansionism.

The Japanese, too, were not idle. They had already, in the 1870's, defined their task as political and economic modernization. But the problem of national security had not yet been very acute. It had been bound up with the question of treaty revision. In the 1880's, however, the country's military policy came to be more clearly defined. As a government memorandum of 1882 noted, in view of the "developments in the world," positive measures had to be undertaken to strengthen military defenses. A system of universal military service was adopted, the General Staff was organized, a naval expansion program was launched, and a deflationary fiscal policy was taken in order to curtail import and expand export trade with a view to industrialization and raising government revenue. In 1888 Yamagata Aritomo wrote in an influential paper that improvements in transportation and communication had made armament expansion the most fundamental need of the nation. As railroads were built and canals opened everywhere, the problems of national security demanded greater attention and larger resources than before.

In this way, as new definitions of national security were developed everywhere in the world, American–East Asian relations entered a new stage. From the 1880's to World War I, the United States and East Asia became enveloped in the "diplomacy of imperialism." The phrase refers to a distinctive era in the history of international affairs, though it is not easy to say precisely what made those years special. Imperialism as an attempt by one country to extend its economic and political influence over another has always existed, and it was present almost from the beginning in the West's relations with Asia. The Marxist-Leninist interpretation does define imperialism as a distinct stage in the development of capitalism, but such an approach is not particularly useful when one tries to apply it to international relations. For international relations are relations between nations, not between classes; and no class concept can explain them adequately. Moreover, international relations are not rational developments to be postulated by economic laws; rather they are a series of incidents with many causes—not all of them rational, and not all economic.

It probably will not do, either, to say that in the few decades after the 1880's imperialism was more pronounced than at other periods. The earlier type of "informal empire" was giving way to more formal, modern empire, reflecting the modernizing nations' adaptation to technological advances, which scattered the products of civilization far and wide and shortened distances between men. Even so, the political and economic control by the metropolitan powers over their colonies, semi-colonies, spheres of influence, and other areas may not have been as extensive as it would be later. American influence in Asia was minimal in 1880 compared with half a century later. What is of crucial significance is that in the age of the diplomacy of imperialism people everywhere became self-consciously imperialistic or anti-imperialistic, justifying or decrying expansion for its own sake, proposing and rejecting moral arguments for overseas domination, and exulting in or bemoaning the new vistas of world politics. This was the time when awareness of Western predominance drove men to postulate theories of international relations; when Asia became part of the world in Western consciousness; and when men awakened to the fact of racial and cultural diversity.

The Conflict of Civilizations

Americans, as they looked across the Pacific, were now no longer displaying the same stable, self-assured optimism that had characterized them a generation earlier. Asia seemed suddenly very close and presented problems as well as opportunities. "The great modern inventions," as a writer said in 1893, "have brought men intellectually as well as materially into closer contact." In such a situation, "the thought and life of one portion of [the world] can no longer be a matter of indifference to another, even the most remote." This proposition would have been accepted as axiomatic by every writer. But it could lead to different paths of inquiry and divergent views of civilization. For one thing, there emerged for the first time serious skepticism about the vitality, permanence, or supremacy of Western civilization. The mid-nineteenth-century view had been that American civilization, as the latest development in the West, manifested the highest qualities of mankind and that other civilizations had risen and fallen to prepare the way for the coming of this new culture; but by the same token less advanced peoples of the world could ultimately partake in the benefits of higher civilization. Now many American writers were not so sure. "It is a truth which it is perfect folly for us to ignore," said an article in *Arena,* "that our civilization is in the most vital part of its decadence, and unless some effective measures are soon adopted and strictly enforced our case will be irremediable." What the author was asserting was an organic theory of civilization: "it is born, it grows, culminates, declines, dies." While such a theory had been applied by earlier writers to all but Western civilizations, it was now held that the West was no exception. The confidence and assurance with which one had looked at Western civilization were gone. In the writings of this time one detects a tone of uneasiness. Note, for instance, that Charles Eliot Norton began an essay on "Some Aspects of Civilization in America" by asserting, "Beginning the century as a small, weak people, we end it one of the greatest and most powerful nations that the earth has known"; but that he concluded by asking, "thus we are brought face to face with the grave problem which the next century is to solve,—whether our civilization can maintain itself, and make advance, against the pressure of ignorant and barbaric multitudes."

There is no question that the tone of uneasiness in these writings resulted from the discovery or rediscovery of the disparateness of the elements of civilization as well as the diversity of humanity. Earlier it had been assumed that the political, economic, religious, and cultural aspects of a civilization were interrelated. Democracy, Christianity, and commerce were considered indispensable aspects of American civilization, not one of which could exist in isolation from the rest. The development of science and technology caused many to doubt such a view of civilization. In an article entitled "Commerce, Civilization, and Christianity in Their Relations to Each Other," a writer noted in 1885 the disparity between commercial and religious aspirations of the West. Commercial aggression and territorial expansion, he concluded, "affect most seriously the propagation of spiritual Christianity." Another wrote of the impact of science on all aspects of civilization. "For the first time in history," he wrote, "scientific thought and mechanical invention have become ruling factors. [Science] dominates all thought, and profoundly modifies literature, art, religion, philosophy, and morals." Could, then, Western civilization be defined as the civilization of science? Would it not then lead to the inference that the West was essentially materialistic? Conversely, could it not be said that scientific discoveries and technological inventions transcended the West and affected other societies as well? If that was the case, what still distinguished the West from the non-West? Few now were optimistic enough to believe in the ultimate transformation of the East in the image of the West. Rather, it began to appear more and more likely that East and West were two entirely different kinds of civilization. While earlier most thinkers had regarded them as two stages in the development of mankind, some came to concede that the two were living realities, existing simultaneously and even struggling for supremacy. One should cease, a writer of the period pointed out, "to identify humanity with the little ethnic, or geographical or religious group to which we may chance to belong." The West was now felt to be only a part of humanity. This discovery made men self-conscious; they could no longer take for granted the identity of America with the West, and the West with the world.

How, then, did East and West stand in relation to each other? This was a question that fascinated numerous American writers in the last years of the nineteenth century. Some took a bellicose stand, fortified by a Social Darwinist idea of the survival of the fittest. The vogue of Social Darwinism itself is a symptom of the West's self-consciousness. As applied to international problems, it rationalized the West's supremacy, developed a theoretical framework in which war and other types of human conflict could be explained, and assured the continued dominance of the West so long as it maintained its vitality. In this sense Social Darwinism may be taken as a defensive response to the new situation in which the West became conscious of the non-West. It also disputed the rationalism of the preceding age which had assumed the oneness of humanity and perfectibility of all men. Now the world was seen in all its diversity. Many came to view racial characteristics as fixed, and cultural development as historically determined. Such a point of view gave rise to arguments that the West's destiny as well as its duty was to confront and control the rest of the world. As John Fiske noted in 1885, the history of mankind was a history of constant struggle between East and West. The East with its "barren and monotonous way of living and thinking," and the West with devotion to the task of "making life as rich and fruitful as possible in varied material and spiritual achievement," had fought against each other, with the obvious ascendance of the latter over the centuries. This was to be again the main question of the future. President Andrew Raymond of Union College echoed these views, saying, "the history of the world is the conflict of civilizations." There had always been struggles between higher and lower forms of civilization, although on the whole there had been progress. Now, at the end of the century, there were in conflict two great types of civilization, Eastern and Western, inferior and superior. He had no doubt that the latter would eventually win the contest, but the very fact that he thought the West had not yet done so is significant. Earlier the superiority of the West would have seemed axiomatic, but now it still seemed to be in the middle of a struggle for survival with the East.

The new view of East-West relationship is a most interesting phenomenon. It was a response to the rapid Westernization of the East. Initially, this was what Americans had hoped and indeed considered their mission to perform. As Asian nations began to absorb the West's military and economic techniques, however, a strain of uneasiness became evident. What if the non-Westerners, occupying the bulk of humanity, were to become Westernized? Would they not threaten the supremacy of the genuine West? Would the West still be able to claim certain values that were their own and not to be easily imitated by the rest? Or could Westerners rest assured that no matter what happened to the East, East was still East, and West West? But didn't this merely bring one back to the original question of East-West relationship? How could the West be sure that its supremacy would be everlasting?

One of the most perceptive American thinkers, Alfred T. Mahan, raised and tried to answer many of these questions in an article entitled "A Twentieth-Century Outlook," published in *Harper's* in 1897. He writes that for centuries Eastern and Western civilizations have existed apart, not only physically but also spiritually, for they spring "from conceptions radically different." What has been happening, he goes on to say, is that the physical distance between the two has been bridged, as have physical differences between them. The East "is rapidly appreciating the material advantages and the political traditions which have united to confer power upon the West." Mahan recognizes that the new movements in the East were originally the West's doing. "The history of the present century has been that of a constant increasing pressure of our own civilization upon these older ones, till now, as we cast our eyes in any direction, there is everywhere a stirring, a rousing from sleep, drowsy for the most part, but real." Characteristically, Mahan argues that this phenomenon is a cause for great alarm. It is "our duty to the commonwealth of peoples to which we racially belong, that we look with clear, dispassionate, but resolute eyes upon the fact that civilizations on different planes of material prosperity and progress, with different spiritual ideals, and with very different political capacities, are fast closing together." The alarm is primarily derived from the fact that the non-West is appropriating the material products of Western civilization without appropriating its spiritual values. The non-West may be all the more powerful and ferocious as it is not encumbered by Christianity even while it modernizes itself. Thus "whether Eastern or Western civilization is to dominate throughout the earth and to control its future" becomes a fundamental issue of human history. It is to be noted that the question is posed in this fashion and at this time precisely as the East is becoming fast Westernized; a half-Westernized East is more of a threat to the West than a dormant East. The only guarantee for the survival of Western civilization would in theory be a heroic effort by the West to Christianize the East, "to receive into its own bosom and raise to its own ideals those ancient and different civilizations by which it is surrounded and outnumbered." This, however, would in practice be an impossible task. Thus Mahan must fall back upon the physical resources of the West; its "great armies" and expansionistic "blind outward impulses" are the only assurance that "generations must elapse ere the barriers can be overcome behind which rests the citadel of Christian civilization."

These ideas were shared by an increasing number of Americans during the last years of the century. The fear that an industrialized Asia might pose a threat to the West was implicit in Brooks Adams' statement that "as, by means of electricity and steam, all peoples are welded into a compact mass, competition brings all down to a common level. . . . Even now factories can be equipped almost as easily in India, Japan and China, as in Lancashire or Massachusetts, and the products of the cheapest labour can be sold more advantageously in European capitals, than those of Tyre and Alexandria were in Rome under the Antonines." The fear of Asiatic competition had earlier taken the form of agitation against Chinese labor. Now voices began to be heard about the possible danger of cheap imports from Asia. "Should China ever launch a great commercial war with modern industry," warned the San Francisco *Chronicle,* "boasted Western civilization would struggle simply to hold its own." Already in 1893 some congressmen were complaining of Japanese competition with the American silk industry. The view that Japan, with its cheap labor and government-sponsored industrialization, would not only exclude foreign imports but undersell Western goods in Korea and China, became a constant theme after the 1890's. American exports to Japan, it is true, always exceeded those to China, but in the business journals one notes a curious unconcern with the Japanese market as a potential. Greater attention was paid to the China market, and because of this very fact possible Japanese competition was a nightmare. In the generally accepted business view, China was still far behind Japan in industrialization, and there seemed great opportunities for Western products before China industrialized itself and competed successfully with foreign imports.

Japan's emergence as a Westernized country was greeted with particular interest and concern. Some continued to speak the language of the preceding generation. John Russell Young, for instance, wrote in 1895, "Japan is thrilled by the dawning light of Western civilization." Especially after the Sino-Japanese War of 1894–1895, newspapers and magazine articles expressed admiration of progress in Japan. Many of them had accepted the Japanese foreign minister's assertion that the war represented a conflict between civilization and barbarism. But there was also another strain. No matter how progressive or civilized Japan had become, it was still an Asian nation. Its Westernization was perhaps cause for gratification for Americans, whose ancestors had opened the door of Japan; but they should not delude themselves into believing that Japan was another Western nation. In the 1880's, writers had already begun to note the qualitative, not merely quantitative, differences between Japanese institutions and ideas and those in the United States. In his *Soul of the Far East,* Percival Lowell, one of the earliest and most articulate authors on the subject, asserted that the Japanese mentality was the precise opposite of the Western. "Ideas of ours which we deem innate find in them no home, while methods which strike us as preposterously unnatural appear to be their birthright." Lowell thought he found a clue to the understanding of these differences in "individualization." As he put it, "the sense of self grows more intense as we follow in the wake of the setting sun, and fades steadily as we advance into the dawn. America, Europe, the Levant, India, Japan, each is less personal than the one before." The United States and Japan stood at opposite poles in this scale of individuality. Theoretically this was a quantitative difference, but for Lowell the contrast was so great and permanent as to make it a qualitative difference. Japan, which many assumed was daily becoming Westernized, remained the least Western of countries. Even at the height of the Sino-Japanese War, an observer pointed out:

> The underlying sentiments, the emotional movements which sway the multitudes, the ways of looking at nature, at the ruler, and at human life, remain essentially the same as those to which "Old Japan" was subject during hundreds of years. As respects these matters, the differences between the old and the new are superficial.

Such a reminder served to rationalize the Western sense of superiority and prepare the West psychologically for an unpleasant confrontation with the changing East that might eventually come to pass.

There were, however, some who refused to believe that just because the East was still East it was necessarily hostile to the West. The distinctive features of Eastern civilization might never disappear, and there might continue to exist East and West as separate entities. But this did not necessarily mean that they had to struggle for supremacy. Would it not be just as plausible to say that the two were complementary and would coexist together to enhance the general level of human civilization? This was the view most forcefully presented by Ernest Fenollosa. In a poem called "East and West," written in 1893, he envisaged the future union of the two types of civilization as a synthesis of the masculine West and the feminine East. Five years later, he repeated the theme; East and West were to be united, not through conquest but through fusion. Just as the contact of Greece and India through Alexander the Great had resulted in a union of cultures "from which sprang modern Europe," a still "broader mankind" was to be created out of the impending fusion of East and West. As Fenollosa eloquently put it,

> It is not merely that the West shall from its own point of view tolerate the East, nor the East the West; not even that the West shall try to understand the East from the Eastern point of view—but that both, planting their faith in the divine destinies of man, shall with co-operation aim at a new world-type, rich in those million possibilities of thought and achievement that exclusion blindly stifles.

Fenollosa's was a noble dream, and his vision of one world offered a sensible alternative to the fatalistic view of East-West conflict. But he was crying in the wilderness. His voice was drowned in the shrilling chorus chanting the praises of expansion, national power, and empire.

Japan Adopts Imperialism

East and West were no closer to mutual understanding in 1900 than they had been in mid-century. The West was definitely more self-consciously aggressive, economically, militarily, and religiously. What was more, the East, too, was becoming self-conscious. The emergence of Japan as a Westernized country might have brought the world one step closer to the Fenollosan union of all civilizations. In fact, Japan symbolized the gulf separating East and West, and the rise of the island empire merely created one more problem in the confrontation of the West with the non-West.

Japanese leaders, it is true, continued to couch their policies and programs in the language of Westernization. "The nation and the people must be made to look like the European nations and the European peoples," said Foreign Minister Inoue Kaoru. It was this kind of determination that drove the government in its task of modernization and enabled it, in the 1890's, to bring about partial revision of the treaties. As earlier, there was no worship of the West for its own sake. Itō Hirobumi talked of the non-belligerent war in which the powers were engaged; they were struggling with one another to expand their commercial and industrial interests abroad, and when they did not seek territories they coveted markets. According to Yamagata Aritomo, when things were quiet in Europe the powers were making plans to advance to the Orient; "the heritage, property, and resources of the East are like a piece of meat thrown among a group of tigers." Kurino Shin'ichirō, a veteran diplomat, warned in 1897 that the attention of the powers was turning increasingly to Asia, particularly China, and it was likely that they would economically and politically intervene in the Ch'ing empire. The drama of world politics would not leave Asia alone, said Fukuzawa Yukichi.

The Japanese leaders' response was to make their country one of the advanced nations of the world, not because those nations embodied anything inherently good, but because there was no other alternative. Only by becoming one of them could Japan survive. As Fukuzawa said, Japan's independence could be secured only if Japan "left Asia." So long as Japan was regarded as Asian, traditionalism, cruelty, superstition, and national weakness would be associated with Japan. This would be extremely detrimental to its interests. Therefore, Japan should forget about its being in Asia and act together with the civilized nations of the West. It should deal with Asian neighbors just as Western countries did. It is obvious that practical considerations underlay such a thought. Kurino, representing the views of the diplomats, heartily agreed. For him, too, it was of fundamental necessity for Japan to join the "European league" of nations expanding jointly in China. Unless it did so, Japan would be left behind while the European countries swallowed up China. But membership in the elite group of nations required evidence of power and achievements. Consequently, Kurino said, Japan should invest money in China in order to establish its claim to power politics.

In accordance with these views Japan started on its road to empire. This took the form of a two-pronged expansionism, directed toward Korea and Taiwan. Traditionally, these two had different values for Japan. Korea's importance was primarily strategic. After the 1880's it became axiomatic that Japanese security demanded Korean "independence." It was considered absolutely essential to prevent the peninsula from falling into hostile hands. The potential threat could come from China, as it had traditionally maintained suzerainty over the peninsular kingdom. However, in the 1890's the Japanese were much more apprehensive of Russia. As Yamagata pointed out in his memorandum of 1890, in the event of the completion of the contemplated railroad across Siberia, Russian power would readily come to weigh heavily in East Asia and "our line of independence running through the Tsushima Islands will have been confronted with a dagger." Talk of a Russian-controlled Korea as a dagger aimed at the heart of Japan was already a cliché. But it did not necessarily follow that Japan should or even could cope with the potential threat singlehandedly. In Yamagata's view, Japan should seek the co-operation of Britain, Germany, and others interested in the independence of Korea. In the end, however, Japan went to war, not against Russia, but against China, as the latter seemed intent upon obstructing Japanese policy in collusion with Russia. But Japan took every diplomatic step to make sure that the powers would not intervene. The policy succeeded, as did the war, but when Japan demanded the lease of the Liaotung peninsula as a price of victory, it was met by opposition from Russia, Germany, and France. The idea that the southern protrusion of Manchuria should be turned over to Japanese control had been implicit in the determination to secure Korean independence. Only by entrenching itself in the Liaotung peninsula would Japan be able to secure the desired neutrality of Korea and prevent others from intervening in the peninsula. This design was frustrated by the tripartite intervention, but Japan did secure China's acknowledgment of the independence of Korea.

Taiwan, on the other hand, did not have the same strategic significance. It was considered important primarily as a base of operation in south China and also possibly in the South Seas. If Japan was to establish its claim as a power, the acquisition of a sphere of influence was vital. Since China was everywhere being encroached upon by the powers, Japan should take possession of Taiwan and then seek to expand in the areas beyond the Taiwan strait, into Fukien and Chekiang provinces. It might even be possible to turn southward and aim at the Philippines. This objective was never seriously entertained after the United States succeeded Spain as the colonial power over the islands.

These were intensely nationalistic years for Japan. There was no contradiction between the continued tempo of Westernization and the self-conscious adoption of nationalistic programs. The cabinet system of government was established, the constitution promulgated, the Diet convened, and modern amenities ranging from the telephone to coffee were one by one introduced. But by becoming Westernized, Japan was also emerging as a power, able to assert its national identity and its unique tradition. The government could choose from various models in the West instead of absorbing indiscriminately what attracted its attention. Foreign teachers would gradually be replaced, and instruction in English and German would soon become a rarity. The essence of Japanese tradition and history would be emphasized in schools. Paradoxically the more Westernized the country became, the easier it became to emphasize its traditional aspects.

Popular thinking was even more explicit in pointing up the duality of Japan's position in the world. A good illustration of how the Japanese people considered foreign affairs at this time is given in Nakae Chōmin's "Three Drunkards' Discussion on National Government," written in 1887. The drunkards represent three divergent views on national affairs. One asserts an outright expansionism; Japan should attack China, capture its rich resources, and use them to achieve military and economic strength. The second takes the opposite view; Japan should curtail its armament, persist in a peaceful foreign policy, and concentrate its energy internally, in order to create a truly democratic country. The third view is a compromise between the two; the nation should tread a cautious path, realistically responding to each developing situation, with a view ultimately to creating a constitutional regime at home. One factor common to all three viewpoints is the absence of a moralistic picture of international politics. They differ on how Japan should behave in an immoral world, not on whether the world is immoral or not. Some would stand aloof from it, others would actively join the game, while still others would take an opportunistic course. The third was obviously the policy followed by the government, and the other two may be considered reactions to official policy. Though they are diametrically opposed to each other, they share the belief that Japan should act independently of other countries, instead of timidly following their lead.

These two views were found in uneasy coexistence in the developing notion of "Pan-Asianism," an idea which symbolized reaction against the government's Westernization program as well as the West itself and demanded that Japan take the initiative in Asia and stem the tide of Western expansionism. Pan-Asianism emphasized Japan's role as an Asian nation and asserted that there were special ties binding Japan to Asia and vice versa. Japan should either establish its own leadership and even hegemony over Asia, or it should renounce aggressive designs and strive to bring freedom and independence to Asian peoples. These two currents of thought, flowing in opposite directions, could also be found simultaneously. It was difficult to distinguish clearly Japan's moralistic ideals and naked ambitions. What bound the exponents of these ideas together was the sense of Japanese identification with Asia and a conscious rejection of what they took to be the West. Of course, in advocating that Japan use military power to control China, or that civilization and freedom should be spread over Asia, these men were resorting to Western tools and even talking in the language of the modern West. But all of them were trying to assert Japan's Asian-ness. At a time when thinkers in the West were talking of incompatibility between East and West, these Japanese writers were confirming the fatalistic image of the world divided between two irreconcilable civilizations.

Reform in China

In China, too, Westernization and nationalism developed hand in hand after the 1880's. This was still the time when the scholar-gentry class dominated the political scene. But an increasing number of scholars, especially young degree candidates, were joining high officials in urging the reform of the country's institutions. Schools were founded specializing in curricula outside the traditional Confucian pedagogy, and study groups multiplied where students devoted their energy to the discussion of how best to modernize the country. Newspapers and journals began to be published, carrying fresh ideas and knowledge of the world. The humiliating defeat at the hands of the Japanese in 1895 was a decisive factor that drove the Chinese intellectuals to a serious study of the West in order to save the nation. Though the movement for political reform was often frustrated by die-hard conservatives, as evidenced by the failure of the "hundred days' reform" of 1898, the reform-minded officials and scholars persisted in their efforts, especially at the provincial level.

Ironically, this was just the moment when the threat to Chinese integrity increased, as the powers began exacting leases and concessions from China and dividing up the empire into spheres of influence. China became a laboratory where the powers tried out their new conception of national security. Relative strengths in Asia were considered an index of those in Europe, and for this reason there was determination to obtain exclusive rights and prevent others from dominating over the scene. Railway and mining concessions were sought, not only because these would serve to strengthen economic ties between the mother country and East Asia, but more fundamentally because the economic rights were a prelude to political influence and would enhance the relative power of the country. The result was the establishment of spheres of influence, among which an uneasy balance obtained. After the Sino-Japanese War, Japan too joined the game, and after the Spanish-American War the United States seemed to have decided to do so. This was the physical fact that confronted the Chinese reformers.

The Chinese view of the West was necessarily affected by these developments, domestic and external. On the one hand, the West was a model; there was no alternative to learning from it if the country were to hold its own. For the reformers, whatever the West offered that was relevant should be studied and adopted. Western works were translated one after another, either from the original or from the Japanese translation. Numerous treatises were written comparing China and the West. Typical was Yen Fu's view that "the greatest difference between China and the West . . . is that the Chinese are fond of antiquity but neglect the present. The Westerners are struggling in the present in order to supersede the past." Here were qualitative differences between East

(China) and West. Yet Yen Fu and most of the reformers did not think that China could not therefore become like a Western nation. Rather, they emphasized fundamental differences between the two in order to combat the complacent view, held by high officials, that certain aspects of Western life could be singled out and transplanted to China in isolation. But even these officials were ready to concede the need to study Western civilization. As Chang Chih-tung wrote, "if we wish to make China strong and to preserve Chinese knowledge, we must study Western knowledge." [1]

These views of the West were basically utilitarian. As in Japan earlier, Westernization programs would be pushed in order to withstand the pressure of the West. In fact, some believed the Chinese could even surpass the West by learning the secrets of its power. As Hsüeh Fu-ch'eng wrote in 1890, "Learning from others does not necessarily mean that there is no chance to surpass them. How can we know that after several thousand years the Chinese cannot carry further the knowledge of Westerners and develop once more the genius of creation, so that the Westerners will be astonished and dazzled by us?" [2] Such a view expressed confidence that China as a state would survive intensive Westernization; in effect here was a separation of politics and values. It assumed, of course, that in the West, too, the two were distinguishable. Western values that underlay its strength should be learned by China; this would not make the country Western but serve to preserve its independence. But Western political domination over the world, which might spring from the same values, must be resisted with all force. How the Western values of freedom, democracy, and progress were related to the physical fact of world domination was never clearly explained except by reference to Western energy, force, and dynamism. There is some evidence that the term "imperialism" was introduced to China via Japan in 1895. With so much being written in contemporary Europe and America in defense or attack of colonialism, the vocabulary of anti-imperialists could not have failed to be made known in Asia. The Chinese mind, however, was not yet receptive to theories of imperialism. Ironically, it was only after the Boxer crisis, the last massive out-

[1] Cited in Ssu-yü Teng and John K. Fairbank, *China's Response to the West, A Documentary Survey 1839–1923* (Cambridge, 1954), pp. 150–51, 169.
[2] *Ibid.*, p. 145.

burst of blind anti-foreignism, that the Chinese intellectuals made anti-imperialism a cardinal doctrine and a frame of reference.

The Waning of American Influence

The United States, which was self-consciously identifying itself as a Western nation, was to Chinese and Japanese by no means the most important of the Western nations. In fact, when they talked of the West they usually had in mind the nations of Europe. This reflects the fact that at this time the presence of European powers in Asia was more conspicuous than that of the United States. Even after the Spanish-American War, however, the Chinese seem to have given much less weight to America than the Japanese. But in Japan, too, there was a decline in the relevance of American ideas and institutions to the country's modernization. The basic framework for constitutionalism and military strengthening was patterned after the European, particularly German, model. One by one American educators and advisers disappeared from the scene, as Japanese bureaucrats and technocrats came of age and began managing national affairs on their own. This was the time when the modern Japanese bureaucratic structure was systematized, to which were recruited men of talent and ambition, regardless of their background. Many now passed recruitment examinations who had been too poor or too far away from positions of power to study abroad.

More than earlier, the flow of men to America was characterized by the aspirations of those who had not found a niche in Japanese society. Those who wanted to get away, who failed to make good at home, and who aspired to something different and less stifling went to America. In addition, there began a significant exodus of peasants as laborers in the sugar plantations in Hawaii. Some of them began to move farther eastward and find occupations in the mines and farms on the west coast. For most of these men America was still a land of promise and freedom. Typical was Baba Tatsui, who came to the United States in 1886 to make it his home. The erstwhile champion of human rights had found life at home unbearable and decided to exile himself in America. For a man of this type, American society was still a free and open one, where he could write what he chose. At the same time, it is notable that several Japanese in America were strongly attracted to socialist thought. Uchimura Kanzō, coming to the United States in 1888, was among the first to sense the deep-rooted problems of industrialization. The America he found was not the same country he had imagined as a Christian, the country where all worshiped God and led a spiritual life. Instead he was deeply impressed with the prevailing materialism and with the social vices that accompanied it. This was the time when Americans, too, were becoming acutely aware of social and economic problems and talked increasingly about the ills of modern civilization. It was natural, then, that Japanese visitors were impressed with these problems and attracted to socialist thought. Men such as Katayama Sen, Takano Fusatarō, and Abe Isoo identified themselves with American labor leaders and teachers of socialism. It was these men, most of them Christians, who became the founders of Japanese socialism. There were curious ties connecting Japanese socialism, Christianity, and America.

There was also a change in the Japanese attitude toward Americans in Japan. As nationalistic goals and traditional culture became emphasized in schools, there was a shift away from American teachers. Their educational philosophies and practices seemed less and less relevant to what Japan needed. An interesting example of the gulf between American teachers and Japanese students was provided by a student "strike" at a girls' school in 1892. The school, located in Sendai, had been founded and run by American missionaries. Several girls left the school in protest against what they considered an excessively American-oriented curriculum. They wanted to learn more about Japan and things Japanese. Similarly, among Christian churches in Japan a movement was under way to make them more independent of American missionary influence and control. This nationalizing of Christianity had the effect of reducing the importance of foreigners in the Japanese religious scene. There were, to be sure, individual Americans, such as Ernest Fenollosa and the Greek-born Lafcadio Hearn, who gained the respect of Japanese students and others during their long stay in the country. But they were specialists in their own fields who found Japan relevant to their intellectual concerns, not educators and engineers who served Japan in its formative years of modernization.

At the official level, the Japanese government continued to take American good will for granted in treaty-revision negotiations. The Japanese strategy at this time, however, was to concentrate on the British, who had proved the toughest to deal with. The Tokyo government was becoming increasingly conscious of the Anglo-Russian rivalry in Asia and the opportunities it created for Japanese maneuver. It was through an effort to impress Britain with a need to settle the treaty matters quickly that Japan finally achieved partial success, including the abolition of extraterritoriality. It was assumed that the United States would sign a new treaty at any moment.

A similar expectation of American good will but not of positive assistance underlay Japanese policy toward the United States during the Sino-Japanese War. Japan turned to the United States as a neutral for the protection of Japanese nationals and interests in China during the war; on the other hand, there was no thought of counting on American good offices to bring the hostilities to an end. The Tokyo government was anxious to prevent the intervention of third powers and to resolve the conflict bilaterally with China. When Russia, Germany, and France did intervene in the peace arrangement to force Japan's retrocession of Liaotung peninsula to China, Japan belatedly turned to the United States for whatever support the latter might be able to render. However, it was soon found that the United States was in no position to depart from its long-standing policy of noninvolvement. It is perhaps an index of the prevailing Japanese view of America that there was no bitterness over the latter's failure to be of positive assistance to Japan. As Foreign Minister Mutsu Munemitsu wrote in 1895, the United States was considered the country most favorably disposed to Japan. It was merely that the Japanese recognized the limited value of such good will in view of the known reluctance of the United States to play an active role in overseas affairs.

It is after 1895 that one begins to note a slight strain in Japan's official relations with the United States. Partly this was because of Japan's new sense of power. Intoxicated with the taste of a victory that had astounded the world, and self-consciously emerging as an imperial power, Japan's image of itself changed; it was no longer that of a small Asian nation desperately trying to win independence but that of a strong nation whose voice should be taken seriously in world affairs. More important in terms of Japanese-American relations was the fact that just at this time the United States, too, was expanding territorially in the Pacific. An abortive attempt at Hawaiian annexation had been made in 1893, and five years later the islands were formally incorporated into the United States along with the Philippines, Guam, and Wake Island. All of a sudden the United States was a Pacific power.

The simultaneous emergence of Japan and the United States as colonial powers in the Pacific added a new dimension to the relations between the two countries. From the official Japanese point of view, this was on the whole a situation to be welcomed, but not without some cause for concern. The Japanese at first refused to recognize that the United States had a prior sovereign right over the Hawaiian Islands. Because the Japanese immigrants there outnumbered those from other countries, and because the islands could be held as an outpost of Japanese overseas expansion, the Tokyo government took the view that the United States had no right to annex the islands. In 1897 a warship was dispatched to demonstrate against American annexation. The Japanese official on board, who was to demand reparations for injuries done to Japanese immigrants, later attempted a suicide in protest against what he took to be the government's irresolute attitude on the matter. In fact, all that the government was willing to do was to protest; lacking the support of other powers, there was little Japan could do to influence the course of events in Hawaii. Similarly, though there were some within the government who wanted to expand in the Philippines, the official policy in 1898 was to welcome American annexation. The main concern of the Japanese government was to prevent a potentially hostile power from getting hold of the islands. For this reason American or British control of the Philippines was considered a desirable outcome. Emilio Aguinaldo and other insurgents turned to Japan for help against the American colonial administration, but the Tokyo government was in no mood to champion their cause and invite friction with the United States. Rather, it was considered best to acquiesce in the American rule of the islands as a contributory factor to the balance of power in the Far East. There is no question, however, that when Japan was barred from expansion into the Philippines, its attention was turned almost exclusively to the Asian continent.

In China, too, more attention was paid to the European powers than to the United States. Chinese officials and scholars seriously studied Western diplomacy, ideas, and institutions, but these were mostly European ideas and institutions. During the Sino-Japanese War, it is true, the Peking government turned to the United States as well as to others to intercede on behalf of China. It does not seem, however, that China placed particular trust in American good offices. In fact, it must have been disappointing that the United States failed to join the tripartite intervention to force Japan to return the Liaotung peninsula. After the war, Chinese diplomacy was engaged with the questions of foreign loans to pay the war indemnities to Japan and of railway and mining concessions granted to foreigners. Here again the role of the United States was minor. China turned to Russia and its ally France for initial loans and possible military protection against Japan. At the same time, China sought to balance Britain and Germany against these two in order to prevent the predominance of a particular power. With much of the politics of imperialist diplomacy, of course, the Chinese government had little to do. The imperialist powers consulted each other more often than they did China in dividing the empire into spheres of influence. But to the extent that China had any say, it followed the policy of seeking to balance the European powers against one another. The United States was not considered in the same category. There was no thought of courting American assistance against some of the European powers. Neither was the United States regarded as a valuable source of money.

China's railway diplomacy tells a great deal about its official view of the United States. The American China Development Company, organized in 1895, sought railway concessions in China. Ch'ing officials were at first willing to grant a concession to the American company to build a major line between Hankow and Peking. As Sheng Hsüan-huai, in charge of railway management, wrote in 1897, "America has no designs on China. . . . It is very far from China and has no intention of seeking our territory." In the end, however, the concession was given to a Belgian syndicate, as it was felt that Belgium, a "small country," would be less harmful than the United States. Moreover, the American-proposed terms were considered excessively harsh; if the concession were granted to the American firm, the Chinese feared other foreigners would be outraged. The Chinese officials soon became convinced that the Belgian syndicate was in fact a front for French and Russian interests and regretted having given the Hankow-Peking line to Belgium. This accounted for their willingness to give the concession to build a Hankow-Canton line to the American China Development Company, with a proviso later added that the right should not be transferred to another foreign group.

By this time the awakened Chinese intellectuals and reform-minded officials were crying for fundamental renovation of the Chinese state. Here again they drew major inspirations from Europe rather than the United States. Yen Fu, the principal voice of the new generation of intellectuals, always talked in the British or French framework of thought. In his famous "one-thousand word memorial" he suggested that the emperor tour the world to convince Britain, France, Russia, and Japan that they should jointly guarantee Chinese security. Nothing was said about the United States. In 1897 Chang Chih-tung sent forty students to study in England, France, and Germany. Later Japan was added to the list. On the whole it seems fair to say that the Chinese reformers had Europe in mind when they talked of the West. More often than not they specifically mentioned Europe instead of the West. It would be wrong to conclude that they never thought of the United States or that they consciously excluded it from their view of the West. It was simply that the examples of England, France, Germany, and Russia were already overwhelming. Above all, they were conscious of developments in England and France and compared China with these two. This is in great contrast to the situation in Japan, where the West almost invariably meant "Europe and America."

Alarms over Asia

The decline of interest in the United States felt by the Chinese and the Japanese was in sharp contrast to the almost nationwide concern with Asia that the American people showed in the last few years of the nineteenth century. All of a sudden China and Japan seemed to have become economically and politically important to America. This was basically because of the technological advances in production and transportation, as already noted. Given the view that the world was becoming smaller, industrial and agricultural production rapidly increasing, non-Western peoples astir, and the techniques of warfare improving, it followed that the Americans could no longer be indifferent to what happened in other parts of the world. Above all, the United States should not be left behind other industrial countries in expanding their trade with Asian peoples. The image of East Asia, in particular of China, as a vast potential market for American goods had existed since the early 1800's. What characterized the 1890's was a sense of desperation because of the view that man's productive forces were expanding much more rapidly than his ability to consume. One need not take seriously such a hysterical outburst as that of Jerry Simpson: "We are driven from the markets of the world!"; or even of the more respectable A. J. Beveridge: "American factories are making more than the American people can use; American soil is producing more than they can consume. Fate has written our policy for us; the trade of the world must and shall be ours." Essentially, these statements are notable for their defensive nature, and this characterizes American economic writings at this time. As Brooks Adams said, "Eastern Asia is the prize for which all the energetic nations are grasping." Since all the industrial powers were pictured as seeking an outlet for their surplus goods, and since China seemed to be their primary target, the United States should not be left out in the competition. It was assumed by many that the competition would not be a free competition under conditions of laissez-faire. Brooks Adams was an exceptional case when he wrote, "Our geographical position, our wealth, and our energy pre-eminently fit us to enter upon the development of Eastern Asia and to reduce it to part of our own economic system." America's economic supremacy, however, did not offer much consolation to many of Adams' contemporaries, who felt that the foreign governments were energetically pushing their nationals' economic activities, thus interfering with the natural law of selection. Under the circumstances, it seemed essential that the United States government, too, bestir itself and make the promotion of trade in China a primary goal of its policy. It was in this spirit that the New York Chamber of Commerce urged the State Department to take "such proper steps . . . as will commend themselves to your wisdom for the prompt and energetic defense of the existing treaty rights of our citizens in China, and for the preservation and protection of their important commercial interests in that Empire." The "proper steps" meant many things to many men, but to the advocates of vigorous policy they would include assisting Americans in China to obtain concessions, guaranteeing these concessions, using force to protect them, engaging in active diplomacy to increase American weight in East Asia, and to protest against any infringement by China or other powers upon the rights and interests acquired by Americans. In other words, the United States government was being asked to depart from the long-standing policy of leaving overseas economic activities to private citizens.

Coupled with the economically motivated views was a new emphasis on Asia in American military thinking. Japan's emergence as a power, followed immediately afterwards by America's emergence as a colonial power in the Pacific, naturally shaped the orientation of naval thought in the United States. The two events were not necessarily related; the decision to acquire the Philippines had little to do with purely military considerations. Nevertheless, at least in American naval circles, there was a logic behind the acquisition of the islands in the Pacific. It was to fulfill the Mahan-type idea of the United States as a sea power, with a two-ocean fleet, an Isthmian canal, and overseas bases and coaling stations. The need for the last in the Pacific seemed to have increased as a result of Japan's rise as a power. The Hawaiian episode of 1897 was symbolic. From that year on, one finds in American naval writings the mention of Japan as a naval rival. The acquisition of the Philippines, so close to the Japanese colony of Taiwan, naturally raised serious problems of defense. Now that the definition of American security had been extended to cover these islands thousands of miles away from the west coast, East Asia naturally became a matter of great concern for naval strategists. The security of the Philippines would require not only the fortification of one of the harbors there and the strengthening of the Asiatic fleet but also energetic diplomatic efforts to prevent a big-power coalition against the United States. This would necessitate paying much closer attention to East Asian international politics than earlier. Moreover, some navalists insisted on obtaining naval bases on the China coast; they would complete the island chain of defense in the Pacific and link up the Orient more completely with the Atlantic coast.

Finally, mention must be made of a religious interest in Asia, in particular China. By the 1880's American missionaries had already been in the field for nearly half a century. As noted earlier, they had on the whole been more successful in Japan than in China. After the 1880's, however, conditions in these countries, coupled with developments in American religious life, conspired to bind missionaries and China closely together. While in Japan there was a trend toward nationalism even among Christians, the new wave of reform and Westernization in China gave American missionaries just the right atmosphere for their energetic work. In the United States there was emerging the "social gospel" movement, emphasizing the social aspects of Christianity. The churches were interesting themselves in fighting corruption in politics, slums of the cities, and the injustices of an urban society. The trend, although by no means predominant at this time, was inevitably reflected in overseas missionary activities. There was now less emphasis on individual salvation through the personal experience of redemption and regeneration; schools and hospitals were considered important tools of evangelization, and missionaries were encouraged to teach lay subjects such as the English language and the sciences. In a sense the emphasis shifted from individual salvation to national regeneration. The missionaries came to believe they were attacking the ignorance and poverty of the whole Chinese nation, and they would liberate the people from these ills as much through education as through personal redemption. That the missionaries' view of the Chinese had not totally changed may be seen in Arthur H. Smith's *Chinese Characteristics*. Published in 1894, the book still abounded in the by then standard references to the alleged weaknesses of the Chinese character, such as their disregard of time, their love of money, and their "absence of nerves." There is no reason to doubt that this was a view generally held among American missionaries. However, such a negative image of the Chinese seems all the more to have propelled the Christian workers to devote their lives to the regeneration of China. While Chinese characteristics had not apparently changed, the missionaries noted the great potentiality of the field. China seemed to be on the eve of a great transformation, and it was an attractive prospect to lend a hand in the process of national rebirth.

It is against the background of an aroused national interest in East Asia, whether economic, military, or religious, that one must consider the policies pursued by the State Department. It becomes evident at once that the official policy of the United States, in spite of the promptings by business, naval, and missionary circles, remained on the whole passive and at times even negative. The State Department forswore joint mediation with other powers in the Sino-Japanese War and vetoed the suggestion by Minister Charles Denby that the United States act vigorously during the war with a view to enhancing its influence in East Asia. After the war, the State Department evinced no interest in actively promoting private business in China; it refused to intercede on behalf of the China Development Company when the Chinese awarded the Hankow-Peking railway concession to a Belgian syndicate, and it declined to act together with Britain to keep China from being carved into colonies and spheres of influence. The government in Washington was guided by the principle that economic activities abroad should be left to private initiative. Neither was the State Department impressed with the need to obtain a naval base in China. The security of the Philippines did not seem to demand the acquisition of such a base.

It is this negativism that inspired the Open Door notes of 1899. Contrary to what historians have maintained, the notes did not mark a commitment by the United States government to a positive policy in China. John Hay, it has been argued, was different from John Sherman, whom he replaced as secretary of state in 1898, just after the Spanish-American War, and unlike his predecessor, Hay was determined to assert America's rights more vigorously in East Asia; he would use diplomatic and even military means to protect and extend American business interests in China. This, coupled with his eagerness to co-operate with Great Britain, made him inclined to take up suggestions by men like William W. Rockhill and the Englishman Alfred E. Hippisley for an enunciation of policy toward China. The result was the sending of notes to the various governments inviting their adherence to three principles: non-interference with the vested interests within the existing spheres of influence in China, the uniform application of Chinese treaty tariffs at all ports within these spheres, and non-discrimination regarding railroad charges and harbor dues in these spheres. In thus defining America's position, Hay is usually pictured as having declared the principle of equal commercial opportunities and let it be known that henceforth American interests would not be tampered with in China.

The Open Door policy has become a myth. No American account of American–East Asian relations has failed to mention it as a central factor. Many have indeed described the subsequent history of American-Japanese and American-Chinese relations in terms of the policy; whether in defense of the United States' East Asian policy or in criticism of it, it has been taken for granted that the Hay notes marked a new stage in America's relations with East Asia. East Asian historians, too, have tended to agree. Even those extremely critical of American policy, such as Marxist writers in Japan and virtually all Chinese historians today, interpret the 1899 policy as a positive principle that was intended to serve the interests of American capitalism. The Open Door is seen as a logical expression of the policy of dominating the China market by preventing others from excluding American interests.

What in fact happened in 1899 was precisely the opposite of what is usually assumed to have happened. The Open Door policy as enunciated by Hay that year was a negative response to the public demand for positive and vigorous assertion of American rights and interests in China. Hay reassured the business interests that they would continue to be safeguarded, though no sanction was mentioned. He refused to affirm any policy concerning concessions in or loans to China. He was entirely silent about naval bases. In other words, his notes had nothing concrete to satisfy the demands for a vigorous policy in East Asia. What he was saying in effect was that the State Department would continue the policy of passive economic foreign policy, protecting American business interests where needed but without resorting to drastic measures. There was no interest in playing a role in power politics. Neither did Hay believe that the security of the Philippines required more forceful measures. Thus in a sense the 1899 notes were addressed to the American exponents of vigorous policy, as much as to the foreign governments. That is why many individuals and groups continued to talk as though he had not spoken. Businessmen did not stop their agitation for an Open Door in China even after the enunciation of the allegedly Open Door doctrine, and navalists went on to press for an adequate harbor on the China coast.

Similarly, neither Japan nor China took particular interest in the Hay notes. The Japanese government responded favorably, viewing the American note as a reiteration of the most-favored nation principle. The Hay message confirmed the impression the Japanese had of the passive nature of American policy in East Asia; certainly it was in marked contrast to the more aggressive policies being pursued by other powers. But the Tokyo government did not believe the Hay note would make much difference in the East Asian scene. The Ch'ing court, too, was not particularly impressed; the note had not even been addressed to China, and as the Chinese saw it there was little cause for satisfaction. It was an American policy, intended to safeguard American interests, and there was no reason why the Chinese should feel interested.

What one notes in the evolution of mutual images among Americans, Chinese, and Japanese in the last years of the nineteenth century is the gap between reality and perception. Physically, the United States was expanding into the western Pacific, and the distance separating the United States and East Asia was narrowing. Moreover, Japan was entering the expansionist stage of its modernization, and China was taking steps toward reform and Westernization. However, America had hardly penetrated Chinese consciousness, and the Japanese were little aware of the implications for the future of the simultaneous emergence of Japan and the United States as Asian imperialists. In the United States, those who grasped the momentum of change in Asia tended to view it within the framework of East-West confrontation. It remained to be seen whether the three peoples would look more realistically at one another and develop a new conception of American-Asian relations.

4

Imperialism—Japanese and American

Between 1900 and 1905, the views China, America and Japan held of each other underwent subtle changes. For the first time in history Americans fought on Chinese soil by participating in the Boxer expedition. For this and other reasons the nascent public opinion of China was aroused against the United States as the foremost imperialist. The Japanese, although they also fought in China, were considered in a more favorable light, and a growing number of Chinese turned to Japan for inspiration and help. In time American opinion had to adjust itself to the rise of an Asian imperialist across the Pacific, and some current of anti-Japanese sentiment was felt already at the end of the Russo-Japanese War (1904–1905). In some quarters this was combined with a changing attitude toward China, a friendly and sympathetic feeling. Japan and China came to embody two different types of Asian development. All in all, these were years of crucial importance for the future course of American-Chinese-Japanese relations, and they are worth examining in detail.

Anti-Imperialism in China

In China, what in retrospect appears as an opening shot of anti-imperialism was fired in 1901 by Liang Ch'i-ch'ao in an article entitled "On the Development of Imperialism and the Future of the World in the Twentieth Century." Liang represented the voice of China's new intellectuals, determined to renovate the country to match the power of the West. They read widely of world affairs, refused to be drawn into the barren dispute over tradition versus modernization, and conceived of China as a nation-society whose survival and growth was their chief preoccupation. In a word these intellectuals were emerging as opinion leaders of the new China. They were active in schools and study societies, edited and contributed to numerous newspapers and journals, and even took to the streets to spread ideas. It is no wonder that they stressed "public spirit" and talked of "public opinion." As they viewed their country and their people, there was still excessive and exclusive concern with personal affairs; the country lacked any organic national unity. It was this situation that the reformers were eager to remedy as the first step toward China's regeneration. The recognition of precisely the same problem had driven Japanese leaders to mass education and indoctrination.

Liang Ch'i-ch'ao was undoubtedly the greatest and most prolific writer of the new generation. Determined to arouse national consciousness, he talked of differences between China and the West and sought to create a new national body politic after the pattern of Western nations. But he was not merely imitative of the West. He was profoundly fearful of it. By 1901 he had come to take anti-imperialism as axiomatic. He seems to have gotten his ideas of imperialism, which remained crude and unrefined, mostly from Japanese writers or Japanese translations of Western writers. It is well to recall that anti-imperialists were as active as supporters of imperialism in England in the 1890's. Those who opposed overseas expansionism and colonialism talked of "economic imperialism" where empires were created and expanded as outlets for surplus capital of millionaires at home, who found it more profitable to invest abroad than to spend the money at home to promote the welfare of the lower classes. For some polemicists imperialism was an inevitable and necessary stage in the development of capitalism; one could oppose it only if one were willing to oppose capitalism. On the other hand, other anti-imperialists felt they could object to specific features of colonialism as immoral and wasteful without necessarily challenging the basic framework of the state. In fact, there were those who believed imperialism would end up destroying the fabric of the society at home by creating an overseas military administration and colonial armies. All these ideas were spread outside of Europe; in the United States the second category of anti-imperialism predominated, whereas in Asia the first category, viewing imperialism as an economic inevitability, became popular.

It is not surprising, then, that Liang Ch'i-ch'ao readily subscribed to the economic interpretation of imperialism. It gave a world view in which the problems facing China were explained. It was no longer the issue of Chinese versus barbarian culture, nor of uncivilized Westerners invading the Chinese empire. China's recent past was seen as a page in human history; Chinese history was integrated into world history. As Liang pointed out in the abovementioned article, Western imperialism had resulted from the search for overseas markets, which in turn was necessitated by technological advances. Expansionism, territorial aggrandizement, and the policy of aggression were all aspects of the same thing. A century that had opened with the suppression of Filipino rebels could not be called a century of freedom. Rather, struggle between independence and imperialism would characterize the twentieth century. China's only hope lay in national unity and a strong foreign policy. The people must unite with officials to resist foreign encroachment, and together they must modernize the country and emerge as a strong nation.

This was the framework in which virtually all Chinese reformers, official and non-official, spoke at the turn of the century. There were, to be sure, various shades of opinion on concrete problems, and the revolutionaries, aiming at the overthrow of the Manchu dynasty, were sharply opposed to the reformers. These differences in time led to crisis, and by 1912 the dynasty had been overthrown. Such developments, however, should not be made to obscure the basic agreement in China on the nature of imperialism and the necessity of saving China by drastic measures. The West was something to be feared, and China was to respond to the challenge constructively. It is interesting to note that this amounted to the idea of a white peril. As Liang wrote, the Aryan race had "dropped its mask and showed its true face." The white race was rapidly expanding, bent on subjugating the colored races. Japan, of course, would be an exception, but little was said at this time about Japanese imperialism. Japan simply seemed to follow the lead of the Western powers. The threatened extinction of the Chinese race was at any rate a common theme in Chinese writings.

It is not surprising that the United States was regarded no differently from other imperialist powers. In fact, to many Chinese America was the imperialist power par excellence. The acquisition of the Philippines, the suppression of the Filipino rebels, and the participation in the allied expedition to Peking during the Boxer crisis seemed to epitomize America's new imperialism. As Liang wrote, "Now that the famous expansionist, McKinley, has been elected President, there is no knowing what big things the United States might not do in the twentieth century."

Japan and America in China

Unlike the Chinese, the Japanese did not have to worry about the immediate problem of national survival. Few talked about the white peril; the most serious question of the moment was the Russian menace, which seemed to be in the way of Japanese aspirations in Korea. Japan's role as an imperialist power was accepted by most Japanese. They congratulated themselves on their participation in the Boxer expedition, in which Japanese troops marched side by side with those from Europe and America. This episode was symbolic of Japan's new status as a power. It had been accepted into the "community of nations," hitherto dominated by the Western states. At the same time, some observers were well aware that this achievement produced more serious questions about the country's future. As an influential newspaper *Jiji shimpō* noted in 1901, Japan had been accepted as a member of the civilized community of nations; at the same time, Asia was likely to be the principal theater of human endeavor in the new century. Much more exacting tasks therefore awaited Japan than mere Westernization. How should Japan, as a Westernized Asian nation, behave in Asia at a time when that part of the world was increasing in political importance? This was the question raised by Fukuzawa Yukichi and many of his contemporaries.

Japan's policy makers were at this time guided by what they took to be the rules of the game of imperialist politics. As they saw it, each power was entitled to a loosely defined sphere of interest but it also recognized the preserves of other imperialists. Imperialist politics was based on some sort of general consent to a status quo. Japan's diplomatic attention was turned to the question of more clearly defining the status quo, as during the Boxer episode Russia seemed to challenge the existing equilibrium by threatening to extend its control southward from Manchuria to Korea. With the United States, Japan had few quarrels. In the Japanese government's view, there was tacit agreement that the two imperialists would recognize each other's colonial possessions and other rights in Asia. Thus Japan would not interfere with American rule over the Philippines. In return, it was expected that the United States would respect Japanese claims in China. The Tokyo government was considerably agitated when, in 1900, the State Department hinted at an interest in obtaining the lease of a port in Fukien province, which the Japanese considered to be part of their sphere of influence. During this episode, Minister Takahira Kogorō in Washington thought Japan might give its consent, as this would cement ties between the two countries. It is characteristic of Japan's imperialist policy that Foreign Minister Katō Takaaki vehemently opposed, saying Japan should not be guided by friendly sentiments alone.

This episode was also significant in terms of American policy. For the Boxer crisis did present new problems to the United States in Asia. In terms of economic interests, there was nothing new about internal disorder in China; American lives and properties would be protected with all available forces, and the United States hoped that peaceful conditions would return as quickly as possible. It was rather the military implications of the Boxer incident that were sensed as something new. First of all, a large-scale civil war in China could affect the security of the Philippines, where American forces were still combating the rebels. The commander of the American Asiatic Station was unhappy about diverting his men from their task in the Philippines to China in order to suppress the

Boxers. Moreover, dissident elements in China and the Philippines might co-ordinate their action to revolt against established authority. Expeditions by the powers to China would mean that much strength added to foreign establishments, so close to the American colony. The expeditionary forces of the various countries might take advantage of the opportunity to entrench themselves in China, thus virtually carving up the country. On the other hand, if American forces did not co-operate with them, not only might American lives be endangered but this might be taken as a sign of weakness by the Chinese.

All these problems confronted American policy makers, for whom the question of security in the western Pacific became suddenly very real. The navy stepped up its demand for a port on the China coast, and its requests were supported by Minister Edwin Conger. It is against this background that Hay's second policy enunciation, issued on July 3, 1900, must be examined. It shows that he once again vetoed the navy's suggestion for obtaining a base in China. Instead, Hay insisted that American security could best be safeguarded if China's "administrative and territorial entity" were preserved "in all parts" of the empire. The circular also stated that the United States still recognized the existence of the Peking government, although the country was in a state of virtual anarchy. The State Department, in other words, believed that a unified China was a better prospect for maintaining the security of American possessions than a China weak and divided. It was in line with such a policy that the Asiatic Station sought jealously to prevent other nations' navies from establishing a permanent foothold in China and that the United States presented less harsh terms of settlement of the Boxer crisis than those offered by most other nations.

The incident involving the premeditated lease of a port in Fukien was entirely out of line with the general policy being pursued by Hay, and should not be made to obscure his fundamental approach. Only once and very briefly did he capitulate to navy pressure. After Japan offered firm resistance, he never again mentioned the port. To say, as some have done, that neither Hay nor President Roosevelt had any intention of vigorously opposing the partitioning of China by other powers is to miss the point. Hay's disclaimer in the July 3 circular was as much directed toward the naval positivists in the United States as toward the foreign governments. He was well aware that the United States could not singlehandedly support Chinese integrity. All he implied was that for the time being he did not consider the partitioning of China to be in the best interest of America. His basic objective was the security of the Philippines. Thus it is not surprising that while the State Department enunciated the policy of China's integrity, plans were under way to augment the Asiatic fleet and to build a permanent base in Luzon.

Outside the government, the Boxer crisis and its aftermath served to sustain public interest in Asia. Those who had spoken or written about China and America's role in Asia believed their views had been vindicated. Mahan was certain his predictions about the aroused masses of China had proved true. His view was that an unstable condition in any part of the world was a menace to civilization; chaos in such a vast territory as China must be brought to an end in the interest of humanity. At the same time, Mahan visualized Asia as an arena where the future of the world was going to be decided. He postulated a conflict between land power (Russia and France) and sea power (Britain and Japan). The balance between the two could ensure stability of the Asiatic continent, and it was essential for American interests to maintain the balance. Since Russia seemed intent on extending its power, thus threatening to upset the equilibrium, it was essential that the United States stand with the sea powers. Fear of Russia, coupled with fear of the Chinese masses, was a theme often found in American writings at this time. Whether ignorant and barbaric, or industrialized and armed with modern weapons, the Chinese under Russian support or domination would be a formidable threat to the rest of the world. The United States particularly seemed to be in danger, as China would not only exclude American goods but try to export cheap industrial goods to America. Such an argument was used by the exclusionists, those who wanted legislation permanently excluding Chinese immigrants, but they were by no means alone. It is illuminating that business groups were among the most vigorous advocates of the use of force to suppress the Boxers. Underlying this attitude was the image of the Chinese united in anti-foreignism. For the first time, Americans came to fear Chinese. Just as the United States epitomized the "white peril" for some Chinese, China, possibly under Russian domination, was synonymous with the "yellow peril" for many American writers.

Rehabilitation of China

For China the greatest issue after 1901 was rehabilitation and regeneration. The degree of optimism in post-Boxer China seems hollow in the light of subsequent events. Modernization and nationalistic foreign policy had to be carried out at the very time when the Russian government sought to consolidate its political and economic hold on Manchuria. Other governments seemed little inclined to resist Russia; moreover, they had acquired new rights as a result of the Boxer affair, such as the right to station troops between Peking and the sea. Still, after the Boxer crisis the Chinese came to believe that the powers did not really want to partition China into outright colonies. Though this was small consolation, it seemed just possible that it was not yet too late for the Chinese to undertake decisive reform.

As tension mounted between Russia and Japan over the Manchurian question, practically all high Ch'ing officials expressed the view that no matter what happened to the two powers, China should augment its military forces and otherwise carry out modernization programs. Thus prepared, the Chinese were not driven to panic when war did break out between Russia and Japan in February 1904. They were determined to maintain strict neutrality and meantime step up their effort to strengthen the country. As one official informed the throne, steps must be taken to exterminate internal bandits, promote commerce, and strengthen provincial defenses in order to cope with the situation after the war. This was a formidable task, but at this time there at least was a unity of purpose and purity of determination.

It is not surprising that in such a frame of mind the Chinese should have made the United States a target of their nationalistic thinking. They would have agreed with Liang Ch'i-ch'ao that the policy of preserving Chinese integrity was a new form of imperialism, constituting economic aggression. There was no point in congratulating themselves that the United States would commit itself to a principle of non-aggression. The fate of American Indians and

Filipinos might befall the Chinese unless they resolutely resisted foreign expansionism. The vision of America, once a land peopled by Indians, where the whites subjugated the latter, appealed strongly to Chinese sensitivity, especially since nearer home Filipinos were fighting a losing battle against superior American forces. Besides, there was not much expectation that the United States would assist China to repel Russian influence from Manchuria. During the war a small minority believed that the United States should be counted upon to mediate between the two combatants. As the Chinese minister to Italy pointed out in December 1904, the treaty of 1868 had mentioned America's readiness to offer good offices to help China. China should therefore ask that country to mediate. This was, however, distinctly a minority view, and the Chinese government continued the policy of neutrality and inaction.

The Russo-Japanese War, in fact, was regarded by some in China as a struggle between the white and the yellow races, and between constitutionalism and dictatorship. The minister to Belgium expressed the opinion that the war was a racial conflict; if Japan won, the Europeans' fear of Japan might express itself against China as well. The best policy for China was to increase contact with Western powers so as to obtain their confidence. Some writers outside the government were more sanguine. An article in the influential *Tung-fang tsa-chih* (*Eastern Miscellany*) noted that the war was about to determine the questions of "the glory or decline of Asia and Europe, the rise or destruction of the yellow and white races, and the victory or defeat of despotism and constitutionalism." Another writer pointed out that if Japan won, obstacles in the way of the yellow race would have been removed and the situation in Asia would gradually improve. The Chinese should do what they could, in the meantime, to reform their institutions, extend their knowledge, recover national power, and seek independence and strengthening of the country. As seen here, Chinese writers regarded the Russo-Japanese War as a turning point in the history of Asia and of China. At last the tides seemed to be turning against the Western domination of Asia, and in favor of political reform at home. Few were as naïve as a writer who said Japan was fighting China's war, motivated by a sense of justice to help the neighboring country. Most officials and writers expressed concern over what Japan, if victorious, might do after the war. Even so, they welcomed Japanese victory, not only because of its racial implications but also because it would prove the strength of a constitutional regime. As an official wrote, Japan was bound to win since national opinion, unlike that in Russia, was united. Liang Ch'i-ch'ao lent his prestige to the notion by writing that the war was "a testing ground to compare the strengths and weaknesses of despotism and a free country."

This was the time when the Chinese rediscovered Japan. On the one hand, there was the recognition that Japan had joined the ranks of the imperialists. As Yüan Shih-k'ai noted during the war, "After the Russo-Japanese War Japan's influence in Asia will increase day by day. As Japan's territory is small and people poor, it never ceases to crave for Chinese territory." On the other hand, Japan's role in China's reform was well recognized. An official stated, "Of all the countries in the world, China and Japan are the two most intimate. China is now undergoing reform so as to become like Japan. Their common interests now and in the future are limitless." It was this feeling that motivated the official encouragement of students studying in Japan. Their number increased tremendously in 1904 and 1905, reaching 8,000 in the latter year. The Chinese minister in Tokyo acted as superintendent of Chinese students. Minister Yang noted that since Japan's military schools sought to inculcate students in the principles of loyalty to the emperor, patriotism, and absolute obedience to the superior, it would be a good thing for the provinces in China to send their boys to Japan for military education; conditions in world affairs made it essential to train students in military affairs. But the minister also saw advantages in the students' going to Japan to study law and politics. In a report to the throne submitted in January 1905, he pointed out that Japanese political institutions were more useful as models for Chinese reform than the republican institutions of France and the United States, or the purely European institutions of England and Germany. Moreover, since Japan had recently rid itself of extraterritorial and other features of the treaty system, there was much that the Chinese could learn from Japan in their own effort to modify the treaties.

Political Consciousness in China

For the Chinese the war between Russia and Japan was only one of many new developments. The coincidence of the war with the increasing tempo of political reform is probably the most important fact at this time. A few years earlier there would have been much less public concern with external affairs, and the war would not have served as a point of departure for many a discussion of politics. In fact, modern public opinion was emerging just at the time the war broke out, thus giving impetus to the movement for constitutionalism, reform, and nationalism. As a writer noted late in 1905, for a few years newspapers had been trying to arouse the people to the danger to the nation. Happily, the people seemed to have been aroused. "The preservation of national independence and rights has become a well-accepted slogan even among the lower classes." For the first time in China's history, the people began to organize themselves into political groups and *ad hoc* committees and assert their right to have a voice in decision making. They wrote letters and sent telegrams to the Foreign Ministry, not in the spirit of rebellion but in order to assist the officials in their effort to regain national rights.

The United States was the first target of aroused Chinese nationalism. It is true that groups of Chinese bitterly denounced Russian penetration of Manchuria, but it was against America's immigration policy that modern Chinese opinion showed its effectiveness and demonstrated its power. The immigration question came to a head as the United States Congress discussed and finally passed a bill in 1904, permanently excluding Chinese immigration from American territories. In an effort to show their displeasure and support their government's negotiations to seek revision of the immigration regulations, Chinese merchants in Shanghai, Canton, and elsewhere resorted to a boycott of American goods and services. Propaganda materials circulated during the boycott pointed out that America's material growth had been achieved to a large extent at the expense of China; China had absorbed cheap American goods, which displaced Chinese workers, who migrated to the United States to build railways and work in the factories. The United States should therefore be grateful to China and treat the

Chinese as their equals. The boycotters, however, consciously refrained from indiscriminate anti-Americanism. They attributed Chinese exclusion to the agitation of American labor, not to the American people or even government. "The harsh regulations [against the Chinese] are only supported by American labor, and the enlightened people in America are opposed to them. Other civilized countries all disapprove of these regulations." Or, as a magazine entitled *Women's World* noted, the United States was the country where women's rights were most advanced. Chinese women, therefore, were only following the American example when they stood up and opposed the Chinese exclusion act.

The boycotters self-consciously referred to their protest movement as a "civilized action." In their view, and quite justifiably, their movement was the first expression of modern Chinese nationalism. As an article put it, "This is the first time since the country was opened to foreign trade that various groups of men of all classes co-operated together and through civilized acts sought to recover rights. Truly this is evidence that the people's knowledge is gradually increasing. Protesting against this and that American regulation is not the whole story." The anti-American boycott was not an end in itself; it was significant as an example of the aroused national consciousness of the Chinese people. The leaders of the movement believed the whole world was watching them; if they resorted to violent xenophobia, there would be a revival of the Boxer incident and the world would conclude China was not fit to be counted as a civilized nation. The successful execution of a peaceful boycott would prove that the Chinese, too, were capable of organizing themselves and making their voices heard. When five American missionaries were killed near Canton during the boycott, the boycotting merchants immediately disclaimed any connection between the two events. It was crucial that the boycott not be regarded as another outburst of blind anti-foreignism.

The boycott gradually lost its force, and its effect on American immigration policy was negligible. But it served to demonstrate that henceforth an organized and educated public opinion would be a factor to be reckoned with. Ch'ing officials, too, became aware of this; while they were wary of seeming to condone the boycott, both for fear of American retaliation and of its developing into undisciplined disorder, they recognized that the movement represented something new in the Chinese political scene. The governor general at Canton expressed sympathy with the boycott as a peaceful, civilized, public-spirited demonstration of the people's anger with the American exclusionist policy. Since, however, there was a possibility that the movement might get out of hand and disrupt public order, it was best to urge caution on the people while doing the government's best to try to modify the existing immigration regulations of the United States. The governor general at Nanking agreed. Chou Fu thought the boycott originated in public indignation at the mistreatment of Chinese laborers in America, and that it proved the Chinese were capable of unified and organized action. However, he also felt the boycott was more harmful to Chinese than to American merchants, and feared that unless it was brought under control, "ignorant people" might create confusion. Since by the end of August 1905 the United States had promised to treat Chinese merchants and travelers in America fairly, the governor general saw no reason why the anti-American movement should continue. Later on, when the American minister in Peking demanded the punishment of Tseng Shao-ch'ing, a Shanghai merchant regarded as the ringleader of the boycott, Chou Fu strongly objected. He wrote to Peking that such an act would infuriate the merchants, not only because Tseng was merely a spokesman for a popular movement, but also because the United States had been the guilty party to begin with. If stringent action were taken against Tseng the matter would not end there but invite a storm of protest. "Even though our system of government is authoritarian," Chou wrote, "we cannot simply summon merchants and tell them they have to trade with so and so . . . or may not trade with so and so and will be punished if they do."

In this way the anti-American movement revealed not only the nationalism of Chinese merchants and students but also the receptivity of a majority of officials to the emergence of a new force in the Chinese political scene. The point will become even clearer when we consider another episode involving the United States at this time. This was the Sino-American dispute over the concession awarded to the American China Development Company to finance, construct, and operate a railway from Canton to Hankow. In the spring of 1904 Chang Chih-tung, who was in charge of railway affairs, became aware that a Belgian syndicate had bought a majority of the stock of the American company, in contravention of the stipulation in the contract prohibiting such a transfer. Chang asked the governor of Hunan province, through which the railway would run, to unite the strength of the officials and gentry in the province to cause the cancellation of the loan contract. Chang was taking advantage of the Hunan gentry's known animosity toward the American concession. It has been suggested that the rich gentry wanted to stop the railway construction, as it was bound to compete with a Yangtze steamship company they had organized in 1897. Chang Chih-tung, however, was interested in railway construction itself, as it would enrich the provinces through which it ran. But he was opposed to the financing of the railway by a potentially dangerous foreign group.

The situation changed in January 1905 when the Morgan Company bought back the shares of the China Development Company that had been transferred to Belgian hands. Chang could thus have sanctioned the loan contract as originally given to the American company. This time, however, he began urging the redemption of the railway contract and ended up borrowing money from the Hong Kong government to buy back the contract. In effect Chang had merely shifted from American to British financiers. This seems to have been due to several factors. First, by 1905 railway redemption had become part of the widespread rights-recovery movement. Not only the provincial gentry, merchants, and students, but those studying abroad sent telegrams to the court and to Chang Chih-tung, calling on them to redeem the American contract. It was not that these groups were economically motivated; students would be unable in any event to contribute funds to buy back the concession; the gentry in Hupeh and Hunan proved likewise unable to assist financially; and even the more wealthy gentry and merchants in Kwangtung were not equal to the task. All these groups failed to respond positively to pleas from Chang and the provincial governments to lend money in order to pay the American creditors. Money had to be sought elsewhere, and in the end British money was borrowed. But this was considered better than to honor the existing American agreement, which had specified creditor control and management of the proposed railway. The loan agreement with the Hong Kong government was not without unfavorable terms; China promised to turn to Britain for construction of the Canton-

Hankow railway if the terms proposed by the latter were the same as those offered by other countries' capitalists. Even so, this seemed better than the continuation of the existing American arrangement. Equally important, there existed a climate in China in 1905 that was unfavorable to the United States. The whole railway episode coincided with the anti-American boycott relating to the immigration dispute. In June, when some American financiers tried to obtain a railway concession in Chekiang province, they were immediately opposed by merchants, gentry, and students; one hundred and sixty of them organized a meeting to oppose the scheme. As a result, nothing came of it. Thus there was greater reluctance to borrow money from America in 1905 than from any other source.

Japan in an Imperialist War

The Japanese view of the United States was shaped by a fundamental national concern, the struggle with Russia over control of Korea. After the Boxer incident, the Japanese became extremely sensitive to what they considered evidence of Russian designs on south Manchuria and north Korea. Policy makers in Tokyo were agreed that a free hand in Korea was an essential ingredient of national security which could never be compromised. The Anglo-Japanese alliance of 1902, from their point of view, was calculated to obtain Britain's support of this contention as well as to neutralize France, Russia's ally, in case of war between Japan and Russia. But Japan's top policy makers were realistic diplomats; they did not believe Japanese-Russian antagonism was destined to be permanent, nor did they think Russia was committed to expansionism in East Asia to the detriment of its interests elsewhere. They felt, therefore, that some way could be found for mutual agreement on the two nations' essential spheres of interest. There did not seem much point in risking a war, which could upset the status quo in other parts of Asia. The Japanese were so desirous and confident of obtaining some agreement with Russia that they were willing to promise non-fortification of the Korean coast if Russia otherwise gave Japan a free hand in the peninsula. In return, they would offer to recognize Russia's sphere of interest in Manchuria.

Unfortunately, the strategy was destroyed from two sides. Russia, despite its general inclination to concede Korea to Japan, wanted insurance against Japan's use of the peninsula against Russian interests to the north. From time to time the Tsarist government demanded the creation of a neutral zone in north Korea and nonfortification of the whole of Korea. On the other hand, the Japanese army was restless; even if temporary settlement were reached, it doubted that war could be totally avoided. On the contrary, some conflict was considered inevitable, simply because the two powers were felt to be incompatible in East Asia. Consequently, aggressive army officers maintained, negotiations were needless and harmful, since a day's delay gave that much time to Russia to prepare itself. As the Tsarist government refused to grant Japanese conditions for compromise, in time the Tokyo leaders came around to the army's viewpoint. It was considered a waste of time to continue to talk indefinitely. By the end of 1903 the Japanese leaders had accepted as inevitable, though regrettable, the impossibility of reaching a satisfactory compromise with Russia. War came in February 1904.

Throughout 1903 Japanese diplomats were authorized and at times urged to co-operate with their British and American counterparts to present a common stand on the Manchuria question. Minister Takahira Kogorō in Washington frequently saw State Department officials and solicited their views on the changing conditions in Manchuria. Summaries of American press opinion were forwarded to Tokyo. Basically, however, Japanese officials were pessimistic about obtaining United States help in East Asia. In the official Japanese view, American interests there were primarily and almost exclusively economic, and the Russian presence in Manchuria did not seem to threaten or concern American security; it was felt that the Washington government would acquiesce in the situation as long as American trade was not hindered. Japanese observers also judged that the American public was on the whole unconcerned with Russian-Japanese differences, and that there were strong currents of pro-Russian opinion. At the same time, the Japanese did not view the United States as a hindrance to its policy. The military assumed that the United States would remain neutral in case of a Russo-Japanese war. The navy's proposal for expansion, submitted for Diet consideration in 1903, talked of the need to keep up with the European powers in expanding naval strength. While it was noted that the United States was emerging as an important naval power, it was not expected that much fleet strength would be placed in the Pacific.

The outbreak of the war brought about a clearer Japanese attitude and policy toward the United States. The first official policy was a negative one; it was considered vital to keep the United States from assisting Russia. Recognizing the need to appeal directly to the American government and people, Baron Kaneko Kentarō was dispatched to the United States, there to stay until the peace treaty was signed. Kaneko had at first hesitated to undertake the mission, as he thought American sympathies and interests were overwhelmingly with Russia. His pessimism seemed confirmed, and he accepted the mission from a sense of supreme self-sacrifice. At his first dinner party in New York he felt that eighty per cent of those present, mostly businessmen, were pro-Russian. But his spirits improved rapidly after he saw President Roosevelt in Washington.

Kaneko had been specifically instructed to squelch any suspicion that Japan sought to dominate Asia or that Japan and China were going to stand together against Western countries. The Tokyo government was very sensitive to the notion of the "yellow peril" and believed Russia might well take advantage of it. Kaneko was satisfied, however, that the people he met in the United States saw nothing in the idea. Roosevelt, Hay, Senator Henry Cabot Lodge, and many others assured him that they did not believe in Japan's alleged intention of excluding Western influence from Asia. These talks were so encouraging that within a few weeks of his stay Kaneko had come to believe that eight or nine out of ten Americans were pro-Japanese.

It was also during the war that an image of America as a financier of Japan emerged. Interestingly enough, initially there had been no thought of turning to the United States for money. American investments had been conspicuous in some Japanese industries, but the Tokyo government had at first sought money for war purposes only in England. It soon developed, however, that as much as half the amount Japan sought could be raised in America. This was a providential break for Japan; in an age when political meanings were read into financial transactions, an American loan, in addition to a British loan, seemed to be full of political significance, implying American sympathy with the Japanese cause. But the view of America as a source of capital could also cause embarrassment to Japan. American financiers might attempt to open enterprises in China detrimental to Japanese interests. It is extremely illuminating that the Japanese government, at the very time that it was seeking American sympathy and support against Russia, refused to approve of a scheme presented by an American firm to construct a railway between Amoy and Hankow. The proposed line would run through Fukien, Japan's sphere of influence, and the Peking government was unwilling to sanction the concession without Japanese approval. This twin phenomenon—America's financial assistance to Japan and ability to compete with Japanese rights in China—was to remain a central theme in the subsequent history of Japanese-American relations.

Among the people of Japan the one group that made itself conspicuous, the anti-war group, was noted for its American connections. Many were leaders of nascent Japanese socialism who had lived and studied in the United States. They were conscious of their American education when they advocated socialist or humanitarian measures and opposed the war with Russia. Kinoshita Naoe's wartime novel, *The Pillar of Fire,* had a hero who had become a socialist and a Christian while in America. He viewed the Russo-Japanese War as a clash between "Two despotic empires, two barbaric governments," and considered all forms of relations between nations and between peoples as relationships between the expropriator and the expropriated. The other prominent opponents of the war, Katayama Sen and Uchimura Kanzō, had also lived in the United States. However, this fact did not cause the United States to be castigated by the supporters of the war. Yano Ryūkei's influential *Future of Japan in the World,* published in February 1905, exhorted Japan to deepen contact with the United States, the nation that practiced the principles of human rights, in order to contribute to the peace and welfare of the country and of the world.

Although, in the initial Japanese conception, the war against Russia was started to assert once and for all Japan's control over Korea and indirectly to promote the nation's expansion in south China, it did not take long before a third objective was added: transfer of Russian rights in south Manchuria to Japan. This not only meant a momentous redefinition of Japanese national interests but also marked the beginning of Japan's continentalism. Japan's civilian and military leaders were infatuated by the vision of a continental empire, and they persuaded themselves that they had to acquire south Manchuria, since expansion was the way of international politics. In time south Manchuria became the cardinal factor in Japanese policy, but unlike Korea and even Taiwan, the decision for Manchuria was made with little deliberation and only as a by-product of the war with Russia. This fact was to cause unending crises and create insoluble problems for Japan for decades to come. What is striking is that in deciding to add south Manchuria to the Japanese sphere of influence, the Japanese leaders did not believe this would violate the framework of power politics in East Asia. It did not seem that the status quo would be upset radically by a mere transfer of Russian rights to Japan, or that the basic principle of understanding with the friendly powers would be destroyed. There was no doubt that the United States would approve of the Japanese policy; as they drafted peace terms, Tokyo's leaders never entertained the thought that Washington might object to the transfer of the Liaotung leasehold to Japan. Through Baron Kaneko and Minister Takahira the Japanese government continued to explore these peace terms with President Roosevelt, and the latter gave no indication that there would be trouble in Japan's demanding superior rights in Manchuria, in addition to those in Korea.

The fact that it was to the United States that Japan looked for mediation indicates Japan's continued confidence in American sympathy. Japanese officials were immensely grateful for President Roosevelt's efforts to bring the Portsmouth Conference negotiations to a close. They were not bitter that the President sought to discourage them from asking an indemnity; the Japanese policy had been to insist on three conditions as "absolutely imperative," Japan's complete free hand in Korea, evacuation of Russian troops from Manchuria, and the transfer of the Liaotung leasehold and the Harbin–Port Arthur branch of the Chinese Eastern Railway to Japan. The Japanese military, as well as civilian leaders, were satisfied with these demands, which Russia, too, was willing to accept conditionally. But the Japanese government decided at the peace conference to gamble on demands for an indemnity and

Sakhalin island for reasons of domestic politics and of national honor. It seemed a disgrace not to obtain tangible territorial and monetary gains as happened after the Sino-Japanese War. This was poor strategy, for the Japanese knew they would have to yield these points if Russians remained adamantly opposed to them, as they immediately found out they were. The poor judgment shown in this case also marred Japanese-American understanding, as the Japanese people persuaded themselves that they had been cheated out of their rightful gains by their government and, indirectly, by President Roosevelt. Anti-American demonstrations broke out, the first of their kind in Japanese history. Quiet soon returned, but these riots revealed that the much-talked-about friendship between the two peoples might be an extremely superficial phenomenon, not based on any genuine understanding.

The Menace of Japan

The United States was inevitably drawn into the drama of East Asian politics. It was not a matter of its own choosing. As seen above, the State Department had, in 1899 and 1900, defined American policy in Asia as a passive one of defending the Pacific possessions and refraining from political or military control over China. The same policy obtained after the Boxer incident. Hay summed up the policy by saying, in May 1902, "What we have been working for two years to accomplish . . . is that, no matter what happens eventually in northern China and Manchuria, the United States will not be placed in any worse position than while the country was under the unquestioned domination of China." Throughout 1903 the Russian ambassador in Washington was repeatedly given assurances by the secretary of state that Russia's special position in Manchuria was well recognized by the United States. While on occasion the State Department protested the extension of Russian influence in Manchuria, such protest was almost always followed by a denial that the United States intended to do anything about it. The Washington government was content to seek the opening of ports in Manchuria as the best way for preserving American interests and indirectly preventing Russian predominance. It was believed that there was not much the nation could do to stop the deterioration in Japanese-Russian relations. At the base of this passivity was the view of China as weak and lacking in central authority. It did not seem worthy of positive American assistance. More fundamental, however, was the fact that neither President Roosevelt nor the State Department had clearly formulated a set of specific objectives to be attained in China. Apart from the traditional policy of promoting trade, there was as yet no definite policy on more political questions in East Asia.

The Russo-Japanese War finally forced the United States to define more clearly its interests in East Asia. In addition to the established policy of protecting the Philippines and promoting trade in China, some began to add a third principle, to balance Japanese naval power. No policy, however, was as yet formulated toward China.

The problems Japan raised for the United States may perhaps best be comprehended if we look at them through the eyes of an extremely sensitive American observer, Willard Straight. An employee of the Chinese Maritime Customs Administration before the war, a foreign correspondent during the war, and vice consul at Seoul toward the end of the war, Straight was in a good position to watch and ponder the implications of the war and the Japanese victory for the United States. Initially he was rather calm, though concerned with increasing Japanese influence in Korea. In March 1904, for instance, he wrote in his diary, "There are many possibilities for friction in years to come" between Japanese policy and American commercial interests in Korea, but that "established as we are it will only be necessary to make a firm stand and Korea under the Japanese alliance . . . will offer in the future as in the past, a field for American enterprise." Such complacency gradually gave way to strong revulsion against Japan. For one thing, he was disgusted with Japanese conceit and sense of superiority as a result of initial successes against Russia. Already in August of the same year he recorded in his diary, "They all hate us, all of them, officers and men. They have been the underdog till now, they have been the scholars, we the masters and now they're going to show us a thing or two if it can be done. They hate us. God knows the feeling is mutual." Straight felt that basically Japan had not changed, that despite the "thin veneer of European life" the Japanese retained their traditional habits and outlooks, which set them distinctly apart from the Westerners whom they were apparently imitating. As he wrote, "The change has been essentially that of a man who keeps a new suit and rides a new horse—his character won't change." In a telling letter to a friend, Straight wrote,

> For no particular reason, with no real cause for complaint I now find myself hating the Japanese more than anything else in the world. It is due I presume to the constant strain of having to be polite and to seek favors from a yellow people. We cannot know them or understand them and they dislike us thoroughly. Kipling was absolutely right when he wrote "The East is East and the West is West, and never the twain shall meet."

Here was undoubtedly a strain of racism, a sense of superiority, as well as of condescension. All these, of course, were coupled with Straight's genuine indignation with Japanese exploitation of other Asians. The sight of an Asian nation oppressing another Asian nation was a relatively new phenomenon. As Straight saw it, Russians had at least brought Christianity to Chinese in Manchuria, and their railways had benefited Chinese as well as themselves. But in Korea the Japanese seemed determined to pursue their business with ruthless efficiency and give no thought to what happened to Koreans, a "kindly, pastoral, simple farm folk." But what was most ominous was not simply Japanese domination over Korea, but the likelihood of Japanese suzerainty over Asia and the subsequent rise of all Asia against the West. That is why he constantly returned to the theme of incompatibility between East and West. Because of the very incompatibility, the West must strive to prevent the revolt of the East under Japanese domination. What Straight was expressing was a notion of the "yellow peril." Japan's successful war against a Western power was a spectacle which had been forecast by some since the 1890's but which had not seemed a real possibility. Here was the East rising against the West, Orientals against Occidentals.

In its crudest form this anti-Orientalism was expressed as an anti-Japanese movement on the west coast of the United States. Attempts at arousing mass emotion by talking of a Japanese yellow peril had not been successful before the Russo-Japanese War. Agitation was resumed in earnest during the war, this time with a measure of success. The relationship between the anti-Japanese movement and the war was easily established in the minds of the agitators. As the San Francisco *Examiner* put it, "Once the war with Russia is over, the brown stream of Japanese immigration" would inundate California. The kind of Japanese that Straight had found in Korea—uncultured, uneducated, uncouth—would "invade" the west coast, creating all varieties of problems, ranging from labor competition to sexual crimes. The result would be a "complete Orientalization of the Pacific Coast," and it would cease to be truly American. As immigration matters were within the jurisdiction of the federal government, the state legislature passed a resolution, in March, declaring that "the close of the war . . . will surely bring to our shores hordes . . . of the discharged soldiers of the Japanese army, who will crowd the State with immoral, intemperate, quarrelsome men, bound to labor for a pittance, and to subsist on a supply with which a white man can hardly sustain life." The resolution called on Congress to restrict future Japanese immigration.

Such extreme language concealed a fear which was much more widespread than the obviously exaggerated image of a Japanese-dominated California revealed. It was not that the Japanese, drunk with a taste of victory over a white nation, would invade California, but rather that they foretold the coming after them of other Asians, equally determined to modernize themselves and expel Western influence from Asia. No matter how modernized, and therefore "Westernized" an Asian people might be, they were still Oriental, which by definition meant hostility toward Westerners. The days of Western supremacy in the Orient were numbered. Unless something was done to check this menace, what the West had built and stood for was in danger of being submerged under an Asiatic horde. A victorious Japan was a symbol of the passing of an era. The image of East-West conflict that had arisen in the 1890's seemed to have been confirmed. Now there was an even stronger feeling that the West was on the defensive. The *Coast Seamen's Journal* was aware of these larger implications of its exclusionist stand when it pointed out, "Never in history had the Caucasian won out in competition with the Oriental. The Oriental might gain manners and technology, but he would always remain an Oriental. The Mongolian would never adopt the Judaic-Christian philosophy while, racially, the Aryan always disappeared before the Mongolian."[1] Only a determined and united opposition by Westerners could resist such an outcome; even a handful of Japanese in the United States must be dealt with in the same spirit, lest they should become the spearhead of Mongol domination.

There is every reason to believe that President Roosevelt was affected by this type of thinking. His very protestation that he was not worried about a yellow peril belied his concern and awareness of the problem. He may have been amused by the repeated and serious assurances given by the Japanese that Japan had no designs on Western interests in Asia and that, on the contrary, all it wanted was "to become part of the circle of civilized mankind." The president would assure the Japanese that he perfectly understood and sympathized with their position. At the same time, he was fully aware of the implications of Japan's rise as a "great civilized power." As he reminded his correspondents again and again, "Japanese motives and ways of thought" were "not quite those of the powers of our race"; Japan's civilization was "of a different type from our civilizations." While Roosevelt did not share the alarmist view that powers representing different types of civilization must necessarily be antagonistic to one another, he felt differences between them were serious enough to require the most careful vigilance. Above all, the president held the popular impression that at heart Orientals were anti-Occidental. He was expressing a commonly held view when he wrote to Cecil Spring Rice in December 1904, "I wish I were certain that the Japanese down at bottom did not lump Russians, English, Americans, Germans, all of us, simply as white devils . . . to be treated politely only so long as would enable the Japanese to take advantage of our various national jealousies, and beat us in turn."

Unlike some of his extreme countrymen, Roosevelt did not believe it wise to treat Asian civilization as non-civilization and if possible to prevent Asians from acquiring the rudiments of Western civilization lest they should use them against the West. Rather, he felt that the more civilized a country became the less warlike it was likely to be. Japan's rise as a civilized power was to be more welcome than dreaded. Thus he would try to bring out the best in the East and suppress the worst in the West so as to minimize

[1] Cited in Richard Austin Thompson, *The Yellow Peril 1890–1924* (unpublished dissertation, University of Wisconsin, 1957), p. 226.

chances of conflict between the two. The president regarded the west coast's agitation against Japanese immigrants as diametrically opposed to his thinking. The "feeling on the Pacific slope . . . is as foolish as if conceived by the mind of a Hottentot," he wrote on one occasion. Insulting the Japanese was the best way of inviting Japanese hostility and antagonism, which the agitators were trying to prevent. The United States, Roosevelt wrote, must treat Japan "with scrupulous courtesy and friendliness so that she shall have no excuse for bearing malice toward us."

At the same time, the president was fully aware of Japan's potential menace, apart from the ideological yellow peril. The Russo-Japanese War revealed to him that "Japanese soldiers and sailors have been shown themselves to be terrible foes. There can be none more dangerous in all the world." If given a pretext, such as the west coast agitation seemed to be providing, the Japanese could turn against the United States and make Roosevelt's nightmare a reality. "I am perfectly well aware that if they win out it may possibly mean a struggle between them and us in the future," he had written as early as June 1904. This was not because of an inevitability of conflict between East and West. Rather, conflict was considered a possibility between a western Pacific power and an eastern Pacific power, simply because they confronted each other and expanded their navies and military potential. The positions of the Philippines and Hawaii seemed especially precarious. Before the completion of the Isthmian canal, the United States fleet would have to be concentrated in the Atlantic, and its Pacific fleet was no match for Japanese naval strength. Thus he urged speedy fortification of Subic Bay on Luzon island. As he said, "If we are not prepared to establish a strong and suitable base for our navy in the Philippines, then we had far better give up the Philippine Islands entirely."

It is a measure of Roosevelt's thinking that he thought an American-Japanese conflict, if it were to come, would arise out of naval rivalry or racial animosity and not from Japan's continental expansionism. If anything, he tended to believe that Japan's continentalism would be a check on its ambitions in the Pacific. As he saw Japan's immediate future, that country had two alternatives before it: either to develop as a continental or as a maritime power. He was convinced that the Japanese first of all wanted to concentrate on continental affairs, staking out their sphere of interests. Only when their appetites were satiated would they turn eastward and southward and confront the United States. "So long as Japan takes an interest in Korea, in Manchuria, in China," wrote Roosevelt in December 1904, "it is Russia which is her natural enemy." Nor was it likely that Japan would combine with Russia after the war and menace the American, British, and Dutch possessions in the Pacific. The risks in such an undertaking would be enormous.

Such thinking, rather than the usually emphasized *Realpolitik* of balancing Russia and Japan against one another, was behind Roosevelt's policy of encouraging Japan's continental policy short of complete domination of East Asia. He took it for granted that Japan would demand Russian rights in south Manchuria and that the United States should have no objection to the transfer of these rights to Japan. For him Japanese predominance in Korea and south Manchuria merely meant a minor redefinition of the status quo in East Asia, one more advantageous from the point of view of American security considerations than any other imaginable possibility.

China as an Economic Interest

These considerations reveal a still very negative image of China. It was an American market but not much more. It was scarcely relevant to American security. There was no need for the United States to bestir itself to take a more active interest in Chinese politics. As far as Roosevelt was concerned, China presented few problems that could not be handled within the existing framework of passive, economically oriented policy. Even the two dramatic episodes, the immigration dispute and the Canton-Hankow railway question, must be interpreted in this light. Roosevelt deplored these incidents, since they might undermine America's trade and investment positions in China. When the Chinese demanded the cancellation of the railway concession, he did his best to persuade the American creditors to keep the contract even against their best financial interests. The reason was not necessarily because the president wanted to retain the concession as a basis for his political policy, as has been frequently alleged. Rather, he simply thought the concession would pay off in the long run. He summed up his feeling on the matter in a letter to J. P. Morgan: "My interest of course is simply the interest of seeing American commercial interests prosper in the Orient." He thought these interests would be endangered if the Chinese felt they could annul foreign contracts each time they felt like it. He would show that the United States government would be fully prepared to support its nationals' commercial interests. The policy was an old one, if the language was somewhat out of the ordinary.

Nor can it be said that anything new was conceived, on the American side, during the immigration dispute. The administration was worried lest the anti-American boycott should seriously cripple American trade. The interests connected with the southern cotton industry seem to have been most concerned with the outcome of the boycott. As a spokesman testified at a Congressional hearing early in 1906, "profitable returns on millions of dollars of invested capital and the employment at fair wages of thousands of working people" in southern cotton mills were absolutely dependent on the retention and development of the China market.[1] While the boycott itself was not of sufficient duration to leave long-range effects on American trade with China, representatives of the southern textile industry and the export trade pleaded with the government to protect their interests. This took the form of placating Chinese sensibilities by adequate reform of immigration regulations and of employing naval force to prevent wanton attacks on American merchants and goods in China. Such an attitude was reflected in official United States policy. Roosevelt, too, wanted to treat nonlaboring Chinese visitors fairly so as to give them no cause for complaint, and at the same time to protect American trade against a discriminatory boycott.

The importance of the administration's handling of these incidents lies in the fact that it still adhered to a strictly commercial definition of American-Chinese relations. "One of the greatest commercial prizes of the world is the trade with the 400,000,000 Chinese," said Secretary of War William Howard Taft in June 1905. Undoubtedly aided by speculation as to postwar demands, American merchants had shipped an unprecedented quantity of goods to China in the first half of the year. With Japanese victory and the

[1] Cited in Jessie A. Miller, *China in American Policy and Opinion 1906–1909* (unpublished dissertation, Clark University, 1938), p. 93.

anticipated opening of more ports, the China trade could be expected to expand. This the president and his government wanted to foster. Beyond such a policy, they did not envisage a new framework of American-Chinese relations. Japanese victory over Russia and expansion into south Manchuria initially made no difference. Japan's policy in China, wrote Roosevelt, "is the policy to which we are already committed." He rebuffed the Chinese demands that he refuse to sanction the transfer of Russian rights to Japan. On the contrary, he assured the Japanese that they had his support in enunciating a Monroe Doctrine for Asia. As he saw it, Japan was in a position to provide order and stability in East Asia, a condition considered auspicious for the expansion of American economic activities.

•

The few years after the Boxer incident were thus of seminal importance for the development of American-Asian relations in the twentieth century. Considerations of race and power came to define the framework in which Japanese and Americans looked at one another, and they were beginning to be dimly aware of the possibility of conflict. In China the language of confrontation with the West was sharpened and its validity tested through a nationalistic foreign policy. The United States, it must be emphasized, was already regarded as a formidable imperialist power, an impression the Washington government did little to dispel by a friendly attitude toward China. At the end of the Russo-Japanese War it might have seemed that a trans-Pacific confrontation might develop, between China on one hand and America on the other, with Japan contributing its naval power and political influence to the strength of the former. In fact, however, Japanese-American conflict preceded the confrontation between China and the United States.

5
The Genesis of American-Japanese Antagonism

In 1908 Hara Kei, a prominent Japanese politician, visited the United States for the first time. He was deeply impressed with America's economic might and its latent but unmistakable influence in world politics. He felt that even Europe, which he had seen in 1886 and now revisited, had come under America's political, economic, and even cultural influence. He vowed that an understanding with the United States would be a basic prerequisite for Japanese policy. This was because America represented the inevitable trend in human affairs; to him it seemed obvious that the vitality of the American people, nurtured by democratic institutions, indicated the wave of the future. Japan's task was to identify itself with the trend; friendship with America was thus a logical necessity. Ten years later, in 1918, Hara became Japan's prime minister. His image of the United States had stayed with him, but to his dismay he found how difficult it was to effect understanding with America. Relations between the two countries had deteriorated during the preceding decade, and self-conscious antagonism between Japanese and Americans had become as much a fact of international relations as American-Japanese co-operation and compatibility before 1905.

In looking at this phenomenon, historians have tended to view it as a natural development, arising out of the two countries' conflicting policies in China. It is certainly true that harsh language was at times used by Japanese and Americans toward each other; some, moreover, confidently foretold a Pacific war. Self-conscious and often hysterical antagonism, however, tends to exaggerate differences and obscure areas of compatibility in the interests of the countries involved. If it is true that the United States opposed what it considered Japan's excessive and selfish expansionism, it must also be remembered that America never challenged the foundation of the Japanese empire in Korea, Taiwan, and south Manchuria. Before the 1930's the two nations more often co-operated than collided as treaty powers, collectively safeguarding their interests in China. Underneath, the current of mutual suspicion between China and America never totally subsided; America's moral concern for China's national aspirations, which reached a height under President Wilson, was only one aspect of American-Asian relations. Despite the efforts by image-makers, Sino-American friendship had no solid foundation in fact.

It is for this very reason that Japanese-American antagonism after the Russo-Japanese War is such a significant episode. In purely rational, realistic terms—the two countries' naval and trade relations—their interests were never in conflict at this time. But there were other factors, ideological, moral, and psychological, that complicated their relations. Among them, China as an idea played a crucial role.

The Problems of an Asian Power

In the moment of triumph, when the Japanese congratulated themselves on their emergence as a world power, some of them felt a sense of void, of "melancholy," as Tokutomi Roka, a novelist, wrote. What had Japan gained as a result of the war? he asked. An expanded army and navy, some territories and their products, and membership in the community of great powers—these, according to Roka, were not worth a drop of blood. Just becoming a great power did not solve all Japan's problems. In fact, the Japanese victory might elate the colored races of the world and for that reason arouse the suspicion and hostility of the white race. The Russo-Japanese War might thus prove to have been a prelude to an interracial war of the future. The stronger Japan grew, the greater would be its sense of insecurity because of the increased suspicion of Japan by other nations. The only way for the Japanese to find true security and contentment was to renounce expansionism and devote themselves to the cause of peace. They should make it their mission to spread justice in all the seas.

Few accepted Roka's solutions, but many shared his misgivings. They, too, were suddenly aware of the enormous problems that lay ahead of the victorious nation. These problems were no longer the simple problems of security and economic expansion. These could be dealt with as they had been in the past. Whereas before the war the Japanese had not had to worry about too many other questions, they now sensed the more complex issues of race, culture, and national purpose. There was an obsessive concern with the future of East-West relations. It was as if all of a sudden the Japanese were reminded that they were an Asian nation. There was gnawing uncertainty about the position of Japan, a Westernized Asian nation, in the postwar world. There seemed to be mounting tension between East and West, between the colored and the white races of the world. That is why so many writers and officials talked about Japan's mission to "harmonize" relations between East and West, or, conversely, to identify itself with the "awakening of Asia" in opposition to Western civilization. Somehow Japan needed to define its existence in a world of racial and cultural diversity and tension.

It is doubtful whether East-West relations were any more serious then than earlier, or even whether there was such a thing as "East" or "West." However, these were the images the Japanese adopted as a framework of thought as they developed national policy after the war. Officials would still be guided by considerations of security and economic interests, but they were compelled to re-examine their assumptions in response to new developments abroad, and they were inevitably led to postulate theories about Japan's position in the world. Two of these developments—the immigration dispute with the United States, and the political crisis in China—were of fundamental importance to Japanese thinking.

The Japanese had assumed that they could continue to count on friendly relations with the United States. As in the past, they believed that Japan's rights on the continent, now vastly augmented, would require political understanding with and economic assistance of Western nations. "Japan must try at least to satisfy and obtain the sympathies of Britain and the United States," said Itō Hirobumi in 1906. It was imperative to eschew adventurism in Asia, which would cause the nation to lose the confidence of the Western powers, and to deepen economic ties with them so as to finance the newly acquired empire. The acceptance of the military and political status quo after the war, and of economic interdependence with Western powers, was the basic framework of Japanese foreign policy. To their dismay, however, Japan's leaders soon came to feel that the policy was not producing results as in the past. For instance, at the end of 1907, the year when Japan had successfully entered into political agreements with France and Russia to uphold their mutual rights in East Asia, Itō had to admit, "Japan's position in the world is most grievous. The situation is such that there is an unmistakable trend toward Japanese isolation." Despite the alliance with Britain and the agreements with France and Russia, he felt there was abroad an underlying suspicion of Japan and that the nation was not accepted as an equal. Contrary to the general belief in Japan's role between East and West, its position seemed more precarious than ever before. Itō was particularly dismayed by the racial prejudice displayed by certain groups in the United States.

The response of Japan's governmental leaders to the anti-Japanese moves in America is most illuminating. The anti-Japanese movement was naturally a blow to the Japanese, who felt they had done all they could to allay the Western fear of a yellow peril and to continue to act within the framework of understanding with the West. The only way they could explain the apparently incomprehensible phenomenon of race prejudice was by regarding it as a product of irrational minorities in America. As Foreign Minister Hayashi Tadasu wrote, the anti-Japanese agitation was attributable to irresponsible journalists and labor leaders in certain parts of the United States; it could not conceivably lie deeper. It must be a temporary and transient phenomenon, which would pass in due course. Hayashi dismissed war scares on both sides of the Pacific as nonsense. The whole immigration episode would soon be forgotten as an unhappy but by no means inevitable page in the otherwise friendly history of Japanese-American relations. Much more important were the two countries' economic interdependence and general agreement on the status quo in East Asia.

Such a line of reasoning was behind Tokyo's eagerness to show evidence of its continued interest in understanding with the United States. The Root-Takahira agreement of 1908, mutually recognizing the status quo in the Pacific and proclaiming Japan's adherence to the Open Door principle, was one such attempt. Another was the rousing welcome the Japanese gave to the United States fleet in 1909, when it visited East Asia as part of its world cruise. Although after 1907 the Japanese navy postulated a possible conflict with its American counterpart, the United States was not yet considered the most likely enemy. At a time when the introduction of the new "dreadnought" type of battleship was complicating naval planning everywhere, prudence seemed to dictate a policy of avoiding friction with the United States. As the Japanese naval attaché in Washington wrote, the world cruise of the American fleet was obviously intended to demonstrate American naval power in the Pacific. Under the circumstances, he wrote, the best tactic for Japan was to impress American visitors with Japan's genuine interest in peace between the two peoples, so that the American people would give up their anti-Japanese prejudice. The naval and civilian leaders in Tokyo fully agreed and did all they could to show their sincere and friendly sentiments to the visitors. Satō Tetsutarō, a prominent naval strategist, writing after the event, chose to believe that the two nations *must* remain in peace and that Japan must do its part in making it so. This was the "truth" he had come to recognize as fundamental.

Nevertheless, many Japanese were coming to the realization that their relations with America were no longer what they had been. No matter how hard they tried to minimize the racial question, no matter how desperately they clung to an image of East and West harmonized through Japan, Western prejudice did not seem to abate. The gentlemen's agreements, in which Japan pledged to prohibit the emigration of laborers to the United States, did not satisfy the west coast agitators, who pushed for restrictive measures against Japanese already in America. Tokutomi Sohō, who had earlier preached Japan's mission between East and West, now came to admit that the country had no true friend in the world. Writing in 1911, he said that despite alliances and ententes Japan was merely an isolated entity. More than that, there seemed to be no real value in international sympathy and understanding. Japan must henceforth be resolute and carry out what it believed to be in its interests, regardless of other nations' attitudes. As though suddenly shaken out of his illusion, he now concluded that universal brotherhood, East-West harmony, and similar notions had merely expressed Japan's wishful thinking, derived from a sense of insecurity.

If the immigration dispute with the United States brought to the Japanese the awareness of irrational factors in international relations, developments in China likewise forced them to re-examine the policy of co-operative action with the West in East Asia. These were years of momentous political change in China, leading to the overthrow of the Manchu dynasty in 1912. This was also the time when the Chinese began their serious attempt at halting the tide of foreign encroachment. These two currents—the political crisis and the "rights recovery movement"—confronted the powers with serious new problems. Japan in particular was deeply involved, since the country had been a haven for Chinese revolutionaries, and since the Chinese nationalists began resorting to the boycotting of Japanese goods to protest against Japan's expansionistic policy in Manchuria and elsewhere. It was in this connection that some in Japan came to advocate a pan-Asianist approach. Instead of trying to co-ordinate action with the Western powers, they said, Japan should act unilaterally in order to safeguard and extend its position in China. Tanaka Giichi, who, as a staff member of the General Staff's operations section, was instrumental in drafting postwar military policy, believed that Japan should behave as a "continental nation." It was the nation's destiny to establish a predominant position in China. Considerations of understanding with the powers should not be allowed to stand in the way, if a favorable opportunity presented itself for obtaining such an end. Tanaka specifically noted that in its continental expansionism Japan might collide with the United States, since the latter, too, seemed intent on extending its interests in China. Japan must be prepared to implant its influence in south China so as to prevent the United States from doing so.

Before 1912 few visualized direct confrontation with the United States in China. Russia remained the most likely enemy in Japanese strategy. For the civilian government in Tokyo, Japanese-American relations were still primarily economic. America was an ever-expanding market for Japanese silks and an increasingly important supplier of capital. Nevertheless, there steadily grew an awareness that the policies of the two countries might not be entirely compatible in Asia. To a nation already bewildered by racial prejudice abroad and inclined to a defensive pan-Asianism, American policy in China seemed all the more to confirm the fear of Japanese-American conflict. The United States seemed more and more interested in championing China's cause against Japan. In Japanese publications around 1910 one finds a sudden increase in references to American help in China to resist Japan. As a writer put it, "China today is trying to use America. . . . If the situation continues, there will develop a crisis between the United States and China on one hand and Japan on the other. . . . Japan should naturally insist on the status quo, based on its legal and treaty rights. But one should pay the utmost attention to American attitude, as it will directly affect the future relations between the two countries." Somehow Japan seemed to have been made the victim of forces beyond its control. Gone was the self-confident expectation that the powers, including Japan, would mutually define their interests and co-operate in maintaining the status quo in East Asia.

Championing the New China

Another Japanese writer, writing in May 1911, expressed his astonishment that "all of a sudden the United States has acquired tremendous authority to speak on Chinese matters." Before foreigners had time to notice it, America seemed to have gained in prestige and influence in China. Such a feeling was an accurate reflection of the new trends in American thinking and policy. Americans were suddenly discovering a Chinese renaissance and a Japanese peril. Anti-Orientalist thinking and the fear of an industrialized East had existed earlier, but it was only after the Russo-Japanese War that these took the form of anti-Japanese and pro-Chinese sentiment. In the new view of Asia, Japan was pictured as intent on expanding its influence to all parts of the East, championing the cause of "Asia for Asians." To many Americans Japan symbolized Asia's challenge to the West. A resurgent Asia under Japanese domination would doom Western civilization. In more extreme cases such an image of East-West conflict took the form of fatalism, which inspired a literature of interracial wars. As the exclusionist San Francisco *Chronicle* argued, "The California problem was but a part of a pressing worldwide issue as to whether the high standard Caucasian races or the low standard Oriental races would dominate the world." The *Coast Seamen's Journal,* another anti-Japanese publication, frankly admitted that the immigration question was basically a racial one; the threat to American society was the most serious issue involved in the Japanese problem. R. P. Hobson, probably the single most energetic publicist of an inevitable East-West war, spread the idea that Japan was aiming at driving the white men from Asia by inculcating an anti-Western sentiment among Orientals. Writers of war-scare stories, too, argued that Japan was likely to invade American insular possessions in the Pacific and even the west coast. Unless Americans awakened to the danger, they would find half of their continent subjugated by the Japanese.

Few shared these extreme views, but the image of Japan holding sway over much of China was by no means confined to a minority. Earlier, the American public might have been little concerned with the fate of China, but the Japanese victory coincided with a renewed interest Americans felt in China, and together this produced an atmosphere unfavorable to Japan. The "awakening" of China became a popular notion, just as the awakening of Japan had fascinated American readers a generation earlier. The coincidence of all these factors is remarkable. China seriously undertook to reform itself just as Japan defeated Russia and there was created in America a reservoir of anti-Japanese sentiment. From this time on, the American public became keenly interested in the "birth of a new China," in the phrase of A. H. Smith. The American missionary whose *Chinese Characteristics* had given a traditional image of the Chinese, now championed the cause of the new China. He was instrumental in arranging the remission of part of the Boxer indemnity to China. Together with other missionaries Smith wrote articles and made speeches, picturing China as a land of great promise, where the people were dedicating themselves to the cause of modernization. The American press on the whole showed a similar enthusiasm. William Jennings Bryan, who toured East Asia in 1906, came back with the notion of the "great awakening of the flowery kingdom." As he wrote in the Montgomery *Advertiser,* "The sleeping giantess, whose drowsy eyes have so long shut out the ray of the morning sun, is showing unmistakable signs of awakening." [1] While, as earlier, there was the view that a new, modernized China might pose a threat to Western supremacy, such a view was on the whole confined to some of the west coast press. In contrast, the southern press was strongly pro-Chinese, probably reflecting the increasing volume of raw cotton and cotton piece goods the southern mills were exporting to China.

It was natural that there soon appeared the view that the United States should do everything in its power to assist China. By this time there had emerged a myth about the Open Door policy. The United States, it was held, had stood for the principles of China's territorial integrity and of the Open Door, and it had never participated in the exploitation of China. Hence America was in a position to render help to China without incurring the latter's suspicions. Since, however, Japan seemed to be in the way of Chinese reform and nationalism, it was inevitable that the United States would have to oppose Japan. This could be done either economically, politically, or by other means. The most sensational proposal came from the New York *Herald Tribune* in 1908, when it editorially campaigned for an American-Chinese alliance. The idea was to counter the entente powers and assure China of America's political support against encroachment by others. The proposal was either ignored or laughed at even by the pro-Chinese press, but the thesis that the United States had much to contribute to China was accepted as axiomatic.

Changes in official American policy were equally conspicuous, although they did not come about until 1909. President Roosevelt sought to deal with China and Japan within the framework of prewar policy. He was not overly alarmed by Japanese power after the Russo-Japanese War and showed no strong interest in building

[1] Cited in Miller, *China in American Policy and Opinion,* p. 17.

up closer ties with China. That he did feel Japan posed serious problems for the United States was clearly stated in a letter he wrote as outgoing president to the new secretary of state, Philander Knox:

> She [Japan] is a most formidable military power. Her people have peculiar fighting capacity. They are very proud, very warlike, very sensitive, and are influenced by two contradictory feelings, namely, a great self-confidence, both ferocious and conceited, due to their victory over the mighty empire of Russia; and a great touchiness because they would like to be considered in a full equality with, as one of the brotherhood of, Occidental nations, and have been bitterly humiliated to find that even their allies, the English, and their friends, the Americans, won't admit them to association and citizenship.

Roosevelt clearly saw the racial factor as an important element in Japanese-American relations. His policy, as before 1905 with respect to the Chinese, was to show courtesy and consideration while carrying out the policy of exclusion, and to be prepared militarily for the worst contingency. He sought the co-operation of Britain, Canada, and Australia in excluding Asians, and in the meantime caused the speeding up of naval expansion as well as of the construction of a naval base at Pearl Harbor. War Plan Orange, adopted in 1907, for the first time envisaged conflict with Japan.

It is significant that the president envisaged possible friction with Japan because of the immigration question and naval rivalry, but not on account of Japanese expansion on the continent. He was willing to concede Korea to Japanese control, and he was ready to recognize Japan's predominant position in parts of China. This was not because he condoned Japanese expansionism, but primarily because he felt it would serve no useful purposes to oppose Japan in China. As he wrote in 1910, the United States should "not take any steps as regards Manchuria which will cause the Japanese to feel . . . that we are hostile to them, or a menace . . . to their interests." If the United States opposed Japan verbally, without being able to back it up with force, relations with Japan would have been worsened with no assurance that Japan would heed the American protest. The United States was not ready to fight Japan over Manchuria. This view was behind Roosevelt's lack of interest in any political agreement with China. The Root-Takahira agreement of 1908 was his answer to the Chinese hope that the United States would support them against Japanese expansion.

During the second Roosevelt administration, however, there were already some in the government who felt more positively about China. Secretary of War Taft, visiting China in 1907, felt "there never was a time when the Chinese were more friendly than today." Significantly, he added, "this friendliness [is caused by] the suspicion and fear that they entertain toward Japan and Russia and possibly England. They know that we do not wish to take any of their territory and that we don't ask any exclusive privilege." In Shanghai he gave vent to his ideas even more fully. He envisaged the United States as a significant power in the Orient, willing to play a role in helping China. Taft also declared that while in the past the government in Washington had been passive with respect to trade, in the future American merchants would have "no reason to complain of seeming government indifference." Here was a voice calling for stronger American initiative in East Asia.

There were others in the government who agreed with Taft that the United States could and should make a positive contribution to the maintenance of Chinese independence. Willard Straight, consul general at Mukden during 1906–1908, not only believed in an American role but actually carried out certain policies designed to undermine Japanese predominance in south Manchuria. He was willing to turn in all directions just to compete with Japanese influence. He felt that American-educated officials in China would play an important role in bringing the two countries close. Through these officials, wrote Straight, "it should be possible to exert to our profit a strong influence on the industrial awakening which is bound to take place in China, the building of railways and the opening of mines." Meanwhile, the United States, too, should seek to increase its political influence by means of expanded economic activities. As Straight saw it, "diplomacy and commerce should go hand in hand and . . . the political prestige, so necessary to the future of America in the Far East, could only be secured by the creation of substantial vested interests." He was also ready to consummate a political union with Britain and even with Russia and Germany to isolate Japan. His almost fanatical devotion to the cause seems to have been rooted in the combination of racism and moralism that was already noted during the Russo-Japanese War.

He sought to prevent Japanese domination over China, which for him implied expulsion of Western influence from Asia. His dream was to bring about an Asia in which American influence and assistance to the cause of reform and independence would predominate. As Straight wrote to a friend in 1907,

> The more I see of Manchurian affairs the more am I convinced that we, the Americans, are favored above all others and that ours is the opportunity to befriend China in this her time of need and to aid her in straightening out her affairs here. [Once] we had established ourselves in Manchuria we could . . . do a tremendous work in furthering the Chinese Renaissance. The task of not Empire building, but of Empire shaping could with proper handling be ours.

Straight was so convinced of the rightness of his stand that he even employed, with official funds, a public relations agent to counter what he considered excessive Japanese propaganda in Manchuria. The idea was to disseminate anti-Japanese and pro-Chinese materials. Given the general orientation of Roosevelt's policy, it is not surprising that the publicity bureau should have caused embarrassment to, and been dissolved by, the State Department.

It was with the inception of the new administration in 1909 that the philosophy behind Taft's and Straight's views began to influence American policy. It is with the Taft administration that one may date the beginning of a moralistic diplomacy in East Asia. President Taft and Secretary of State Knox were more willing than their respective predecessors to listen to the voices of men like Straight and pro-Chinese missionaries and to make a moral concern with China's destiny a basis of their policy. What Knox wrote in 1910 neatly sums up this new approach:

> Why the Japanese *need* Manchuria any more than does China, who owns it now, or why it is any more "vital" to them than to China is not apparent. . . . I still believe that the wisest and best way for all concerned is for us to stand firmly on our pronounced policy and let it be known on every proper occasion that we expect fair play all round. The Japanese Government certainly is not indifferent to public opinion, and it is much better that we should continue to try to bring Japan's policy in China up to the level of

ours, where we may differ, than to lower our policy to the level of hers.

The Taft-Knox diplomacy has sometimes been described as a "dollar diplomacy." That epithet would apply to their East Asian policy only with respect to the means they employed. They resorted to financial tactics to achieve ends that were basically moral. Most fundamental was the principle of "fair play," as Knox called it. The United States would expect the foreign powers as well as itself to adhere to the Open Door policy, which by this time had become synonymous with the principles of equal commercial opportunity and China's territorial and administrative integrity. What the Taft administration set out to do was, again in Knox's words, "to reduce the theory to practice." In order to do this, the United States sought to undermine the monopolistic position of the South Manchuria Railway by building another railway running parallel to it, and by proposing an internationalization of all railways in Manchuria, whether in existence or to be constructed in the future. An American syndicate was organized to participate in an international banking consortium to finance various projects in China.

There is no question that the chief target of the new policy was Japan. Japanese policy in Manchuria and in Asia in general had inspired the moralistic approach. Japan's predominant position, of course, had been there before 1909; while the Roosevelt administration had acquiesced in it, however, the Taft administration decided to challenge it on moral grounds. There was no assurance that such an undertaking would succeed; it is remarkable that neither Taft nor Knox foresaw war with Japan on account of the Manchurian question, and that no step was taken to augment the Pacific fleet at this time. They were not even sure that the American people would support a war, should it come, that would be fought over a China question. Nevertheless, the administration adhered to a moralistic policy since, as Knox wrote, "it would be much better for us to stand consistently by our principles even though we fail in getting them generally adopted." As it turned out, the United States failed to undermine Japan's hold on Manchuria. On the contrary, the challenge posed by America drove Japan and Russia still closer together. Neither was Britain willing to forsake the Japanese alliance on account of America's moral commitments. Success or failure, however, is irrelevant. The United States was for the first time announcing its entrance into the East Asian world as a morally oriented nation. It was opposed to Japan's amoral policy, which Tokyo's leaders consciously pursued in order to safeguard what they took to be the essential national interests. Here, in a sense, was America's response to the rise of an Asiatic imperialist, subjugating other Asian peoples. Somehow it was felt to be America's mission to help the victims of Japanese imperialism, to side with some Asians against others. At a time when other Western countries were pursuing the usual power-oriented diplomacy, regarding Japan merely as another power, the United States tended to view it as an Asian imperialist, an object of moral concern.

•

The new American attitude toward East Asia was at first little appreciated and even little understood by the Chinese. Some Ch'ing officials, it is true, hopefully turned to the United States as the country that might effectively check Japanese expansionism. Men like Yüan Shih-k'ai and the American educated T'ang Shao-yi agreed that America's financial resources and prestige might help in undermining Japan's influence in Manchuria. There is little evidence, however, that they consistently followed such a strategy or that they regarded the United States as essentially different from other powers. The Chinese eagerly took advantage of America's offer to return the unused portion of the Boxer indemnity so that the money might be spent in sending students to the United States. Some of the "Boxer indemnity scholars" would later achieve prominence in China and constitute a pro-American force. As yet no such trend was visible. The most one can say is that some Ch'ing officials from time to time thought about taking advantage of American-Japanese antagonism to reduce Japanese influence, without really making it a systematic policy. To many Chinese—students, provincial gentry and officials, merchants, and officers of the new army, many of them under the influence of revolutionary ideology —the United States seemed committed to the preservation of the dynasty. Together with Britain, France, and Germany, the United States extended the so-called "Hukuang loan" in 1909, designed to assist the central government to nationalize Chinese railways.

The scheme ran into the direct opposition of provincial leaders, whose protest against railway nationalization was a direct cause of the 1911 uprising. They failed to detect much difference between American policy and the policies of the European governments in the loan arrangements. Huang Hsing, the revolutionary leader, even charged in 1911, "The United States, having no territorial ambitions in China, has therefore pledged to maintain Chinese independence and integrity in order to monopolize foreign loans." [1] The Chinese revolutionaries had looked to America as well as to other countries for financial support, but they had been notably unsuccessful in collecting funds outside of small circles of overseas Chinese communities.

A notion of Sino-American friendship as a distinct phenomenon dates from the republican revolution of 1912. Not only Americans, already disposed to a sympathetic view of China, but the Chinese themselves began mouthing similar sentiments. Interestingly enough, prominent Chinese of diverse political persuasions subscribed to an image of friendly relations between the two countries, so that the image survived the turbulent domestic developments after 1912. These developments can be briefly summarized. The republican revolutionaries, in their moment of triumph, felt constrained to turn to the military leaders of the country to maintain a semblance of political unity after the collapse of the Manchu dynasty. Yüan Shih-k'ai, out of power since 1909, symbolized this unity, and it was through him that a more or less peaceful transition of power was accomplished. He served as provisional president at first, but in time he emerged as the new power. Sun Yat-sen, a symbol of the revolutionary movement, was at first willing to go along with these changes, but the failure of Yüan to sanction a more decentralized and democratic form of government as advocated by Sun and his followers led to the latter's defection, assuring Yüan's complete hegemony.

Americans thus had new heroes in China. They were at first most enthusiastic about Sun Yat-sen. He appeared as the leader of the new China, the father of the "sister republic." He was, as many readily assumed, the George Washington of China. It was particularly gratifying that Sun was a Christian. His advent seemed

[1] Cited in Chün-tu Hsüeh, *Huang Hsing and the Chinese Revolution* (Stanford, 1961), p. 85.

to herald the coming of a new day to Christianity in China. At home a movement soon got under way to press for a speedy recognition of the Chinese republic. As early as February 29, 1912, seventeen days after the abdication of the emperor, the House of Representatives adopted a resolution expressing the American people's sympathy with the course of events in China and their hope that a republican form of government would firmly establish itself.

Toward Yüan Shih-k'ai American sentiments were even warmer. He had always been a favorite figure in American writings. Though, after his temporary eclipse in 1908, he was sometimes maligned as a reactionary, his return to power in 1912 was warmly welcomed. Of all the potential Chinese leaders he seemed to be the most competent, capable of unifying the country in its difficult moment. What was more, Yüan's promise to respect religious freedom came just at the right moment to rally missionaries and their home boards to his cause. A Boston publication of the Congregationalist American Board noted, "A religion which today has liberty for its propagation and which numbers among its followers many of the leading men of the nation is bound to grow in the esteem of the common people. [The overthrow of the Manchus] is to result in the coming of the larger civilization of men which draws no national boundaries and which is controlled by good will. Jesus called it the Kingdom of God." Even after Sun and his followers defected from the Yüan government, in 1913, the favorable image of Yüan stayed. American opinion, whether in China or at home, was decidedly pro-Yüan. It is remarkable that many of the same writers who only a year before had greeted Sun so warmly now turned against him. As one writer put it, "evidently we have been too forward in exalting Sun Yat-sen as a second Washington. . . . Visionary in temperament and socialistic in creed, he seems to have developed into a chronic fault finder." Such a changed view of Sun only served to perpetuate a favorable image of Yüan Shih-k'ai. His regime seemed to merit recognition. Through extending recognition, many argued, the United States could help stabilize political conditions in China, so that together they might contribute to the peace, welfare, and even Christianization of Asia.

Such an outburst of enthusiasm needs an explanation. Certainly American observers of the Chinese scene could not have been blind to the turmoil in China, which Yüan's leadership at the top could not entirely cover up. Provinces were semi-autonomous and government finances were in disarray. Larger portions of governmental revenue were either pledged as security for foreign loans or expropriated by the local governments. The central administration could not function without further foreign loans, to which nationalistic Chinese were opposed as a matter of principle. Yüan's concern with consolidating his power was such that he even connived at the assassination of an opposition leader. His republic was never meant to be a democratic government based on party politics. No wonder, then, that some realists abroad showed skepticism about the new China. In the United States bankers could not bring themselves to lend more money to China because of its political instability. They could not believe that the new republic held much promise. Church leaders and press editors, however, continued to create a rosy image of China. They did so because they wanted to believe in the China that they pictured. This wishful thinking seems to have been rooted in the same psychology as had produced the fear of Japan. There was a psychological need to believe that China would not be another Japan, that it would somehow modernize itself without posing the same threat as Japan seemed to represent. In the view of many Americans the Japanese had parted company with their American benefactors, but it was hoped that the Chinese would remain closely tied to America, or at least to the West. It was just in such a frame of mind that several observers noted the allegedly more Western features of Chinese life, actual or potential. Japanese modernization had been a disappointment, but perhaps China could vindicate the hope of many a Western well-wisher that a non-Western nation could be both Westernized and pro-Western.

President Woodrow Wilson came to power just at this juncture. His assumption of office assured a basic continuity in America's East Asian policy. While it is customary to speak of his "new diplomacy," it must be noted that much of what is usually associated with Wilson had originated with President Taft. The climate of American opinion and Wilson's personal inclinations served to perpetuate a moralistic approach to East Asian problems instead of a return to the Rooseveltian emphasis on economic and security matters. "There must be, not a balance of power, but a community of power," said Wilson, "not organized rivalries, but an organized common peace." He was, in a sense, proposing a new conception of international relations and in fact a new view of human society. He would seek to bring about and maintain peace in the world, not on the basis of a precarious balance of power or on the basis of the big powers' definition of a status quo, but on the basis of the universal adherence to the principles of justice and self-determination. "I am proposing," he told the Senate in January 1917, "that all nations henceforth avoid entangling alliances which would draw them into competitions of power, catch them in a net of intrigue and selfish rivalry, and disturb their own affairs with influences intruded from without." There could be no lasting peace unless all peoples were free and independent. President Wilson was postulating an axiom for a basic harmony of international relations; if only people everywhere lived in freedom and independence, there would be harmony among them and peace would reign.

Wilson's new diplomacy, it is true, was not full-blown in 1913 but developed gradually from the dilemmas of neutrality during the World War. After all, his major preoccupation had been with national politics and domestic reform. A distinctly idealistic, "Wilsonian" approach to foreign policy emerged only in 1916, when he began asserting America's responsibility to "stand for the rights of men" and called for the creation of a "universal association of the nations" in order to guarantee "territorial integrity and political independence" in all parts of the world. Verbal idealism, moreover, did not imply a policy solely based on moral considerations. Wilson's high-handed actions in Santo Domingo, Haiti, and Mexico, no matter what justification was offered, perpetuated the practices of the old diplomacy. There is little doubt, however, that a new approach toward East Asia was a major concern of the Democratic administration from its inception—a concern that had to be balanced against other concerns, but was nevertheless a significant issue to which America's moral stand was considered relevant. For Wilson it was axiomatic that the international situation surrounding China was most unnatural; the Chinese were denied their rightful sovereign rights, and the powers determined Chinese affairs among themselves, often without bothering to consult the Chinese. To assist China regain its rights was a theme running through eight years of the Wilson administration. The policy was advocated by Secretary of State Bryan, who had already been a champion of Chinese nationalism, and others such as Paul S. Reinsch, minister to Peking, and E. T. Williams, a former missionary who headed the Far Eastern division of the State Department. Unlike the preceding administration, there was less interest in financial collaboration with the other powers; for Wilson an international banking consortium was an immoral imposition on China. Rather, the United States would employ more unilateral tactics to do what it could to help China. The recognition of the Yüan Shih-k'ai regime, a step taken independently of the other powers, was one such example. For the government in Washington Yüan seemed to represent the hope of the new China; even the assassination of his major political opponent, Sung Chiao-jen, did not affect the initial American attitude toward Yüan.

Friendship Reciprocated

The Chinese themselves returned these friendly feelings emanating from across the Pacific. Perhaps for the first time since the mid-nineteenth century, there emerged the view of America as a friend, in fact the only friend of China. The new image was in part traceable to the realization that the United States was the only power that might be expected to check Japanese expansionism. America was simply the most available friend to oppose Japan's ambitions. The moment the United States appeared willing to acquiesce in Japanese policy, therefore, such a picture of American friendship would evaporate. For many Chinese, however, the United States was more than just one of the powers; America impressed them as a nation endowed with special resources that were relevant to the young republic.

There are certain indices to reveal the new Chinese attitude toward the United States. More and more students were going to and returning from America, which had replaced Japan as the country from which Chinese would obtain an education. Though the number of Chinese students in America was never large, two or three thousand at most, they included prominent representatives of Young China—Wellington Koo, Hu Shih, Ch'en Kung-po, and others. Four of the twelve members of the first cabinet of the republic had studied in America. It has been suggested that most of the Chinese students in the United States were poorly prepared and performed unsatisfactorily in American schools and colleges. Once they returned to China they were unable to adjust themselves to rapidly changing conditions at home. It is possible, however, that such a situation could make the students' nationalism all the more potent and radical. If their education had been superficial, and if, on their return home, they were often arrogant and despised native manners and institutions, their devotion to the ideas of national independence and progress could make a tremendous impact on public opinion in China. They evoked in the Chinese minds an image of America standing for progress and freedom. The United States, in their view, represented something new, and it supplied symbolic guidance for the movement for national regeneration. "The ideals of China and the United States," declared Huang Hsing, who found himself an exile in America after his failure to overthrow the Yüan regime, "are now absolutely the same, and the sympathy of the American people with China in its aims would have tremendous effect at home." [1] The revolutionary leader who, only a few years earlier, had denounced America's financial schemes in China, was now saying that the Chinese hoped to fashion their revolutionary government after the United States.

A Chinese youth who did not have an opportunity to study in America could study in one of the three thousand schools founded and managed by Americans. There was an increasing number of Chinese teachers in these schools who had been educated in the United States. One hundred and forty hospitals established by American funds symbolized America's help to the Chinese people, as did 2,500 Protestant missionaries, who consistently tried to spread the image of a new China. A reader of Chinese magazines would have found that it was quite rare to read an issue without some mention of American life and society. Such diverse aspects of American culture as the children's library, mineral resources, the iron and steel trust, and the housewife occupied the pages of monthly and weekly publications, serving to bring America closer to the Chinese public. It was as though American ideas, institutions, and customs were found to be suddenly relevant to the emergence and development of a new society in the Orient.

[1] *Ibid.*, p. 172.

Japanese-American Enmity

The self-conscious antagonism between Japanese and Americans came to a climax during World War I. It is revealing that the Japanese navy, which had earlier eschewed continentalism and pan-Asianism lest these should create trouble with the United States, now came to view Japanese-American relations as critical and heading toward a showdown. The continued anti-Japanese agitation in the west coast and the opposition of the United States to Japanese policy in Asia were driving the naval strategists in Japan to a fatalistic view of their relations with the American navy. One of them wrote in 1913, "The sudden emergence of the California question, coupled with the China question, impels us to action and gives us a great opportunity to promote a great union of Japan and China." The espousal of such a pan-Asianist view by a naval spokesman revealed a fundamental change in the Japanese view of America. Four years later, in 1917, although the two nations were now allies against Germany, the Japanese navy formally adopted the policy of viewing the United States as the most likely enemy. According to Navy Minister Katō Tomosaburō, war with the United States was possible because of five factors: America's Monroe Doctrine, restrictive immigration policy, Open Door policy in China, opposition to Japanese possessions in the South Seas, and continued naval expansion. "Although vast differences in the two nations' material wealth make it impossible for us to compete with the United States numerically," he said, "we must do our best to maintain our armament in a state of readiness. We must make preparations for controlling the Asiatic seas in case of emergency and to adopt plans to overcome the enemy by holding these sea lanes." Half a year later, in February 1918, a staff officer of the Navy General Staff urged a Siberian expedition in order to prevent the United States from controlling Siberia, since it could then close in on Japan from the north, west (China), east (Hawaii, Guam), and south (Philippines). Should the United States oppose a Japanese expedition to Siberia, Japan should not hesitate to go to war with it.

These views reflected a changed estimate of American power in East Asia. The Japanese now viewed the United States as a potential enemy, now that the two powers seemed destined to struggle for supremacy in the western Pacific and the continent of Asia. On this latter point, the Japanese exponents of wartime expansionism justified their policy by pan-Asianism. The European war seemed a heaven-sent opportunity to entrench and solidify Japanese influence on the continent of Asia so as to prevent Western powers from overwhelming Japanese interests. Because of the notion that the nation was not entirely accepted as an equal, bold action seemed needed to take advantage of the West's distress so that its postwar counteroffensive would not materialize. This was the psychological background of the Twenty-One Demands negotiations, schemes to detach Manchuria and Mongolia from China, the "Nishihara loans," and other policies and machinations pursued during the war. By 1918 Japan had succeeded in obtaining Chinese consent to the perpetuation of its rights in Manchuria and Inner Mongolia, to the transfer of German rights in Shantung to Japan, and to the formation of closer military and economic ties between the two countries. In pursuing these aims, the Japanese naturally were aware of American disapproval, and the image of the United States as a major obstacle in the way of Japanese policy in China became firmly established.

At the same time, it would be wrong to say that the two naval powers were destined to collide in China. Actually, many Japanese, especially civilian bureaucrats, leading businessmen, and some influential politicians clung to the view that the interests of Japan and the United States were still not incompatible. After all, trade between the two countries expanded by leaps and bounds during the war, and American capital continued to pour into Japan. Nor was the United States challenging Japan's treaty rights in China. Just because the two navies were expanding rapidly in the Pacific, this did not mean that they were fated to collide. Thus reasoning, prominent groups of Japanese sought to consolidate the framework of understanding with America. They wanted to assure America of Japan's peaceful intentions, so as to prevent the former from coming to China's assistance. Only if the Chinese despaired of obtaining American support would they acquiesce in Japanese rights and interests; to bring about this end it was essential to guarantee to America that these rights did not infringe upon American rights. Instead of regarding Sino-American co-operation as inevitable, therefore, Japan should try to protect its interests through closer economic and political ties with the United States. Such a view of Japanese-Chinese-American relations was behind the dispatch of Baron Ishii Kikujirō to Washington in 1917, to explore the possibilities for entering into a modus vivendi with the United States. The resulting Lansing-Ishii agreement, despite its secret protocol upholding the status quo in China, was considered a significant achievement by the Japanese. They could use it to impress the Chinese with the hopelessness of courting American help against Japan.

It is evident that the Japanese exponents of understanding with America underestimated the depth of pro-Chinese sentiment in that country. Among American policy makers, it is true, there were some who were more or less in agreement with the Japanese definition of international conditions. Robert Lansing, counselor of the State Department until he succeeded Bryan as secretary of state in 1917, viewed American–East Asian relations in security and economic terms. America's interests for him consisted of expanding trade and investment activities in China and Japan, and safeguarding territorial possessions in the Pacific. From such a narrow definition of American interests, it naturally followed that for the United States to concern itself with China's integrity was nothing less than "quixotic." He would view Japanese predominance in East Asia as a fact to be reckoned with, as long as America's security and economic interests were not compromised. In fact, he felt that war between Japan and America would be so catastrophic that he even considered the sale of the Philippines to Japan in return for certain concessions on Japan's part. Lansing spoke the language the Japanese understood and appreciated, and if he had had his way he would have entered into some sort of political agreement with Ishii. The Lansing-Ishii agreement, however, was as much Wilson's making as Lansing's. The president vetoed the secretary's suggestions for political bargaining. Only Colonel E. M. House supported Lansing, and this episode revealed the upper hand held by exponents of the new diplomacy within the American government.

The First World War saw America's sympathy with China and opposition to Japanese policy reach new heights. In official statements and memoranda there was an air of desperation and urgency. Japanese policy after 1914 seemed to confirm the fear of Japanese domination of Asia. As Minister Paul S. Reinsch wrote during the Twenty-One Demands episode of 1915, the demands "would make China politically and in a military sense a protectorate of Japan and establish a Japanese monopoly in the commercial resources of China most requisite for military purposes." If Japan controlled China, echoed E. T. Williams, head of the Far Eastern division of the State Department, "Japan, which is not restrained by the scruples of the West, and which declines to enter into peace pacts, becomes a greater menace than ever to the U.S." Significantly, Williams continued, "If we can succeed in reducing the demands, it seems to me that we ought to insist upon China's putting her house in order and making herself able to defend herself. We can and ought to assist her in this, and in so doing we shall be building up a strong defense for ourselves." It is easy to see where these officials' real fear lay. Unless the United States took a lead in encouraging Chinese resistance against Japan, the island empire would emerge as the overlord of Asia and would menace the West. If China was to be Westernized, the process ought to be assisted by the West itself, in order to prevent China's following Japan's path of modernization. It was with such ideas that the United States enunciated the principle of "non-recognition"; it would not recognize any demand imposed on China that compromised its political or territorial integrity.

The spectre of Japan's absorbing China was a popular one outside the government. The vision of future conflict between Japan and America began to seem less and less fantastic. The crisis literature was voluminous, and two themes were usually presented. On the one hand, a Japan predominant in Asia was so dangerous that the United States should do all it could to help China resist Japan. On the other hand, it was felt by some that it might be impossible to hold Japan in check in Asia. Perhaps Western power could not be salvaged there. This all the more necessitated the need for racial segregation. The fear of mixed marriages between races, specifically between the white and yellow races, was heard more and more loudly. No matter what happened to Asia, it was absolutely essential to keep the white race pure and intact, since miscegenation would ultimately demoralize the Western peoples and lead to their atrophy. By coincidence some of the most influential books on the subject were published in 1916: Madison Grant, *The Passing of the Great Race, or the Racial Base of European History;* Carl Crow,

Japan and America; and James F. Abbott, *Japanese Expansion and American Policies.* They all talked of the menace presented by the mixing of races. With Japan predominant in Asia, the Japanese in America would pose a serious threat to the fabric of American society. It was essential either to check Japan in Asia or, barring this possibility, to keep the Japanese out of the Western hemisphere.

It will be noted that there was a curious dichotomy in these views with respect to China. On one hand, China must be helped to resist Japan; on the other, Chinese were Asians, and if they came under Japanese domination, they could not be helped. Undoubtedly there was some genuine sympathy with China's plight and its valiant effort to stand up against foreign encroachment. But, for these writers, concern for China's welfare was ultimately linked to concern for racial purity and for American safety. It was natural, then, that the expressions of sympathy for China were frequently coupled with pleas for naval expansion. An adequate defense force, not merely to protect the Philippines or Hawaii but as a shield against Japanese expansion, seemed more and more needed. Only the determined might of the United States would, it was felt, deter Japanese invasion of America. Undoubtedly such thinking was behind Congressional debates on naval construction programs. Though Germany was as much an imaginary enemy as Japan in 1916, these discussions revealed sensitivity to the growing power of Japan and willingness to augment fleet strength in the Pacific as well as in the Atlantic.

In 1917 the United States and Japan became allies against Germany. But America's suspicion of Japan did not abate. If anything, mutual antagonism increased as a result of Japan's bold expansionistic acts in China and Siberia. The distance between the two countries widened as the United States now emerged as the recognized champion of the new diplomacy. America's participation in the war ensured that its role would increase at the peace conference and that its ideas would be given respectful attention. The picture was somewhat complicated because Russia under the new Bolshevik leadership renounced the old diplomacy and advocated a complete overhaul of international relations. Wilson and Lenin stood as the two figures heralding the coming of the yet undefined new age, and the Siberian expedition took on the symbolic appearance of Wilson opposing Lenin. Nevertheless, these developments did not affect the already defined pattern of America's relationship with China and Japan. The United States encouraged China's entry into the war so that the latter might emerge as an influential nation after the war, and meanwhile the government in Washington did all it could to discourage Japan's unilateral expedition to Siberia. It is significant that even the realistic secretary of state, Lansing, had by 1918 come to believe in the need to take a firm attitude toward Japan. He felt that all attempts at compromise had been taken advantage of by Japan's military expansionists. It would thus be imperative for the United States to restrain them by all possible means.

America's opposition to wartime Japanese policy confirmed the Chinese view that the United States was the one power most likely to render help to China against Japan. Men as different as Yüan Shih-k'ai and Huang Hsing expressed confidence that their country could count on the sympathy of the United States against Japanese expansionism. Such confidence is particularly impressive in view of the fact that Chinese pleas for specific American help against Japanese ambitions were often turned down. In 1914, for instance, when the European war broke out, the Peking government immediately sought America's assistance to keep East Asia out of the conflict. Yüan Shih-k'ai hoped that the American force in China and the fleet in the Pacific might be augmented as a check on the Japanese. During the Twenty-One Demands episode, the Chinese government leaked the demands to the American press in the hope of obtaining foreign support of China's stand. In 1917, as China followed the lead of the United States to break off diplomatic relations with Germany, Peking sought to obtain American funds to train a new army in preparation for war against the Central Powers. None of these hopes was fulfilled. On the contrary, the Chinese were bitterly resentful of the seeming American capitulation to Japanese expansionism, as embodied in the published texts of the Lansing-Ishii agreement. The Peking government lodged a strong protest, and the rival regime in Canton denounced the accord as "offending the spirit of American friendly policies toward China." Moreover, America's apparent support of Yüan's imperial ambitions did not endear the United States to his opponents. Although Frank J. Goodnow, a Johns Hopkins professor and adviser to Yüan, never explicitly advocated the adoption by China of a monarchical form of government, his skepticism about the universal validity of republican institutions was well known. President Wilson, Minister Reinsch, and other American officials refused to endorse joint action by the powers to oppose Yüan's imperial scheme. After his death in 1916, China was divided into rival regions and regimes, some of which openly staked their existence on a co-operative policy toward Japan. The wonder is, therefore, that through such turmoil the image of Sino-American friendship survived. This was fundamentally due to the impact of Wilsonism. By 1918 President Wilson had become the symbol of the new world order. The Chinese avidly took to the Wilsonian vocabulary of national sovereignty and self-determination. Just as Japan seemed to persist in the old diplomacy of power politics, the United States under Wilson represented the principles of the approaching new order. No matter what the political chaos at home, the Chinese could turn to America for inspiration and moral leadership.

It would be interesting to speculate on the impact of such a Chinese view of America as China's special friend on American politicians and writers for whom these were formative years. They would undoubtedly carry with them the memories of wartime friendship as they reached positions of influence and leadership in the 1930's. It should be emphasized, however, that the Chinese turned to the United States for what they believed America stood for. So long as the United States challenged the designs of aggressive powers and championed the cause of small nations, so long as efforts were made to realize the lofty ideas of President Wilson, so long would the Chinese continue to hold an image of close friendship between the two countries. By its unilateral acts the United States had raised the level of expectations of the Chinese for changes to come in international relations. By infusing morality into diplomacy, hitherto defined in military and economic terms, Americans had introduced a new yardstick, by which they themselves would be judged in the years to come. It remained to be seen whether the much-talked-about friendship between the two countries would become an actuality.

6
Chinese Nationalism and the United States

By 1918 Chinese nationalism had emerged as one of the forces of international life. The United States had done much to make it so. Chinese national aspirations would have been held in check if all the treaty powers had been interested in suppressing them or in meeting the Chinese challenge in co-operation so as to minimize its impact. Wilsonian diplomacy, however, had defied the old practices and ideas of international relations and made the nationalism of weak nations respectable. But this was not all. Japan's propensity to act alone in extending its influence in Asia, the disappearance of Germany as an imperialist power as a result of its defeat, and the defection of Russia under the new regime from the ranks of the imperialists, all served to undermine the status-quo policy that had been the foundation of the diplomacy of imperialism. There is no question that even without the developments in China these changes would have brought about the demise of the old order in East Asia. The contemporaneous rise of "Young China," which was assisted by the collapse of the old framework of imperialist diplomacy, ensured that these changes would be permanent.

Nor was Japan free from internal changes. Just as in other countries the "forces of change" were challenging the "forces of order," there grew in Japan a new political and intellectual movement under the impact of democratic ideas abroad and the wartime boom and postwar recession at home. Intellectuals again interested themselves in politics, and they were strongly influenced by internationalism and democracy, which, according to them, were the current "trends in the world." They called for universal suffrage at home and more peaceful policy abroad. Civilian bureaucrats and party leaders, too, staged their counteroffensive against the military who had pushed the limits of the empire. There were voices calling for reassessment of foreign policy, and many asserted the need to return to the principle of co-operation with the West. Business leaders, too, supported such a stand. They saw the impossibility of meeting continued and increasing expenditures for armament in competition with the United States, when trade with that country was expanding rapidly.

Anti-Japanese Sentiment

It is not surprising, then, that as soon as the war came to an end there emerged a trend toward rapprochement between Japan and the United States, and between Japan and China. It was, nevertheless, not until the Washington Conference (1921–1922) that a degree of amity returned to Japanese-American relations. For one thing, within the United States official and non-official suspicion of Japan reached a new climax during 1918–1921 despite Japanese protestation of their desire for understanding. The title of an influential book by the exclusionist Valentine S. McClatchy, *The Germany of Asia,* best exemplifies the American attitude toward Japan just after the war. By its acts during the war and in the Siberian expedition, Japan had created an impression among Americans that it was behaving like Germany—aggressive, humorless, and barbaric. McClatchy visited East Asia in 1919, and from then on till his death in the 1930's he was a consistent foe of Japanese policy and of Japanese immigrants. He pictured Japan as being intent on the conquest not only of Asia but of America. Japanese immigrants were agents of this plot, and their exclusion was absolutely imperative if America was to be spared Mongolization. Like many of his contemporaries, McClatchy deplored interracial marriages. The American and the Japanese ways of life were simply incompatible, and they could not coexist or cohabit together without damage to the fabric of American society. These views were even more forcefully presented by T. Lothrop Stoddard in his dramatically titled *Rising Tide of Color Against White World Supremacy*. Published in 1920, the author conceded that the whites probably could not hold Asia forever. However, if they had to withdraw from Asia they should also make sure that the nonwhites would be kept away from other parts of the world. That such racial views were by no means simply ignorant extravagance may be seen in Stoddard's effort to present his case in scientific language. Indeed these were years when "scientific" studies were made of primitive societies and of human races; their bone structures were measured and compared, and their speech patterns were analyzed, all purporting to show the superiority of the Nordic race. The United States Congress itself endorsed these views by passing various immigration laws, designed to establish a quota system weighed heavily in favor of Western Europeans. Many a Congressman must have felt his views were confirmed when, in 1922, a noted anthropologist testified that the mental capacity of the black man was 80 per cent of that of the white man, and the yellow and brown races' capacity averaged 95 per cent. Hence the evil of miscegenation, as children of mixed marriages were bound to have mental capacities below that of the white parent.[1]

Anti-Japanese sentiments, however, were by no means confined to the exclusionists and racists. E. T. Williams represented the voice of East Asian experts in the State Department when he wrote, in 1919, "The spirit of Japan is that of Prussia, whom the Japanese leaders openly admire and whose government they chose for a model." Williams' successor, John V. A. MacMurray, fully subscribed to the view that Japan was like Germany just before the war. The government of Japan, he wrote in 1921, "is an oligarchy of military clansmen and their adherents, all alike imbued with the same materialistic political philosophy, differing among themselves only in the degree to which their nationalistic aspirations are tempered by considerations of prudence in dealing

[1] Thompson, *The Yellow Peril*, pp. 48–49.

with the rest of the world." MacMurray believed that there was a growing realization in Japan that the United States could not be ignored, "not only because of their relative geographical situation, but also because the whole fabric of Japan's industrial life is dependent upon trade with the United States." On the other hand, there was also the possibility that the Japanese had already decided to consider conflict with America as inevitable, because of "a fundamental belief on their part that our civilization threatens to overwhelm theirs, that our national position is a menace to their political ideal of a hegemony of the peoples of eastern Asia." Whatever the actual intentions of the Japanese, MacMurray suggested that the United States maintain a strong fleet in the Pacific to ensure protection against reckless Japanese action.

As earlier, part of the anti-Japanese sentiment was traceable to the feeling of sympathy with China. In the above memorandum, MacMurray wrote that the United States had not done enough to help China, despite the fact that "the Chinese regard the United States with a degree of confidence and friendship which may be termed singular among international relations." The United States had failed their confidence, he felt, as it had not successfully checked Japanese aggression. It was time, therefore, to give what encouragement America could to "the element in China which is seeking to preserve and to develop China as a nation." It is well known that part of the strong senatorial opposition to the Versailles peace treaty was due to the feeling that the treaty had wronged China by failing to provide for Japan's relinquishment of control over Shantung. The Shantung question took on a moral aspect, and America seemed to be deeply involved. Because President Wilson had failed, despite his urgent efforts, to induce the Japanese to surrender the rights they had acquired over Shantung during the war, the pro-Chinese sentiment was aroused and undoubtedly influenced the outcome of the "great debate" in the United States. Some State Department advisers, including Lansing, had advocated a strong stand on the question, but the President had yielded on the issue in order to gain Japan's participation in the League of Nations. From the point of view of his critics and even of his supporters, this was an act of betrayal of the confidence the Chinese had placed in America.

The Shantung episode, in fact, epitomized the state of Japanese-

American relations. It illustrated what sort of compromise the Japanese had in mind when they resumed the policy of rapprochement with the United States. It is revealing that Prime Minister Hara Kei, who took some energetic steps as soon as he came to office in September 1918 to demonstrate his desire for friendly relations with China and with the United States, should have been adamant on the question of Shantung. He was ready to cut back political loans to China and reduce the number of expeditionary forces in Siberia. He envisaged co-operative action with the United States in East Asia, and he endorsed in general America's idea of a new international consortium to assist China. Nevertheless, neither Hara nor his cabinet seems to have understood the implications of the Wilsonian new diplomacy. There were a few, such as Makino Shinken, who talked of the American-inspired new diplomacy. "Some Japanese," he said in 1919, "still entertain pro-German feelings. [However] today it is the trend of the world to respect the principle of peace and reject that of oppression. The so-called Americanism is promoted everywhere on earth. Conditions have entirely changed from the days of the old diplomacy." This was a correct interpretation of the international scene. It is ironical that it was the same Makino who was named plenipotentiary at the peace conference and, perhaps against his will, held out adamantly against concession on the Shantung question. For, despite the recognition of the need to seek understanding with the United States, the Japanese leaders were still guided by the assumptions of the old diplomacy. They assumed that if they made certain concessions the United States would recognize Japan's prerogatives in parts of China. Shantung was just such an example. In return for Japan's joining the League of Nations it was felt that Wilson would offer to acquiesce in the Japanese position in Shantung.

It was natural, then, that these years should have seen the Chinese more anti-Japanese than ever before. The aroused nationalism of China, now having emerged as a victor in the war, was crystallized into a social movement in 1919, as the Chinese revolted against the Versailles settlement, which had failed to restore Shantung unequivocally to them. The force of public indignation was such that the government in Peking refused to sign the treaty. A nationwide boycott of Japanese goods was started, leading John Dewey, just then visiting China, to exclaim that a new nation was being born. The Chinese were tremendously disappointed by the failure of President Wilson to deal more firmly with Japan, but significantly this did not make them anti-American. Compared with the mob violence in Asia and Africa in the 1960's, often government-backed, the actions of the Chinese nationalists seem very well disciplined. With rare exceptions they shunned physical violence and instead resorted to peaceful measures and fundamentally to an intellectual campaign to reach the masses. Because the May Fourth movement which thus ensued was predominantly an intellectual movement, its leadership was assumed by students, professors, and journalists, many of whom were American educated. There were far more graduates of American colleges than European institutions, and they played leading roles in a number of colleges founded in China. A few Chinese intellectuals, it is true, were fascinated by the Bolshevik revolution and applied themselves to the study of Marxism. Many, too, were impressed with the new Soviet government's repeated offers to renounce the old treaties and enter into an equal relationship with China. Before 1921, however, the impact of the Soviet revolution and diplomacy was still limited. To the Chinese intellectuals who led the fight against Japan and for a cultural rebirth of the country, the United States remained the source of encouragement and inspiration.

The Washington Conference

From such a perspective, it is obvious that the Washington Conference marked a successful consummation of Japan's effort to effect rapprochement with the United States, while it also signified a temporary end of China's infatuation with the image of Sino-American friendship. The United States under President Harding was no less committed to the new diplomacy than under Wilson, and all attempts by Japan to come to terms with America through political bargaining had failed. For instance, sensitive to American objection to the Anglo-Japanese alliance in its existing form, the Tokyo government was willing to renounce it and conclude a new tripartite pact, in which the two and the United States would explicitly honor the principle of the Open Door in China. Even this gesture was rejected by the State Department, as it was reminiscent of the old diplomatic practice of collusion among the big powers. Thus during the course of the Washington Conference the Japanese decided to accept the inevitable. They would do everything to avoid conflict with the United States, and to this end they would be willing to embrace the principles of the new diplomacy, as embodied, among others, in the Nine Power Treaty which enunciated a series of principles of Sino-foreign relations to replace the existing particularistic arrangements. All of this was based on the recognition that Japan was in no position to fight against the United States. As Admiral Katō Tomosaburō, Japanese plenipotentiary, said, modern warfare required enormous funds, which Japan had no choice but to obtain from abroad. Since, however, America was the only possible source of money, there could be no thought of fighting against that country. Thus the former Navy Minister who in 1917 had asserted the likelihood of war with America now declared, "it is imperative to avoid war with the United States."

Japanese realism and America's concerted effort to challenge the old diplomacy had brought about rapprochement. From the Chinese point of view this was nothing but an about-face on America's part. The Nine Power Treaty, it is true, reiterated the adherence by the signatories, including China, to the principles of independence, integrity, and sovereignty of China as well as of the Open Door. Moreover, America offered its good offices as the Chinese and Japanese delegates met outside the conference proceedings to discuss the Shantung question, producing Japan's readiness to restore the rights it had acquired in the peninsula to China and withdraw troops. Despite these and other concessions on Japan's part, the Chinese were bitterly disappointed that the conferees failed to restore to China a full sovereign status. They resolved "to provide the fullest and most unembarrassed opportunity to China to develop and maintain for herself an effective and stable government," and to put this principle into effect resolutions were adopted providing for gradual revision of the treaties. The Chinese, having come to expect more, were dissatisfied. They sought to persuade the United States to take more forceful steps, but the latter was disinclined to do so. It was enough, from the American point of view, to have demolished the old imperialist diplomacy and forced Japan to beat a retreat. These steps should have cleared the path for the Chinese to evolve a stable and modern government. President Wilson might have gone a step further and identified American policy with Chinese nationalism to its logical limits. The basic inspiration of the postwar American counter-offensive in Asia, however, was to challenge Japanese predominance. Once they satisfied themselves that Japan had cut back its wartime excesses, they assumed that orderly change in the Chinese treaty system was the best way to assist China. Having expected much more from America, China's nationalists refused to accept the Washington Conference treaties as the framework for postwar foreign policy.

Leninism in China

Chinese nationalism, in fact, took a decisively radical turn in the 1920's. The Chinese now clearly distinguished between modernization and Westernization, and their view of the West was couched in the vocabulary of anti-imperialism. It should be remembered that the theme of "European decline" was world-wide, not limited to the Chinese perception of the West. In postwar European writings one finds evidence of inner doubt about Western civilization.

"Europe is sick, perhaps dying," said Anatole France, while Thomas Hardy remarked that another Dark Ages might be preparing to descend upon Europe. Francesco Nitti, Italian prime minister, probably expressed the feeling of postwar European statesmen when he observed that a smile had vanished from every lip in Europe. The 1920's saw vast numbers of treatises about civilization, in particular Western civilization. Analysis after analysis was written about the evils of scientism, technological civilization, democracy, the rise of the masses, and nationalism. "In a state of drunken illusion," wrote Hermann Hesse in 1922, Europe "is reeling into the abyss and, as she reels, she sings a drunken hymn such as Dmitri Karamazov sang. The insulted citizen laughs that song to scorn, the saint and seer hear it with tears." In talking of the decline of Europe, writers naturally had in mind the rise of Bolshevik Russia, the growing influence of Americanism, and, most important, the rediscovered vitality of Asia. All of a sudden European intellectuals became fascinated with "the East." To many a weary mind of Europe, the "Eastern way of life" seemed to offer a new escape from despair and anarchy. Because the West had failed with all its ideas and institutions, they felt, the gods of the Orient must be the true gods, and its philosophy the way of truth. "Our Western world is weary; not weary of life, but of strife and hatred," noted a German journal in 1921. "Men are looking to the East unconsciously, and therefore sincerely. . . . The world of Asia draws us with its promise of something new and something that will liberate."

The re-evaluation of Western civilization that characterized the Chinese intellectual world in the 1920's must be comprehended within the world-wide disillusionment with the West. Controversies on East and West and on science versus humanism were especially sharp in China because Chinese intellectuals with modern educations had come of age and were in leading positions in the universities and bureaucracies. It cannot be doubted that most of them were profoundly skeptical of the values of the West's spiritual heritage. They would have agreed with Hu Shih that the "difference between the Eastern and Western civilizations is simply a degree of success or failure in the process of breaking away from the medieval ideas and institutions which once ruled the whole civilized world." This process was seen as a technological change; the modern West seemed characterized by material advances and technological innovations. These the Chinese could and should adopt, as they were not a monopoly of Westerners and they were essential if China was to cope with the might of the big nations. But China could dispense with the spiritual aspects of Western civilization. Christianity, for instance, seemed irrelevant to modern civilization, and to the extent that it had been part of the West, it had not prevented the calamitous war. China with a different cultural heritage should therefore not try to graft the West's spiritual values and religious institutions on itself. There were, of course, those who were ardent Christians and who continued to assert the necessity for spiritual as well as materialistic Westernization. Which way the wind was blowing was, however, clearly revealed in 1922 when a world congress of Christian students, scheduled to meet in Peking, was adjourned due to a nationwide protest movement. There was a revolt against what the Chinese considered the Christian churches' excessive influence in their country. Within the churches, too, there was a movement to replace foreign preachers with Chinese, and to weaken the control held by the missionary boards. Since Chinese nationalism in its inception had owed much to Christian missionary inspiration, the nationalism of the 1920's was of a distinctly different character.

An equally crucial factor was the Chinese conversion to anti-imperialism. The number of Communists was always small, as was that of the Kuomintang left. But the Leninist theory, in its necessarily simplified versions, had an enormous impact quite out of proportion with the strength of the Communist Party or even of the Kuomintang. The Chinese, as noted earlier, had long been accustomed to the term "imperialism" and had looked upon the Western nations and Japan in that framework. However, Leninism gave it a distinctly scientific touch, as imperialism was seen as a phase of human history. Just as imperialism was an inevitable historical fact, however, anti-imperialism was a necessary force, eventually to triumph over the former. In the Leninist analysis, the imperialist forces were trying to perpetuate their domination over the colonial and semi-colonial peoples by means of supporting the "feudal" elements in these societies. At the same time, the anti-feudal and anti-imperialist groups in China and elsewhere were joined in their struggle by the anti-capitalist masses in the imperialist nations. The Chinese were thus engaged in a world-wide movement against the forces of oppression. There was a definite direction in which they were moving. Such a theory of action, combined with the twenty-year-old nationalism and the reappraisal of the West, imparted dynamism to Chinese thinking.

It was thus a changed climate in which Sino-American relations developed after the Washington Conference. The Chinese view of America would be determined in a large measure by what they took to be America's attitude and policy toward the new Chinese nationalism in its external and domestic manifestations. Sun Yat-sen provides a good example. In his life he had turned in all directions, including the United States, for financial and moral support. In the early 1920's he was still eager to grasp at any foreign friend that might be willing to help him as he tried desperately to establish leadership in Canton and ultimately emerge as a national figure. In 1921 Sun sent a direct appeal to President Harding to solicit America's support of his cause; Sun referred to the United States as "the champion of liberalism and righteousness, whose disinterested friendship and support of China in her hour of distress has been demonstrated to us more than once." In February 1923 the revolutionary leader expressed the hope that the United States might "send a strong man, Mr. Hughes for example, who as a neutral person would be able to bring together the now mutually suspicious leaders of China and make it possible for them to unite for the carrying out of some scheme of Government." By early 1923, it is true, Sun had entered into negotiation with Adolf Joffe, the Soviet representative in Peking, and the two had issued their joint manifesto, signaling the first step toward an alliance between Russia and the Kuomintang. But at this time Sun was also toying with the idea of union with any foreign government that was willing to support his cause. It was only late in 1923 that Sun turned definitely to a Russian alliance as the basic strategy and adopted anti-imperialism as the Kuomintang's central ideology. A crucial determining fact was the "Canton customs episode" in the fall of 1923. As the Nationalist government at Canton announced its intention of seizing part of the customs revenue in order to finance various city projects, the foreign powers, including the United States, sent naval vessels to demonstrate. Sun, who thought that perhaps the foreign governments might consent to his scheme, was bitterly disappointed. He said of the United States,

> America was the inspiration and example when we started the revolution to abolish autocracy and corruption in high places. . . . We might well have expected that an American Lafayette would fight on our side in this good cause. In the twelfth year of our struggle towards liberty there comes not a Lafayette but an American Admiral with more ships of war than any other nation in our waters.

To a group of students at the American-founded Canton Christian College, Sun predicted that within ten years there would be a world war between China, Russia, Japan, Germany, and India on one side with the imperialists on the other. Then the United States "would see how it feels to have a Chinese fleet in San Francisco harbor."

After January 1924, with the consummation of a Kuomintang-Communist alliance, Chinese nationalism became totally identified with anti-imperialism. The reorganized Kuomintang declared the principle of "the liberation of China by the Chinese people," and categorically asserted that all "unequal treaties are to be abolished." Internally, the Nationalists were to fight against the Peking government and the warlords who stood behind it. Even the warlords and northern officials, however, were beginning to speak the language of revolutionary nationalism. "We wish to remind the friendly powers," said C. T. Wang, then Peking's spokesman, late in 1924, "that China has a right to her own existence. Any conditions derogatory to her rights to exist as a free and independent nation must by necessity be rectified by mutual arrangement as quickly as the exigency of circumstances requires." Chang Tso-lin, the warlord behind the Peking government, sought to persuade the United States to effect mild treaty revision to undermine the strength of the radical nationalists. Both north and south thus were eager to attack the existing framework of Sino-foreign relations.

America was put on the defensive, and it remained in that position until after 1925. The general decline of American influence in postwar China was, of course, partly traceable to the attitude of the Chinese themselves. At the same time, it cannot be denied that this resulted from conscious decisions by certain key groups in America, above all, State Department officials and businessmen. As they saw the political situation in China, it was helplessly chaotic and unsafe for expansive business activities. The lives of foreigners were more than once endangered, and there had emerged no central government lasting for more than a few months and commanding the loyalty of all the provinces. In December 1922, when an American merchant at Kalgan was fatally shot without provocation by a band of Chinese soldiers, Secretary of State Hughes responded by declaring that the incident was "further evidence of increasing disregard by Chinese authorities for the rights of American citizens in China." He instructed Minister Jacob Gould Schurman in Peking, "Should the [Chinese] Government fail to deal with the case energetically and promptly, without quibbling but with manifest sincerity, you may indicate that this Government regards the matter as a test of confidence which may be placed by it in the Government of China." Schurman drove the message into the Chinese with still more force by telling C. T. Wang, "American-Chinese relations had reached a crisis. The attitude of the United States toward China had always been one of benevolent helpfulness. . . .

The American Government now wished to know whether it was the intention of the Chinese Government to prevent the United States from continuing that attitude." These were strong statements, indicating that less than a year after the conclusion of the Washington Conference American officials had begun to feel frustrated by the disparity between what they expected of China and the reality.

China's domestic instability and danger to foreigners, however, had always existed. Conditions in the 1920's do not seem to have been much worse than those in the preceding decade. The United States under a Wilson might have offered moral and financial assistance to stabilize conditions in China rather than simply lamenting the lack of stability. In the 1920's, too, the State Department considered extending loans to the Peking government and/or regional governments if there was no central government. This time, however, American bankers were least enthusiastic about such loans. They had lent millions of dollars of money to the Chinese government during the war, and they had not been repaid. Most of the loans had been either unsecured or inadequately secured, and there seemed to be little prospect of redeeming the money. Under the circumstances, the financiers could not be persuaded to extend more loans until stability returned to China and some means had been devised for debt redemption. Indeed, there was a definite shift in the financiers' interest from China to Japan. Japan's loan market was more promising and profitable, and its political conditions seemed much more durable. Since the Japanese seemed to have fully subscribed to the Washington Conference formula, businessmen needed to have no moral scruples about doing business with that country. There even appeared some who were eager to undertake co-operative enterprises with Japanese in China. New York bankers' interest in lending money to the Oriental Development Company, a Japanese firm doing business in China, is a good example.

An Economic Friendship

The mention of business and of Japan leads to a characteristic feature of American–East Asian relations in the 1920's. There was a return to the pre-Taft policy of economic diplomacy. Now that the Washington Conference had cleared the path of obstacles, the way seemed to have been reopened for principally economic relations between the United States and China and Japan. Since business prospects were not bright in China, it is not surprising that the State Department remained passive in the face of revolutionary nationalism there. Also, the Harding and Coolidge administrations, unlike Wilson's, were reluctant to act unilaterally in China. A loan proposal of 1922, for instance, met determined opposition of Japan, and the State Department was unwilling to force the issue. It was felt that a co-operative framework of action was best suited to maintain the new system of multilateral treaties worked out at the Washington Conference. In the official American conception, the major "Washington powers" were to co-operate in promoting the evolution of an independent China. There was no thought of pursuing an independent course of action. This is not to say that the suspicion of Japan had totally disappeared. Many members of the State Department who had shared the Wilsonian principles were still with the department, and they continued to look upon Japan's attitude toward the continent with misgivings. That is why the State Department refused to allow bankers in 1923 to lend to the Oriental Development Company, for fear that the money might be spent to the detriment of the Open Door in China. Still, there is no question that there had been a perceptible change in the official American image of Japan in the early 1920's. A good example is the immigration question, which reached a climax in 1924, with the passage of the Oriental exclusion legislation.

The Japanese exclusion act of 1924 was a triumphant culmination of the agitation that had begun during the Russo-Japanese War. Assisted by the postwar vogue of racism and fundamentalism, the exponents of Japanese exclusion could successfully argue their case. From their point of view the Washington Conference settlement had not diminished the threat of Japanese invasion of America; now that political amity had been restored between the two countries, the Japanese would redouble their effort to migrate peacefully and compete economically with Americans. In fact, the policy of peaceful competition which Japan pursued seemed even more dangerous than outright military aggression, given Japanese industrial power and technological skills. The administration in Washington had always opposed total Japanese exclusion, but this time private expressions by officials revealed a deep resentment of the exclusionists and the Congress that had gone along with them. It is illuminating that MacMurray, chief of the Far Eastern division, who had been a staunch advocate of opposition to Japanese expansionism, now bitterly denounced the Congressional action. The exclusion act, he wrote, was directed against "a friendly people who have shown themselves disposed to put aside mutual distrust and rivalry and to cooperate loyally with us in our traditional Far Eastern policies that were formulated with a new precision and adopted by the recent Washington Conference." In January 1924 he warned that the immigration bill, if enacted in entirety, would "make difficult, if not impossible, that sympathetic and wholehearted cooperation, in the area of the Pacific Ocean, which the results of the Washington Conference have brought within the range of practical realization." More than anything else, these lamentations indicate a new view of Japanese policy. From one of America's antagonists in East Asia, Japan was being pictured as a partner to maintain the peace in the Pacific and in Asia.

Such felicitations were reciprocated across the Pacific, at least by civilian officials and most intellectuals. Japanese leaders consistently spoke of the "new epoch" in international relations. Prime Minister Takahashi Korekiyo, for instance, stated that the Washington Conference had ushered in a "new stage" of international politics and opened up a "new vista" in the foreign policies of the powers. The Tokyo officials agreed with their American counterparts that the newness consisted in an assumption of international peace, political harmony, and economic interdependence. Above all, in Japan as in America there was emphasis on the economic aspect of foreign policy. Since the United States was Japan's biggest customer and largest supplier of capital, it followed that friendship would be the basic framework of relations between the two countries. Among Japanese intellectuals, too, peaceful relations with America were the point of departure. If the United States under a Republican administration did not inspire as much enthusiasm among Japanese as Wilsonism, at least peaceful relations with the United States symbolized Japan's own friendly intentions and dedication to the cause of internationalism. As in China, the Soviet revolution and Marxist thought attracted a great many intellectuals, especially college students, but unlike their

Chinese counterparts the Japanese intellectuals did not of necessity lose faith in the merits of Western civilization. Parliamentary democracy was still the most immediate goal, and there was no cynicism about international co-operation.

There, however, remained a residue of anti-American sentiment which was fortified as a result of the immigration act of 1924. For one thing, the architects of military planning continued to view the United States as the most likely enemy. Though an American war was at the moment unthinkable, both the army and the navy continued to base their strategic planning and annual estimates on the possibility of future conflict. Outside the government and the military, right-wing organizations considered America as the epitome of Western civilization standing opposed to the essence of the Japanese national polity. The anti-Japanese legislation in the United States gave these organizations a much-needed spur. They sponsored protest meetings and disseminated anti-American propaganda, and their influence grew as the feeling of indignation against America's racial prejudice spread. There was inevitably a pan-Asianist strain in these movements. The Washington Conference structure of international relations which the civilian government upheld was seen as a white-sponsored system for the perpetuation of Western domination of the world. Instead of following the whites' lead and ending up rebuffed by them, it was asserted, Japan should once and for all renounce its allegiance to the West and work for the solidarity and strengthening of the colored races. It will be seen that America had become a symbol in the Japanese mind of the postwar framework of international relations. It was natural that the Japanese view of America fluctuated in accordance with the benefits the postwar world order brought to the Japanese. On the whole the decade of the 1920's was a depression decade, and this undoubtedly helped to divide national opinion sharply between the elites, identifying their interests and outlook with amity with America, and the rest of the population, increasingly resentful of the nation's leadership and therefore of America.

China: Anti-Foreignism Among All Factions

The death of Sun Yat-sen in March 1925 brought about a crisis within the Kuomintang, now split between right and left, and to

Chinese politics, as his death had removed from the scene a national figure who might yet have avoided civil war and united the country through peaceful means. From this time on till the victory of the Nationalist armies over the northern warlords and the Nationalist unification of China in 1928, there was hardly a central government capable of speaking in the name of the people. Perhaps for this very reason, a strong current of anti-imperialism was visible in all factions and all regions. They vied with one another in denouncing foreigners and competed with each other to put an end to the unequal treaties most quickly and successfully. The result was that by the end of 1928 most of the major powers had agreed to tariff revision and expressed willingness to discuss extraterritorial matters as well. What is remarkable is that initial steps in this direction were taken not by the radical Nationalists but by the more moderate Peking government. This was the time when even a warlord was constrained to talk of equality and independence. The Nationalists' "three people's principles" (people's rights, livelihood, and nationalism) were answered by Sun Ch'uan-fang's "three principles of love" (love of the nation, the people, and the enemy), and Chang Tso-lin's "three rights" (national, human, and people's rights).

There is no evidence that the United States was excepted from China's anti-imperialism in the mid-twenties. The Chinese, it is true, well understood the expediency of having to deal with one imperialist or at most two at a time; it would be dangerous to denounce all the powers together and invite their joint intervention. Initially the British were the target, then the Japanese were added to the list. The United States was never singled out for attack. Indeed, during the initial phase of the Nationalist Northern Expedition in 1926, it is reported that the tactic was to "fight the British; be friendly to the Americans, and ignore the Japanese." Nevertheless, there was no particularly friendly disposition on the part of the Chinese toward the United States. On March 24, 1927, when a band of Nationalist soldiers ransacked foreign establishments and killed a number of foreigners in Nanking, Americans were not excepted. The molesters reportedly told an American consul, "You Americans have drunk our blood for years and become rich. We are busy now killing Fengtien [i.e. northern anti-Nationalist] soldiers but we will soon be killing all foreigners in

Nanking regardless of what country they are from." An American educator was among the casualties of the Nanking incident. Pearl Buck vividly describes how she and her family had to hide in a hut all day long to escape Nationalist wrath. "The nightmare of my life has come true. We are in danger of our lives because we are white people in a Chinese city." Thus reasoning, she felt her familiar world departing there and then. It did not seem to matter that she was an American, a true friend of the Chinese. She and other Americans were branded along with other whites for their past transgressions. Pearl Buck no doubt exaggerates the racial aspect, for the Nationalists attacked the Japanese with equal vengeance while their Russian advisers marched side by side with them and perhaps even instigated some of the anti-imperialist acts. Still, it is perfectly true that Americans could not expect to be spared Chinese animosity. They would regain Chinese friendship only if they responded positively and with specific action to the Chinese call for equality.

Sino-American relations after the Nanking incident were inevitably bound up with the internal rift within the Kuomintang, which led to the rupture of Kuomintang-Communist and of Kuomintang-Russian relations. Contrary to the subsequent accusations by anti-Nationalist writers, however, there is no substantial evidence that the right-wing Kuomintang under Chiang Kai-shek followed a pro-American policy from the very beginning. Even after his coup against the Communists and leftists in Shanghai, he declared that anti-imperialism was still his basic goal. In fact, to the extent that he thought of obtaining foreign support of his cause, Chiang seems to have turned primarily to Japan. It was only gradually, and as the Chinese feared Japanese intervention, that they once again turned to America. Thus in the fall of 1927, when the Chinese heard of a premeditated American loan to the South Manchuria Railway, they immediately protested to the United States. Kuomintang leaders told an American, "Such loans would enable Japan to increase her activities and strengthen her grip on Manchuria and . . . the United States would thus unconsciously help Japan to extend her influence in the internal affairs of China and would give evidence of a change from the past friendly American attitude toward China." The mention of "the past friendly" policy is perhaps significant. The Chinese time and again reminded Americans of the policy to put pressure on the United States. Thus President Coolidge received a telegram from the "representatives of the provincial assemblies" of Manchuria declaring, "We deem it highly unwise and decidedly unfriendly for the United States to help Japan financially infringe upon our inalienable rights and interests and that therefore in view of friendly relation [sic] between two sister republics we sincerely wish Americans stand for justice as she did in the past." The American-educated diplomat, Wellington Koo, telegraphed that the American loan "not only endangers traditional friendship of Chinese toward America but sows seeds of future trouble for which America will have to bear responsibility." Fortunately for the State Department, it did not have to answer these pleas as the loan negotiation was cut off.

The Tradition of Sino-American Friendship

It was in the spring of 1928, when the Nationalists, now purged of Communists and leftists, resumed the Northern Expedition, that they once again turned to America for support. They feared diplomatic isolation, and the United States seemed the only country capable of helping them now that Britain, Russia, and Japan had one by one alienated them. They were eager to settle the Nanking incident with America before they dealt with other governments. In May, as Nationalist troops in Shantung clashed with Japanese soldiers, sent to protect Japanese lives in the path of the Chinese forces, the Nationalist government telegraphed President Coolidge, appealing for American sympathy. The telegram reminded the president of the past efforts by the United States to settle the Shantung question and asked what policy he proposed to take, now that a grave situation had been created by the Japanese. Despite the small-scale war with the Japanese, known as the Tsinan incident, the Nationalists pushed northward and conquered Peking in June. Immediately thereafter, they approached the United States with a view to effecting treaty revision. C. C. Wu, an American-educated official and son of the famous Chinese minister in Washington earlier in the century, Wu Ting-fang, had already appeared in Washington in May as the representative of the Nationalist government. In July he formally presented a note to the State Department requesting negotiation "for a new treaty between the two countries on a footing of equality and reciprocity." Wu referred to "the traditional friendship between the United States and China" and insinuated that the new leaders of China were particularly desirous of concluding treaty revision with the United States before beginning negotiations with other countries. The Nationalists were so desirous of achieving diplomatic victory that they consented to the retention of the most-favored-nation clause in the new treaty on tariffs that was concluded at the end of the month. Thus the United States became the first "Washington power" to extend *de facto* recognition to the Nationalist government in Nanking and to grant tariff autonomy in principle to China.

In these modest achievements the Nationalists were considerably aided by the fact that American foreign policy was conducted by Secretary of State Frank B. Kellogg. Unlike his predecessor, Hughes, Kellogg was not unwilling to depart from the principle of co-operation with other countries in Chinese matters and from the provisions of the Washington Conference treaties. He pictured in his mind the "awakening of the national spirit in China" and believed the United States should take the lead in responding positively to that awakening. He was convinced that tariff and jurisdictional autonomy was "the trend of modern events in relation to all self-governing countries." By helping China regain such autonomy he felt the United States could encourage the impression that it was the friend of China, thus exempting it from much of the antiforeign feeling. He rather consistently followed this policy; even in the face of renewed civil strife in China in the spring of 1926, he vetoed the suggestion of his subordinates that the United States withdraw recognition of the Peking government. America should not be the first, Kellogg thought, to "notify China publicly that she has no Government. [Even] if we believe there is no chance of a central government strong enough to carry out its treaties, we should not take the lead and bring upon us the hostility of the Chinese people." Even if political stability were a myth, America should not declare it as such and sacrifice its potential value as a friend of China.

Kellogg, to be sure, was more than once exasperated by the continued anarchy in China. At one point, early in 1927, out of desperation he challenged the Chinese minister to tell him "who the Chinese Government was and who would negotiate" for treaty revision. The secretary stated, "it was almost impossible for him to find out what [the Chinese] wanted; that they were not united and conditions were getting worse; that he was not prepared to negotiate with Canton and Chang Tso-lin and then with some one else who might appear." Nevertheless, he held to the belief that someday soon the Chinese would organize a representative government of their own. Such optimism underlay his famous statement of January 27, 1927, in which he reiterated the willingness of the United States "to enter into negotiations with any government or delegates who can represent or speak for China" for the restoration of tariff autonomy to China. He had to wait for over a year before he satisfied himself that a government had appeared in China that met the test. In mid-July 1928, a month after the Nationalist capture of Peking, Kellogg concluded that the Nanking government was "demonstrating a capacity to establish itself in China as the accepted government." In a public statement he presented the image of "a strong China . . . in process of emerging from the chaos of civil war and turmoil." In October the secretary wrote to a friend,

> So far as the Nationalist Government is concerned, it is the first time since I have been Secretary when there seems to be a fairly united government in China. It is not pro-Communist but rather is opposed to the Communists. . . . I cannot, of course, guarantee the absolute and continued stability of the Nationalist Government but it gives more hope for such a government than has existed for many years. In my judgment, the more support which can be given to the Nationalist Government the better for all the powers interested in China. It gives a greater assurance that the Communist influence will not be dominant in China.

It is expressions such as these which have led historians, mainly of pro-Communist persuasion, to accuse the United States of collusion with the right-wing Nationalists against the more liberal elements of China. It is certainly true that after mid-1928 the United States dealt only with the Nanking government as the government of China; and it cannot be denied that American policy was anti-Communist, whether Chinese or Russian. But there is no foundation to the charge that the United States supported or, worse, instigated Chiang Kai-shek's coup in 1927 against Communists and leftists. In fact, American officials in China remained mostly in the dark about the anti-Communist plot carried out by the right-wing Nationalists in Shanghai on April 12, which marked Chiang Kai-shek's "counterrevolution." Clarence E. Gauss, the American consul general in Shanghai, reported on April 4, "Those who have been endeavoring to persuade Chiang to . . . align himself with moderates are reported to be very much discouraged." Four days later Gauss telegraphed Washington that though there was some evidence of a gradual breach between Chiang Kai-shek and the leftist Nationalist regime at Hankow, "he still refrains from taking strong action against local Communist and racial elements." Minister MacMurray reported from Peking on April 9, "Nobody viewing the situation from the standpoint of China can seriously entertain a doubt that the Russians are now the masters of the whole Nationalist movement which prevails in the South and is sweeping northward like a prairie fire." Despite various rumors circulating, American officials and residents in China were mostly unaware of the developments which led to the Shanghai coup.

Nor did the elimination of Communists immediately suggest a new line of approach to the American representatives in China. Minister MacMurray even surmised that the appearance of a fundamental split within the Kuomintang was the result of a tactical maneuver by the Russian advisers to divide responsibility for the Nanking incident, so that the foreign governments would have difficulty in enforcing their demands. In Washington, in contrast, there grew some willingness to consider Chiang Kai-shek "the leader of the Moderates." By the end of April the State Department sensed the effort "being made by the moderates to drive the radicals from the control of the Chinese Nationalist Government." Nevertheless, the failure of the allegedly moderate wing of Nationalists to assume responsibility for the settlement of the Nanking incident made American policy makers cautious. In a personal letter written in mid-May, Nelson T. Johnson, chief of the Far Eastern division, wrote that there were at least three recognizable governments in China. They were represented by "three competing and very vocal Ministers of Foreign Affairs, namely, Wellington Koo [in Peking], Eugene Chen [at Hankow], and C. C. Wu [in Nanking]." He felt that "in the end it will be a race to see which one will be the most radical in his views of foreign relations." Far from settling on the Nanking government as the object of support, the State Department in 1927 was still searching for a moderate and responsible government that might yet emerge in China.

Among non-official Americans in China, there were many who were strongly impressed with the Nationalists. Protestant missionaries in the interior of China reported how well disciplined they found Nationalist soldiers. They seemed willing to pay for their purchases and lodgings, behavior unprecedented in the annals of warlord politics. Journalists, notably John B. Powell, editor of the *China Weekly Review,* considered the Nationalists as the representatives of modern Chinese nationalism. While foreign businessmen insisted on calling the Nationalists "reds," Powell and several influential missionaries pictured them as no more "red" than the British Labour Party. There were a few Americans who worked actively for the Kuomintang. Robert S. Norman, erstwhile legal adviser to Sun Yat-sen, had stayed close to Chiang Kai-shek as the latter plotted against the radicals. Norman urged strong American support of the Nanking government after its formation in April 1927. He wrote Nelson T. Johnson, "I have the utmost faith in the ultimate success of that government. It has the support of all classes, and the very material backing of the merchants. While in regard to China's just aspirations it will pursue a very patriotic policy, the government will move, if it is allowed to do so, along moderate and sound lines." All these pro-Chiang voices, however, must be distinguished from official American policy. Johnson's reply to Norman best summed up Washington's attitude in 1927: "Why does not General Chiang establish in the eyes of the world the fact that he is the man which all of his admirers claim that he is by an outright cleaning of the Nanking [incident] without marring the situation by insisting on negotiations. Nationalist soldiers outraged innocent and unoffensive foreigners living in their homes in the City of Nanking."

Neither can it be said that America's business circles were overly impressed with Nationalist performance. Before the Nationalist unification of China in 1928, they remained skeptical about political stability in that country. It is illuminating that Thomas W. Lamout of the Morgan Company, with substantial interests and experiences in East Asia, wrote in the fall of 1927 that Manchuria was "about the only stable region in all China." In his view American resources might be spent much more profitably in co-operation with the Japanese than independently in China. American merchants and industrialists in China, too, were not at first enthusiastic about the Nationalists, right and left, and it was only after mid-1928 that some of them began to show an interest in aiding the reconstruction and rehabilitation of China. Even so, before the world economic crisis American business was predominantly Japan-oriented.

The Prospect of Japanese-American Conflict

After 1928 Sino-American relations became bound up with the critical developments in China's domestic politics and in Sino-Japanese relations. The factions and warlords still opposed to the Chiang Kai-shek group circulated the myth that the latter was subsidized by the United States. Due to Chiang's connections through marriage with the Sung family, with educational and financial ties with America, and due to the American education of some of his advisers, the Nanking government under the Kuomintang right inevitably gave the impression of relying on the United States for its existence. Nanking officials themselves eagerly cultivated American friendship in the hope of obtaining financial and technical assistance. They constantly reminded Americans of the particular ties between the two peoples, in order to induce the United States to take the lead in abolishing extraterritoriality and otherwise abrogating the existing unequal treaties. The new leaders were especially desirous of American help as Sino-Japanese relations worsened. As the Nationalists steadily extended control to north China and spread their influence in Manchuria, it was inevitable that they would eventually have to confront squarely the question of Japanese rights in these regions. The Nationalist leadership was determined ultimately to regain complete national independence, including the retrocession of foreign leases and concessions and abolition of special foreign rights. Though there was little thought of outright conflict with Japan, it was generally expected that Japan would remain adamant about these rights, especially in Manchuria, and that America's friendly attitude toward the treaty question could add tremendously to China's moral prestige. Already before 1930 Chinese writers were referring to the possibility, even the inevitability, of Japanese-American conflict in East Asia. Chiang Kai-shek himself stated in 1929 that a second world war among imperialists would come in about fifteen years; the imperialists would surely clash in China again, but if the Chinese diligently prepared themselves for the eventuality, they could take advantage of the war to free themselves completely from imperialist control. Though Chiang did not specify Japan and the United States, several of his contemporaries explicitly wrote about the inevitable Japanese-American conflict in China, as the two countries pursued different policies, and as America had been willing to support China against Japan. Consequently, many argued, the Chinese could hope that in case of Japanese aggression the United States would not stand idly by.

It is interesting to note that such an image of Japanese-American conflict was shared by the opposition groups in China. By the late 1920's the bulk of the Chinese intellectuals had been alienated from the Nanking government. They felt that the new Nationalist leadership stifled creativity by its policy of suppressing radical thought and leftist activities. Many of them were Marxists. They were among the most violently opposed to Japanese rights in Manchuria. They were also anti-American, as they were dogmatically anti-imperialist. In a book on the history of Sino-American relations, one of the Marxists, Chiang Kung-shen, wrote in 1930 that the United States was no less aggressive than other powers. The Open Door policy was never meant to uphold China's integrity and otherwise help China against the encroachment of other nations, but merely to prevent them from controlling China; the ultimate aim was to establish America's own dominant position. The so-called friendly attitude of the United States toward China was mere propaganda; it was intended to hide its aggressive designs. Traders, missionaries, and educators were all agents of American policy. This type of polemic has characterized Chinese Communist writings ever since. Even from such a point of view, however, it was not denied that the United States might collide with Japan in China. As the two most aggressive imperialists, they might collaborate from time to time to perpetuate the subjugation of the Chinese people, but they were bound to clash as each sought a monopolistic position in the China market.

The inevitability of Japanese-American conflict in East Asia was also assumed by certain groups in Japan, especially the right-wing and the military. Their anti-Americanism had been given fresh impetus after the passage of the Oriental exclusion act in 1924. In the last years of the decade the emotional sentiment of resentment against America was reinforced by a more sophisticated view of future Japanese-American conflict that was advocated by some army strategists. Most influential was Ishihara Kanji, assigned to the Kwantung Army as its staff officer in 1928. He visualized the "final world war" in the near future. The World War had been fought primarily among European nations, and it was not therefore truly a world war. The next war would be participated in by all races, and it would be a war of extermination, due to advances in military techniques and especially in aviation. Nations, not simply armies, would then engage in a mortal combat, and only through effective national mobilization and an economically self-sufficient state organization, could a nation expect to survive such conflict. Ishihara believed that this was likely to be fought principally between Japan and the United States; Japan was trying to emerge as the central force in Asia, and the United States in the West. Hence the next war would be fought between the two. This obviously was circular reasoning, but it should be noted that Japanese expansionism in China was here justified as an integral part of the course of Japanese-American relations. As Ishihara said in 1929, "We must not hesitate to declare war on China and establish control over Manchuria and Mongolia, if these steps are needed in preparation for war against the United States."

Under ordinary circumstances, such thinking might not have had much influence outside a tiny circle of military strategists. The last years of the twenties, however, were no ordinary times. China's radical foreign policy, the economic crisis of 1927 which two years later merged into the world economic crisis, and the concomitant shrinking of Japanese-American trade, all had the effect of seriously undermining the civilian leadership of Japan. Under General Tanaka as prime minister, it is true, Japan undertook expeditions to Shantung to protect nationals in the paths of the Nationalist expeditionary forces, and in May 1928 there developed a small-scale war between the two countries' troops in Tsinan, the capital of Shantung. The expeditions were hailed by many in Japan as evidence of a "positive policy" toward China. In other respects, however, the Tanaka cabinet followed the policy of sympathy with Chinese nationalism and friendship with the Western powers. The army's dissatisfaction with Tanaka had much to do with his resignation in mid-1929. His successor, Shidehara, further alienated the military and civilian malcontents by his continued profession of understanding with China and the West. He sought to develop a co-operative framework between Japan, the United States, Britain, and China as the basis for the peace, stability, prosperity in East Asia. Japan's concessions at the London Naval Conference of 1930, convened to limit the number of cruisers, destroyers, and submarines, were meant to exhibit Japan's sincere desire to remain on friendly terms with America and Britain. By this time, however, the civilian government's authority had been seriously undermined by the social and economic problems generated by the world depression. With trade with China and America falling, there was nothing tangible that the Tokyo government could show its people as evidence of the soundness of its policy. To the dissatisfied, the civilian bureaucrats represented wealth, education, and Western orientation. Under the circumstances, attack on the government's foreign policy could lead to a wholesale denunciation of the Japanese establishment and its pro-Western outlook.

It will be noted that on the eve of the Manchurian incident of 1931, concern with China's radical diplomacy was only one of the main currents of Japanese thinking. Equally significant, and essentially bound up with it, was the fatalistic view of Japanese-American relations. To the military, America represented the inevitable antagonist. To the right wing, America's racial prejudice was driving Japan to seek its destiny in Asia. Above all, to the economically and socially deprived, America symbolized the existing order, both domestically and externally. The Japanese leadership had educational and business ties with the United States, and it seemed to have unwarranted faith in America. It was no less than a revolt against the established order that the military and the discontented sought. China alone was not an end in itself. Underneath all there was an apocalyptic vision of future struggle with America.

America's response to the mounting tension between China and Japan was such as to belie the expectations of the Chinese and Japanese prophets. On the one hand, there was interest in assisting

National China in its programs for national rehabilitation and reconstruction. American advisers were in a majority among foreign advisers to the Nanking government. A mission headed by the economist Edwin W. Kemmerer was sent to China in 1929 and did invaluable service in recommending fiscal reforms. The myth of the China market revived, although this did not alter the quantitative superiority of the Japanese market. American funds were particularly attracted to such relatively new fields as public utilities and aviation. Among officials, too, there was sympathy with China's determination to abolish extraterritoriality. Though no outright surrender of the judicial privileges was foreseen, the U.S. government was notably more willing than other governments to proceed along liberal lines.

Assistance to China, however, did not seem to be incompatible with continued amity with Japan. Apart from the navy, whose strategic planning was still postulated on the likelihood of an "Orange war," there was unwillingness to believe in Japan's sinister designs on China. There were, in retrospect, some far-sighted people. Consul General Myrl Myers at Mukden, for instance, early suspected Japan's aggressive designs on Manchuria. In the spring of 1928, as the Tsinan incident broke out, the Nationalists captured Peking, forcing the withdrawal of the warlord Chang Tso-lin, and as Kwantung Army officers caused the death of Chang by bombing his train proceeding northward, Myers definitely concluded that Japan was intent on creating an autonomous state in Manchuria under Japanese influence. The Japanese were "extremely anxious to force provocations," he reported. At this time, however, the warning did not sound convincing. Edwin Neville, chargé in Tokyo, stood by the country to which he had been accredited. He did not believe anything was contemplated in Manchuria "beyond assuring the safety of the South Manchurian Railway and its allied activities." Decrying the alarmist views such as Myers', Neville wrote privately, "I don't see anything in the situation out here to get het up about. . . . [There] are a lot of persons who get het up over our leadership and prestige and our duty to humanity. I don't think there is anything in any of it." The State Department on the whole sided with the more complacent position. Despite some misgivings over Japanese action, officials in Washington remained convinced that there should and could be no real conflict between Japan and the United States. As Nelson T. Johnson wrote, "All of the evidence seems to point to the friendliest of feelings between us and the Japanese which should continue more or less indefinitely. I find it difficult to see where Japanese and American interests can come into conflict in the Far East to such an extent as to make for hostilities."

The idea that the United States could maintain friendly relations with Japan, while helping the Chinese with their task of rehabilitation and nationalistic foreign policy, seemed even more plausible after 1929, when Shidehara returned to the helm. Thus on one hand one finds Secretary of State Stimson talking glowingly of America's "help and advice" to China; on the other hand, he was tremendously impressed with Japan's conciliatory attitude during the London Naval Conference. There seemed to be no reason why there could not be perfect amity among the three peoples. It is symbolic that on September 17, 1931, the day before the outbreak of the Manchurian incident, Stimson told the Japanese ambassador that there was no important pending question between the two countries. The secretary was leaving on the 19th for a conference with President Hoover on the Rapidan on the European debt question, and the Japanese ambassador was to take a vacation at the end of the month and would be gone for a few months. Nothing urgent seemed to be in the offing.

There were some officials who expected a Sino-Japanese clash. Throughout the spring of 1931 American consuls in China noted that the situation of the days of the Twenty-One Demands was reviving and Chinese leaders were showing only hatred and disgust toward the Japanese. Americans also saw a developing rift between civilian and military circles in Japan and felt a crisis might be precipitated by the latter despite the good intentions of the former. On September 10 a member of the National government handed a memorandum to the American minister citing evidence to show that the Japanese military had resorted to "repeated provocations in Manchuria in order to provide excuses for the use of force, as well as an intensive propaganda campaign designed to blind the eyes of the world to the facts of the situation." But Minister Johnson did not feel that a Sino-Japanese war was imminent. As he wrote to Ambassador W. Cameron Forbes in Tokyo, "There is plenty of powder lying around but I think that it is hardly dry enough yet to explode." When Johnson was told, on September 11, that Japan might occupy Manchuria within the next three months, he replied, "It seemed fantastic that at this time the Japanese would act in this way, particularly as they were able to exploit Manchuria while all of the expenses of administration and government would remain on Chinese shoulders." Ambassador Forbes shared the optimism. He spent most of his time in Japan traveling, as "there wasn't such an awful lot to do" in the summer of 1931. His greatest preoccupation in September was with the visit of Charles Lindbergh to Japan.

In retrospect all these remarks sound hollow. What is of fundamental importance, however, is not so much that American officials failed to predict the Japanese invasion of Manchuria as that they had much less time after 1929 to devote to the study of East Asian matters. The world depression took up much time and energy of the keenest minds in the administration. In 1931 Secretary Stimson was absent from Washington during the crucial months of June, July, and August visiting London, Berlin, Paris, and Rome to talk with European officials about the debt question. East Asian matters were relegated to a position of relative insignificance. If they were given some recognition, it was in connection with the country's over-all economic policy. The silver interests in the Senate, for instance, proposed the sale of silver to China to counteract the depressing price of the metal in the world market. The Commerce Department considered selling to the Chinese government large quantities of wheat, cotton, and other farm products on long-term credits. The London Naval Conference, too, was partially motivated by President Hoover's fiscal retrenchment policy. Under the circumstances there was no possibility of evolving a systematic policy toward East Asia at a time when Chinese nationalism and Japanese policy were fast moving toward a showdown. American–East Asian relations were back to where they were at the turn of the century. These relations were basically defined as economic, and the awareness of East Asian matters in America had become dimmed.

III
Sino-American Co-operation Against Japan

7
America's Failure to Assist China

On the morning of September 19, 1931, Ambassador W. Cameron Forbes in Tokyo was about to leave his house for Yokohama, there to sail for the United States on a vacation, when he was apprised of a clash between Chinese and Japanese soldiers in Manchuria. He telephoned Edwin W. Neville, counselor of the embassy, and asked if he should cancel the sailing. Neville replied, "It couldn't be as bad as that" but went to the Foreign Ministry to get the official facts. After being assured that "there would be no war nor did the Japanese want a war," Forbes decided to proceed with his scheduled sailing, since to do otherwise would "make it felt by the public that we regarded the situation as very dangerous." Thousands of miles away, in Washington, Secretary of State Stimson was leaving for a conference with the president on the Rapidan when the news came from Manchuria. Stimson's first thought was that it must have been a military mutiny.

"Can it be possible that the Americans and the English do not understand what it means that Japan has taken Manchuria?" Pearl Buck was asked in China. "There will be a second World War," the Chinese said. For many Chinese, officials, Communists, and intellectuals, direct action by the Japanese military had been foreseen, and they were quick to view it as a prelude to a much larger war. And most of them saw in the Manchurian incident the beginning of the Japanese-American conflict that they had long expected. As they looked back on the history of Chinese-Japanese-American relations, they thought they clearly saw a pattern through the decades. As one writer noted, after 1899 there had always been possibilities of conflict between Japan and the United States, since the former sought to establish a dominant position in China and the latter stood for the principle of the Open Door. The Open Door doctrine, another asserted, had stopped the trend toward the partitioning of China. China's territorial integrity had been dependent on the American policy; hence the inevitability of a clash between the United States and Japan. A third author hopefully wrote that the Open Door principle might change its nature from one of merely maintaining equal opportunity to one of positively upholding the peace in East Asia. All these writers, whose views seem to have been shared by most Chinese officials, were obviously indulging in wishful thinking. They saw in the past what they wanted to see, something that would assure them of American help. Few of them, however, were optimistic enough to believe that the United States singlehandedly would wage war against Japan just to help China maintain its integrity. It was generally believed that American intervention would depend on international circumstances; if the United States could be sure of obtaining the backing of other major powers, a possibility which did not seem promising in 1931–1932, it was hoped that America would undertake something positive to stem the tide of Japanese aggression. Regardless of the actual state of Japanese-American relations, however, there was little doubt that the latent contradiction between the interests and policies of the two would ultimately affect the course of events in China.

The Triumph of Military Thinking in Japan

The Manchurian crisis was brought about by a handful of Kwantung Army extremists to establish firm control over a large part of Manchuria. The Mukden incident of September 18, 1931, which ushered in the crisis, had been carefully plotted months in advance by a few staff officers in Manchuria, in conjunction with their sympathizers in the Tokyo supreme command. Their idea was to respond forcefully to the challenge of Chinese nationalism and incorporate much of Manchuria as an integral part of Japan's defense structure, so that the nation would better be prepared for future warfare. They were willing and even determined to ignore the civilian government in this task, as they thought Tokyo officials were too timid and tied to the existing order at home and abroad to sanction such drastic action. Once the critical point was passed on the night of September 18, the Kwantung Army, in co-operation with the army stationed in Korea, extended its sphere of operation and spread its action beyond the treaty-stipulated zones along the South Manchurian and other railways. In time the Tokyo supreme command realized the need to restrain Kwantung Army extremism, lest the latter should establish itself as an autonomous colonial army and defy Tokyo's authority. But the staff officers in Manchuria always took the initiative; while they did not wish openly to rebel against the supreme command and the civilian government, ultimately it was the latter that ended up sanctioning the acts committed by the field army. One such act was the penetration of north Manchuria, confronting Soviet power. Another was the creation of Manchukuo, an autonomous state under Japanese military control.

Viewed purely as a military episode, therefore, the Manchurian crisis can be characterized as the revolt of part of the military against established authority. In the light of subsequent events, it is natural that historians should have since regarded the Manchurian incident as the opening shot of Japanese militarism, a militarism which would not be silenced until 1945. However, viewed as an ideological phenomenon, the crisis was much more than the machination of a few army insurgents. It marked the return of security considerations as the basic framework of national policy, and it also signaled the emergence of pan-Asianism as an official ideology. These two phenomena are interrelated and of crucial importance. On the one hand, the Japanese acts in Manchuria and later in China were justified in terms of national survival. Japan must subordinate all other considerations, it was argued, to the basic task of safeguarding national security. "Security" was very broadly defined so as to mean Japan's control over Manchuria, Inner Mongolia, and eventually most of China. The nation, it was held, must compensate for its small size by incorporating these areas into its defense system. Only then could Japan hope to guarantee its survival in a world apparently dominated by large powers. Considerations of peace, amity, and respect for treaties were secondary. In this sense Japanese policy was defined anew militarily; the whole history of Japanese expansion in the 1930's may be characterized as a revolt against ideology and a triumph of military thinking devoid of idealism. At the same time, the new concept of national security was from the beginning bound up with and was eventually even dominated by pan-Asianist thinking. At first this took the form of justifying the violations of existing international agreements. Instead of honoring the fiction of international co-operation while seeking to maintain rights in China, and instead of talking about Japan as a respectable member of the Western community of nations while it had peculiar ties to Asia, Japan was now to act boldly and independently in defense of its essential prerequisites for survival. The withdrawal from the League of Nations in 1933 was a symbolic act of defiance of the Western precepts of international relations. Eventually, in the late 1930's, pan-Asianism would even come to take precedence over more mundane and realistic calculations of national security.

Interestingly enough, the Japanese exponents of new expansionism did not initially envisage direct conflict with the United States. This was because of the view that in purely political terms the two powers were not incompatible. The Japanese, to be sure, were constantly reminded of American opposition to their scheme—by Secretary Stimson's enunciation of the "non-recognition doctrine," by the ominous concentration of the United States fleet on the west coast in 1932 and 1933, and by America's stiff attitude during the Shanghai incident of early 1932, when Japanese expeditionary forces clashed with Chinese troops. America's opposition was to have been expected. Kwantung Army officers had believed that they were adding Manchuria to Japan's imperial domain in order to prepare for future warfare, very likely between Japan and the United States. It was natural, then, that they should have disregarded Stimson's repeated warnings against extending hostilities. There is no evidence that they paid much heed to his voice. At the same time, after 1931 the Japanese army's attention was turned once again to the Soviet Union as the imaginary enemy. The navy, it is true, held to the notion of the United States as the most likely enemy. The Washington and the London naval treaties were considered inimical to Japanese security, as they established an inferior naval ratio for Japan vis-à-vis the United States. It became the Japanese naval strategists' main concern to establish parity with American fleet strength and to prepare for southern expansion to control key areas in south China and southeast Asia. Before the late thirties, however, there was little thought of war with the United States in the near future. This was partially because of the Soviet build-up in the Manchurian-Siberian border, which forced reorientation in Japanese strategy. More fundamentally, there was emerging a new image of America, as a country that delighted in moralism and condemned Japanese action but that was not likely to challenge Japan with force. So long as America tacitly acquiesced in the *faits accomplis* in East Asia, there was no need to worry about possible conflict with the United States.

Such an image of America was shared by the civilian government. Initially, the Tokyo government decided on non-extension of hostilities in Manchuria. A major factor in this decision was concern with Western reaction. For Foreign Minister Shidehara, the Kwantung Army's action was a serious blow to his effort to base Japan's East Asian policy on the foundation of co-operation with the United States and Great Britain. His sensitivity to American reaction was communicated to and to some extent shared by the army supreme command, but it was ineffective vis-à-vis the Kwantung Army. After December 1931, when Shidehara went out of office along with his cabinet, there no longer was genuine interest in maintaining the façade of understanding with America. At the same time, it did not seem that the two countries were fated to clash. America was less than a sympathetic bystander, and more often than not it seemed to delight in increasing its nuisance value, but fundamentally it appeared that the United States would grudgingly acquiesce in the new situation in East Asia so long as Japan did not compromise American security or directly challenge American interests in Asia. The foreign policy of Hirota Kōki, who either as foreign minister or as prime minister played the most important civilian role between 1933 and 1938, was in line with such a view.

It is a measure of changed circumstances that in the 1930's he was known as an advocate of "co-operative" foreign policy. He spoke of "co-operation and harmony among all the nations." He talked of the need to improve relations with China and with America. But his brand of international co-operation was based on the recognition of Japanese hegemony over Manchuria and, in the mid-1930's, north China. Whereas Shidehara had sought to seek understanding with the United States as a prerequisite for Japanese policy in Asia, Hirota would first establish the fact of Japanese control over China and then seek American understanding on that basis. This was based on the assumption that the two nations were not really incompatible in Asia; as long as they refrained from infringing upon their mutual preserves, there was no reason why they could not be totally friendly. This was the new realism the Japanese boasted in the 1930's. Thus on one hand Hirota stated in 1934 that Japan's position in China was so different from that of other countries that "Japan must do everything it can to accomplish its mission in East Asia, regardless of whether other powers will recognize it or not." It was Japan's responsibility to maintain peace and order in Asia. Accordingly, Japan should be prepared to "destroy" other countries' programs of military, political, and economic assistance to China. These ideas were incorporated into the famous "Amau doctrine" and had the effect of discouraging American financial assistance to China. On the other hand, Hirota tried to obtain America's explicit recognition of Japanese predominance in East Asia by proposing a new agreement between the two countries which would more or less divide up the Pacific into the American and Japanese spheres of influence. For once he met with a rebuff. The State Department was not interested.

The reluctance to believe in Japanese-American conflict in Asia was not confined to the government and the military. Professional writings in Japan as well as more popular accounts on Japanese-American relations exhibited a tendency to discount talk of war. There were, to be sure, sensationalist books and articles depicting the two nations' road to war, but these were mostly prompted by the presence of the United States fleet in the Pacific, not by America's China policy as such. As far as the policies of Japan and the United States were concerned, it was generally believed that they were different but not fatally incompatible. Unlike the Chinese, Japanese writers were reluctant to subscribe to the simplistic formula of Japanese-American conflict over China because of America's adherence to the Open Door policy. As Ashida Hitoshi wrote in 1934, United States policy was periodically swayed by sentimentalism and idealism, and because of the Americans' sympathy with the underdog, they had often stood with China against Japan. But since, as the Japanese saw it, morality in international affairs was a relative matter, the United States was not necessarily in the right just because Americans believed so. Japanese historians and specialists on international law were all exasperated by what they considered to be the legal ambiguities and imprecision inherent in United States policy in East Asia. At any rate, since American and Japanese policies were derived from different sources, the latter from the nation's security and economic needs, and the former from moral considerations, these two could not be equated. They could even be perfectly compatible, for unlike the Chinese, the Japanese did not see that for economic or security reasons the United States and Japan were fated to clash over China. Because of the very moralism of American policy, conflict with that country seemed extremely unlikely.

The celebrated "Fundamentals of National Policy," adopted by the premier and the foreign, finance, war, and navy ministers in August 1936, revealed the same complacent view of the United States. It was stated that Japan should co-operate closely with Manchukuo and China, prepare against American and British interference, and defend Manchuria against the Russian menace. Mindful of the fact that the naval disarmament was to expire that year, the five ministers decided that Japan's naval strength should be augmented to the extent necessary for control of the western Pacific. In the "principles of Japanese diplomacy" which accompanied this decision, it was stated that Japan's immediate objective should be the removal of the Soviet threat to the empire. Consequently, Japan was to adopt an attitude of caution toward the United States, in view of the latter's ability to obstruct Japanese policies toward Russia and China. "Japan should respect America's trade interests in China so that the United States may understand our fair policy, promote good relations between the two countries on the basis of Japanese-American economic compatibility, and try to prevent America's interference with Japanese policy in Eastern Asia," the document concluded.

Morality in International Relations

Across the Pacific, the Manchurian crisis lent itself to much generalizing which on the whole tended to confirm the Japanese image of American policy. Much has been written about America's blunder in 1931, whether in failing decisively to check Japanese aggression or in unnecessarily and meaninglessly irritating Japan. From either point of view, American policy in the Manchurian crisis has seemed a crucial factor in the subsequent history of East Asia. It has seemed, for example, that the failure to stop an act of aggression at its inception encouraged further aggressive acts by the aggressor. Had the United States and others resolutely opposed Japanese military conquest, it is argued, the peace structure of the world, patiently built up after World War I, might yet have been saved.

There is no question that the United States could have acted differently in Asia during the first half of the 1930's. It might have opposed Japan by resorting to an economic boycott or giving aid to China. It might have demonstrated its disapproval of Japanese action by fortifying bases in the Pacific or reinforcing the fleet in East Asian waters. On the other hand, it might have done nothing; it might have passively watched the course of events in Asia without passing moral judgments on them. What was in fact done was to condemn Japanese acts as immoral and a threat to peace but not to resort to specific measures to counter Japanese aggression. To have taken the more positive alternative would have meant challenging Japanese hegemony in East Asia and implanting American influence there; while the passive alternative would have entailed withdrawing American prestige and power from that part of the world. It is obvious that at bottom was the question of America's position in Asia. Should America concern itself with the course of events in East Asia? Should Asian matters be left to Asians, or should the major powers, which meant Western nations, intervene to save Asia for their influence?

Secretary Stimson's response was derived from his perception of Asia as no different from other parts of the world, where the rules of moral conduct equally applied. Asia should not be exempted from these rules; aggression was aggression whether it occurred in Asia or elsewhere. It must be stopped lest it should endanger the fabric of world peace and security that had been woven after the Versailles Peace Conference. Stimson's recourse to the League of Nations is illuminating. It was the world's responsibility to do something about the East Asian crisis. His sense of chagrin grew as he was time and again disappointed by the Japanese leaders' inability to check Kwantung Army advances. He had assumed that Japan's civilian leaders had accepted the norm of moral international behavior, but in fact it seemed that they condoned aggressive action in Manchuria. Japan was making itself a lawbreaker and must be treated as such. If Japan persisted in wrongdoing, the United States and other countries should be willing to consider, as far as practicable, resorting to some drastic measures such as economic and even military sanctions. It was not necessarily that Japanese acts in Manchuria immediately posed a threat to American security and economic interests. It was rather that these acts were immoral and a breach of the confidence the world had placed in Japan. If no other nation went along with America's opposition to Japan, America should be ready to stand up alone and be counted.

In retrospect, Stimson's thinking appears as a precursor of moral globalism; he saw little distinction between Asia and Europe as theaters of international conflict. His policy of non-recognition implied that he would not recognize any Japanese rules that were not universally applicable. Just because Japan was an Asian nation, it did not follow that it had the right to enunciate new principles and policies and disregard the existing precepts, however Western oriented these might be. It is noteworthy that throughout the Manchurian episode Stimson phrased his policy primarily in the form of rebuking Japan, not of helping China. China happened to be the victim of Japanese invasion, but Stimson's main concern was with restoring the peace, and in his view the most fundamental necessity was to bring Japan back to its senses. Assistance to China for its own sake was not the issue. Once aggression was checked, he assumed that things would return to normal.

It was this ambivalent attitude toward China that came more and more to characterize America's official attitude toward East Asia as the decade of the 1930's wore on. It may be said that the "non-recognition" policy came to mean not only refusal to recognize the fruits of Japanese aggression but also reluctance and unwillingness to render positive assistance to China. In fact, even under Stimson there were those who were unhappy about his approach. They felt that East Asia was essentially beyond America's zone of vital interests. With a few exceptions the officials of the State Department and their representatives abroad shared Stimson's moral concern with the course of events in Asia but objected to his moralistic approach to foreign policy. So long as America's security and vital economic interests remained unaffected, as appeared to be the case, they saw no reason why the United States should assume the responsibility of publicly castigating Japan and run the risk of war. War with Japan on the question of Manchuria was unthinkable. Unlike Stimson, these officials felt the Manchurian incident was an isolated Sino-Japanese affair and not likely to involve the United States unless it chose to be involved. Under the circumstances, it was best to leave Asians to settle their affairs among themselves. It was premature, in their view, to identify America's interests with China's cause. President Herbert Hoover was definitely more inclined to these views than those of his secretary of state. He would be ready to censure Japan but not to alienate the country so as to provoke it.

The mixture of moral globalism and fear of military involvement in Asia also characterized American press opinion. On the whole it endorsed Stimson's non-recognition doctrine as a novel approach to peace, but this approval seems to have been based on the assumption that there would be no open conflict with Japan because of Stimsonian policy. One could apply to East Asia the principles of peace and justice, provided that this would not involve the United States in war. According to the February 13, 1932 editorial of the Washington *Evening Star,* "For the United States to go to war with Japan to prevent the seizure of China or to compel its release if seizure were already effected, would be a monstrous injustice to the American people, a sacrifice of American lives and treasure, for which there would be no justification." Chastising Japan for its misconduct was psychologically an easy performance, but helping China was something different. Concern with China's plight was thus not the basic motivating factor in the general endorsement of the non-recognition policy.

"We have expected the Japanese to react as we should react," wrote William R. Castle, formerly under secretary of state, in 1933, "and when they have not done so we have been disappointed." The "disappointment" had become a generally felt sentiment of Americans toward Japan when Franklin D. Roosevelt assumed office. The Japanese had not responded as expected; they had openly defied the existing principles of international conduct. The question, of course, was what could now be done about it. On the whole it is fair to say that most Americans, officials and non-officials, had made up their minds not to do much about it. It was not worth trying harder to force the Japanese to behave if this involved further expenditures in the form of armament or assistance to China, and if there was a grave chance of conflict with Japan. Obviously the Japanese had not been deterred by considerations of Western reaction. In the words of Castle, "The Japanese accept the postwar treaties as expressions of wholly admirable opinion, but not as obliging them to forgo actions for the good of the state." It did not seem worth war to force Japan to conform to the Western principles of good behavior. At the same time, there was no need to regard Japanese conduct as acceptable. It must still be censured, but otherwise it was best just to consider East Asia as lying beyond the realm of America's real concern.

Numerous official memoranda written at this time on the East Asian question were rationalizations for the basic lack of policy and of interest in East Asia. Moral globalism and political parochialism could only be reconciled by tortured argument, and the officials were engaged in countless experiments in such argument after 1933. First of all, there was the view that America's basic interests in Asia were economic, which did not seem to be threatened by Japanese acts in Manchuria and China. Writing in June 1933, Minister Nelson T. Johnson asserted that these Japanese acts did not concern the United States directly. "It probably does not mean the loss of a dollar from an American purse," he wrote. "On the contrary, the development of [Manchuria] under Japanese enterprise may mean an increased opportunity for American industrial plants to sell the kind of machinery and other manufactured goods that will be needed where so much energy is being displayed." Here Johnson was going back to the pre-Taft tradition of America's East Asia policy, giving primacy to economic interests. Such a view had many advocates, including Ambassador Joseph C. Grew in

Japan. From this point of view Japanese aggression, no matter how repugnant morally, was no great cause for alarm so long as it did not interfere with American business activities. This in effect was economic globalism. Economic considerations should have priority over moral considerations, especially since American security itself was never considered to be in doubt. The only problem would arise when Japan was found not to subscribe to the same principles of economic relations.

A second rationalization for the policy of passivity was to argue that the United States should not provoke Japan unnecessarily before military preparedness was sufficiently advanced. Japanese behavior might be immoral, but the United States should not lightly take steps to counter it unless it was ready and strong enough to fight. In fact, President Roosevelt's initial naval construction programs were linked to the domestic economic recovery plan and not primarily thought out as part of preparedness against Japan. The expert naval view in the mid-thirties was that Japanese predominance in the western Pacific could not be easily broken unless more ships were built and bases fortified. There persisted uncertainty as to whether the Philippines, promised independence as of 1946, were to be defended in case of war with Japan. For all these reasons, it seemed crucial to avoid trouble with Japan under the existing relative strengths. American security in the western Pacific seemed to depend on maintaining a degree of normal relations with Japan and on avoiding unnecessary friction with that country. This reasoning on the basis of relative strengths, however, was essentially tautological. The United States could not challenge Japanese action because of military unpreparedness; but the nation was unprepared because of lack of serious interest in the East Asian crisis. There was little sense of involvement in East Asian affairs because America's security was not at stake and because America's influence was not so great as to enable it to alter significantly the course of events there.

Another argument was that no matter how outrageous Japan might be, China was not much better. The victim of Japanese invasion was pictured as weak and divided, not deserving of American assistance. Edwin Neville expressed such a sentiment, which was shared widely among representatives abroad, when he wrote in December 1935, "I cannot see where any interest of the United

States . . . would be served by laying ourselves open to a rebuff by protesting on behalf of a people who apparently are incapable of political action and unwilling to make any sort of common cause against what they complain of as aggression." Neville obviously had in mind the continued struggle for power within China, between the Nanking government under Chiang Kai-shek and dissident elements, in particular the Chinese Communists. The history of republican China seemed to indicate an utter inability on the part of the Chinese to evolve a stable and centralized government instead of engaging in apparently endless factional struggles. While they were always extremely radical with respect to external issues, they had failed to put their own house in order. They had been unable to unite and repel the Japanese attack resolutely. For the United States to help such a people would necessitate an almost superhuman effort on the part both of Americans and Chinese. Ironically, such a view of China was becoming more and more unrealistic. At the very time when American officials rationalized their inaction by picturing to themselves the image of a weak and divided China, the Chinese were steadily stirring themselves up to bridge the gap between their nationalism and political instability. Moves were under way to rehabilitate the economy and reunite the country on the basis of a broad "united front" against Japan. The Sian incident of December 1936, involving the temporary capture of Chiang Kai-shek by Chang Hsüeh-liang under Communist instigation in order to force him to establish a united front, was a climax in this trend and an unmistakable sign of national determination. American officials, however, saw in the episode what they wanted to see in order to reassure themselves of the correctness of their estimate of the Chinese situation. They failed to connect the Sian incident with China's determined effort to resist Japan; instead, they tended to see in it another episode in the ever-shifting drama of warlord politics. It was considered to be merely a scheme designed to enhance Chang Hsüeh-liang's political and economic influence.

Such a complacent view was reflected in the general ignorance about the Chinese Communists. According to Dr. Borg's study of American official documents on the subject, American officials in China were not unaware of the existence of a persistent Communist movement to challenge the authority of the Nanking regime. In fact, the Nationalist-Communist antagonism was part of the American image of a divided China. However, most reports on the Communists were limited to their military moves, in particular during the "Long March" of 1934 to 1936. Their moves were reported just as the military maneuvers of other warlords and factions had been reported. There was little interest in Communist ideology. Partly this was a reaction against the official Japanese view, which stressed the threat of international Communism. The Japanese, it seemed, harped on the theme in order to justify their aggression. No wonder, then, that American officials in China should have felt that the alleged danger of Communism was by and large a Japanese fabrication. At most the Communists were a minority of bandits, not very different from those that had periodically appeared in Chinese history to challenge the established authority. This view of Chinese Communism helped to discount the reality of mounting nationalism in China and the trend toward a united front. Communists, in other words, served both as a symbol of China's instability and lack of nationwide determination to unite against Japan.

American public opinion on the whole seems to have been in accord with the official attitude toward the East Asian crisis. There is no question that the majority of the American people were sympathetic with the Chinese and critical of Japan. By coincidence, Pearl Buck's *The Good Earth* was published in 1931, and within a few years it is believed to have sold two million copies, disseminating an image of the Chinese as earthy, hard-working, and persevering under adversities. There was nothing comparable with respect to the Japanese. This itself is interesting. Somehow Japanese life did not seem to lend itself to a descriptive and sympathetic novel. There already was a climate of intellectual opinion in America which was receptive to the information transmitted by a novel like *The Good Earth*. This psychological environment never disappeared, but after the failure of Stimson's crusade there was a noticeable decline in public concern with the East Asian crisis. Once America's moralistic initiative was found unworkable, the public refused to take a next step and consider constructive alternatives. As Tyler Dennett pointed out as early as July 1933, "Americans are a funny folk. They applaud lofty moral sentiment but they are rarely ready, outside the Western Hemisphere, to take the next step, to make effective the sentiment which they applaud." Dennett himself, in fact, was converting himself to diplomatic parochialism. His monumental *Americans in Eastern Asia,* published at the time of the Washington Conference, had paid a glowing tribute to John Hay and his Open Door policy as an example of a "co-operative" approach to East Asian problems. East Asia was an arena where the United States, in co-operation with other nations, could contribute to the peace and welfare of its inhabitants. Writing a biography of Hay in 1933, however, Dennett reversed himself, saying the Open Door policy had never been meant as something that had to be imposed by force. Dennett now talked about Hay's "brazen opportunism" as a realistic approach to East Asia, "a region where American interests were actually very small." This was a rationalization of the policy of passivity, and the fact that many equally eminent historians and jurists of the time wrote numerous articles on the subject reveals their self-consciousness in attempting rationalization. Asia was beyond the zone of immediate American national interest because American interest there was small. It was such circular reasoning which led writers to examine just what were these interests. Quite naturally they concluded that basically America's stake in Asia was economic. It was not America's responsibility, therefore, to intervene in the Sino-Japanese conflict.

Press opinion, too, mirrored this type of reasoning and revealed unconcern with the future of Asia. The East Asian crisis, editorialized the Hearst publications in 1934, "is not OUR business. It interests us. We SYMPATHIZE. But it is NOT OUR CONCERN." Starting from this conclusion, newspaper and magazine editors sought to rationalize it. As with the officials, there was created an image of China as a disorganized nation that was incapable of helping itself, and that of Japan as a sensitive nation which might be provoked by hostile American action. The general unconcern with Asian affairs was part of the isolationist psychology of the 1930's as well as of the social values of the time, which gave primacy to economic factors. Business journals quite naturally abounded in references to trade as a way to peace and understanding among nations, and the promotion of America's economic interests in East Asia, which generally meant Japan, seemed the most plausible alternative available to the United States. Economic universalism coupled with political isolationism was shared by newspapers and journals. Considering the sanguine interest in political affairs of Asia in the 1910's, however, the whole parochial outlook in the 1930's is nevertheless striking. It was as though Asia ceased to exist in American consciousness except as a market—a very traditional view of that part of the world. This perhaps indicates that the isolationism of the 1930's, at least with regard to Asia, was quite in line with historical American relations with China and Japan.

There were, however, a few who raised serious questions about the future of American–East Asian relations. Granted that the role of the United States in the East Asian crisis was and had to be limited, there still remained the question of what shape the future of Asia should and would take. America itself might not be able to influence it to any great extent, but at least it was worth raising this question. Would American interests be best served by a strong Japan dominating the whole of East Asia, or by an Asia made up of equal, independent states, or by somehow freezing the status quo? Should stability in Asia, obviously a prerequisite for economic activities as well as for peaceful relations among peoples, be dependent on the continued existence of Western colonial empires, on a balance of power maintained among them or between some of these on one hand and Japan on the other, or on Japanese or Chinese hegemony? Basically, how was Asia to be related to the rest of the world? These are questions that are asked even today, and it is perhaps a great credit to a handful of Americans that they raised some of these issues in the 1930's. Once again William Castle must be mentioned. He wrote in 1933, "Nothing else would so advance American interests in the Orient as the real peace and progress which would result from a close friendship and understanding between Japan and China." This general proposition contained a profound truth as Castle saw it; stability in Asia was dependent on Sino-Japanese co-operation. Without it no external pressure would be sufficient to safeguard American interests. It is evident that Castle envisaged Sino-Japanese co-operation under Japanese terms, in view of Japan's superior power position. A similar opinion was expressed by John MacMurray, several years retired from active service, in a memorandum written in 1935. In this famous paper the idea was expressed that Japanese power in East Asia was a fact that must be accepted. To challenge it would serve no useful purposes; the defeat of Japan at America's hands might simply open the way for Soviet domination of Asia, or make America "not the most favored, but the most distrusted of nations" because of such impetuous action. Peace and stability in Asia could be built on the fact of Japanese hegemony, which the United States could at least have recognized. Indeed, MacMurray believed that Japanese hegemony would have been less unpleasant for the United States to face if the latter had realistically sought to work together with Japan in the 1920's so as to restrain Japan's naked aggressiveness. As matters stood in the mid-thirties, MacMurray believed that a semblance of order in Asia had to be imposed by some power, and Japan might as well be that power. Theoretically, these arguments could have been countered by another, asserting that China, rather than Japan, should be the stabilizer in East Asia, or that only when China regained its sovereignty could there be real peace in Asia. Before 1937, however, such views had not been advanced by any influential official.

Finally, President Roosevelt did not depart from the general official thinking about the East Asian crisis. His sympathies were unmistakably with China, not only because of his familial ties to the Orient through the China trade, but also because he self-consciously inherited the Wilsonian moralistic foreign policy with regard to Asia. He felt that the United States could not remain unconcerned with developments outside the Western Hemisphere, and he was often willing to use strong language to show his displeasure with Japanese action. In January 1936, for instance, the president spoke of the "dictators" in the world, meaning Germany, Italy, and Japan, who were engaged in aggression, which might ultimately lead to another world war. He was strongly opposed to the neutrality legislation being promoted by an isolationist public and Congress. He remained an advocate of a discretionary arms embargo, which would give the president authority to forbid the export of arms to a belligerent. A mandatory embargo, which the isolationists advocated, would deprive the United States of freedom of action in case it wanted to sanction an aggressor. Nevertheless, during his first term President Roosevelt left East Asian affairs largely to the State Department. Despite his awareness of the Japanese threat in Asia, he did not feel the problem was serious enough to warrant much executive leadership and education of the public. There were other more pressing matters. It is noticeable that while the president shared the anxiety that there might be war between Japan and America in the future, he responded to this fear by a naval construction program in the Pacific rather than by massive aid to China.

Chinese Hopes for American Aid

The Chinese view of America was optimistic. Much, of course, depended on the factional struggle within China, and it would be wrong to regard the views of all the factions as uniform. The Chinese Communists echoed the voice of Moscow, and at least with regard to external affairs there was no distinctly "Maoist" theory at this time. They viewed the Manchurian incident as a prelude to the final struggle between Japanese and American imperialism in East Asia, and for this reason expected American opposition to Japanese action. At the same time, the Communists feared that Chiang Kai-shek might come to some compromise with the Japanese, and sought to take advantage of the crisis in Manchuria in order to spread their own influence. As the Nanking government nevertheless pushed its anti-Communist campaign and forced the Communists to move out of their base in Kiangsi province, they in time came to call for a united front against the Japanese imperialists. This again reflected the Soviet strategy; after 1935 the Comintern began calling for a popular front against fascist aggressors. The United States, too, could be part of the popular front. The restoration of diplomatic relations between America and Russia, effected in 1933, made it psychologically easier to embrace the notion of America as a friend in need. The Communists never gave up the view that the United States was an imperialist, but there grew an ideological distinction between a fascist imperialist and a non-fascist imperialist. The Leninist theory of imperialism and the new strategy of the united front both led the Chinese Communists to believe that sooner or later the United States and Japan would come to an open clash.

In domestic affairs the Nanking government under Chiang Kai-shek was determined to crush the Communist insurgents, until the latter induced the former, after the Sian incident, to give up the effort and instead unite national strength against the external enemy. Nanking's view of America, however, was in actuality strikingly similar to that held by the Communists. Gone was the self-confidence and optimism of the 1920's, when the National government felt emboldened to define a new framework of Sino-foreign relations by its own fiat. After 1931 one once again finds references to China's "weakness" and "powerlessness." It seemed out of the question to repulse Japanese attack singlehandedly. There was thus a psychological need to believe that other countries would not sit idly while the Japanese mounted their aggression. In particular, it was a soothing thought that Japanese aggression would inevitably provoke American retaliation. Since such a view of Japanese-American relations was born of the feeling of desperation concerning China's own helplessness, it was natural that the Chinese government should have interpreted every move on the part of the United States as an indication of the latter's determination to resist Japan. The Chinese were quite excited, for instance, by the Roosevelt administration's naval expansion programs. There was little sympathy with Japan's pan-Asianism, with which the Japanese tried to lure the Chinese away from their reliance on Western help. When the Amau statement was issued in 1934, explicitly enunciating a "Monroe Doctrine for Asia," the Foreign Ministry in Nanking immediately countered, saying, "China believes that the maintenance of international peace is dependent upon the co-operation of all the nations in the world. Those interested in maintaining long-lasting peace in the world must promote a sincere spirit of mutual understanding and eliminate the basic causes of serious problems. No nation in the world can assert that it alone has the responsibility to maintain international peace." The Chinese view was to contradict Japanese particularism and present the East Asian crisis as a common problem of the world, as a specific issue in a particular stage of world history. It was as much the West's responsibility to come to the aid of China as it was the latter's task to do all it could to resist Japan.

By the same token, the sense of disappointment was great when the Chinese felt the United States was not acting as expected. It is possible to distinguish official Chinese attitude toward America before and after 1934. For about two years after the outbreak of the Manchurian incident, American response, from Stimson's nonrecognition policy to Roosevelt's naval programs, seemed to fit the Chinese conception of American-Japanese antagonism. After 1934, however, the feeling grew that the United States was not likely to risk alienating Japan by coming to the aid of China. The Japanese government's apparent determination to avoid trouble with America made extreme measures by the latter seem even more unlikely. From the Chinese point of view, such things as the Silver Purchase Act of 1934 and the discouragement of loans to China were evidence that the United States had ceased to champion China's cause. The Silver Purchase Act, in particular, dismayed even pro-American officials, as it had the effect of draining silver out of China, causing financial chaos to the silver-monetized economy. It was natural, then, that for some time after 1934 the Chinese should have looked more hopefully to the developing tension between Japan and the Soviet Union. The latter's increasing interest in assisting China was most welcome, as was Britain's belated effort to help China by sending a team of financial experts to undertake currency reform. Chiang Kai-shek told government, army, and party leaders in March 1934 that the rapid progress of the Soviet Union's second five-year plan, due to be completed in 1937, might precipitate Japanese-Russian conflict. His view was that the best course for China was to concentrate on internal reform so that the country could fully take advantage of an external war. It is no accident that it was just around this time that Chiang Kai-shek initiated the "new life movement," emphasizing China's cultural heritage and the relevance of Confucian virtues to contemporary China.

The tide changed again after 1936. As China successfully tided over the financial difficulties of 1934–1935, and as the Japanese army resumed its offensive in north China, the Nanking government was put under pressure to establish a union of all factions and turn the nation's energy against Japan. In this process the United States, as well as Britain and Russia, came to be looked upon once again as a friendly and potential ally. Within the Nanking government, the "pro-Anglo-Saxon" men, such as T. V. Soong and H. H. Kung, gained power. They would make serious efforts to press for substantial aid from America. Their faith in America seemed vindicated when the Treasury Department adopted the policy of purchasing silver from China at a fixed price, the proceeds from which could be accumulated in New York as credit for purchases of goods. After the Sian incident a curious marriage was effected between these pro-American officials and the Communist theorists, both of whom were confident of ultimate American intervention against Japan.

Public opinion in China, expressed in the press as well as in student movements and street demonstrations, was consistently nationalistic and called for stiff resistance against Japan. The public's view of the United States, however, fluctuated roughly parallel to the official attitude. Initially, as noted earlier, Chinese writers interpreted the Manchurian crisis as a prelude to a Pacific war between Japan and the United States. This view was always there, but opinions varied as to the timing and degree of America's positive opposition to Japanese invasion. At first the Chinese welcomed Stimson's non-recognition policy and, after the policy proved ineffectual in stopping Japan, they thought President Roosevelt was determined to implement something more concrete to counter Japanese expansionism. As one author wrote, in his review of American foreign policy for the year 1933, America's policy toward Japan had departed from the merely verbal principle of non-recognition and entered the stage of positive preparation. Proof was the naval construction program, the wheat loan to China, restoration of diplomatic relations with the Soviet Union, and the reluctance to grant Philippine independence. "America and Japan are as incompatible as water and fire, and there is no prospect for compromise in the near future." Through naval competition between the two countries, wrote another author, the curtain had risen for the drama of the world war. There was no question, he added, that the restoration of American-Soviet diplomatic relations was aimed at checking Japanese expansion. Few were optimistic enough to believe that the United States would immediately declare war on Japan; America, it was felt, was not ready to sacrifice itself on account of China, and there was always the danger that Japan might seek to effect rapprochement with the United States. Thus Chinese commentators almost invariably concluded that ultimately China's own self-strengthening was the only salvation for the country. Only when the nation stopped its internal warfare and became united, would China gain the respect of foreign governments and would they feel warranted in taking a stronger attitude toward Japan. Unless it did so, China, weak and divided, would become involved in the power struggle among the imperialist nations. Only through their own effort could the Chinese people expect to turn to their advantage the vicissitudes among the "advanced imperialist nations."

As these writings revealed, Chinese opinion viewed China as a victim both of the imperialist power struggle and of its own endless civil strife. America was an imperialist, but it was an anti-Japanese imperialist, and the two imperialists were sooner or later destined to collide. However, the Chinese could benefit from such a collision only if they were prepared to take advantage of it. It is no accident that in the early 1930's there appeared numerous articles tracing the origins of Japanese-American conflict in China. Most writers subscribed to the simplistic formula of Japanese continentalism clashing with the American policy of the Open Door after the Russo-Japanese War. As the Chinese saw it, both Japan and America were latecomers to the international scene, and when they emerged as imperialists they saw China had already been exploited by the European powers. Hence the American policy of the Open Door, designed to preserve the political status quo in order to secure the China market for America's economic activities. Japan, too, went along with the Open Door policy until after the Russo-Japanese War, when it took up the Western policy of imperialism and went further than Western nations in expanding in China. Hence the clash between America and Japan. From such a point of view, not only was Japan considered the foremost aggressor to be resisted with all might, but the United States was viewed as no selfless third party. The Open Door policy, as one put it, was no glory for China; there would have been no Open Door policy to begin with if China had been strong enough to maintain its own integrity. China was still the victim of big-power diplomacy, and if the United States happened to come to the aid of China for its own interests, this did not mitigate China's task ultimately to seek its own salvation.

The theme of China's self-help was repeated more and more forcefully as the Chinese sensed the apparent unwillingness of the Roosevelt administration to stop Japan by force. Writing in the July 1934 issue of the *Diplomatic Monthly,* a commentator noted that after 1931 China had turned to the League of Nations and hoped for American help, but all such attempts had been in vain. American policy toward Japan was sometimes firm and sometimes conciliatory, and it was "beyond comprehension." There even seemed to be a movement for settling Pacific problems peacefully among the big nations. It was to be hoped that Chinese interests would not be sacrificed, but in the end the Chinese people's united effort alone would save the nation. At any rate, "we should never forget that our country is an important factor in international politics. Toward Japan and other countries we must adopt a policy in response to the trends of the times." Here and elsewhere there was no sympathy with Japan's "Asian Monroe Doctrine." The Chinese seem to have shared no illusion about pan-Asianism, a theme Sun Yat-sen had harped upon before his death. Rather, there was a view of the Sino-Japanese struggle as part of the world scene. Since Japan had joined the ranks of the imperialists, there was no use talking about Asia for Asians unless Japan renounced its colonialism and aggressive policies. If the Chinese were powerful, a writer asserted, they would destroy both the Asian Monroe Doctrine and the Open Door strategy and establish a realm of complete equality in East Asia.

The emphasis on self-help assumed increasing political importance in China, as the Nanking government, before the Sian incident, was still pushing the anti-Communist campaign, whereas public opinion was urging national unity. At the same time, the Chinese continued to view the East Asian crisis as part of the world crisis and the first chapter of the impending world war. Events of 1935 and 1936 in Europe, Africa, and Asia seemed to confirm such a view. Humanity seemed to have reached another Dark Ages, wrote an author in January 1937. Racial and international struggles were evident everywhere, and a final tragedy in human history seemed approaching. China's suffering was part of this global drama of human folly and ambition. This, of course, was no consolation to the Chinese, victims of aggression, but such an image enabled them to retain a sense of perspective even while they persisted in their call for an anti-Japanese united front. It seemed obvious that sooner or later an anti-Japanese coalition would develop to restrain Japanese expansionism; as of 1936–1937 it seemed particularly possible that the United States and Britain would patch over their differences and take bold steps to resist Japan in Asia and Germany in Europe. Here again, these countries were pursuing their own interests. While their policy might work to the advantage of China, the Chinese should never indulge in the illusion that their own efforts were not essential. As one writer asserted just after the Sian incident, while the Chinese might congratulate themselves on the emerging national unity, they should never lose sight of the developing international tension in East Asia. Unless China made its own effort, it might repeat the tragedy of Spain, as the foreign powers would struggle against one another on Chinese soil. The aim of all these powers, whether Japan, America, or Russia, he wrote, was the acquisition of more rights in China. The United States, probably in co-operation with Britain, would sooner or later intervene against Japan, but such an expectation did not lead the Chinese to view America as any less selfish than Japan, Germany, or other countries.

Global Implications of a Crisis

The triangular relations—the Japanese resolutely pursuing their goal of establishing a new Asian order, Americans morally denouncing but in reality acquiescing in Japanese policy, and Chinese confidently looking to a Japanese-American war—underwent subtle changes after July 1937, when a mysterious clash between Japanese and Chinese troops in Peiping ushered in a full-scale although undeclared war between the two countries. For several months after the outbreak of the Marco Polo Bridge incident on July 7, 1937, the Japanese persisted in the attitude that had by now become fixed. The Japanese military, as before, did not want trouble with the United States immediately, but neither did they feel a re-evaluation of their view of America was called for. America was still pictured as a source of supply of raw materials and machines, which were needed in increasing quantities as the war progressed; politically, the United States was considered a nuisance but not really a formidable opponent of Japanese military policy. As though unconcerned with possible American reaction, the Japanese military in China closed the Yangtze to foreign navigation, bombarded Chinese cities with foreign populations, and blockaded the China coast south of Shanghai. Though there is no evidence that the *Panay* incident of December, involving the sinking of the American gunboat, was a deliberate act on the part of the Japanese navy, there is little doubt that such an incident could have been prevented if the military had taken a more serious view of the United States. As it was, they thought the *Panay* incident serious enough to require their prompt apology. The incident is a good example of the Japanese attitude toward the United States; it was felt that the latter could be pushed with impunity so long as Japan did not provoke it to actual hostility. Throughout 1937 and even in 1938, available evidence reveals that the Japanese army, both in Tokyo and in China, visualized little possibility of war with the United States on account of the war in China. A typical memorandum, written by the Kwantung Army headquarters, noted, "We must respect [America's] rights in the Philippines and Kwangtung, promote economic and cultural co-operation, and if necessary bring about an improved atmosphere by proposing a Pacific defense agreement solely between the two countries." The navy, on the other hand, was studying specific plans for control of the western Pacific and an eventual advance southward, but no strategic connection was seen between the prosecution of war in China and hostilities with the United States.

Such views of America were complacent but not inaccurate, at least so far as official American policy was concerned. However, few Japanese were at first aware of the tension their warfare was creating in official circles in the United States as well as in American public opinion. Superficially, the State Department continued the policy of avoiding trouble with Japan, while denouncing its behavior in China more and more loudly. Secretary of State Hull, as earlier, characterized Japanese action as a breach of the peace in Asia and a violation of the principles of justice and humanitarianism. But in actuality the State Department remained cautious. According to its view of American–East Asian relations, the time had not yet come for the United States to involve itself more actively in East Asia. If anything, steps were taken to minimize chances of direct confrontation between Japan and America in China; officials of the State Department favored the withdrawal of Americans from areas of danger in China and disapproved of arms shipment to China in defiance of the Japanese blockade. At bottom, as in the past, was the perception of the East Asian conflict. While it was a moral issue, one involving the peace of the whole world, it could still be defined as a Sino-Japanese affair as far as American policy was concerned. It is suggestive that Ambassador

Nelson T. Johnson, who clearly saw the Japanese military's ultimate goal of dominating China, should still have concluded, in November 1937, that the struggle was "essentially one between the Japanese and the Chinese." As he wrote to Ambassador Grew, "We want to live in peace and friendship with both sides."

It was bound to happen, however, that the gap between moral universalism and political parochialism would become so great that an effort would be made to bridge the gap, or the fiction that the Sino-Japanese War was of no immediate concern to American interests would become less and less plausible until a new image of the East Asian crisis would develop itself. The inner tension in the American perception of East Asia grew as Japanese forces moved steadily southward and all attempts at cease-fire failed. By the end of the year 1937 it was obvious that a full-scale war had developed involving the question of the future of China and of East Asia. Japanese control over the whole of China seemed no longer an academic proposition. Under the circumstances it is not surprising that more and more voices began to be heard, lamenting the United States government's inaction and parochial approach. Some critics spoke the old language. The navy, for instance, asserted that Japanese domination over China was a threat to American interests. It was felt that the policy of not resisting Japan in China would aggravate the danger to American insular possessions as well as to prestige in the Pacific. As Admiral Harry E. Yarnell, commander in chief of the Asiatic fleet, saw it, a point of no return had been reached in the Sino-Japanese crisis by the end of 1937. The United States could not long refuse to clarify its position; it must unequivocally oppose further extension of Japanese power. From a moralistic point of view, Norman Davis deplored the State Department's passivity vis-à-vis Japanese aggression. Davis represented the United States at the Brussels conference, convened late in 1937 to discuss the East Asian crisis. He had come to the conclusion that mere "preaching" had not prevented Japanese aggression in China and that to be effective the West should once and for all be firm, resorting to sanctions if necessary, so as to prevent the Japanese from believing that they could go on feeling complacent about Western reaction. This was a Stimsonian response to Japanese aggression; essentially Davis sought to apply universal moral principles, backed by force, to an

Asian situation. His efforts were frustrated by a State Department that clung to the policy of non-involvement.

It was, however, the Treasury Department that distinguished itself as the clearest advocate of a new approach to the East Asian crisis. Before 1937 the Treasury Department had already proceeded ahead of the State Department in aiding China, through its purchases of silver. The philosophy behind the assistance, however, had not been clearly defined as other than that of extending sympathy to a troubled nation. A Treasury Department memorandum of September 1937 marks a first instance of a branch of the United States government speaking a new language. It said, "The peace of the world is tied up with China's ability to win or to prolong its resistance to Japanese aggression. It is our opinion that a Japanese victory increases greatly the chances of a general world war." Here moral universalism was coupled with political universalism. Japanese aggressive acts were not only immoral; they would encourage aggression elsewhere and eventually force the peace-loving countries to stand up in defense of their own security. Japanese victory over China would not end the Asian conflict but would be a prelude to global warfare. President Roosevelt must have subscribed to such a view, if one is to judge from his "quarantine speech" of October 5, 1937. Though there is considerable scholarly argument as to what the President intended with the speech, the content itself is entirely clear; he compared the acts of "bandit nations" (Japan, Italy, and Germany) to an epidemic and suggested, "When an epidemic of physical disease starts to spread, the community approves and joins in a quarantine of the patients in order to protect the health of the community against the spread of the disease." The use of medical analogy is suggestive; as contagious diseases spread through land and sea routes, so was "the epidemic of world lawlessness" considered likely to spread unless checked carefully. It is evident that Roosevelt was thinking in global terms. Though he failed to spell out clearly how international banditry could be contained, his speech declared his interest in finding an effective means toward this end.

These instances reveal the growing concern with the global implications of the East Asian crisis. It may be said that various Americans were coming to accept the long-standing Chinese view that the Sino-Japanese conflict was a prelude to world war. However, it should be noted that Japanese expansion was the primary object of concern, not China as such. China was a victim of aggression, but America's immediate concern was with Japan. Editorials and civic groups called on the nation either to join in a boycott of trade with Japan or to persist in isolationism to avoid war with Japan. Both these extreme views reached a new height after the quarantine speech, as the President seemed prepared to lead the nation to a resolute stand against aggression overseas. The question of whether the United States should extend help to China was always bound up with the question whether to risk fighting Japan. It was not surprising, then, that little thought was given to the complexities of internal Chinese conditions, political and ideological.

The Resolution to Stand Alone

If Americans had read what Chinese were writing at this time, they would have found that the Chinese were getting discouraged at the poor prospect of American help, just as American opinion was coming to recognize the need to restrain Japan. It may be said that the last few months of 1937 marked a nadir in Chinese estimate of America. Although the view persisted that Japan was threatening the peace not only of Asia but of the world and therefore that the United States would sooner or later become involved in the East Asian conflict, the Chinese grew discouraged as they saw little evidence of active American support while the Japanese army was taking city after city. "Principal countries such as England, France, and Russia sympathize with us," wrote one author, apparently intentionally omitting to include the United States in the list of sympathizers. Initially, also, there was much expectation that Germany would help China. The best that could be said about the attitude of America was that American opinion would in the end come to co-operate with other countries against Japan. "We are dissatisfied with America's attitude, but we are not pessimistic," noted an article. An editorial in the Hankow *Takungpao* bluntly asked, in late September, if America's passivity while China was being devoured was all that the American people would show to respond to the trust that the Chinese had placed in America for half a century. The Chinese were fighting with their blood for America, for American interests would be directly menaced by a pan-Asian empire of

Japan. As such a hysterical outburst indicates, in the Chinese imagination the United States had forfeited the position as the number-one friend of China. President Roosevelt's "quarantine speech" and American participation in the Brussels conference momentarily soothed Chinese anxieties, but the inconsequential result of the latter conference again disappointed the Chinese. The Shanghai *Takungpao* noted after the conference that isolationists were still strong in the United States and seemed to nullify the efforts of the American government and people to reassert their leadership in Asian affairs. The United States appeared to be merely passively watching the undermining of its historical position in East Asia and the destruction of its economic interests there. However, the newspaper still hoped that the enlightened people of America would surely determine not to abandon what they had acquired in Asia since the 1840's. They would surely not sit idly by while Japan replaced the Open Door policy with an Asian Monroe Doctrine.

Two weeks after the above editorial was published, in mid-December, the Shanghai newspaper, one of the oldest in the country, closed its offices. The editors would not surrender to Japanese censorship, and the cessation of publication was the only honorable way they could see. In the final issuc, the reader was told to think of the crisis in historical perspective. It was just a passing phenomenon in the 5,000-year history of 450,000,000 people. Surely the time would come when peace would return and the people would enjoy independence. Until then, only three words, "never to surrender," should be the policy for all. Help from friendly powers had not materialized, and the Chinese must rely upon their own determined effort to seek salvation.

8
Toward Pearl Harbor

For about ten years after 1938, Sino-American co-operation against Japan defined both East Asian politics and what the three peoples thought of their relations as they faced each other. For most Chinese the American alliance was merely a fulfillment of what they had foreseen; for most Japanese the Sino-American coalition signaled a final obstacle in the way of their attempt to establish a new Asian order; while for Americans the new tripartite drama dissipated the tension that had existed between their moral universalism and political parochialism. By 1948, however, Chinese were denouncing the United States for interference in their domestic politics and for trying to resurrect Japanese militarism; Americans were becoming upset over the Chinese civil war; and Japanese were turning almost exclusively to America for help and advice, material and spiritual.

It is a measure of the superficial nature of American-Chinese-Japanese contact that such drastic transformations should have taken place in their mutual perceptions in less than ten years. Looked at historically, however, it also becomes evident that these changes were not as unnatural as might appear. For Americans, China had become a moral question. If sentiment dictated support of a tragic China during the war, it also called for rejection of a hostile China after the war. Security considerations, on the other hand, had necessitated the policy of American resistance to Japanese expansionism; after Japan's defeat the same considerations would result in a policy of containing China. In the long drama of Sino-American confrontation, it was the brief moment of co-operation that was exceptional, rather than the mutual antagonism that followed the war. For this very reason, the years of direct American involvement in China merit serious study as an extraordinary interlude in otherwise friction-ridden relations.

American Policy and Global Security

The American-Japanese war was brought about by Japan's decision to extend its control over southeast Asia and by America's determination to prevent it. Beginning in 1938, the Japanese military pushed their China campaign southward to offshore islands and eventually to French Indochina. Their undisguised aim was to achieve the control of the Dutch East Indies as well as Singapore. The inclusion of all these regions would enable Japan to form a gigantic Asian bloc, presumably an impregnable fortress and a source of most raw materials that were needed for national defense. It was such moves that ran counter to the American policy of defending the status quo in southeast Asia. The survival of the British, Dutch, and French colonics in Asia necessitated America's involvement in that part of the world and led directly to war with Japan. It is obvious that southeast Asia became a crucial factor in American-Japanese relations because of developments in Europe after 1938. Japanese penetration, actual and premeditated, of southeast Asia was prompted by the German victories and the expectation of further victories in Europe, while America's opposition to Japanese "southern advance" was designed to prevent the collapse of the British empire, which was, Americans thought, essential to the survival of England itself. A Japanese victory over China would release resources for southern expansion, whereas a prolonged Sino-Japanese war would tie the Japanese military down on the continent of Asia and prevent them from penetrating the colonial empires to the south.

Thus, ultimately as a result of the European war, the Sino-

Japanese war developed into a Pacific war via southeast Asia. The United States became involved in the East Asian conflict because the survival of Britain in Europe and in Asia was considered vital to America's own security. Seen from such a perspective, it is clear that no single road led to Pearl Harbor. Without the German-British war there might not have been a Japanese-American war, and without the collapse of France in Europe there might not have developed a southeast Asian crisis. The Sino-Japanese war did not automatically result in war between the United States and Japan. There had, after all, been no war between the latter before 1941, and no grave crisis before 1938. From new situations in Europe and in southeast Asia grew distinct possibilities of armed conflict in the Pacific.

But if those were the realities of prewar American–East Asian relations, what was perceived was very different. There still exists the myth, shared by many scholars in the three countries, that the United States and Japan went to war over China, and that, whether for moral, economic, or other motives, the United States was determined to prevent Japanese domination of China. Such a view of the recent past is convenient on many counts. For Americans it gives a psychologically satisfactory explanation for the origin of the Pacific war: America had gone to the rescue of the beleaguered Chinese. It is just a step from that to the corollary that the Chinese have betrayed American generosity, that they have bitten the hands that fed them. For the Chinese, also from the postwar perspective, the Pacific war appears as the beginning of America's unmistakable intervention in Asia, leading up to the postwar policy of interference in Chinese domestic politics. Many American, Chinese, and Japanese historians picture Japan as intent on establishing a predominant position in China ever since the Russo-Japanese War, and the United States as countering this intent with the policy of the Open Door. In fact, many still see in the Pacific war a culmination of the American-Japanese conflict in China that emerged after 1905.

Some contemporaries in the United States, China, and Japan, however, clearly saw the key issues in the late 1930's. In America, there is no doubt that, beginning in 1938, the conviction grew that the East Asian crisis was no longer an isolated phenomenon but was part of a developing world crisis. Italy and Germany had revealed their intention of altering the status quo by force even before 1936, but there was a time lag between these developments and the realization in the United States of the seriousness of the crisis. The crucial factor seems to have been the series of diplomatic crises in Europe in 1938, culminating in the Munich fiasco. It was in this connection that Japanese action in China throughout 1938, conquering Hankow and Canton and enunciating the principle of a new order in East Asia, appeared particularly ominous. In the minds of American policy makers, a clear link was established between the developments in Europe and in East Asia. There emerged the possibility, as they saw it, that the aggressive nations, in particular Germany and Japan, might band together and collectively menace the status quo and peace in the whole world. It seemed imperative to respond to the challenge if America's security and its concomitant, peace in the world, were to be maintained. Aggression in Asia must be resisted to discourage lawless action in Europe. Moral globalism was given official status by security considerations.

A few examples will illustrate the new language of global security. In July 1939 Secretary of State Hull told the Japanese ambassador,

> We consider the preservation of peace so supremely important to the future of all nations that we draw the line between honest, law-abiding, peaceful countries and peoples, without reference to their form of Government, on the one hand, and those who are flouting law and order and officially threatening military conquest without limit as to time or extent; . . . we will work in a friendly spirit with every peaceful nation to promote and preserve peace, without serious thought as to who they are.

In this unusually strong language Secretary Hull, the symbol of caution before 1938, put forth the philosophy of globalism in its simplest form. It is to be noted that he stressed the division of the world into peace-loving countries and aggressors "without serious thought as to who they are." It did not matter whether the aggressor or the victim of aggression was in Europe or in Asia, a democracy or a socialist state. What mattered was the distinction between the party of order and that standing for forceful alteration of the status quo.

From Hull's and his colleagues' point of view, Japan's self-styled new order in East Asia was the epitome of lawlessness. At the end of December 1938, the United States openly rejected the Japanese contention that a new situation had arisen in East Asia, necessitating changes in the principles of international conduct. The United States government did not admit, it declared, "that there is need or warrant for any one Power to take upon itself to prescribe what shall be the terms and conditions of a 'new order' in areas not under its sovereignty and to constitute itself the repository of authority and the agent of destiny in regard thereto." In a similar vein Ambassador Grew made his famous speech at an America-Japan Society meeting in Tokyo in October 1939. He reiterated the belief that international peace was dependent on law and order; this was particularly the case, he said, since nations were economically interdependent. Grew reminded the Japanese that "the present trend in the Far East, if continued, will be destructive of the hopes which [the American people] sincerely cherish of the development of an orderly world." The new order in East Asia ran counter to the American aspiration for "security, stability, and progress not only for themselves but for all other nations in every quarter of the world."

As often happens, military strategists perceived most clearly the trend toward global conflict. Before 1938 American naval and army planning vis-à-vis Japan had been conceived in terms of an "Orange war"—war in the Pacific against Japan. After 1938, however, strategic thinking was centered around a "Rainbow war," that is, war involving the Atlantic as well as the Pacific, Germany and Italy as well as Japan. Various possibilities were considered, depending on the timing of the war, capabilities of the belligerents, and geographical distribution of armed strengths. There was little doubt, after 1939, that the United States would co-operate with Britain to fight against an Axis alliance. Here the question of priority had to be raised; should the United States concentrate its resources first in the Atlantic or in the Pacific? Much depended on specific situations, and of the five Rainbow plans that were drafted in 1939, three envisaged a strategic defensive in the Pacific, while two specified an offensive. In the end the strategy of defeating the enemy first in Europe and then in Asia was adopted, but the tradition of global strategy had been firmly established by the end of the 1930's.

Now that Japan was identified with Germany, the psychological transition was made to identify China with the democracies in Europe. As Hull's statement indicates, the United States was to assist the victims of aggression regardless of their form of government. America would help China resist Japan just as it would encourage British and French opposition to German militarism. Before 1938 the United States had not been moved to come to the aid of China in any substantial degree, and had rationalized its passivity in numerous ways. Now a sudden turn to positive action was accompanied by the image of the world divided between two camps. Without the awareness of the global crisis, one suspects, there would not have been a shift of attitude toward China. One notices, for instance, that American business publications began denouncing Japan and expressing support of China only after 1940. Some of them, in fact, maintained an awkward silence on the East Asian situation throughout 1940 and then began attacking Japan in 1941. It is obvious that the shift was due to the awareness of the European war and its implications for East Asia. Opinion polls, too, began to show signs that the American public was now willing not only to express themselves unequivocally in sympathy with China but to approve of certain measures short of war to restrain Japan. The feeling was that the crisis in China was closely related to America's own security problems, now that Germany and Japan were emerging as the twin threat to the peace of the world. It is interesting to note, too, that such specialists on American East Asian policy as Paul W. Clyde and A. Whitney Griswold were subtly changing their attitude toward the East Asian question. Earlier they had expressed the view that America's basic interest in Asia was economic and that whatever Japan did in China was not America's business. Griswold's classic *Far Eastern Policy of the United States,* published in 1938, may be regarded as characteristic of the era of isolationist writings on the subject. He eloquently pled for America's non-involvement in East Asia so long as its essential economic interests were not injured. For him the whole adventure in Asian politics, begun in the 1890's, had been misplaced politically and confused morally. Clyde had written much in a similar vein. By early 1941, however, they were talking of the relevance of the East Asian crisis to America's security. In an extremely lucid analysis, Griswold pointed out that the East Asian crisis and the European crisis had been merged and that America's and Britain's security had become menaced. The best safeguard for Anglo-American security seemed to lie in an undeclared peace in East Asia and an undeclared war in Europe. The idea was that the United States should do all it could to assist the British effort at survival, and to this end it seemed best to take a cautious stand toward Japan. Clyde declared that Japan's new order rested upon "a system which, whatever its merits may be, is the antithesis of every ideal represented by a century of American policy in China." Although he had tended to be sympathetic toward Japan's aspirations in China and critical of America's unilateral adherence to the Open Door policy, he now came around to a solid denunciation of Japanese action.

Since they were predisposed to thinking in terms of global security, it was natural that Americans should find Japan's alliance with Germany, consummated in September 1940, final evidence that the two arch-aggressors had combined forces to challenge the democracies and conquer the world. In American thinking a point of no return seemed to have been reached when the Japanese recklessly, as it appeared, entered into a pact for universal aggression. The spectacle of Japan and Germany subjugating the weak nations and dominating the Atlantic and the Pacific was frightening. Should England and the British empire fall, their rich resources and naval power would have been at the service of Germany and Japan. The United States would be surrounded by a formidable combination of hostile forces. The only safeguard, then, was to prevent the collapse of the British empire. "The United States is isolated except for one great power and that's the British Commonwealth," Secretary of War Stimson wrote down in his diary, "and I already see signs of a realization of this among the thoughtless." He had long realized the need for co-operation with Britain, but even the "thoughtless" isolationists were slowly coming around to such a view. Perhaps the clearest exposition of the new state of American–East Asian relations was made by Ambassador Grew in his "green light message" of September 1940, a few days before the signing of the Axis alliance. In the telegram Grew, who had tried to understand the Japanese side of the East Asian question for nearly a decade, explicitly castigated Japan as "one of the predatory powers." He went on,

> American interests in the Pacific are definitely threatened by her policy of southward expansion, which is a thrust at the British Empire in the East. Admittedly America's security has depended in a measure upon the British Fleet, which has been in turn and could only have been supported by the British Empire. If the support of the British Empire in this her hour of travail is conceived to be in our interest, and most emphatically do I so conceive it, we must strive by every means to preserve the *status quo* in the Pacific, at least until the war in Europe has been won or lost.

Here was a clear rationale for new action to deter Japan in southeast Asia. Stripped to essentials, Grew's message bespoke the fundamental truth, as he saw it, that American and British security were interdependent. That belief became the guiding principle of American policy and strategy, as well as of popular thinking from this time on.

The New Order in Asia

The Japanese, too, perceived that Japan's new order was a threat to British and American security, although few at first were willing to accept the logical connection between the new order in Asia and the possibility of conflict with the United States. Even those who did accept it disagreed as to which stage of Japanese expansion in southeast Asia would provoke forceful American intervention. This, however, was a question of military strategy, not of policy.

Southern advance was a basic Japanese policy after 1938. Partly this was a military move, an aspect of the new definition of national security. The military had explained their acts in Manchuria and China as an attempt to create an economically self-sufficient and militarily impregnable "defense state." The bloc embracing Japan, Manchukuo, and China was obviously far from being self-sufficient. From this point of view there was a logical necessity to include southeast Asia, with its rich mineral and vegetable resources, in the Japanese empire. Such a new order would help reduce Japan's dependence on American supplies of oil, iron, and other materials. Thus from a military standpoint the new order was often conceived of as an alternative to Japanese-American trade. The navy in particular, with its absolute need for fuel oil, came to view a southern advance as an inevitable choice forced upon Japan by America's policy. Since, in naval reasoning, unrestricted trade with America was being endangered by America's policy of opposing Japan in Asia, the latter would have no choice but to strike southward. By 1940, when southern advance was made a national policy, top naval circles had also come to the conclusion that Japanese action in southeast Asia would bring about conflict not only with Britain but also with the United States. This was because of the view, held by the navy, that Britain and America could not be separated; once Japan struck at British colonies, the United States would be bound to intervene. The question, therefore, was whether war with these two powers justified the policy of southern advance. By late 1940 section chiefs of the Navy Ministry and the Naval General Staff came to the belief that since war with America was sooner or later inevitable, Japan should take the initiative and advance into southern Indochina and the Dutch East Indies to secure naval bases and strategic raw materials. Circular reasoning here is notable. For naval strategists, the policy of southern advance would make conflict with the United States inevitable; since war was bound to occur, Japan should advance southward to prepare itself for the conflict.

The idea of a new order in Asia, however, was not totally a military notion. More and more civilian officials became believers in "pan-regions," several blocs into which the world was to be divided. Each bloc would be dominated by one or two superpowers, and all blocs would coexist harmoniously among themselves. World peace would be maintained on the basis of a balance of power among them. Japan was obviously to be the overlord of Asia, the term that came to include not only China but southeast Asia. The "expulsion of Anglo-American influence" from Asia, to use an oft-employed phrase, was clearly a first step toward realizing this end. Already at the end of 1938 the Tokyo government had explicitly enunciated its new policy when Foreign Minister Arita Hachirō stated, in a note to the United States, that Japan was building a new order in East Asia and that the old ideas and principles of diplomacy would no longer serve to establish permanent peace there. At the same time, Japan's policy makers believed that the pan-Asian order was compatible with peaceful relations between Japan and the United States, once the latter recognized the new order.

How it was felt that Japan could go on building a new order while avoiding open conflict with America, provides a clue to Japanese thinking. According to Matsuoka Yōsuke, who as foreign minister in 1940–1941 was the major ideologue behind Japanese policy, Japanese-American relations would form part of the global system in which Japan predominated in Asia, Germany and Italy in Europe, the Soviet Union would remain neutral, and the United States would keep its hegemony in the Western Hemisphere. As he wrote in January 1941, "The world is to be divided into the great East Asian zone, the European zone (including Africa), the American zone, and the Soviet zone (including India and Iran), though Australia and New Zealand may be left to England, to be treated in a similar manner as Holland." Matsuoka seems to have been completely sincere in stating again and again that the Axis alliance and Japan's non-aggression pact with Russia, both part of the bloc policy, were designed to prevent war between Japan and the United States. America's influence in Asia and hostility to Japan were such, he thought, that only by presenting a determined stand would America be deterred from entering the war against Japan. Matsuoka's view of America is revealed in an informal statement he made in September 1940 at a government conference. He remarked that Japan was confronted with a choice between the United States and Germany. To choose understanding and co-operation with the former would entail a settlement of the China war in accordance with America's dictates, abandonment of the new order idea, and submission to Anglo-American influence for at least half a century. Amity with America and Britain would bring material benefits to Japan, he conceded, but the Japanese should remember what happened after the First World War, when Japan was their ally. Moreover, the Chiang Kai-shek regime would be emboldened and openly insult Japan. Thus Matsuoka justified the Axis alliance as essential to the completion of the new order. Japan would force American acquiescence in the new order by its very existence and splendor. From Matsuoka's and his supporters' point of view, the crisis with America had progressed to such an extent that only a bold new stroke of policy would work in maintaining Japanese-American peace. They were so captivated by their own logic that they did not note the primitive circularity of their reasoning. Nevertheless, their perception of America was realistic in that Americans, too, had come to view their relations with Japan in the light of the new order in East Asia.

Outside of the military and the government, there was in Japan a great deal of theorizing about what was called the Great East Asian Co-Prosperity Sphere. It is remarkable that the Japanese, who had developed few ideas of international relations, suddenly poured forth treatise after treatise about the meaning of East Asian conflict. A good example of Japanese thinking after 1938 is an article by Ozaki Hotsumi, a Marxist thinker, entitled "The Idea of the 'East Asian Co-operative System' and the Objective Bases of its Formation," which appeared in the January 1939 issue of *Chūōkōron*. Although he had China specifically in mind rather than the whole of Asia, the author wrote that nationalism was a basis of the new order. The co-operative state system in Asia would be a "regional, racial, cultural, economic, and defensive combination," which would shield itself against the West's imperialistic expansionism. There must be genuine co-operation among the member states, although it would be justifiable for Japan to assert its special status within the combination. The new order seemed economically inevitable, as an increase in productive power in Asia was destroying the equilibrium in the colonial societies. Their liberation and welfare would be promoted by economic co-operation within the East Asian bloc. This was also the best way for Japanese capitalism to survive in competition with Western capitalist nations. At the same time, Ozaki emphasized the need for Japan's internal economic and political transformation so as to enable it truly to play a central and leading role in the new order. Here an avowed Marxist was justifying Japanese policy while advocating internal reform, a response common to a vast number of Japanese liberals and leftists at this time. There was something appealing in the idea of a new Asian order, liberated from Western influence and truly integrated economically and politically. Such an image of Japan's mission was shared by a whole range of Japanese writers, from traditional ultra-nationalists to Marxist intellectuals. They had come to interpret the history of modern Asia as a story of Western capitalist exploitation. Japan was leading a crusade to free Asia. In the new dispensation the language of harmony would replace that of force, and the principle of co-prosperity would take the place of capitalism, materialism, and individualism. America was the symbol of the West, and the establishment of a new order necessarily meant rejection of America's role in Asia. It goes without saying that much ink was spent rationalizing the alliance with Germany and Italy while theoretically rejecting the West. Somehow these countries were seen as an antithesis of the United States and other democracies and therefore as more "Japanese." Such were the extremes to which the ideology of the new order led Japanese thinking. At any rate, the image of Western exploitation of Asia lay behind Japanese policy toward China, southeast Asia, and the United States.

China: The Expectation of American Aid

The Chinese, too, believed that Western imperialism had been a key factor in China's deterioration. But they saw an even greater foe in Japan. A few of them, in particular those that joined Wang Ching-wei's Nanking government under Japanese sponsorship and control, were ideologically motivated by anti-communism; but they were far from enthusiastic about the Japanese-proclaimed new order in Asia. They seem to have reasoned that the United States would not intervene in the East Asian war and therefore Japan would subjugate Chungking. It seemed best, therefore, to salvage what was left of China if the only alternative was continued desolation of the land or an increase in Communist strength. By the last years of the 1930's, however, the vast majority of Chinese were confident of American support. Though they had been disappointed by America's passivity before 1937, they were encouraged by the gathering clouds in Europe which, in their view, were bound to involve the United States in East Asia. The critical situation in Europe after 1938 afforded evidence that they had been right in predicting the coming of a world war as a result of Japanese aggression. Chiang Kai-shek was only reiterating a popular and long-standing conviction when he declared, in January 1939, that international conditions were favorable to the defense of peace and justice; people in Europe and America, he said, were more and more loudly denouncing aggression.

There was particular reason for the Chungking government to desire American help. With Germany approaching Japan, and Britain adopting an appeasement policy, Nationalist China's only substantial friend before 1939 was the Soviet Union. For obvious reasons Chiang Kai-shek was unwilling to rely solely on Soviet assistance, no matter how valuable and timely it had proved. If he was to resist Japan and at the same time forestall Communist subversion, the only avenue of help had to be the United States. If no American aid could be obtained, China would either have to continue a hopeless war against Japan, inviting further internal chaos and deterioration, a condition favorable for Communist subversion, or it would find itself more and more deeply tied to the Soviet Union, with the same probable result. Close ties with the United States would help solve both the external and domestic problems.

It was no coincidence, then, that the view of America as China's closest ally emerged after 1939, the year of crisis in Europe and resumption of Kuomintang-Communist rift in China. It is undeniable that there was an element of "self-fulfilling prophecy" in Chungking's image of the United States. It was psychologically imperative to believe that moral commitment as well as strategic interest moved Americans to support Kuomintang China; believing that, the government could ask for more and more help, hinting at China's defeat by Japan or take-over by the Communists unless it was given. Because the Nationalist leaders were confident of obtaining American assistance, they could play with time, making a gesture of seeking settlement with Japan or preparing themselves for an eventual show-down with the Communists.

Chinese Communists, on their part, never departed from the theoretical framework of Marxism-Leninism, to which was being added "Maoism," through Mao Tse-tung's idea of "the people's new democracy." According to Mao, China was defined as a semicolony ruled by a collective dictatorship of all revolutionary classes. The country was neither a bourgeois state nor a proletarian dictatorship, the two types of states that Lenin had identified. Advanced capitalist countries of the West as well as Japan belonged to the former, while only the Soviet Union qualified for the second category. Between the two there were a host of colonies and semi-colonies, which went through a transition stage of "new democracy" on their way to proletarian dictatorship. These societies could not immediately transform themselves into socialist republics but had to go through the stage of collective government by revolutionary classes under the leadership of the proletariat. "Revolutionary classes" were defined tautologically; they were anti-imperialist and anti-feudal, such as proletariat, peasants, intelligentsia, petty bourgeoisie, and national bourgeoisie. These classes would bring about a "new bourgeois democratic revolution" as a necessary stage in China's ultimate development as a socialist state under proletarian dictatorship.

Internally, this theory was at least consistent; all anti-communist groups could simply be branded as feudal and therefore outside the pale of the revolutionary struggle. Externally, strain existed as soon as the imperialists fought not only among themselves but often in alliance with semi-colonial states. So long as the United States and Japan, for instance, clashed over their rights and possessions, such a conflict could be regarded as a purely imperialist power struggle. Actually, some imperialists were more friendly to China than others; and some were closer to the Soviet Union, the only socialist state, than others. The Chinese Communists had to explain away within the framework of "new democracy" such disparate phenomena as the German-British war, the German-Soviet neutrality pact, to be followed by Germany's invasion of Russia, and the Japanese-Soviet non-aggression pact. The theory of coalescence of all revolutionary classes could justify the view that the democratic imperialists, such as the United States, Britain, and France, would come to the aid of China against fascist aggressors. These bourgeois nations might co-operate with the socialist Soviet Union to help China, just as petty and national bourgeoisie in China worked together with the peasants and proletariat to eradicate feudalism. The fact remained, however, that the bourgeois nations were by definition imperialists. The war in Europe was inevitably characterized as the "second imperialist war," fought among imperialists who were alike motivated by anti-Soviet and anti-revolutionary principles. Soviet overtures for temporary rapprochement with Germany and with Japan were defended as necessary tactics to strengthen the socialist state by taking advantage of imperialist politics. These two views of the Western democracies, as imperialist and as anti-fascist, could be reconciled by a view of the state that distinguished between the ruling (bourgeois) class and the masses. Though a bourgeois society was by definition imperialistic, there were the "people," other classes in society, that remained democratic and potentially revolutionary. They could be expected to be in sympathy with the revolutionary struggle abroad. Thus the United States, too, was imperialistic but its people were opposed to imperialism; they were sympathetic to the Chinese as they fought against the Japanese aggressor and against feudal elements at home. Nevertheless, so long as the class structure in a capitalist state remained unchanged, the only reliable ally for the Chinese people was the Soviet Union. It is not surprising, then, that in 1940, in the middle of crisis at home and abroad, Mao Tse-tung should reassert the need to "lean to one side." He wrote, "As the conflict between the socialist Soviet Union and the imperialist Great Britain and the United States becomes further intensified, it is inevitable that China must stand either on one side or on the other." It was simply impossible to be neutral.

It is very difficult to evaluate general Chinese thinking on the United States apart from Kuomintang or Communist party dogma. Many pamphlets and articles written at this time reflected either one of these dogmas. Nevertheless, the two views were not wholly contradictory. All were agreed that the United States was an imperialist power and also that it stood in the way of Japanese aggression. It remained the task of publicists and general writers to apply such theories to concrete situations and somehow present a coherent picture of American policy in East Asia. Chou Chi-ch'üan's *American Far Eastern Policy,* a hundred-page tract published in Changsha in 1940, offers a good example. The book reiterated the clichés about America's Open Door policy as an expression of the country's economic interests and as the antithesis of Japan's policy of monopolistic control over China. But he also emphasized the fact that the United States had developed as a Pacific power, with influence and interests in the western Pacific and East Asia. Japan was challenging this role played by America. As the author saw it, the question was soon to be settled whether American influence would be expelled from Asia. So long as the United States persisted in the policy of the Open Door, such an outcome seemed unlikely. America would resist with all its force Japan's threat to its interests in Asia. However, if it was to continue to play a role in East Asia, it must recognize the mistake of continuing trade with Japan and resolutely come to the aid of China. Americans, the author concluded, should clearly determine what destiny they sought to obtain in Asia. As revealed in such an outline of American–East Asian relations, the Chinese were aware that the United States was confronted with two aspects of the East Asian conflict, one in China and one in the Pacific. The United States was pictured as a naval power in the Pacific whose policy in China had been that of insisting on the Open Door. Japan's aggression in China compromised the second principle, while its southern advance would threaten the former position. Like the Japanese and the Americans, the Chinese saw that the war in China was becoming part of a Pacific struggle for power, which in turn was an aspect of the global crisis. American policy in China, they felt, would be determined by global considerations. On the whole it is fair to say that pro-Kuomintang writers tended to play up the China aspect of American policy, emphasizing the absolute incompatibility of Japanese and American policies in China. The United States had traditionally opposed the ambitions of a third power to dominate China, and such a long-standing principle could not be surrendered without a fight.

Communist-oriented writings, on the other hand, tended to emphasize the Pacific and international aspects of United States policy. They also agreed that Japan and America stood opposed in China, but Communist and pro-Communist writers put all of this in a Leninist framework. According to Chin Chung-hua, editor of *World Culture,* American involvement in the East Asian crisis was inevitable because the question was being decided as to who was to control the large market of China and who was to dominate the Pacific Ocean. Due to the war in Europe, American capitalists were being forced to turn their attention more and more seriously to the potential market of China. Not that the Japanese market was unimportant. As so many Chinese writers noted uneasily at this time, even after 1940, when the United States repudiated the commercial treaty with Japan, the trade between the two countries went on. A writer bluntly predicted that the United States would come to the aid of China only when its ruling capitalist circles judged that the loss of trade in China due to Japanese aggression outweighed the advantages of continued trade with Japan. However, most authors agreed that trade with Asia was but a part of America's global strategy. More fundamentally, the United States was challenging Japan's bid to establish a new Asian order, with itself as the overlord of the Pacific. As Marxist writers saw the Pacific struggle, there was also a third party, the Soviet Union, which complicated the picture. China's struggle, Chin noted, "is one aspect of the three-cornered struggle in East Asia, involving Japan, the Soviet Union, and the Anglo-Saxon powers." Reflecting Soviet dogma, Chinese Communist writers on occasion expressed anxiety over a great imperialist collaboration against the socialist state. The United States was pictured as oscillating between its hostility toward Japan and toward Russia while trying to prevent rapprochement between them. At any event, from the Chinese Communist point of view, America's opposition to Japan in the Pacific and in China was of great help to the Chinese people, but they should not delude themselves that such help was selfless. They should try to understand America's global policy and utilize it wherever possible so as to make it serve their struggle for national liberation. In the end only the Chinese people had the key to the future of their country.

Toward War

Despite the theorizing of all concerned, the road to Pearl Harbor was basically a military road. On the American side, of the five Rainbow plans considered after 1939, Rainbow Five was eventually adopted, with its emphasis on the defense of Britain in Europe. The crucial decision was made by the highest authorities in the winter of 1940–1941, based on the recommendation of Admiral Harold R. Stark, chief of naval operations. Called Plan Dog, his proposal called for an offensive in Europe and a defensive in the Pacific. Until British survival was ensured, it was considered best to delay decisive action vis-à-vis Japan. At the same time, Japan's southern advance must be prevented, as it would threaten the British empire, and necessary measures would have to be taken in order to prepare for an eventual conflict with Japan. More specifically, while diplomatic delaying tactics should be employed so as not to provoke Japan, Pacific islands should be fortified, the United States fleet should be retained at Pearl Harbor, and staff conversations should be held with British and Dutch commanders in southeast Asia with a view to joint defense. These measures would serve as deterrents against rash Japanese action, while diplomatic action would postpone final confrontation. There was, of course, a fine distinction between military measures as deterrents and as stimulants. Certain steps might actually involve the United States precipitously in war with Japan instead of serving the aim of postponing the showdown. In retrospect it appears that while military leaders in America generally sought to concentrate on the Atlantic theater of war, specific measures were taken in the Pacific which did not help postpone war with Japan. After July, when Japan sent troops to southern Indochina, the United States stepped up joint strategic planning with Britain, the Commonwealth, and the Dutch East Indies, and these countries were implicitly assured of American intervention should Japan attack Singapore or the East Indies. Meanwhile Japanese funds in the United States were frozen, bringing about a cessation of trade and cutting off the supply of fuel oil, vital to the Japanese navy. The bulk of the United States fleet was still kept in Hawaii despite the urgency of the struggle in the Atlantic.

American action in the Pacific prior to December 1941 reveals a view of Japan that was a product of wishful thinking. There was the idea that strong determination on the part of the United States would keep Japan in check, that force was the only language the Japanese understood and that concessions would encourage further aggression. Since Japan was pictured as inferior militarily and economically to the United States, it was not expected to risk American retaliation by precipitous action. At the same time, delaying diplomatic action would serve to gain time for the United States and keep Japan from becoming desperate. In other words, the Japanese would behave as Americans would if placed in a similar situation. America's show of determination, backed up by superior economic resources and military potential, would moderate Japan and prevent it from challenging the United States. There is no question that here was an element of self-complacency. American military leaders as well as American policy makers wanted to believe that the measures they were taking would suffice to hold Japan in check. Some, notably Ambassador Grew, tried to warn that the Japanese could be extremely erratic and irrational, that out of desperation they might resort to extreme measures. President Roosevelt and his senior advisers, however, held to the view that war could be avoided or at least postponed through military preparedness coupled with diplomatic talks.

It was such a view of Japan that was put to a severe test as months went by in the year 1941. As seen already, some in Japan, particularly naval officers, had come to believe in the inevitability of war with the United States. The point of no return had been reached in Japanese-American relations, they argued; therefore Japan should worry only about how to wage war against the United States most effectively. Advocated most forcefully by the navy's section chiefs, such a view came to be accepted by their superiors as well as by army strategists. After the spring of 1941 both the armed services were in virtual agreement on the inevitable logic of coming events; Japan would strike southward, the United States would retaliate by imposing a total embargo on exports to Japan, and Japan would finally decide on war with America. The Japanese military became so captivated by their own logic, which, it must be admitted, was not far wrong, that it became more and more difficult for them to transcend it and think of alternatives. The only logical alternative they could accept would have been restoration of normal trade with the United States, which would ensure the navy of continued oil supply and render unnecessary the forceful seizure of southeast Asia. It was this alternative that the civilian government in Tokyo sought to pursue in the peace talks in Washington. Put simply, Japan's leaders embraced a clear formula of choosing between American oil and southeast Asian oil. Believing that the United States would welcome a deal, they carried on their last-minute negotiations with Secretary of State Hull and sought to hold a leaders' conference in Honolulu. The burden of the Japanese offer was that Japan would give up its southern advance if the United States would consent to the resumption of trade. The Japanese, too, were guided by military considerations. Even the navy advocates of war admitted that it was doubtful if Japan could win an American war; war, however, was considered preferable to the continuation of the stalemate, with the stock of oil running out. If war had to be faced, the decision must be made quickly. It would be impossible to wait past the end of November 1941.

The Japanese attitude throughout 1941, like the American, reveals an image of its potential antagonist. That the Japanese prepared for war against the United States as they advanced southward indicated that they could not separate America from Britain and the Dutch East Indies. The United States, they realized, was to enter the scene as soon as Japan attacked British and Dutch possessions in southeast Asia. At the same time, they recognized that America desired peace in the Pacific in order to concentrate on the Atlantic. Furthermore, in the Japanese view, the United States would be ready to buy peace with oil and iron; it would be willing to resume trade if Japan refrained from attacking southeast Asia. Such a view of America persuaded the Japanese government that it was worth while pursuing a modus vivendi with Washington. The idea that the United States really did not want war with Japan encouraged some optimism. Thus the Japanese tended to read into America's policy statements what they wanted to find there, as revealed for instance when Ambassador Nomura Kichisaburō misrepresented Hull's remarks to Tokyo. Though the secretary's tone was always uncompromising if not belligerent, the ambassador desperately sought in it some indication of a conciliatory spirit. The conviction that the United States in the end would compromise explains why the Japanese regarded Hull's November 26 note as an ultimatum and decided on war.

The "Hull note" visualized the return to the status quo, not of 1940, 1939, or even of 1937, but virtually of 1931, by demanding that Japanese troops be withdrawn from Indochina and China in return for resumption of trade with the United States. The presentation of the note signaled the end not only of negotiations in Washington but also of the fiction of peace between the two countries. This was well recognized by leaders in Tokyo as well as in Washington. What is crucial, however, is the intrusion of the China question at the very last moment. American and Japanese military planning, as well as Japan's civilian diplomacy, had visualized the alternative of war or peace in terms of southeast Asia, not of China. The Japanese had hoped for a compromise on the issue of oil, and the American military had sought to prevent

Japan's southern advance. In the fall of 1941, as the sense of crisis heightened on both sides of the Pacific, serious thought was given to averting war on the basis of the resumption of limited trade in return for Japan's abstention from a southern thrust. In Washington the military planners felt such a bargain was worthwhile, in order to gain time and wait for the outcome of the European conflict. It was considered imperative to prevent Japan's advance into Malaya and elsewhere and this could be done, it was felt, only by agreeing to the resumption of trade. It was at this point that the question of China assumed decisive proportions. Partially it was a military question. Japan might refrain from advancing into southeast Asia and even withdraw forces from Indochina, but it would still be predominant in China. There was no assurance that Japanese troops might not again attempt to thrust southward. Moreover, the British were adamant on the question of China. Winston Churchill believed that the collapse of China would menace the British position in southeast Asia. Thus he would have the United States insist on total evacuation of Japanese troops from Indochina, and he also opposed concessions in China. The United States, committed to joint defense with Britain and the Dutch, had to consider such views.

More fundamentally, however, there was American revulsion at the idea of sacrificing China in order to arrive at a deal with Japan merely to gain time. Here was, as Americans saw it, a moral question. It seemed morally wrong to compromise with Japan without considering China's destiny. Harry Dexter White, assistant secretary of the Treasury, was expressing a commonly held opinion when he wrote, in August 1941, "To sell China to her enemies . . . will not only weaken our national policy in Europe as well as in the Far East, but will dim the bright luster of America's world leadership in the great democratic fight against Fascism." The dualism in American thinking, dividing the world into fascist aggressors and peace-loving peoples, dictated the conclusion that the destinies of America and China were bound closely together, as two free, democratic nations fighting against totalitarianism. When the State Department considered accepting a temporary modus vivendi with Japan in November, Treasury Secretary Henry Morgenthau wrote a note, drafted by White, opposing such moves. "No matter what explanation is offered the public of a 'truce' with Japan," the note asserted, "the American people, the Chinese people, and the oppressed peoples of Europe, as well as those forces in Britain and Russia who are with us in this fight, will regard it as a confession of American weakness and vacillation." From Chungking, Owen Lattimore, adviser to Chiang Kai-shek, telegraphed, "A relaxation of American pressure while Japan has its forces in China would dismay the Chinese. Any modus vivendi now arrived at with [Japan] would be disastrous to Chinese belief in America and analogous to the closing of the Burma Road, which permanently destroyed British prestige."

Similar statements can be multiplied. Here was moral concern with the destiny of China, or rather with an image of Chinese-American relations. America was pictured as having built up good will in China; Free China, a phrase that began to be used in official documents, looked to the United States for support and co-operation. Any compromise with Japan would do irreparable damage to the state of Sino-American relations. It was simply unthinkable to betray the Chinese trust in America. In the light of what we now know about Chinese Communist thinking at the time, the American image of China appears hollow, a product of the liberal American imagination. There is no question that America's view of China was part of its global picture, a picture in which the democracies of the world were seen as fighting against dictatorships.

Some, undoubtedly, were unhappy with such a characterization of American–East Asian relations. Ambassador Grew, while absolutely opposed to Japan's southern advance, remained unconvinced that the United States should take up China's cause against Japan with military force. As he wrote in September 1941, "I question whether it is in our own interest to see an impoverished Japan reduced to the position of a third-rate Power." He would have liked to see Japan continue as a stabilizer in East Asia, especially against the Soviet Union. Grew's colleague in China, Ambassador Clarence E. Gauss, wrote to the president in November, "it is important that we bear in mind that the defeat of Japanese aggression does not necessarily entail, as many Chinese think, our crushing Japan militarily. The complete elimination of Japan as a force in the Far East would not be conducive either to order or prosperity in this area." Both Grew and Gauss were thinking in the framework of power, rather than of morality, and were championing a cause that was daily becoming unpopular with the administration in Washington. "Japan has no friends in this country, but China has," wrote Secretary of Interior Harold Ickes. America's friendship with China was not on account of any consideration of power politics but was by then a moral concern for China's plight and heroic struggle against odds. Given an image of the Chinese placing their trust in American friendship, and an image of the American people eager to help the Chinese, there was no psychological possibility of coming to terms with Japan, however temporarily, if it meant sacrificing China. Unlike the Soviet leaders, who cavalierly entered into a non-aggression pact with Japan for their own national interest and later thought of reasons to justify it, American leaders were psychologically bound to an idealistic image of Chinese-American relations.

In view of the American attitude what is striking is not that no compromise with Japan was possible because of American-Chinese ties, but that there was any thought at all of such a compromise. A temporary modus vivendi with Japan was basically a military idea; it seemed imperative from the military point of view to postpone war with Japan, if only for three months. In the end military considerations were subordinated to moral principles, reinforced by concern for British security in southeast Asia. These two strategic and moral concerns remained the basis of American thinking as the United States entered war with Japan. Subsequent developments, however, were to demonstrate the tension between military objectives and more political and ideological concern with the fate of China.

The Chinese, too, had an image of friendship with America, but, as earlier, their view of Sino-American relations was by no means uniform or unqualified. Communist writers had a difficult time adjusting themselves to rapidly changing conditions in international relations—the Axis alliance, the Soviet-Japanese non-aggression pact, the German invasion of Russia, Japanese-American negotiations in Washington, and other developments. As expected there was less emphasis now on the alleged machinations of imperialist countries to collaborate against the Soviet Union. America was pictured as having emerged as the leader of the global war, determined to assert prominence in the world. In particular, the

United States was perceived as stiffening its attitude toward Japan and willing to step up assistance to China. The Japanese-Soviet pact was hailed as encouraging to China; now that there was no immediate prospect of war in the north, the Japanese imperialists would surely strike southward, thus inviting conflict with the United States. Such a situation would undoubtedly induce the latter to increase its aid to China, paralleling Soviet help to China. Though Communist writers initially warned that despite such help the Chinese people must in the end rely upon their own effort for national salvation, after the German invasion of Russia in June there emerged an unequivocal image of an international anti-fascist front against Germany, Italy and Japan. An author noted that the Soviet Union was the leader of the anti-fascist coalition, America was in its front line, and China was its pillar in the East. The United States, Britain, and the Soviet Union were termed the three greatest nations of the world, jointly defending humanity against the aggression of the fascist states. Throughout the summer and fall of 1941 there was a note of uneasiness concerning Japanese-American negotiations, but it is remarkable that few openly referred to United States imperialism and monopoly capitalism. A minority expressed the view that the United States might come to terms with Japan because the former would need the latter's assistance in a postwar struggle against socialism. But even these writers remained confident that America would not sacrifice China entirely. Huang Yaomien, writing for *World Culture* in mid-November, perhaps offered a psychologically most acceptable explanation of American policy by picturing the United States as divided between fascist-oriented isolationists and the anti-fascist majority of the population. The former were finance capitalists, and the latter democrats. The government's policy was swayed by the tug of war between the two, but some influential leaders seemed to take a compromising course, trying to take advantage of the global anti-fascist coalition in order to establish American hegemony in the postwar world. The implication here was that the United States would remain in the democratic camp so long as its policies reflected the aspirations of the people, but that there always remained reactionary propensity. Such a theory would explain almost anything, and for the time being the apparently uncompromising stand of the Washington government toward Japan satisfied Communist writers that the world coalition of democratic peoples was still secure and would in the end triumph over the forces of fascism and militarism.

Pro-Kuomintang writings naturally underplayed the role of the Soviet Union in the East Asian conflict. They expressed their regret at the signing of the Soviet-Japanese non-aggression pact as a betrayal of Sino-Soviet friendship. Still, most writers remained convinced that the United States would step up aid to China and that sooner or later Japan would advance southward, thus inviting a clash with America. There was an optimistic image of America as economically and militarily a far superior nation to Japan; these writers believed, therefore, that no matter what happened in areas outside East Asia, an eventual Pacific war would bring about Japan's downfall and China's salvation. In contrast to Communist-oriented writers, official and semi-official Kuomintang spokesmen held to an image of Sino-American friendship as a basic factor in the way of Japanese ambitions. In their view China was a member of a democratic alliance in the world, and the United States was its leader. There was every reason why the two should co-operate in Asia. The German invasion of the Soviet Union at first gave rise to the fear that by reducing pressure on Britain the new situation might delay America's intervention in the war. Soon, however, the Chinese recognized the emergence of a coalition among the United States, Britain, and Russia, and expressed the hope that the alliance would function as effectively in Asia as in Europe. Throughout the fall of 1941 Kuomintang opinion remained confident that the tides were changing in favor of China and that by determined economic and military co-operation Japan would be isolated in the Pacific. The Chungking regime naturally opposed the modus vivendi proposal discussed between Tokyo and Washington late in November, but it does not seem that the Chinese leaders really believed compromise was possible between Japan and the United States. They had come to view America's commitment to assist China as axiomatic; China's survival was considered vital to American security, and there could be no compromise between an aggressive, fascist Japan and the democratic United States.

Nationalist thinking on the United States in 1941 may further be illustrated by a speech made by Sun Fo, son of Sun Yat-sen and a high Kuomintang official, to a meeting of college students.

He pointed out that for many years China alone, under the National government, had shouldered responsibility for fighting against aggression and defending human justice and world peace. America, Britain, and other nations, he said, had failed to comprehend the historical significance of the Manchurian incident, regarding it as an isolated occurrence in East Asia. It was only after the outbreak of war in Europe, in particular since 1940, that the friendly powers came to realize that China's struggle against aggression was intimately linked to world peace. Now they recognized the truth that only through supporting China could peace be maintained in Asia and in the world. America, in particular, was determined to extend all necessary help to China. Such friendly support had been won by the Chinese people's persistent effort and perseverance. After the war China would emerge as one of the four major powers, in addition to America, Britain, and the Soviet Union. Unequal treaties would be abolished, the humiliating status as a semi-colony would disappear, and China would gain complete equality as one of the strongest nations in the world. Though the enemy disseminated the propaganda that China was not a democracy and did not deserve help from democracies, this was complete nonsense. China was a state governed by the "three people's principles" under the leadership of the Kuomintang, and there was no doubt that the nation was marching toward a democratic form of government.

Finally, for the Japanese, too, the developing crisis with the United States had more than a purely military meaning. At bottom was the image of Japan as the leader in Asia, opposed to the policies of the United States which stood for "the maintenance of the status quo, the conquest of the world, and the protection of democracy," as a General Staff memorandum noted. Under the circumstances, Japanese-American conflict was a "historical inevitability." As the Imperial rescript on the declaration of war stated, the United States and Britain had created chaos and confusion in Asia by supporting the Chungking regime, interfered in Japan's peaceful foreign commerce, and seriously menaced the nation's existence. Japanese existence was so defined as to include domination over Asia. Acceptance of the Hull note would have been tantamount to the rejection of the ideology that had underlined Japanese policy for a decade.

In the end, the Japanese navy's strategic decision to attack

Hawaii, as well as the European colonies in southeast Asia, demonstrated the failure of American policy, a policy that had been unable to imagine either the degree of Japanese military recklessness or the irrationality of pan-Asianism. For the Japanese, the ensuing attack on Pearl Harbor was a symbol of Asia's revolt against the West. Only the Chinese saw no need to reorient their thinking after the Pearl Harbor attack; they had foreseen it for a decade.

9
Images of the Pacific War

Americans, Chinese, and Japanese had never been more conscious of one another than during the Pacific war. It is only in the 1940's that one may rightly speak of international, rather than interstate, relations with respect to these countries. For this reason the wartime images, propaganda, and myths should not be lightly dismissed. They were part of the historical process in which these three peoples grew in awareness of one another. In the history of misunderstanding across the Pacific, the war years mark, not an extraordinary period of distortions and misconceptions, but rather a stage in the gradual expansion of interest in and knowledge about each other. What one should look for, in recalling the recent chapter in American-Asian relations, is evidence, not exclusively of mutual suspicion and mistrust, but also of an effort to grapple with common problems. The remarkable wartime experiences emerge as a significant chapter in American-Asian confrontation, in which a failure to understand was an index, not only of the inherent difficulties but also of the effort to overcome these difficulties in cross-cultural relations.

The facts of military developments can be summarized briefly. The Pearl Harbor attack transformed the Sino-Japanese war into an East Asian war, and Chinese soldiers began to be equipped with American materiel and assisted, sometimes directed, by American officers. Since Allied victory was expected sooner or later, however, the Chinese contribution to the Pacific war in terms of manpower and resources was less than during the preceding years. Instead, the rival factions in China spent their energy in preparing for a postwar confrontation. The Kuomintang, the Communists, and various warlords developed their own armed camps, in effect dividing up the unconquered part of China into several semi-autonomous zones. At the end of the Pacific war, the Communists controlled strategic areas and the countryside in north China, while the Nationalists were strong in western and southern China.

More active Chinese participation in the war, which would undoubtedly have affected Kuomintang-Communist relations, was precluded by the actual course of the war in the Pacific as well as in the Atlantic. In a total-war situation, developments in Asia and in Europe were closely linked, and America's decision to give priority to the defeat of Germany necessitated military adjustments in Asia. A strategy of defense was undertaken toward Japan, and instead of resorting to a counterattack from the China-Burma-India theater, "island hopping" tactics and the bombing of Japanese territories were adopted. Submarines and airpower were the crucial means of destroying Japan, rather than ground troops of the Allied nations. Then, too, the Soviet promise to enter the war against Japan reduced the strategic importance of the China-Burma-India zone. More than anything else, the development of the atomic bomb brought the conflict to a close much sooner than anticipated. All these developments had the effect of minimizing China's and southeast Asia's role in the war against Japan. Although Japan's invasion of these territories had led to the Pacific war, the war had in fact become naval and air warfare between Japan and the United States. After the initial successes, Japanese naval operations were gradually curtailed until, in 1945, all resources had to be mobilized to defend the home islands. But American airpower, climaxed in the dropping of two atomic bombs, proved superior to Japanese, and the emperor, overcoming the opposition of die-hard military leaders, moved to take the country out of the war. The failure to induce the Soviet Union to mediate between the combatants, and actual Soviet participation late in the war, were additional factors that contributed to the termination of the conflict in August 1945.

An intellectual history of the Pacific war yet remains to be written. A study of how the various participants in the war rationalized their roles and incorporated the exaggerated notions of wartime into their own self-images would offer a fruitful and meaningful field of inquiry. Here only a bare outline is offered, in the hope that wartime images would be viewed as a historical phenomenon, related to the past as well as to the present.

The Overcoming of Modernity

In Japan the intellectuals grasped the meaning of the Pacific war as "the overcoming of modernity." The struggle against Anglo-American civilization could be viewed as an effort to transcend the Western-dominated stage in modern history and establish new concepts of international relations. It is illuminating to note that in Japan there was a widespread sense of rebirth at the news of the opening of hostilities with the United States. The poet Takamura Kōtarō, for instance, wrote as he heard the news of the Pearl Harbor attack, "The world has entered a new stage; history has just ushered in a new epoch. It looks as though yesterday were a long time past. The present has been raised to a new height in order to march toward the future, on a steady course, with a pure and profound meaning, and emanating light." World history seemed to have entered a new stage, and all of a sudden the history of Japan from times past and especially since the coming of Perry seemed to make sense. Japan was going to be reborn, to throw off the shackles of superficial Westernization, and assume a new path of renovation and mission, to bring justice and harmony among the nations of the earth. The sense of exaltation and the recognition of rebirth were phenomena particularly noted among Japan's intellectuals. It was as though the bold military stroke against the dreaded Western power had served to drive away the mist of self-doubt and clouds of ambiguity and skepticism that had characterized the thought of Japanese intellectuals since the Meiji Restoration. It was felt that the nation had at last come to grips with its real enemy—not China, but Western power and culture. As a writer noted, the Japanese had been groping for a principle, an ethic based on a new world view. The struggle against Anglo-Saxon civilization and imperialism, the construction of a new zone of culture in Asia—these were the principles Japan had just discovered. Like the naval battle of Salamis, the Pearl Harbor attack would mark a turning point in the cultural history of the world. Japan was at last liberating itself from Anglo-Saxon influence, wrote an old novelist, and marching on the path of autonomy and independence. Japan's national life seemed to have been purified and raised up as a result of the blow delivered to the Americans at Pearl Harbor.

From the Japanese point of view, the meaning of the Pacific war—their Great East Asian War—was so self-evident that all Asians should fully co-operate with them. It was hard to understand why the Chinese should continue to resist Japan; why they remained content to work as tools of non-Asians. Japan and China shared the mission to destroy the influence of Anglo-Saxon democracy and Soviet Communism and restore Asia to Asians. Apart from a core of Communists, who had refused to join their comrades in the mass recantations of the 1930's, there were few who questioned these theses. For both ultranationalists and leftist thinkers, the spectacle of Asia's counteroffensive against the West was gratifying. It seemed as though Asia, under Japanese leadership, was evolving a new culture, distinct from the humanism, democracy, and inherent hypocrisy of the West. "Rise, peoples of Asia," sang a poet, "rise and resurrect yourselves to the sun. . . . Restore to yourselves what is yours." Officially, pan-Asianism was given expression in 1943, when a Great East Asian Conference was held in Tokyo. Representatives of Japan, China, Thailand, Manchukuo, the Philippines, and Burma adopted a declaration asserting that these countries were co-operating to liberate Great Asia from the yoke of Britain and the United States. The nations of Asia would further work together to promote cultural and economic integration among themselves and contribute to world peace and friendship.

Much was written about the United States by Japanese in wartime, yet little was said. Every official, writer, and even schoolchild penned his thoughts about the past and present of Japanese-American relations, but what they wrote displayed almost identical clichés and stereotypes. First of all, there was a mushrooming of what might be called a literature of eschatology. Titles such as *The Final Reckoning with America and Britain, The Beginning of the Decline of America and Britain, A Chronology of the Anglo-American Invasion of East Asia,* and *A History of the Anglo-American Invasion of Asia* give some idea of the predominant attitude. This last book, written by the leading theorizer of pan-Asianism, Ōkawa Shūmei, typified wartime Japanese thinking: the war, Ōkawa said, was only a final chapter in the century-old struggle against British and American imperialism, which had subjugated Asia by enforcing capitalism and the Western political status quo. The imperialists had applied the principle of justice only to themselves and opposed Japan because it stood for true justice for all. "They have for many years wanted war with us, and now they have been given what they wanted."

A view of America as materially superior but spiritually inferior to Japan, a common wartime image, was implicit in such ideas. Some took America's economic and natural resources seriously. Ishihara Kanji, who had earlier advocated preparedness against the United States, is said to have predicted, on December 8, 1941, that Japan would surely lose the war because it simply could not compete with America's material power. But even the optimists did not deny that Japan was inferior in potential economic and military strength; that was the reason why they had decided to strike the first blow. After Pearl Harbor, the Japanese held it to be virtually certain that the United States would in time stage a comeback, confronting Japan with its profound resources. In the realm of the non-material aspects of the war, however, the Japanese indulged in much wishful thinking. To them America, the embodiment of capitalism and individualism, seemed morally unfit to fight the more dedicated Japanese. Americans were described as capricious, selfish, and incapable of group action. They were so accustomed to luxury and democratic life that they would be unable to achieve national mobilization. They would find the tension of war unbearable. Sooner or later the fabric of American society would break down.

Such complacency in time gave way to a sense of desperation. Because America, together with Britain, had come to symbolize the modern era which the Japanese were seeking to "overcome," the Japanese leaders were willing to turn in all directions just to escape a defeat at the hands of the American enemy. They offered a truce with Chungking, even suggesting the liquidation of the Nanking regime, and they sought to negotiate with the Soviet Union so as to keep it out of the war. In the spring of 1945 the Japanese government was ready to give up Sakhalin and even Manchuria in order to purchase Russian neutrality. It is suggestive that the Japanese leaders who began sounding out possibilities of a negotiated peace, and eventually accepted the Potsdam terms for peace, did so in the hope that Japan's imperial institution and other "essences" of the polity would be kept intact. Even more striking is their assertion that surrender was necessitated because the enemy had resorted to the use of a cruel inhuman weapon, the atomic bomb. Defeat could be accepted as a material, military failure of the nation against a wealthier foe, without questioning the moral basis of the Pacific war.

A New Spokesman for Asia

The Chinese had anticipated the coming of a Japanese-American war for so long that they needed little reorientation of their thinking when they became formally allied to the United States. At the same time, the Pacific war affected their world views in many ways. A good example is given by the speech by Sun Fo, made on the day Japan struck Pearl Harbor. As a result of the Japanese attack, he said, the alliance of the United States, Britain, the Soviet Union, and China in the Pacific had now become a reality. They must now firmly co-operate until the German and Italian, as well as Japanese, aggressors were completely wiped out. From then on the world would be "a world of America, Britain, China, and Russia." Gone was the fear that the United States might enter into a temporary modus vivendi with Japan, thus leaving the latter free to subjugate China. Now that the United States had entered the war, Japanese defeat became a foregone conclusion.

As we have seen, the earlier pessimistic, defensive self-image of China as a weak country, the victim of imperialistic aggression, now gave way to a much more confident view. China, it was held, was fighting alongside the democratic forces of the world for the sake of peace and justice. At the end of the war the nation would emerge as one of the triumphant and one of the greatest powers. As long as the Asian conflict and the European war had been separated, Sun Fo noted on another occasion, there was the fear that China might not occupy a prominent seat in the postwar peace conference. But now "a global structure of war" had been completed, in which the world was divided between the forces of aggression and anti-aggression, between civilization and barbarism. As a spearhead of the anti-aggression movement, China must expect to hold a leading position in the postwar world.

China, however, would be a unique power after the war because of its semi-colonial past. As a writer noted in Chungking, "China will be the stabilizing force in the Pacific. It will have responsibilities for the oppressed peoples of Asia, but it will exercise no arbitrary power over them. China is powerful, but it has no ambitious plans for aggression." An article for *People's Diplomacy,* published in Chungking, pointed out in 1943 that the postwar peace must be maintained on the basis of three principles: respect for the weak nations' interests and status, removal of racial prejudices, and elevation of democratic ideas to the level of world politics. China would champion these causes; in fact it would emerge as the spokesman for the oppressed peoples of the world. This was the meaning of the war. Underlying these thoughts was the persistent belief that ultimately the predicament of China had been brought about by imperialism, Japanese and Western. It followed that not only Japanese militarism but other kinds of imperialism must be eradicated if Asia was to enjoy a lasting peace after the war. Though there seems to have been no agreement as to what this meant in specific detail, Chinese writings in wartime suggest that they visualized the restoration to China of all the territories foreigners had snatched away after the Opium War, and the independence of Korea, Vietnam, Burma, India, and the Indies. The United States had already promised Philippine independence. Only on the basis of independent states in Asia could peace be secured in the whole world.

Chinese wartime views of the United States were related to such images of the postwar world. To the extent that Americans, too, talked of China as one of the big four powers and of racial equality and international justice, their words fitted into the Chinese perception of the United States. The Chinese were naturally gratified that in 1943, at last, the American and the British governments signed new treaties with China, abolishing extraterritoriality and otherwise relinquishing the vestiges of special rights. As Chiang Kai-shek noted on the occasion, by their acts the United States and Britain had shown that they were indeed fighting for humanism and justice. The frustrations and failures of the Chinese Republic had been due to the existence of the unequal treaties, Chiang said. Now that independence and liberty had been restored, the Chinese must be united and so successfully consummate their revolution. The year 1943 was indeed a historic moment for modern China. The United States revised its immigration laws, enabling a limited number of Chinese to immigrate; Roosevelt and Churchill announced the unconditional-surrender formula at their meeting in Casablanca; and later on in the year Chiang Kai-shek joined them for a meeting in Cairo. There the Allied leaders endorsed a peace plan that would strip Japan of all the territories it had obtained from China. Chiang's *China's Destiny,* which was also published that year, reflects a sense of self-confidence amid such diplomatic victories.

At the same time, from the Chinese point of view, there was some uncertainty as to the degree of America's commitment to China's cause as well as to the Kuomintang regime. The Chinese were fearful that the United States might concentrate on the European theater of war and ignore the immediate needs of China against Japan. Some expressed concern that the United States and the Soviet Union might co-operate closely without seeking Chinese advice. When Nicholas J. Spykman's *America's Strategy in World Politics* (see page 242) appeared, some Chinese, sensitive to trends in American thinking, were deeply impressed. The book seemed to reveal the persistent influence of the balance-of-power school of thought. It was appalling, as Sun Fo remarked, that some Americans had not learned that "realism" had been the basic cause of the world catastrophe. It was nonsense to say, as Spykman did, that China would come to threaten world peace after the war. At the same time, Sun Fo went on to say, postwar peace would never be long-lasting so long as foreigners isolated China through their prejudice, fear, and suspicion. China must be given an absolute equality of opportunity, and the views of the Chinese people, who comprised one-fifth of the world's population, must be heard in the building of a constructive peace.

The over-all attitude of the Chinese in Chungking, however, was one of trust in American friendship and support. More than anything else, they had to believe that the United States would continue to deal with the Kuomintang and assist its effort to unify Free China. While the Chungking government consistently talked of the great alliance with the Soviet Union and Britain as well as with the United States, its references to America were usually the most impassioned and warmest. From about 1943, when some Americans began to murmur complaints about Chiang Kai-shek's handling of the war, and Communist strength and defiance of the Kuomintang became marked, the Nationalists had the need to depict their relations with the United States as most intimate and perpetual. This was a way of assuring themselves that America would continue to support them. A Kuomintang publication of July 1943, for instance, referred to the "two great peoples, whose sentiments are in harmony and who have very close ties, because they share similar spiritual foundations for the building of their respective nations." While the assistance of Russia and Britain to China was also noted, the United States was pictured as the only country that had consistently supported China against Japan after the Manchurian incident. Madam Chiang's visit to America that year was another demonstration of Chungking's effort to secure American help against both the Japanese and the Communists.

By 1944, when the Chinese Communists began pressing for the establishment of a coalition government in China, all factions and groups took it for granted that the United States was in a position—and had the power—to influence the course of events inside China. Chiang Kai-shek kept telling Americans, as he told Vice-President Henry Wallace in 1944, that the Chinese Communists were more communistic than the Russians and thus a subversive group in Free China. A coalition with them, which would enable them to share in the arms and supplies provided by the United States, was therefore out of the question. Throughout 1944, when the Japanese resorted to a final offensive in China, the Chinese forces offered little resistance, in order to save men and ammunition for an eventual domestic showdown. Chiang was confident of continued

American support, since the United States would not dare forsake him in the middle of a war; he took a calculatedly stubborn attitude toward his American chief of staff, General Joseph Stilwell, who was demanding the distribution of American arms to all forces in China. After Stilwell's recall, Chiang worked successfully to assure the support of his successor, General Albert Wedemeyer, and the new ambassador, Patrick Hurley. At the same time, there was a need to demonstrate his sincerity in striving for a more unified and democratic government. In 1944 and 1945 he talked apologetically of the delay in bringing about a constitutional government and promised steps to eradicate the corruption of officials and the hardship of the common people. All this was designed to answer American critics and maintain his position as the leader of Free China.

The Chinese Communists, too, recognized the enormous influence of the United States in Chinese domestic politics and sought to bend it in their favor. Before 1944, however, they were relatively quiet about the internal strife in China, stressing the united front against Japan. During the Pacific war, "imperialism" came to mean Japanese imperialism. The United States was not referred to as imperialistic for most of the duration of the war. Instead, the Communists stressed in glowing terms America's role in the war. The abolition of the unequal treaties in 1943 made it easier to do so. It is remarkable that the Kuomintang and Communist references to the new treaties were almost identical; in the words of Chu Teh, the army leader, the treaties had not only swept away China's unequal status in the world but also strengthened China's union with Britain and the United States. The nation must further co-operate with the anti-fascist allies, noted the *Liberation Daily,* so that Japanese imperialism would be eradicated and the Chinese people would win final victory and liberation. At the same time, the signing of the treaties was made another occasion for stressing the need for co-operation between factions in China. As a Communist commentator noted, during the first united front between the Communists and the Kuomintang considerable progress had been made in revising the existing treaties; the achievement of 1943 was also brought about by the wartime united front. China must therefore continue to be united, not only to crush Japanese imperialism, "our only enemy," but also to build a new nation after the war.

After 1944 the Communists' views of the United States came to depend on the latter's support of their demand for a coalition government. At first they seem to have been confident of America's sympathy for such a program. To the American journalists and officials who visited their headquarters in Yenan, Communist leaders stressed the need for a democratic government and called on the United States to use its influence to induce Chungking to give up its opposition to the scheme. The Communists must have been encouraged by the growing criticism of the Kuomintang in the American press and among official circles. While the existence and influence of anti-communist groups within the United States were recognized, it was hoped that the Communists could win American support by picturing themselves as the representatives of the democratic forces in China, fighting resolutely against the Japanese imperialists.

After Stilwell's recall, the Communists became more and more concerned with America's continued recognition of Chiang Kaishek as the government of China, a policy known as the "Hurley strategy." In the absence of massive Soviet aid, and in fact due to the Soviet policy of dealing with the Chungking government, the Chinese Communists had still to reckon with the power of the United States to influence the course of events within China. Somehow it was necessary to appeal to the "progressive" elements in American society so as to prevent the United States from backing up Chiang. Mao Tse-tung's "On Coalition Government," a statement of policy issued in the spring of 1945, best summarizes the Chinese Communist attitude just before the end of the war. "Americans," he said, "whom we used to think were very far away, have now become our neighbors." He expressed the hope that they, together with the peoples of Britain, Russia, France, and other countries, would strive to construct a lasting peace in the world. In particular, he thanked the United States for its role in opposing the Japanese aggressors and noted its sympathy for and assistance to the Chinese people. America was defined by Mao as an antifascist, democratic country. At the same time, he called on the American and British governments to "pay attention to the voice of the Chinese people, so that their foreign policies would not impair the friendship with the Chinese people." He recognized that certain groups in America supported the reactionary elements in

China, and explained this phenomenon by postulating that there were progressive and reactionary, democratic and anti-democratic elements within the United States. It was the latter, represented by Hurley, that dominated the thinking of the government in Washington. However, Mao asserted, the combination of reactionary cliques in America and China was but a transitory phenomenon, for it ran counter to the currents of history. "In the present world, democracy is the main current, and the anti-democratic reaction is only a counter-current." Thus the American people, representing the historical current, would surely rise and restore friendship between the two peoples by terminating ties with the Chungking regime. The point was further stressed in another speech Mao made at this time. "We must distinguish," he said, "between the American people and their government, and between the decision makers within the government and the lower-ranking, ordinary officials." It was incumbent upon the lower officials and the people of America to repudiate the Hurley strategy and deepen ties with the Chinese people as represented by the Communists.

Kuomintang-Communist differences, however, should not be made to obscure the basic identity of views among all groups in China as to the shape of postwar East Asia. The Communists were in complete agreement with the Nationalists that China must emerge as a strong power, an equal member of the international community at the end of the war. As Mao Tse-tung said in April 1945, important international problems in the future must be solved through co-operation by the United States, Britain, the Soviet Union, China, and possibly France. He also called for the independence of India, Burma, Malaya, Indochina, the Dutch East Indies, and Korea. Such an image of postwar Asia was identical with the one pictured by the Nationalists. No matter who emerged as the leader of China, then, the Chinese were serving notice that they would not be satisfied with anything less than a status as one of the major powers in the postwar world.

War for a Democratic Asia

In America, meanwhile, many "lessons" were being drawn from the cruel fact of war in the Pacific. "We must never forget what we have learned," said President Roosevelt in his address of December 9, 1941. America had learned that there "is no such thing as security for any nation . . . in a world ruled by the principles of gangsterism." While this kind of globalism had underlined official American thinking since the mid-1930's, the Pearl Harbor attack seemed to illustrate the truth more forcefully than ever before. For, as Roosevelt continued to say, "We have learned that our ocean-girt hemisphere is not immune from severe attack—that we cannot measure our safety in terms of miles on any map." War had become total, not only involving civilians and home industries, but also the entire world into conflagration. The corollary of this lesson was the all-too-late realization that the United States should have intervened more actively when predatory nations had begun showing their designs. "War began in 1931 when Japan invaded China," as Secretary of State Hull stated. Since then Japan had been bent on the conquest of Asia and, in conjunction with Germany and Italy, of the entire world. Americans should have recognized that evil and stood up resolutely in defense of freedom. Since the State Department under Hull had been in charge of America's foreign affairs during the time that the secretary said the nation should have resisted aggression, it was natural that he should have come in for a good deal of criticism immediately after Pearl Harbor.

The lesson that freedom was indivisible and must be defended resolutely whenever it was threatened has stayed with the American consciousness. This explanation of the origins of the war obviously implied that the Second World War would end only when the forces of freedom and democracy triumphed over those of totalitarian tyranny. The latter must be crushed and prevented from ever again asserting themselves. More specifically, Japanese militarism must be totally eliminated, so that Japan would never resort to violence in the future. There was considerable debate as to how the objective was to be achieved. Many called for dissolution of the *zaibatsu* (financial combines) and agrarian reforms, on the theory that the social and economic foundation of Japanese militarism must be removed. Others pointed out the need for a wholesale "psychological disarmament," so that the Japanese would never again delude themselves into thinking that they were invincible and a law unto themselves. Still others insisted on the abolition of the Imperial institution, as they equated militarism with the emperor system. Some officials, notably former ambassador Grew, came under criticism since they favored the retention of the institution. This in fact became official policy, although it was never clearly stated so as not to compromise the principle of unconditional surrender. There was basic consensus among the American people and officials, however, that sweeping social, economic, and educational reforms would have to accompany the destruction of Japanese militarism and imperialism in order to foster a sense of security in postwar Asia.

Such thoughts were directly related to the American views of the postwar world. The war was being fought, said a typical writer, "for the construction of a democratic, rationally managed, fully productive world order, without which the military struggle cannot result in victory, and without which the fruits of victory cannot be realized." Because of America's military involvement in East Asia, it was natural that visions of the postwar world should have allotted a significant role to the countries of Asia. There were two aspects to that role, as seen by most American writers. It was taken for granted that China, victorious over Japan, would emerge as a strong power and replace its enemy as the central force in East Asia. Secondly, peoples of Asia were pictured as likely to shake loose from the colonial order and assert their independence.

One of the clearest and most widely read views on the second point was Wendell Willkie's *One World*. He made a forty-nine day trip around the world in 1942 that left him impressed not only with the world's oneness but also with the emergent importance of the East in the world's politics. He wrote, "Brilliant victories in the field will not win for us this war now going on in the far reaches of the world. . . . [Only] new men and new ideas in the machinery of our relations with the peoples of the East can win the victory without which any peace will be only another armistice." He, like most of his fellow Americans, took the Atlantic Charter seriously and believed the Allies stood for much more than the military defeat of their enemies. Only by bringing freedom to the colonial peoples could the United States and its Allies be said to be fighting in a noble cause and for an enduring peace. If "we hope to prevent war in the future," as Willkie wrote, "we must know what are the forces at work" in East Asia. As he saw that part of the world, the Chinese were identifying themselves with these forces, the forces of freedom and independence. The United

States must work with them and try to bring Chinese national aspirations to fruition. "If we are wise, we can direct forces which are in being throughout the East toward world co-operative effort for peace and economic security. These same forces, however, if they are flouted or ignored, will continue to disturb the world." The fact that *One World* was received enthusiastically by reviewers and sold over one million copies indicates the receptivity of the American public to such ideas. Other writers joined the chorus, demanding freedom, independence, and democracy in postwar Asia. "A plan for a democratic new order in Asia, based on India and China, but including also all the other Asiatic peoples," was called forth by *The New Republic*. "Only a firm stand on the principle of human equality for all peoples," Pearl Buck reminded her readers, "will give us the final victory necessary for a real peace in this world. If we do not make that stand now by speaking out clearly and independently to reassure the great people of the East, then while we fight this war we are begging the next one." What she, Willkie, and others visualized for China was a country rid of foreign colonies such as Hong Kong and foreign privileges such as extraterritoriality and concessions. But above all, they pictured an Asia emerging out of centuries of backwardness and Western subjugation into fully equal status. From such a perspective, it was not difficult to conceive that the war was "somehow the war of a democratic world revolution which bursts the neat and trim confines of Anglo-Saxon superiority," as a commentator noted. What underlay these views was an idea of history—the Pacific war was comprehended historically so that the Japanese-American war was fitted into the picture of an awakening East coming into its own and blossoming into co-operation with the West. In this sense the war was truly global; it was not merely a fratricidal conflict among nations of the West, but one accompanying a world-wide democratic upheaval which would result in the defeat of the forces of imperialism and oppression and triumph of the forces of genuine democracy and international co-operation.

While everyone may have shared a vision of East-West equality, the translation of this vision into a practical democratic social order was another matter. Thus only a small minority of American writers protested vigorously against the administration's apparent lack of initiative in promising independence to the people of East Asia.

At home, prejudice against the Chinese did not abate. There was no question, however, that whether they approved of it or not Americans would have to reckon with the possibilities of change in postwar Asia. It was virtually unanimously held that without stability and economic progress in East Asia there would remain the danger of another global conflict, and that such stability and progress depended to a great extent on the emergence of China as a central force. It is a theme commonly found among wartime American writings that the postwar peace would have to be guaranteed within the framework of co-operation among the United States, Britain, the Soviet Union, and China. Secretary of State Hull said, in 1944, "there is no hope of turning victory into enduring peace unless the real interests of this country, the British Commonwealth, the Soviet Union, and China are harmonized and unless they agree and act together. This is the solid framework upon which all future policy and international organization must be built." Joseph Stilwell told T. V. Soong in 1943, "A powerful and independent China . . . could take the lead in the organization of an Asiatic League of China, Siam, Burma, and India. The Pacific Ocean would be controlled jointly by the United States and China, with no conflicts of interest in the Dutch East Indies, Australia or the Philippine Islands." The view of postwar China as an Asian power was written into official policy, as the Roosevelt administration obtained the acquiescence of Britain and the Soviet Union to count China as one of the big four in the forthcoming United Nations organization.

Not everyone, it is true, had an idealistic vision of the Asian future. There were some "realists," perhaps best illustrated by Nicholas J. Spykman, whose *America's Strategy in World Politics* was published in 1942. He found continued validity in the traditional concepts of geopolitics and applied them to current international affairs. For him the balance of power was still the basic mechanism for preserving peace, and national self-interests were the legitimate motive of foreign policy. What is notable, however, is that he agreed with the more idealistic writers and officials that China would emerge from the war as one of the strong powers of the world. The "power potential" of China, he wrote, was infinitely greater than that of Japan, and a "modern, vitalized, and militarized China" would be in a position to control the whole of southeast Asia by its air power. To balance it the United States should preserve Japanese power and seek a regional agreement in Asia to check Chinese power. Such "realism" was immediately attacked as too traditionalist and insensitive to the new currents in international affairs. Those were times of change, as Ruth Benedict wrote, and any attempt to perpetuate the old concepts and practices of diplomacy was bound to fail. Many reviewers reassured the Chinese who, as noted above, expressed shock at Spykman's ideas, that these by no means represented the thinking of most Americans.

What these writers and officials said was one thing. While they talked of China's future as a great power, actual policy toward that country was dictated more by military developments, not only in Asia but elsewhere, than by sentiment. In fact, President Roosevelt may have encouraged the vision of "four big policemen" in order to bolster Chiang Kai-shek's ego while the Generalissimo's requests for more military aid had to be turned down. As the importance of the China-Burma-India theater of the war declined, moreover, Roosevelt referred less and less to the theme of American-Chinese co-operation in postwar East Asia; he was much more committed to an idea of American-Soviet co-operation. On the eve of the Yalta conference in February 1945, the president reportedly admitted that "three generations of education and training would be required before China could become a serious factor." Such a reappraisal of China's strength may have made it psychologically easier for the president at Yalta to make certain concessions to Stalin which clearly impinged upon Chinese sovereignty. By promising to the Soviet Union, in return for its entry into the war against Japan, most of the rights Tsarist Russia had enjoyed in Manchuria before the Russo-Japanese War, Roosevelt was making it unlikely that China would emerge as a sovereign power after the war.

Which China?

The question whether China was to emerge as one of the big powers after the war was intimately connected with American perceptions of Chinese domestic politics. If China was to become a major force in East Asia and co-operate with the United States to preserve peace and freedom, it followed that postwar China would and should be a truly free and democratic nation. All the "four big policemen" were by definition free—forces against tyranny and aggression. If the Chinese, and in particular the Nationalists, were found to be not as free and democratic as Americans had pictured them, some reorientation of American thinking was necessary.

Those Americans who were skeptical of China's claim to big-power status were on the whole more willing to be cynical about the alleged qualities of heroism and democracy among the Chinese. As many wartime correspondents have testified, the glowing picture of China that was being depicted by the American press at home was not shared by seasoned diplomats and the bulk of the newly arrived American officer corps in Chungking. They mistrusted colorful rhetoric and were prone to see in China little more than a mass of miserable and xenophobic people ruled by a corrupt and equally anti-foreign government. They did not believe that the war had transformed the Chinese people and purged them of their inherent anti-foreignism. In the view of these Americans, the Chinese were constantly feuding against one another, were untrustworthy, valued human life little, and secretly hated the white man. Some Americans even suspected that the Chinese must have been pleased to see the mighty United States and the British empire humiliated by the Japanese navy. Thousands of young recruits who were sent to China found an ill-smelling land filled with filth and disease. For these Americans, the talk of China's becoming a major power was nonsense if not ridiculous.

For the majority of Americans who stayed home, and for a significant handful of American officials in China, the vision of Sino-American co-operation in postwar Asia was no fantasy. They sincerely believed in the possibility of such co-operation. For this very reason, they were troubled by the gap between image and reality. Literally millions of Americans had come to picture the Chinese as a heroic, hard-working people struggling against a superior enemy with fortitude and perseverance. The outbreak of the Pacific war had brought the Sino-Japanese war nearer home; since America's war goals were defined in terms of the defense of freedom and democracy, it followed that the Chinese, too, were devoting themselves to the same cause. America and China, typically wrote one author, were "two large democracies whose combined populations represent more than one-quarter of mankind."

It did not seem entirely facetious to compare Chiang Kai-shek to George Washington and T. V. Soong to Alexander Hamilton. The Chinese people's "dogged struggle for independence," "magnificent spirit and courage," and "hardened and valiant" army were oft-heard clichés.

It did not take long before reports began arriving from Free China which did not seem to corroborate these facile images. One of the earliest alarmist writings appeared in *The New Republic.* In its November 16, 1942, issue, Michael Straight pointed out that "500,000 of the Generalissimo's best troops are engaged in besieging their fellow Chinese, the communists, in Shansi. Wherever the communist soldiers are moving down to fight the Japanese they are executed." Straight thought the trend toward a one-party state in China was unmistakable and closely linked to the failure of the major Western powers to allot a meaningful and equal status to China; the more the Westerners disregarded Chinese aspirations, the more reactionary the leaders in Chungking could become, because a dictatorial government might seem to be the only logical way to achieve national greatness. Straight thus suggested that Britain, Russia, and America must first of all raise China "to a position of full partnership in the United Nations" and then "mediate between the Kuomintang and the Chinese communists, in order that China's civil war may be ended." From this time on, *The New Republic* came to take a distinctly anti-Kuomintang line in its descriptions of Chinese politics. China, earlier built up as a great democratic nation, was shown to be torn by internal dissension. It was natural therefore that the Chungking regime should be criticized for its apparent lack of determination to fight the Japanese and its interest in consolidating its own power at the risk of perpetuating the civil strife. "Many of the men around Chiang Kai-shek come very close to being fascists," was one way of explaining the unpleasant news coming out of wartime China. This was the "moral crisis of the war." If the United States was fighting not only for its own survival and security but also for a saner world order and for nobler principles, the idea of an alliance with a fascistic government was obviously repugnant.

The picture of the Chinese Communists as more truly representative of the people of China offered a plausible solution to the dilemma. If one had a vision of the future of China as an independent and free country, in alliance with the United States, and if one yet found in China a regime apparently ridden by corruption and dictatorial tendencies, the discovery of a more democratic and efficiently organized group of men was an attractive alternative. This line of reasoning began to be heard more and more prominently after 1943. In the celebrated article in the *Far Eastern Survey,* "China's Part in a Coalition War," T. A. Bisson bluntly characterized Nationalist China as feudal China, representing the old and the backward, unworthy of American alliance and of participation in a global democratic coalition. There was, however, a second China, represented by the Communists, that might be called democratic China. Democracy here was defined in the vein of Marxist historiography; Bisson held that China, like all other societies, went through the feudal and bourgeois stages, and the Chinese Communists were bringing their country to the latter stage, the period of bourgeois democracy. Instead of a feudal political structure based on an agrarian economy, segments of China under Communist control were undergoing a transition to a free enterprise system with a minimum of political control. This was not Communism. In other words, the Chinese Communists in this view were allotted a historical task of bringing China into the modern era. Since their opponents, the Kuomintang, represented the counter trend, it was evident with which group the democratic forces of the world should identify themselves.

While such a view of the Chinese Communists has been attacked as naïve, if not downright subversive, it must be noted that the simplistic image of China was fundamentally a product of the vision of Sino-American co-operation in Asia. There could be no co-operation between democratic America and totalitarian China. If the Chungking regime was found to be not as liberal or democratic as had been thought, there was an intellectual need to find some groups that fit the American conception of Free China more accurately. If one could somehow persuade oneself that the Communists' main objectives were "putting an end to landlordism, and aiding education and industrialization," as a writer put it, then it would become easy to subdue nascent and unwelcome doubts about the reality of Chinese-American co-operation. It was perhaps for this reason that many stressed the Chinese aspect of the Chinese Communists and underplayed their Communist and Soviet aspects.

The Communists were above all Chinese patriots; they were no tools of Soviet Communism. It followed that partnership between America and Communist China was not only possible but even desirable. Close ties between them would not only prevent the resurgence of Japanese militarism but also guard postwar Asia against whatever expansive designs Soviet Russia might possess. These views were put forward with special vigor by a group of American officials in China who worked with the military advisory corps. As John P. Davies, one of them, wrote in November 1944, "we must make a determined effort to capture politically the Chinese Communists rather than allow them to go by default wholly to the Russians."

At any rate, all Americans were agreed on the need to work out a coalition government in China. After 1943, magazine articles and official reports were more and more taken up by this question. Few were at first willing to see Chiang Kai-shek victimized and dropped. He had embodied the Chinese people's heroic struggle against Japan, and his wife's visit to the United States in the same year served to perpetuate the image. At the same time, if there were unmistakable signs of Kuomintang inefficiency and dictatorship, the way must bc opened for a more representative government. A *New Republic* article of March 13, 1944, candidly observed, "If in China Chiang Kai-shek is using our help to enthrone reaction at the expense of the war, our pressure should be the other way. We can't say we believe in our own system and at the same time, wherever a choice is possible, turn our back on it, all over the world." In other words, pressure must be exerted on Chungking as much as and even more than on the Communists, in order to encourage the emergence of a multi-party system of government in China. If, as it appeared likely, the Nationalists insisted on retaining their power and refused to share it with other groups, the implication was that the United States must be prepared to start actively supporting these groups, especially Communists. Throughout 1944, many civilian officials, especially those stationed at Chungking, came to accept such a conclusion.

Many, including officials in Washington, however, were reluctant to antagonize Chiang Kai-shek by openly defying him and championing the dissident groups. The National government was still the government of China, and it must be made the core of the new coalition. Since the organization of a coalition government entailed the question of distribution of American arms, the Communists were clamoring for a share of them. This, these Americans felt, would only perpetuate the internal division of China. The first essential thing was to get all the factions together, while confining American arms to the Chungking government. This amounted to putting pressure on the dissident groups instead of Chungking.

What would have happened if the war had been prolonged is not easy to say. In the absence of an unexpectedly quick victory in the Pacific, made possible by the atomic bomb raids on Japan, the China theater of war might have taken on much greater significance, and the problem of coalition might have become a real challenge to the United States. Then it would have had to choose between the continuation of the existing unsatisfactory situation and an active support of anti-Chungking elements. Either way the United States would have been deeply involved in Chinese internal affairs and opened itself to the charge of partisanship and interference by whatever faction it did not happen to support. As it is, the Pacific war ended before such a choice had to be faced, saving the United States from an embarrassing situation. Even so, the problem had been raised, and unless the nation decided to leave postwar East Asia to itself, its intervention in Chinese politics to some degree was inevitable.

It may be pointed out that whether Americans were Nationalist- or Communist-sympathizers, their vocabulary was almost always taken from the familiar language of Western history and institutions. Willkie referring to the war in China as "truly a people's war"; Stilwell condemning China's inefficiency; his successor, Albert Wedemeyer, visualizing the Kuomintang program in terms of the establishment of a constitutional republic; civilian officials describing the Communists as modern and democratic—these adjectives and phrases served to place China in one's scale of values and one's view of history, both Western. Even to say that wartime China was like wartime Russia, or that Chiang Kai-shek was a fascist, was a way of comparing things Chinese with things more familiar. Political vocabulary was still limited. This is probably one reason why extreme language was often used to describe a single person such as Chiang Kai-shek. Extremely good or bad examples were more easy to come by rather than more subtle comparisons. The very idea of coalition itself was Western. It seemed a simple matter to get all the factions in China together, since they were all at heart united on the war. As one writer noted, "there is no reason why the communists should not become the Left party, represented in a coalition government, just as they were before the war in various European countries. . . . Insofar as China moves toward democratic principles, the conflict between the communists and Chungking will be moderated." All this was perfectly true, if only China followed the European pattern of political behavior. "Loyal opposition," however, has been found to be one of the most sophisticated institutions of the parliamentary West and one of the hardest to graft to another political structure—whether Asian, African, or even South American. It might or might not have worked in China. In presupposing that it must, wartime Americans were reading their history into Chinese affairs and applying their political concepts to a tradition with different historical roots. When they found how difficult it was to bring Nationalists and Communists together, they found refuge in some other analogies from European history.

Wartime American images of China, however, must be viewed as a stage in the evolution of American-Chinese relations. While studies indicate that a majority of Americans still had a hazy notion even of where China was, there is no question that news about China reached the reading public in all sections of the country to a larger extent than ever before, and that China became part, no matter how small, of American consciousness for the first time in history. The very fact that controversy arose on the question of Chinese political institutions indicates the degree of commitment Americans felt toward China.

10
Chinese Communism and Postwar Sino-American Relations

The Pacific war brought sweeping changes in the political structure of East Asia. The end of the 1940's found the area purged of most of the empires, Japanese and European. In this new vacuum the United States had established itself as a super-power, with its nuclear weapons and military bases linking islands in the western Pacific. America, hitherto a Pacific power, had become an East Asian power. At the same time, China, which had been invaded by an enemy and where regional foci of power had challenged the nominally legitimate government, was emerging as a unified nation, already making moves toward administrative centralization and economic modernization. Finally, the Soviet Union had regained its status as an East Asian power as a result of the Yalta agreement, the Japanese defeat, and the Communist victory in China.

If one could somehow ignore the processes through which these results emerged, one would be able to conclude that the simultaneous appearance of three great countries in Asia—the United States,

China and the Soviet Union—was precisely what had been foreseen by many Allied strategists during the war. In terms of power relations, the wartime statesmen who had looked forward to a postwar East Asia whose peace would be maintained by these three, possibly with the co-operation of Great Britain, had been proved right; but instead of the anticipated friendship and co-operation, America and Russia, and America and China found themselves opposing one another—even talking of war. Herein lie the largely unexpected but essential characteristics of the immediate postwar years.

It is probably less surprising that Americans and Chinese should have found themselves in a state of potential antagonism than that they should have thought they were compatible in East Asia. Two such great countries, emerging as powers in the same geographical area, could not have been expected to opt for *a priori* friendship and good will. The wonder is, then, not that they eventually developed mutual hostility but that they should have thought at all about friendly relations. This, of course, was a heritage of the war. Wartime psychology had contributed to an image of Sino-American co-operation in postwar East Asia, and this image died hard, even as conditions that had temporarily brought about such co-operation were fast disappearing. The common Japanese menace was gone, the United States and the Soviet Union sought different objectives in China, and the question "which China?" was once again being decided in battle. In the years between the Japanese surrender and the Korean War, Chinese and Americans sought uneasily to adjust themselves to changing conditions but were unwilling to admit frankly that the two peoples might be in basic conflict. They still remembered wartime co-operation, while at the same time the new vocabulary of ideological confrontation was being introduced. That is why the strain in American and Chinese thinking was enormous.

The Gap Between Power and Policy

What happened in the American perception of China must be distinguished from what happened in China. If the American people had looked at China differently during the war, their postwar response might have taken a different form and a far less violent turn. As it was, the American mind reacted, not to China as such, but to the disappearance of a familiar image of Asia. In the postwar world Americans had at first assumed that the United States would control Japan, that China would be unified and strengthened through the American-supported Kuomintang, and that the Soviet Union would deal with these *faits accomplis,* recognizing the Nationalists as the government of China and meanwhile consolidating its own gains in East Asia. Peace and stability would be maintained on the basis of such understanding; above all, the new China would function as a provider of stability.

The view of Asia as dominated by America, Russia, and China, was derived from certain assumptions. One was that a Kuomintang-led China, if not a Kuomintang-dominated China, was feasible and could become the basis of new stability in Asia. Second, there was the assumption of Russian willingness to accept the emergence of a strong China under the Nationalists. Third, it was assumed that the United States could and should play an active role in helping the emergence of the new China. In the long run, the third assumption may have been the most significant. Few Americans questioned the right of their country to promote a political program in Asia and in particular in China. There was readiness to accept the fact of power and to approximate policy with power. The fundamental problem, of course, was that American power became less than well defined when it came to the continent of Asia. Just what American power implied, apart from the certitude that it could destroy any Asian nation by the use of nuclear weapons, remained unclear. Many assumed, however, that the United States had the power and therefore should have the will to be a determining factor in the course of events in China. The gap between power, actual and potential, and policy, real and intended, provided tension between the making of American policy and its discussion in the postwar years.

For the time being, however, failure of the other two assumptions to prove correct was a more serious matter for American thinking. The assumption that the Soviet Union would agree to accept a Kuomintang-led China was not far wrong. Unlike Eastern Europe, Soviet aims in East Asia were not clearly defined. There was no immediate interest in establishing puppet regimes whose existence depended on the presence of the Soviet army. Moscow was prepared to recognize the Nationalists as the government of China. However, the Russians seem to have assumed that China under the Kuomintang would remain weak and even divided so as not to menace Russian interests—like Austria or the Scandinavian states after the war. Russia did not want a strong China under Chiang Kai-shek, especially if it was backed by the United States. The Soviet leadership did not expect an immediate Communist victory in China, but it was deemed desirable to assist the Communists if only to the extent that China would remain divided and be prevented from entirely falling to the American sphere of influence. This was nothing new in Soviet policy, but wartime American expectations had been that Russia would collaborate with America's China policy. The failure of the expectations to materialize had a profound impact on American thinking.

Finally, the assumption of a strong China led by the Kuomintang proved untenable almost as soon as the Pacific war ended. Because the war came to an end with unexpected suddenness, the Nationalists had not had time to re-establish control over large segments of the country. Instead, key strategic areas were under Communist control. The Communists, contrary to official American expectation, offered stiff resistance to the formation of a unified government if it meant giving up their independent armies and arms before joining the government, as Chiang Kai-shek insisted they do. Thus the American belief, embodied in Ambassador Hurley's efforts, in a new China built around the Kuomintang was challenged, and what was more, the fact began to be recognized in official circles in Washington. By the end of 1945, the American government came to realize that under the circumstances to continue the Hurley strategy was tantamount to aiding one faction in China rather than supporting the government of the Chinese people.

The Marshall mission, which covered a span of over thirteen months, revealed America's continued interest in playing a positive role in postwar East Asia. This is illuminating. In Europe, American intentions were far from clear. The Russian policy of re-establishing control over Eastern Europe was vigorously protested under the principle of self-determination. But the protests were usually little more than verbal, and there was no clear-cut decision whether to entrench American influence in Europe, now that German military power had been destroyed. In Asia, on the other hand, there was a clearer policy of establishing a predominant position in Japan and playing an influential role in China. While postwar American policy toward China has been almost universally criticized, the policy does appear to have been better thought-out than policy toward Eastern Europe. The basic idea was that the United States should look toward China's unification and strengthening through some kind of unilateral American assistance. This was the initial philosophy behind the sending of George C. Marshall to China in December 1945. On that occasion, President Truman said that peace in the Pacific would depend on the replacement of Japan by a unified, democratic, and peaceful China. The United States was ready to accord technical, economic, and military assistance to the country once it set out on its road to unification.

There was nothing wrong about the ideal of helping China become unified and strong through American help. The failure of the Marshall mission should not perhaps lead one to condemn the ideas that underlay the mission. What is more open to criticism is the way Marshall and the State Department actually undertook their mediation efforts, and the way in which American policy makers soon lost sight of the vision of an Asian world order based on Sino-American co-operation, instead turning their attention more and more to meeting the Soviet challenge in Europe. Because the Marshall mission did too much and yet too little, it came to be condemned both by the Nationalists and the Communists. At the same time, the government in Washington began defining American interests in world affairs primarily in terms of retaining American influence in Europe. The result was that by 1947 little had been done to realize the goal of strengthening China as America's partner in Asia.

It does not seem that the policy makers in Washington were so naïve as to think that mere good will on their part would bring about the cessation of conflict in China. They could perhaps be criticized for the belief that the only way to democracy was through a coalition government. They tended to visualize in the two dominant factions of China something akin to two-party politics. If only these factions gave up their independent armies and came together in a coalition government, China would be able to walk the path toward independence, unification, and democracy. Still, President

Truman, Secretary Byrnes, General Marshall, and others were fully aware of the difficulties in their task. They knew that the fact of American power made it imperative for the United States to play some role in the evolution of Chinese politics. At the same time, they were unwilling to undertake massive intervention in China. To do so would have meant giving military aid to the Kuomintang, still regarded by Washington as the legitimate government of China, in return for promise of political reform. Or else, American intervention might have taken the form of withdrawing recognition from the Nationalists and extending massive assistance to other factions to induce them to form a coalition government. Still another possibility is that the United States might have assisted the Kuomintang to hold the southern half of China, leaving the rest of the country to its fate.

The fact that these policies were not adopted and the policy of friendly persuasion, backed up with a small-scale assistance to the Kuomintang, was continued, seems to indicate, not that the American government felt the latter alternative was workable, but rather that the first set of alternatives was untenable. There was little readiness to commit American power to the mainland of China. In other words, the protestation of the need to encourage the emergence of a unified and strong China fell short of direct American assistance to realize this goal.

What one finds in the record of American policy toward China in the immediate postwar years is a curious contrast between the officially proclaimed vision of an emergent strong China and the official reluctance to help China become strong. China, it was hoped, would mainly by its own resources be unified and strengthened. Official complacency about such a state of affairs perhaps revealed lack of concern with Soviet designs in East Asia. At the time of the Marshall mission, China was not regarded by the United States as an arena of American-Russian confrontation. This is in striking contrast to Washington's view of the two-power confrontation in Europe. While officials were wary of Soviet expansion in East Asia, they did not believe that the Soviet Union would make China its satellite. The chance of Russian-Chinese alliance and collusion would have caused American officials to reorient their thinking, but they underrated such a possibility, and before 1949 they do not seem to have believed that China would become a theater of conflict between the two giant powers. The country, it appeared, somehow stood outside the sphere of influence either of Russia or the United States. Consequently, no effort was made to entrench American influence more deeply in China.

The fact remains that the United States did resort to a policy of partial intervention. Apart from verbal exhortations, it offered a limited supply of arms and materiel to the Kuomintang, and American forces were kept in China. Although, beginning in the middle of 1946, the State Department took steps to reduce such assistance, the policy of regarding the Nationalists as the government of China was never abandoned. A policy of complete non-interference might have been better if it had been accompanied by a policy of positive assistance to the peoples of southeast Asia. Since in the long run limited support of the Kuomintang made little difference, American resources might better have been diverted to the countries on the periphery of China. Just after the war there were unsettled conditions in Indochina, Indonesia, Burma, Malaya, and elsewhere, due to struggles between the colonial powers and native populations. A vigorous American policy in these regions, to encourage their political stability and economic progress, would have been far more significant than small-scale intervention in China. The fact that such a policy was never contemplated reveals the official feeling that China was not likely to emerge as a strong and hostile country in the near future, to threaten the peace of southeast Asia. Thus we come to the paradox: the United States had pursued a policy of promoting China's emergence as a unified and strong country, but in time there emerged the opposite image, an assumption of China's weakness in the foreseeable future. Image and reality were mixed up, and few foresaw the rapidity with which the Communists would triumph and transform the nation.

Outside of officials, segments of American public opinion were at least more candid about the implications of the continued civil war in China. Those who had, during the war, begun to lose faith in the Kuomintang and turn hopefully to the Communists, maintained their attitude throughout the Marshall mediation episode. Few went as far as to suggest an outright support of the Chinese Communists; most American writers, while critical of the Kuomintang, supported the Marshall mission as a feasible approach to bring about a peaceful reunification of China. However, some of the writers recognized the logical untenability of a policy that simultaneously sought to help China's peaceful unification and continued to deal with the Nationalists as the government of China. American official policy, no matter how well intended, seemed to exacerbate relations among the factions in China and arouse antagonism toward the United States on the part of the anti-Kuomintang Chinese. The government in Washington, many observers held, should either renounce its pretensions of impartiality or cease to give aid, however limited, to the Kuomintang. And there was an overwhelming sentiment against the first alternative, if it meant explicit support of Chiang Kai-shek.

Thunder Out of China (1946), by Theodore H. White and Annalee Jacoby, seems typical of this line of thinking. If one is to judge from the favorable reviews the book obtained and the fact that it became a best-seller, it must have had a great deal of appeal to the American reading public at the time. The authors graphically portrayed the National government as corrupt, inefficient, and out of touch with the common mass of the people. It had ceased to represent the people but had become an instrument by which a handful of party officials and generals sought to perpetuate their power. The United States, the book pointed out, should see beyond party rivalry and to the revolutionary potential of the people. For there were signs of change everywhere in China. "A revolution is stirring and shaking every province, every country, every village in the land." There was a danger that the Kuomintang might not understand or welcome the change; if China were to be reborn and the people at last gain their due, then the dominant power, the right-wing Kuomintang, the "political expression of Nationalist army leaders, feudal landlords, and the war-inflated bureaucracy," must not be allowed to enjoy their privileged status forever. The United States should never identify itself with this group. Since revolution in Chinese life was inevitable, America must associate itself with it, so as to relate itself directly with the aspirations of the common mass of the Chinese people. Specifically, the authors envisaged America's complete non-intervention in Chinese political-military affairs; once the fact of American good faith was demonstrated, the United States must co-operate with the Soviet Union to encourage the emergence of a multi-party government in China, presumably consisting of the Kuomintang, Communists, and the third parties. Should Russian co-operation not be forthcoming, then America must boldly act alone, in the interest of revolution in Asia. Only by actively identifying itself with the winds of change in China and elsewhere in Asia could the United States secure itself the affection and friendship of the people of Asia. While the authors did not explicitly call for support of the Communists, in case of their victory, they implied as much, since they asserted that the Communist Party stood for change.

Equally candid were those who began voicing concern with the government's passive attitude. While the above view presented the possibility of Sino-American co-operation and friendship within the framework of the encouragement of the Chinese Communists, a minority remained unconvinced that such a course was practical or even logically possible. Essentially, the second view held that the Communist Party in China was an arm of international Communism and therefore that co-operation with it was unthinkable. Rather, it was argued, the United States should continue support of the Kuomintang. This was the only possible way, since confrontation with Communism was what defined postwar international relations. Encouragement of the Chinese Communists was tantamount to aiding the defeat of the anti-communist forces in China and implied appeasement of the Soviet Union.

Whether one advocated abandonment or support of the ruling faction in China, these views were at least frank, in contrast to the government's ambiguous stand. They expressed dissatisfaction with a policy that seemed out of step with the reality of American power. Articulate segments of American opinion were demanding that the nation use the power that it had acquired to shape the destiny of Asia. One group insisted that this could best be done by assisting the Nationalists, while others felt the support of the anti-Nationalists and the middle groups had greater promise of success.

The American Role in a Civil War

The Chinese, too, had to adjust themselves to the reality of postwar politics. Instead of emerging as one of the Big Four, as they had fondly believed they would, they found the country torn by civil strife, the outcome of which seemed to depend on the extent of foreign assistance to the factions. The Chinese viewed the United States in the context of this crude reality. For the Nationalists, there could be only one answer to China's failure to be unified and strengthened as a result of the war. Communism, foreign and domestic, was openly revolting against order and peace. At the same time, convinced of American opposition to Communism, the Nationalists continued to count on United States support.

By depicting China becoming a Soviet satellite, the Nationalists sought to convince Americans of the need to prevent such an eventuality. The National government, it is true, had signed a treaty with the Soviet Union, just before the Japanese surrender, in which the Russian government expressed its promise to consider the Kuomintang regime the government of China in return for the latter's acceptance of the Yalta agreement. There is little evidence that Chiang Kai-shek thought Russia would openly intervene in the civil war. At the same time, after the Pacific war, when the United States and the Soviet Union began colliding in Eastern Europe, it could be hoped that the United States would identify itself with the anti-communist forces in China. In order to establish the claim that he stood for freedom and democracy against divisive and subversive elements, Chiang authorized the convening of a national assembly and the drafting of a constitution, thus inaugurating the third and final democratic phase of the Nationalist revolution. Because Chiang was basically convinced of America's support, however, he never gave up the hope of militarily unifying the country. While accepting Marshall's mediation efforts, he remained ready to seize the initiative whenever opportunities presented themselves.

Such an attitude on the part of the Kuomintang served to impress the anti-Nationalist and neutral groups in China of the identity of interests between the Nationalists and the United States. Even without any American assistance to Chiang Kai-shek, therefore, segments of Chinese opinion would have come to identify America with the Kuomintang, thus imputing to the former the motives and aspirations, generally considered reactionary, of the Kuomintang. As it was, the Chinese Communists had already, before the end of the war, expressed their concern with the continued American policy of dealing with the Chiang regime. In a speech at Yenan, Mao Tse-tung declared on August 13, 1945, that

Chiang Kai-shek was "depending on the support of American imperialism." This marked a break from the Communists' use of the term "imperialism," which had referred almost exclusively to Japan during the war. Perhaps emboldened by the show of force by the Soviet Union against Japan, Mao now denounced United States imperialism as assisting Chiang's ambitions in order to make China its satellite. He exalted Russia's role in defeating Japan and said atomic bombs alone would never settle wars.

Still, the Chinese Communists did not engage in total recrimination against the United States. What they sought right after the conclusion of the Pacific war was some kind of political modus vivendi with the Nationalists on the basis of the military status quo. There was no hope that the Communists could conquer the whole of China in the near future; there was no clear indication of how much support they could expect of the Soviet Union, which, after all, recognized the Nanking government. What was necessary was to prevent a forceful unification of China by the Nationalists. That, in the Communist view, could only be accomplished through American military support. At the same time, the United States might be induced to use its influence with the Kuomintang so as to restrain its ambitions. Because of the experience of wartime collaboration between the two countries, there was a lingering hope, in the minds of the Communists, that the American people would repudiate their leaders' policy and bring about a true era of friendship and co-operation in Sino-American relations.

The Chinese Communist views of the United States between 1945 and 1947, as far as one can judge from their publications, reveal a gradual process of disillusionment and bitterness at America's failure to sever its ties with the Kuomintang. The Communists at first welcomed the American offer of mediation; they interpreted the Truman-Marshall policy of 1945–1946 to mean that the United States would support the immediate reorganization of the Chinese government so as to broaden its base and destroy the Kuomintang monopoly of power. As a Communist spokesman said in December 1945, the Truman proposal for cessation of fighting in China was fair and constructive; the Chinese and American peoples could yet try to promote friendly relations on the basis of the principle of self-determination. Many American diplomats and officers in China, he said, had been generally without prejudice, and their accurate reporting on conditions in China had contributed greatly to friendship between the two countries. It was regrettable, therefore, that American troops were still on Chinese soil, three months after the end of the war. Some of them had exceeded their duty, which was merely to disarm Japanese soldiers. It was to be hoped that these American forces would soon be withdrawn. In another statement, the Communist spokesman accused the Kuomintang of falsifying the intentions of the American government by willfully mistranslating the Truman statement.

A good illustration of Communist thinking toward the United States is provided by a *Liberation Daily* comment on the Byrnes statements of December 4 and 7, talking of America's support for the emergence of a strong, unified, and democratic China, and calling on all the factions in China to compromise and devote themselves to the supreme task. "The Chinese people," the editorial stated, "welcome such a clear and wise policy statement and hope the United States government will truly carry out the spirit of these declarations. . . . We are confident that the American government and people will make a maximum effort to transform their words into action." The writer then went on to note that certain American officials and especially army officers in China had acted in contradiction with the stated policy. The policy of President Roosevelt to assist all groups in China militarily had been sabotaged by Hurley and Wedemeyer, who refused to help the Communist armed units. Even before the Japanese surrender, Wedemeyer had begun using American force to help the Nationalist campaigns and was now contributing to the intensification of the civil war in China. Such military intervention was subverting the basic American policy of promoting a democratic government in the country. The time had come, the editorial concluded, to realize the "common demand of the Chinese and American people, namely, to evacuate all American forces in China and immediately stop participating in the Chinese civil war."

Because the United States did not completely pull out its forces from China, retaining 12,000 men at the end of 1946, but instead continued to recognize the Chiang regime as the government of China and provide it with surplus arms and materiel, the Communists were forced to conclude that the American government could not be counted upon to sever its ties with the Nationalists.

Although Marshall's mediation efforts were still appreciated, other "American imperialists in China" seemed intent upon armed intervention. The Communist press thus loudly called on the United States to stop such interference at once so as not to forfeit the friendship between the two countries. A *Liberation Daily* editorial of June 7, 1946 is typical. Although the Chinese had repelled Japanese imperialist bandits, it was written, "we have not obtained national independence; we are even being murdered by foreign arms." Since the Opium War, imperialism had intervened in Chinese domestic affairs and suppressed the people's movement for democracy and freedom. But "the situation such as obtaining today is wholly unprecedented in the magnitude of [the imperialist threat]." The Communist paper reminded the American people that the two peoples "have maintained a long-lasting friendship; the American people have shown a deep sympathy with the Chinese people's movement to win national independence, democracy, and freedom." The Chinese people would never forget the encouragement and good will shown by President Roosevelt. But a minority of American reactionaries were destroying the friendship of the two peoples, under the illusion that the Chinese were still a weak and disunited people. Americans should realize that they could no more destroy the Chinese people's democratic impulse and national strength than dictate that the sun rise in the west. The United States government must immediately change its policy of "killing the chicken and stealing its egg."

During the course of 1946, the Communists resigned themselves to the fact that the government in Washington was not likely to change its pro-Kuomintang policy. President Truman now joined Hurley, Wedemeyer, and others as objects of their attack; toward the end of the year Chou En-lai stated that no matter how Truman sought to justify his deeds, he could not deny that the United States was manufacturing and promoting the Chinese civil war. At the same time, the Communists continued to postulate a dichotomy between the American people and government. The persisting image of Sino-American friendship fitted the Communist perception of American policy in two ways. On the one hand, United States imperialism could be characterized as more vicious than others because the government could cloak its ambitions by referring to the record of traditional friendship. The United States, it was often held, had established a fund of good will in China, of which the imperialists could take advantage as they aimed at exploitation of China. On the other hand, since the American people were pictured as still friendly to the Chinese, they could be expected to repudiate their leaders and restore amity between the two peoples. As Mao Tse-tung told the American journalist Anna Louise Strong, the people of America would surely rise up against the reactionary policy of their government to suppress the democratic struggle everywhere in the world. Lu Ting-i, propaganda chief, stated that the basic contradiction in the world was not between nations but between democratic and reactionary forces, in particular between the American people and American reactionaries.

Just as Chiang Kai-shek sought to obtain American help by picturing the danger of Soviet penetration of China if the Communists were allowed to challenge his power, the latter tried to minimize the possibility of American-Soviet conflict. Although the two countries obviously stood for contradictory policies, it was unwise to picture their conflict as impending; if so, the United States might use the impending crisis as a pretext for occupying China. America's anti-Soviet propaganda, Mao said, was only a cloak to cover up aggressive designs on China and elsewhere bordering on Russia. The United States would not, because it could not, immediately attack the Soviet Union; before it could do so, the imperialists would be confronted by the democratic forces of the world, including the American people.

By the beginning of 1947, when General Marshall admitted the failure of his mission, the United States government had become closely identified by Chinese opinion with the Chiang Kai-shek regime. Practically all groups were in agreement that the outcome of the civil war was greatly dependent upon American action and that by its policy of partial assistance to the Kuomintang the United States was prolonging the crisis in China. As the Democratic League, representing the "third force" between the Nationalists and Communists, declared in January 1947, the United States and the Kuomintang had been guilty of ignoring the distribution of power in China and trying forcefully to unify the country. But the declaration admitted the essential helplessness of the situation by saying that it was the very lack of unity in the country that had invited American intervention. Only because the Chinese were engaged in factional struggle, it was stated, had the United States sought to take advantage of the situation to pursue an anti-Soviet, anti-Communist foreign policy. China must first of all be unified so as to play a more constructive role in bringing about peace between America and Russia. Few would dispute such an ideal, but the Democratic League itself attested to the dilemma confronting the Chinese people at this time by soon resolving to oppose the Kuomintang openly and identify itself with the Communists.

American Views of Asian Communism

While physical contact between Americans and Chinese steadily dwindled after 1947, their consciousness of each other never lessened. Sino-American relations, in fact, became part of the daily life of both Chinese and Americans. At the same time, ideology, rather than power, remained the framework in which they tried to come to grips with the problem.

On the American side, the years between 1947 and 1950 were a period of determined opposition to Soviet power in Europe without, however, an equal application of the containment policy to Asia. The policy of preventing extension of Soviet power and upholding the principle of national self-determination had been verbalized since 1945, but it was after 1947 that concrete steps were taken to make containment the cardinal principle of American policy. The containment policy, as its architects—notably George F. Kennan—saw it, had two components. First, the United States was to defend the countries still outside the Soviet sphere of influence. Second, the eventual creation of an integrated, prosperous and stable Europe was aimed at. The first component was tactical, showing America's response to whatever region was challenged by the Soviet Union, such as Greece and Turkey. The second was strategic and was expressed most clearly in the Marshall Plan, designed to give encouragement to European integration. The plan was initially intended to apply to the countries of Eastern Europe. As they refused participation, however, the strategy lost force in that region, but the idea of a unified, neutral Europe was always there. Once Soviet expansionism was checked, Europe would cease to be divided between the Soviet and American spheres of influence and emerge as an integrated whole.

It is essential to keep in mind these aspects of postwar American policy when one examines American-Chinese relations. To put it simply, the containment policy evaporated when applied to China. The image of postwar Asia, in which America and China would co-operate to maintain peace and order, gave way before the image of a weak and divided China, unstable and unreliable. It was out of the question to construct the peace in East Asia on the basis of joint action with such a country. Rather, America's position as well as the peace in Asia came to be viewed more and more in connection with the idea of a resurgent Japan. The picture of Japan as an anti-communist bastion emerged just as the image of a unified, strong, and friendly China faded. Beginning in 1948, the United States concentrated on Japan's economic reconstruction, in the hope that social and political stability in that country would prevent its coming under Communist influence. Japan's rearmament, too, began to be considered in Washington; the National Security Council discussed the question at the end of 1948, and in 1949 the policy of concluding a peace treaty as well as a mutual security treaty with Japan was adopted by the State Department. Even so, it should be recalled that there was little expectation that international Communism would choose Asia as the place of confrontation with the United States. In the official American view, East Asia appeared to be headed for a prolonged period of instability and uncertainty; it would function as a buffer zone between the Soviet Union and the United States. It was sufficient that America safeguarded its position in Japan by encouraging its economic recovery. Beyond Japan, on the continent of Asia, the United States would play no positive role.

By 1949, it is true, the United States had officially come to the view that China was coming under Communist control and that the new China was drawing into the Soviet sphere of influence. As Secretary of State Dean Acheson put it, in his preface to the China White Paper, "The Communist leaders have foresworn their Chinese heritage and have publicly announced their subservience to a foreign power, Russia, which during the last 50 years, under czars and Communists alike, has been most assiduous in its efforts to extend its control in the Far East." Acheson referred to China's "foreign yoke." Nevertheless, the whole tenor of the White Paper was to underplay the aspect of Soviet subversion in destroying the

Kuomintang regime in China. On the contrary, the State Department officially proclaimed that the Nationalists had "lost the confidence of its own troops and its own people," and that this, not Soviet activity or American policy, was the cause of the turmoil in China. The Communist victory there "was beyond the control of the government of the United States. Nothing that this country did or could have done within the reasonable limits of its capabilities could have changed that result." If such was the case, the present-day critic may point out, then why did the United States bother at all to give partial aid to the Kuomintang? Here was obviously a logical inconsistency; it could be explained only by looking at the above-noted gap between American power and American will, and at the impact of anti-communist ideology on foreign policy.

The fact remains that the United States government had come to recognize the inevitability of a Communist take-over in China and of the ascendance of Soviet influence in China. The White Paper revealed the official view that all this was tragic but that there was little that America could have done and could yet do to prevent such a situation. Whatever the United States did, short of massive intervention, would now make little difference. However one regards such an attitude, it is evident that the policy was characterized by passivity, in striking contrast to the more positive policy pursued in Europe. Thus the question once again is: why was the United States less determined to check Soviet expansion in Asia than in Europe? The old phenomenon of priority inevitably emerges. For the United States government recognized the threat of Communism as world-wide; it was resolved to discourage Soviet penetration everywhere. There was no reason why a Soviet-controlled China should be any less relevant than a Soviet-controlled Greece. A few Washington officials believed that China under Communists would not quite be a Soviet satellite and would eventually assert its independence. The White Paper expressed the hope that "ultimately the profound civilization and the democratic individualism of China will reassert themselves" and the country would throw off the yoke of Russian imperialism. However, no deed accompanied these expressions of hope. The United States might have encouraged the trend toward Chinese independence of Russia by means of a Marshall Plan for the Communist-dominated China, but nothing like it emerged at this time.

The failure of the leadership to picture a clear image of Chinese-American relations was crucial in producing confusion and mutual animosity among the American people. The view of international affairs in terms of confrontation with Communism appeared so suddenly that for a time this remained the only intelligible framework in which to look at the happenings in China. China was either going to be a friend or a potential enemy of the anti-communist camp; such a dichotomy, more an expression of hopes than of facts, often colored American views of what must be done now that the Communists had emerged as the dominant party in China.

At bottom was the radical shift in American public opinion on the question of war or peace. When the war ended in the Pacific, a poll indicated that only 10 per cent of the people believed future wars were likely. A year later, 70 per cent of those polled expected another world war within twenty-five years; in 1947 the same percentage of men answered the next war would come within ten years. The view that the next war was imminent provided the psychological milieu in which people responded to the phenomenon of a revolutionary China. The vast majority of people who anticipated war attributed the likelihood of new global crises to the threat of Communism; accordingly, they strongly favored measures to cope with the threat, to check Communist extension of power, whether in military preparedness or economic aid.

Since China was obviously becoming a Communist stronghold, it was natural that the American public, now accustomed to viewing world problems in terms of the coming confrontation with Communism, should have been uneasy over the administration's China policy, which seemed to have done little to deal with the situation. The Democratic administration was constantly urging the need to meet the Soviet challenge in Europe and the Middle East with firmness, and the Congress and public opinion gave overwhelming support to measures such as the Marshall Plan and the formation of the North Atlantic Treaty Organization. The singular lack of firmness when the matter applied to East Asia, no matter how justified or defended, could strike critics as inconsistent. Some logical connection between the government's policy of confronting the Communist challenge and its attitude of passivity in Asia was needed, if for no other reason than that the government became vulnerable to attack from the Republican Party and the anti-communist press. Regardless of the administration's dual response to Communism in Europe and Asia, opinion polls indicated little inclination to distinguish the two areas of confrontation; before 1949 a majority of Americans always favored specific steps to assist European countries as well as the Nationalist Chinese to fight against the Communists. To be convincing, the government would have had to explain more fully why the situation in Asia was so different from that in Europe as to make the same policies inapplicable. Or else, it would have been necessary to discard the view of the worldwide struggle against Communism and present the cold war simply in terms of national security and economic interests, rather than in terms of ideological differences. It is difficult to escape the conclusion that much of the attack on the Truman administration was traceable to this logical inconsistency, which in turn resulted from a highly stereotyped image of international affairs.

It is, however, noticeable that Congressional and other critics of the official China policy did not generally regard the Communist victory in China as constituting a grave threat to American security as such. Expressions of concern over possible Chinese menace to American security came mainly from anti-communist spokesmen on the west coast. As earlier in the century, the west coast was more sensitive than the rest of the nation to the military situation in the Pacific. A typical expression was a speech by Senator William Knowland in 1949, supporting an unsuccessful proposal for a $1,500,000,000 aid to the Kuomintang:

> . . . those of us who represent the Pacific Coast states [have] a particular interest in this regard, [for] the waters of the Pacific Ocean wash upon our states. It was not so very many years ago that we had in the state of California, so far as I know, the only enemy [Japanese] shelling of an American submarine. . . . We want no repetition of that kind should the world be so unfortunate as to become engaged in another war at some time in the future.

The burden of Knowland's pro-Kuomintang position as well as the stand taken by similarly oriented individuals and groups was, however, not that the new China threatened America's security but rather that China had become an unfriendly nation. The mere fact that China had turned Communist seemed to indicate a loss to the United States and a gain to the Soviet camp.

The very fact that the attention of the interested public turned to the question of who was responsible for the "loss of China" indicates that the emergence of a Communist China was not widely considered an immediate threat to American interests. Otherwise, more attention would have been paid to the question of how best to safeguard national security and interests now that China had become a potential enemy. The fascination many felt with the first question revealed that this could easily become a domestic political problem in the United States and divide the American people, who would be prevented from probing more deeply into the second question. As is well known, an attack on the Truman administration, in particular on the makers of East Asian policy, began in the spring of 1947, when Congressman Walter Judd, Republican of Minnesota, accused the State Department of having mishandled the country's China policy. According to him, the Far Eastern division of the State Department had blindly subscribed to the Chinese Communist version of the civil war in China and underestimated the strength and merits of the Nationalists. The same sin had been committed by America's academic experts on East Asian matters. The theme was taken up nearly three years later by Senator Joseph R. McCarthy, who at one time declared that eighty-one officials of the State Department were Communist sympathizers and had contributed to the Communist victory in China.

The intellectual exercise of linking the loss of China to United States failings was not confined to right-wing groups and pro-Chiang sympathizers. Those who had a more critical view of the Kuomintang likewise sought factors within America that had brought about the tragic situation in China. Graham Peck, the author of *Two Kinds of Time* (1950), noted that "the present turn of events in China is not so much a success of Russia and Communism as it is a failure for America and Democracy." Peck presented a thesis with a long-range historical perspective; according to him the Chinese revolution had begun with the advent of Western power and economic dislocations of the nineteenth century. When the Chinese began to stir, "Americans had an excellent opportunity to influence the unavoidable revolution into democratic channels, but did not bother to make enough effort." The political and military chaos and upheaval of postwar China was only the last chapter in the long process of social change; the

United States had failed to relate itself to this change and was now in danger of viewing it simply in terms of international Communism. The American people, press, and government had been indifferent to and ignorant of more than superficial aspects of Chinese life; in fact there had been no real communication between the two peoples. Instead, the American people had romanticized their relations with the Chinese, with the inevitable result that they were puzzled by and resentful of China's rejection of the non-communist West. What the United States should have done, Peck asserted, was to refrain from military intervention and to push for a political settlement of Chinese internal affairs. Admittedly, without American military support the Kuomintang would in any event have lost to the Communists. However, such a China would not have held a special grudge against America. The way to salvage Sino-American friendship, the author noted, would be only by an intelligent effort to see China not only as a Communist dictatorship but also as an end product of many decades of economic and political anarchy. Speaking of those who were blaming Acheson, Marshall, and other architects of China policy, Peck wrote, "Hurley and Wedemeyer . . . whose anti-Communist belligerence undoubtedly encouraged the Generalissimo to hope for more American aid than would ever be forthcoming for a Chinese civil war, helped the Communists more than Marshall did."

These varying attitudes toward the making of Communist China produced equally opposing proposals for dealing with it. They ranged from stopping the Communist victory to recognizing the Communist regime in China. On the whole, however, it is noticeable that a majority of writers considered Sino-American amity as not irrevocably lost. Whether one took the pro-Kuomintang or the anti-Kuomintang stand, almost everyone expressed sympathy with and friendship for the people of China, victims of exploitation whether by the aristocratic, feudal elements or by ruthless Communist dictatorship. It was felt that by some action the United States could salvage ties with the Chinese and restore amity between the two peoples. By definition, this implied that the two countries were not incompatible at all; if the United States adopted the right policy, it could once again produce an era of co-operation with China. Trade would flow between the two, and they would consolidate ties and work together for peace in Asia. Here was a fundamental assumption that the interests of the two countries were compatible; there would be no conflict if Americans understood the Chinese revolution, or if they resolved to destroy Chinese Communism, as the case might be.

In this way, while Communism defined for most Americans the framework in which to view the situation in China, few came to the conclusion that China, apart from and independent of its Communism, was inherently a potential enemy of the United States. Looking back, it may be pointed out that concern with Soviet Communism and the image of traditional Sino-American friendship prevented Americans from developing a more dispassionate appraisal of the China problem in terms of power and national interests. There might have been an attempt to comprehend developments in China without reference to stereotypes and clichés. Such an attempt might have shown that China as a nation was inherently neither friendly nor hostile to other countries, and that its actual foreign relations were as much a function of power politics as of its ideological orientation. It is surprising how few writers then talked of reconciling American and Chinese national interests, rather than of accommodating one to the other. The language of confrontation with a hostile China was not yet fully developed.

Chinese Communists View America

In China, too, the picture of American-Soviet struggle provided the framework in which to comprehend events in and out of the country. The Nationalists continued to view their war with the Communists as part of the world-wide struggle between Communism and anti-communism, and therefore to expect further American aid. This was, at any rate, the way they appealed to the United States and American public opinion for massive assistance. As Chiang Kai-shek wrote to President Truman in November 1948, "If we fail to stem the tide, China may be lost to the cause of democracy." He attributed the deterioration of the military situation to Soviet machinations and designs. As he said, "But for persistent Soviet aid, the Chinese Communists would not have been able to occupy Manchuria and develop into such a menace." The Nationalist leader was visualizing his fight against the Communists as a struggle for "independence, freedom, the survival of each individual citizen, world security, and the happiness of humanity," as he stated in 1949. He was standing as the vanguard of the forces of anti-communism. Since the United States gradually withdrew help throughout 1949, he came to view his war as a solitary struggle in the cause of national freedom and justice. At the same time, he sought to organize an anti-communist coalition with the leaders of the Philippines, South Korea, and others who might share his view of international Communism.

Despite the effort of the Nationalists to impress the United States with the urgency of the situation, they had to admit that Americans did not wholeheartedly agree with his diagnosis of the Chinese situation. As reported by Ambassador John L. Stuart, "According to Generalissimo's reports Americans did not believe there was any close connection between Chinese Communists and U.S.S.R., nor that U.S.S.R. was backing [the Chinese communists]." No matter how hard he tried to demonstrate that his party stood for democracy and freedom, segments of American opinion seemed unconvinced and critical of his acts. As the Nationalist foreign minister stated in 1948, "During the past four years and a half, American public opinion has been very critical of us. Some of the criticisms have been justified, whereas others have been malicious propaganda by Communists." Nevertheless, he still hoped that the "permanent and solid" friendship between the two peoples would remain unimpaired, and declared that the Chinese government's policy was to maintain and promote the friendship. Such optimism steadily gave way to more pessimistic views, until, with the publication of the China White Paper, the Nationalists saw clearly how hopeless it was to count on American aid. As a Nationalist spokesman said, the Chinese were disappointed by the American government's passive policy and attack on the Chinese government, attributing to it responsibility for the expansion of Communist influence. The situation in China could never be improved by indulging in objective criticisms and half-hearted reforms. What China needed was more positive assistance, not an explanation by the United States of its past policy of passivity. Yen Hsi-shan, the former warlord of Shansi and now chairman of the Executive Yuan, stated that even if the Kuomintang's alleged corruption and inefficiency were wiped out, there still would be Communist menace in China so long as there was international

Communism. The United States must recognize the international nature of the Chinese civil war and come to the aid of the Nationalists, the vanguard of anti-communism. The *Central Daily* in Taipei, soon to become the organ of the National government in exile, stated even more frankly that America's "immature" policy had brought about the disaster in China. The paper reminded Americans that they must share the responsibility for having invited Soviet penetration of China, for it was the Yalta agreement that opened the way for Soviet entry into Manchuria. Second, the American government had followed a very correct policy in Europe but had been totally mistaken in Asia. Why? Americans should honestly admit that their resources were limited and therefore they must concentrate on the defense of Europe, thus sacrificing Asians to Soviet authoritarianism. Third, no one in the State Department had seriously studied Communism. American officials had believed that the Chinese Communists were more Chinese than Communist, thus justifying their strategy of mediation between all groups in China. But they had failed to understand that any compromise with Communists was tantamount to surrender. Finally, Americans were misled by ideas such as "reaction," "inefficiency," and "oppression," words they used in describing the National government. Granted that the latter was often guilty of these, it must be realized that any undue criticism of the government would only embolden the Communists.

"We should not blame each other about past mistakes," said another Nationalist, "but the two peoples must resolutely co-operate in the task of fighting the Communists, based on the tradition of friendship during the past one hundred years and the experience of co-operative action during the war." It was with such a hope that the Nationalist leaders withdrew to Taiwan, there to consolidate their base in order to plan an eventual counterattack on the mainland. Sooner or later they hoped an opportunity would present itself when Americans would finally come to realize the wisdom of helping them in that historic task.

For the Chinese Communists, naturally, the White Paper was one more evidence of American intervention in China's domestic affairs. Ever since Marshall departed from China, in January 1947, the Communist press and party leaders had been stepping up their denunciation of the United States. While the basic outline of Communist attitude toward American imperialism had already been drawn, it is possible to find new emphasis on certain themes among the Communist writings after 1947. For one thing, they no longer felt it necessary to play down the impending crisis between the United States and the Soviet Union. On the contrary, the overriding seriousness of American-Russian relations could be stressed, so as to identify the Chinese Communists with the world democratic forces led by the Soviet Union. Now that the American government was openly supporting the Chiang regime and opposing the Communists, it was useless to plead with Washington's leaders to desist from intervention in the Chinese civil war. In fact, they came to talk of American imperialism, rather than the Kuomintang reactionaries, as the obstacle to their aspirations. Chiang Kai-shek, in such a view, would become little more than a pitiable tool of the imperialists. As Mao Tse-tung said on Christmas Day of 1947, Chiang Kai-shek's war was really America's war, a counterrevolution, opposed to the independence and liberation of the Chinese people. It was necessary to defeat Chiang so as to get rid of American imperialism. Mao pitied Chiang's "illusion" that the United States was all-powerful and that it would eventually triumph over the Soviet Union. In fact America was never omnipotent; it was being steadily weakened by a coalition of democratic forces in the world. Such thinking was behind Mao's famous justification for "leaning to one side"; since the world was seen as divided between the imperialist and anti-imperialist camps, there could be no middle way. China could never remain neutral in the global struggle against the forces of reaction. The Chinese people must identify themselves with the Soviet Union and lean on Soviet support and assistance to win the war against the imperialists.

Given such a frame of mind, the gradual withdrawal of American physical assistance to the Nationalists had little impact on the Communist perception of the United States. If anything, the American policy of passivity was taken as evidence that American imperialism was bound to lose, given the dedication of the Chinese people to the cause of democracy and the support given them by the freedom-loving peoples of the world under the guidance of the Soviet Union. Imperialism, however, was still considered to be far from dead. If it failed in China, it would try to utilize reactionaries elsewhere to perpetuate the struggle against the peoples of the world. For this reason, the Communists saw no need to maintain even *de facto* relations with the United States. This explains the rather impetuous acts that they committed toward foreigners in China, in particular American officials and businessmen, throughout 1949. Because of the view that the imperialists were in China only to profit at the expense of the people, there seemed to be no justification for permitting their continued residence and business activities in China. Thus foreign trade was placed under the party's supervision, and no initiative was taken to obtain speedy diplomatic recognition by the powers. The wave of revolution, it was felt, would soon envelop the whole world, and there seemed little need to normalize relations with imperialist countries.

The American people, it is true, were still distinguished in Chinese Communist perception from the leaders who, according to Liu Shao-ch'i's "Internationalism and Nationalism" (1948), were controlled by the "eight biggest financial cliques." The ordinary people of America were still pictured as democrats and opposed to the reactionaries. The American people would join the worldwide united front against imperialism and participate in the fight against the forces of tyranny and oppression. However, what constituted the "American people" must have steadily dwindled, as shown, for instance, by the growing debate on the China question within the United States. One notices, in particular, that the Chinese Communists came to lump all American imperialists together, instead of distinguishing some friendly leaders like Roosevelt and Marshall. The publication of the White Paper provided documentary evidence that the American leaders had consistently plotted to intervene in Chinese domestic affairs in order to promote their selfish ends. Marshall, who had earlier been regarded as a man of good intentions, was now castigated as one of the imperialists, in the same company as Wedemeyer, Truman, Stuart, and Acheson. The Marshall mediation episode itself came to be denounced as a sham; it was an attempt by the United States to control the whole of China without resort to force. The Marshall mission in fact had been a device to deceive the Chinese people. Having failed in the attempt, the American government finally decided to use force to obtain its ends. But the use of American force was still limited. Fearful of opposition by the Chinese people and democratic Americans, the imperialists had been trying to let the Nationalists fight America's war. All this was fully documented in the White Paper. The Communist spokesmen especially warned the "liberal, independent" groups in China that they were now the target of American policy, as the White Paper seemed to reveal the policy of courting these groups in order to resist Communist take-over.

The state of Communist-American antagonism was such that the Communist commentators were ready to characterize the whole course of Sino-American relations in black-and-white terms. The White Paper referred to the traditional friendship between the two peoples and also to America's policy of amity, benevolence, and good will in East Asia. The Communists agreed that there had been and still should be friendship between the two peoples—but only between the two peoples, not governments. The American people had no need for aggression in China, but the record of United States policy revealed how hypocritical it was to talk of amity at that level. As a New China radio broadcast pointed out, the much-boasted Open Door policy was merely a reflection of the fact that at the turn of the century American imperialism was not yet ready to monopolize control over China. The principle of equal opportunity had assured the United States the rights the other powers enjoyed at the expense of the Chinese. In fact America had acted together with the other imperialists in 1900 (the Boxer incident), 1919 (support of Japanese rights in Shantung), 1922 (new tariff regulations), 1923 (the Canton customs incident), 1925 (the May 30th incident), 1927 (the Nanking incident). Between 1931 and 1941 the United States was a major supplier of military goods to Japan, and even after 1940 increasing quantities of materiel were shipped to Japan. Down to the eve of Pearl Harbor the Washington government had sought to reach compromise with the Japanese aggressors at the expense of China. In this way, the White Paper provided a unique textbook, as one put it, to study how imperialists tried to cover up their evil deeds and indulged in deceiving themselves as well as their victims.

As a Communist writer stated, despite their traditional friendship, the Chinese and American peoples were losing contact with each other because their respective reactionary leaders intervened between them. While it was hoped that the American people would sooner or later rise against the ruling clique, for the time being there seemed little chance for resuming close ties. The political parties, newspapers, radio, and other mass media in the United States were tools of reaction, and so the Chinese people would completely sever ties with America. The Chinese must be freed from the evil effects of American propaganda. They must learn the truth about the past.

Given these views of American policy, it was natural that Communist propaganda should have placed more and more emphasis on the alleged intention of the United States to resurrect Japanese militarism. Since American influence was declining in China, it was to be expected that the imperialists would beat a tactical retreat and try to consolidate control over the areas adjacent to China. More fundamentally, the Communists viewed the civil war as a continuation of the struggle against Japanese imperialism. The Chinese people, with the support of friendly countries, had defeated Japanese militarism, but found that the struggle for independence, peace, and democracy had still to go on, now that American imperialism succeeded Japanese imperialism as the obstacle in their way. Having crushed the Japanese, the American ruling circles had sought to invade China and fight against the revolutionaries. More than that, since the imperialists realized the impotence of the Kuomintang, they were turning to Japan, there to resurrect militarism and prepare for a new invasion of China. "We oppose," declared Chu Teh in July 1949, "America's long-term occupation of Japan, calculated to make Japan its arsenal and base of aggression, and threatening the peace of Asia and the world." The Japanese cabinet of Yoshida Shigeru was characterized as fascist, and the United States was accused of assisting it in order to establish a hegemony over the whole of Asia.

The final years of the Chinese civil war, then, saw an ideological revolution in which the idea of Sino-American co-operation against Japan, which was so current only a few years earlier, gave way to an image of American-Japanese imperialist collaboration against China. As a corollary, the Communists called on the Japanese people to repudiate their leaders' policy of submission to American authorities. The Chinese and the Japanese people, stated the delegates at an anti-Kuomintang rally on the twelfth anniversary of the Marco Polo Bridge incident, both desired to live in peace and co-operate with each other economically and culturally. But such wishes were being obstructed by American imperialism, intent upon reviving militarism and imperialism in Japan. In order to realize the ultimate objective of the war against Japan, in which the United States, too, had taken part, the Chinese must demand that America give up its policy of turning Japan into its military base and confer with all the former allies for the conclusion of a peace treaty. "The wheel of history can never be turned back," declared the noted writer Kuo Mo-jo, "the peace in the Pacific will be maintained only by the real strength of the people. Only then, will there be a glorious day for mankind, when man will have entered an era of great harmony." Such statements showed how fragile had been the hopes for a postwar Asia in which China and the United States would co-operate to ensure the permanent extinction of Japanese imperialism.

IV
The Sino-American Crisis

11
The Military Confrontation

The history of Sino-American relations since the Korean War is unified by one shared perception: that each country threatens the security of the other. Although ideological issues have by no means disappeared, talk of Sino-American relations now usually revolves around national security and national interest; and as a framework for that discussion both the rhetoric of friendship and the dogma of Communism have been replaced by cool appraisals of each other's power position in Asian politics. Chinese-American relations, in short, have been reduced to the common denominators of military confrontation. Only by viewing this situation in a historical perspective can one transcend day-to-day occurrences and view the future with some measure of detachment. One sees then that American-Asian contact from the beginning has been fraught with romantic images, distortions, wishful thinking, irrelevant generalizations, and logical inconsistencies. Grim as it is, the present Sino-American crisis seems much more conducive to realistic appraisals on both sides than any previous phase of relations.

Since the end of World War II, American-Chinese-Japanese relations have reversed themselves: earlier, China and America co-operated against Japan; now Japan and the United States are allied against China. But these two alliances are different in nature, for the character of "co-operation" itself has changed, as conditions in Asia have changed. Asia in 1938 was still predominantly a colonial area, with Japan the predominant power and China weak and disunited, while the European colonies still went on as in the past. Here Sino-American co-operation simply took the form of the United States discouraging Japanese capture of the southeast Asian European colonies, by tying Japan down in China through economic and moral assistance to the latter. But the United States operated from Washington, with few substantial bases in the western Pacific. By 1950 the United States had armed forces and bases in many parts of Asia and possessed long-distance striking power with nuclear weapons. Thus Japanese-American military co-operation has never been so tenuous as the earlier Sino-American co-operation. Southeast Asia, on the other hand, is no longer secure in European hands, and China, not Japan, has been trying to extend control over this area. Thus the reversal in American–East Asian relations is not simply a reversal. And if the Chinese and Americans have felt themselves to be in potential conflict, it must be said to reflect faithfully the changed power equation in Asia as a result of the Japanese defeat and the independence of southeast Asian countries from European rule.

The Defense Perimeter

Neither the United States nor China expected or experienced direct conflict before the Korean War. Before 1950 the United States had had no anti-Chinese strategy. America had stood for containment of the Communist forces in Europe; in Asia it had only morally opposed Communism. Before the Korean War, moreover, there was no unanimous and clear-cut view of the new China. Owen Lattimore suggested in Senate hearings in March 1950 that four possibilities could be thought of for the future of China—a Soviet satellite, a Communist China independent of Soviet control, a democratic China, and a China under the restored rule of Chiang Kai-shek. By this time the last two possibilities seemed out of the question, unless the United States were somehow to reverse the tide by massive intervention. While some specialists, including Lattimore himself, held to the view that China, although Communist, was not yet a mere Soviet satellite, most officials were ready to regard the new Chinese regime as within the sphere of influence of Russia. American officials were not unanimous, however, in predicting Chinese expansionism. Granted that the country was embracing Soviet Communist dogma, key officials, including Secretary of State Acheson, were not yet convinced that the new China would pose an immediate threat to the peace in Asia. However disagreeable the prospect of a Communist China, there was as yet no proof that apart from ideology it could be a positive force for undermining American interests. Therefore, though formal recognition of the Communist regime was out of the question, the maintenance of a *de facto* relationship was not opposed by the State Department. For instance, the United States was not going to object to the seating of the representatives of the Chinese Peoples Republic rather than the National government in Taiwan at the United Nations as representing China. While the United States would not itself endorse such a change it was willing to go along with a majority view at the Security Council. Also, John Foster Dulles, then working on a peace treaty with Japan, suggested that the representatives of both the Communist and the National governments should send delegates to the forthcoming peace conference. Finally, there was no official policy opposing trade with Communist China.

The best evidence that American policy ignored power considerations in its attitude toward Communist China was the lack of concern with the future of southeast Asia. Karl Lott Rankin, consul general at Hong Kong, had warned, already in November 1949, that through propaganda and subversive tactics Communist China would try to extend its influence over Indochina, Thailand, Burma, the Philippines, Indonesia, Pakistan, and even India. He dismissed as unrealistic the notion that China was weak, or that Chinese Communism was somehow different from Soviet Communism. "In Eastern terms, communist China is a great power, economically, militarily, and politically," Rankin asserted.[1] The famous speech by Secretary of State Acheson, given before the

[1] Karl Lott Rankin, *China Assignment* (Seattle, 1964), 33ff.

National Press Club on January 12, 1950, was in a sense a rebuttal of such alarmist views. In that address Acheson defined America's "defense perimeter" in Asia and the Pacific. The United States, he declared, would safeguard the security of Japan, Okinawa, and the Philippines, but it would not take upon itself the responsibility for defending the territories lying outside the chain of these islands. This was tantamount to excluding power considerations from southeast Asia, as well as Korea and Taiwan. But Acheson warned against emphasizing military considerations and military means in looking at Asian problems. For him the most crucial factor was the revolutionary changes that were sweeping over the countries of Asia and the Pacific. As he said,

> [There] is a new day which has dawned in Asia. . . . It is a day in which the old relationships between east and west are gone, relationships which at worse were exploitations, and which at their best were paternalism. That relationship is over, and the relationship of east and west must now be in the Far East one of mutual respect and mutual helpfulness. . . . [But] we can help only where we are wanted and only where the conditions of help are really sensible and possible. [The] decision [as to the future of Asia] lies within the countries of Asia and within the power of the Asian people.

Nothing was here said about the potential aggressiveness of the Chinese Communists. Rather, they were pictured as having taken advantage of these revolutionary aspirations in Asia to achieve their victory. All these considerations led to the conclusion, in Acheson's view, that the United States should not employ military means to influence the course of events on the mainland of Asia. At bottom there may have been the feeling that East Asia would be in a state of flux for years to come and would even serve as a buffer zone between the American and Soviet power zones, unlike Europe where, as in Berlin, the two confronted each other directly.

The Chinese were also indulging in similar thoughts, in reverse. The Communists had developed a view of American imperialism as the enemy of the Chinese people, and there had also loomed the image of the United States assisting a reactionary clique in Japan. But there was optimism that the overwhelming majority of the world's people supported the democratic revolution and struggle against imperialism. As for the defense of China, the alliance with the Soviet Union, concluded in February 1950, seemed to guarantee national security against attack. There was confidence that the United States would not directly challenge Communist power in China and that it would not resist the extension of Communist power to Taiwan and elsewhere in Asia. While America was China's ideological enemy, it was not considered an immediate threat to the reunified country.

Redefining Asian Interests

The Korean War belied such Chinese expectations. The war itself was intimately linked to the Soviet perception of American policy in Asia. As the architects of Soviet policy saw it, the United States was building up Japan as a satellite but withdrawing from South Korea and elsewhere in Asia. It logically followed that forceful unification of Korea would be accomplished relatively easily and contribute to preventing the resurgence of Japanese militarism. Communist control over the peninsula would be effective in checking Japan's possible repenetration of Korea and thus neutralize whatever the United States was attempting to do in Japan. Moscow may have decided that the risk was worth taking in view of the announced reluctance of the United States to defend South Korea, and in order to divert American attention from Europe. What is interesting, however, is that the Soviet Union, whatever its reasoning, was viewing the Korean venture as accomplishing limited objectives and not as the beginning of a third world war. Nor did the Soviet Union conceive of direct confrontation with the United States in Korea. The conflict was to be a limited one, involving only the North and South Koreans. In other words, the Soviet Union, while pursuing its own cold-war diplomacy, was not ready to risk a global conflict over Korea.

American response was ideologically clear but strategically ambiguous; it nevertheless confounded Communist expectations. Ideologically, the administration in Washington viewed the North Korean aggression as related to international Communism and its expansionist design. To do nothing would be tantamount to acknowledging the Communist power to alter the status quo with impunity and revealing America's lack of determination to resist

Communist expansionism in Europe as well as in Asia. To the generation of American leaders who had gone through the experience of the 1930's, it was axiomatic that aggression, in particular of a world-wide nature, must be resisted with determination in order to discourage the aggressor from further acts of violence. Strategically, however, United States policy was not so clear-cut. Initially, the policy was to localize conflict, to recover South Korea. Soon, however, the United States decided to launch military action in North Korea and extend its military control over that region, as a step toward the reunification of Korea under South Korean leadership. The decision, reached by President Truman and his highest advisory circles in September 1950, was based not only on the estimate that military action in North Korea was necessary in order to discourage further aggression in the south, but also on the calculation that here was an opportunity to establish an anti-communist regime in the whole of Korea.

That crucial decision reveals the cross-currents of assumptions that made up official American attitudes at the height of the cold war. It gave American officials, civilian and military, an opportunity to apply their cold-war policy of containment. This policy, however, was open to two varying interpretations. The strict containment policy, as originally developed by George F. Kennan, required resistance to further extension of Communist power by military intervention, and thus the rescue of the non-communist regime in South Korea. This was conceived of as a local conflict, although part of the world-wide pattern of American-Soviet antagonism. It was a policy of restoring the status quo, of discouraging a forceful change. At the same time, the containment policy had been born of the American image of the confrontation with Soviet power; so long as the latter existed, it seemed by definition expansive. It was natural, then, that some should have begun to advocate not only the repulsion of North Korean forces from South Korea but also the unification of the whole of Korea under a non-communist government. Without such an achievement, they argued, the world would merely be back to where it was before aggression; the aggressors would not have been discouraged but merely halted. Not only the repulsion but the destruction of the North Korean army seemed called for if the Korean people were to live in peace after the war. They could never be at peace so long as the Communist forces north of the thirty-eighth parallel were kept intact. These forces had to be destroyed.

The picture is further complicated by the American officials' reluctance to consider the war in Korea as the beginning of war with China or the Soviet Union. In the American perception, the Korean War, although one provoked by the Communists to extend their sphere of influence, was nevertheless not a prelude to a world war. Here obviously was a logical inconsistency, but its implications could be held to a minimum so long as the fighting was confined to South Korea. The question, now that the extension of hostilities to the north was being considered, was whether American military action in North Korea would bring in the intervention of China or the Soviet Union. President Truman most clearly revealed the uneasiness implicit in the dilemma when he authorized General MacArthur to pursue North Korean troops beyond the thirty-eighth parallel if there was no sign or threat of Soviet or Chinese participation in the war as a result of such action. In a radio message to the American people, on September 1, the president expressed faith that the war would not extend itself to a total war so long as North Korea did not drag in other Communist countries. Truman also spoke of his hope that the Chinese people would not be led to fight Americans, and he reiterated that the United States had no territorial ambitions over the island of Taiwan and other territories in Asia.

The policy of military reunification of Korea, while at the same time avoiding direct clashes with Russia and China, revealed misperception at least of Chinese intentions. The famous Wake Island conference between Truman and MacArthur, on October 15, did little to clarify the situation. General MacArthur's categorical declaration that the Chinese would never dare intervene in the Korean conflict was based on his own reading of the Chinese mind; he assumed that the Chinese Communist leadership would reason as he would, and conclude that Chinese intervention would only be met by American retaliation. Mao Tse-tung would never resort to such a suicidal act, MacArthur insisted. It is clear that his perception of Chinese motives was based on the assumption that the Chinese considered their participation in the war to be the beginning of a world-wide struggle between Communism and anti-communism. If indeed the Korean War developed into a third world war, then the United States would use all its available resources, including nuclear weapons, to destroy the Soviet Union and China. Mao Tse-tung would never want to face such consequences by intervening in Korea. In other words, the spectacle of global conflict would keep China from interfering in the Korean War. President Truman was satisfied with such an explanation; he, too, was intent on localizing the conflict, and was reassured by MacArthur's view of Chinese Communist motives.

The Chinese, in fact, were willing to risk war with the United States. To them, too, the Korean War had come as a rude awakening. Initially, the Chinese Communist leadership had viewed the United States as intent upon regaining South Korea, not unifying Korea by force. While the Chinese press denounced American action and condemned America's alleged aggressive designs on Korea, Taiwan, and Vietnam, no immediate threat to the mainland of China was perceived. So long as the Chinese persisted in a cautious attitude, it was believed that the war would be confined to the southern half of the Korean peninsula. Such considerations were behind the decision to postpone the attack on Taiwan, which had for some time been planned. By the end of August, however, the Peking leaders became aware of the possibility that the United States might seek to unify Korea by force, extending military action to North Korea. In that event Manchuria would become vulnerable to attack. In September the Chinese government openly declared its intention of coming to the aid of North Korea in case it was invaded by the American imperialists. Massive Chinese intervention followed in the next month.

The crossing of the thirty-eighth parallel by American troops, provoking the crossing of the Yalu by Chinese "volunteers," marked the beginning of direct Sino-American confrontation. Tragic and unwanted as these developments were for the majority of Americans and Chinese, it cannot be denied that the new stage of the Korean conflict served to clarify the nature of Sino-American relations, which had been confounded by abstract ideological disputes. To look at the American side first, the Korean War produced the policy of opposing Chinese expansionism while at the same time avoiding direct involvement on the mainland of Asia. The policy evolved from an acrimonious debate within the administration, highlighted by the famous Truman-MacArthur controversy.

Apart from the obvious question of presidential authority over the military, the controversy involved the making of a new China policy where none had existed before. The most immediate question was military strategy in North Korea. If forceful unification of Korea was impossible without large-scale war with Communist China, officials in Washington, both civilian and military, were willing to give up the objective and return to the initial goal of regaining control over South Korea. As President Truman and his close advisers saw it, now that the Chinese had entered the war contrary to expectation, the military situation in Korea had entered a new stage. To combat the Chinese and persist in the goal of liberating North Korea from Communist rule could imply massive military action against China itself, as obviously China would keep supplying "volunteers" to resist American forces. Thus the United States would be inevitably drawn into a land war in Asia. Not only that, the Soviet Union, China's military ally, might intervene, thus inviting a third world war. In such an eventuality, American resources would have to be concentrated on the defense of Europe and the Western hemisphere. Korea would dwindle in significance in an ultimate test of power with the Soviet Union. Actually, the American strategy in case of global conflict had been to surrender Korea and retire American forces to Japan. Under the circumstances, it was logically as well as militarily inconsistent to fight China in Asia while the real enemy was Russia in Europe. As the chairman of the joint chiefs of staff, General Omar N. Bradley, said in May 1951, "Red China is not the powerful nation seeking to dominate the world. Frankly, in the opinion of the joint chiefs, this strategy [i.e., fighting for a united Korea] would involve us in the wrong war, at the wrong place, at the wrong time, and with the wrong enemy." The implications are entirely clear. Since war with China could extend into a war with Russia, in which case the United States could not really concentrate on Asia, it logically followed that war with China was undesirable.

These views were vigorously opposed by General MacArthur, who persisted in his insistence that the Korean conflict be extended to Manchuria and beyond. In his view it made strategically no sense merely to fight the Chinese in Korea; since they came from Manchuria, it was imperative to take such measures as blockading the coast of China, bombarding Chinese supply centers, encouraging the Nationalist forces to launch a counterattack on the mainland, and even dropping atomic bombs at the Korean-Manchurian border in order to create a radioactive no man's zone. More than that, the commitment of massive American power in Asia would enable MacArthur to save Korea from Communism and destroy completely Communist China's aggressive war potential, thus removing from Asia China's capacity to threaten peace for generations to come. Most important of all, the general believed there was no danger of Soviet intervention, since the show of American determination in Asia would deter the Soviet Union from military adventure. If America lost in Asia, it would also lose in Europe. Everything must be done to strengthen defenses in the West, but this should not mean that the United States must retreat from Asia.

From MacArthur's point of view, the administration's policy of return to the limited objective by means of a truce along the thirty-eighth parallel was meaningless. The Korean War was a test of strength with the force of Communism; it was in Asia that "the Communist conspirators have elected to make their play for global conquest." Merely to restore the prewar status quo, therefore, would not deter further Communist aggression; it would be tantamount to a defeat for anti-communism and bring about an inevitable loss of Europe in the future. Here was a great opportunity to destroy China's war potential and make Asia secure for anti-communism. The Truman administration, on the other hand, continued to reason that struggle with world Communism must be played out in Europe, where the United States and its allies had an advantage. It is no accident, then, that throughout 1950 the United States took decisive steps to strengthen the North Atlantic Treaty Organization. Sixty divisions of the NATO force were ordered created and put under command of General Dwight D. Eisenhower, and steps were taken to rearm West Germany. The United States forces in East Asia, in Washington's policy, were primarily intended for defense of Japan, not for defeating Communism on the mainland of Asia. The Truman-MacArthur controversy and the general's defeat revealed America's unwillingness to divide its forces between Europe and Asia, even while the Communist menace was thought to be world-wide.

In retrospect, however, there seems to have been a hidden pattern in America's Asian policy beneath the surface drama of the MacArthur episode. Few if any would now dispute MacArthur's view that Communist China was indeed a member of the international Communist community, intent on aggression. Whether it should have been destroyed by force at that juncture was debatable, but not the nature of the Chinese state itself. The Chinese intervention in the war seemed to reveal that China, in addition to the Soviet Union, now posed a threat to the peace. If the threat went unchallenged, not only the peace of the world but America's own security and interests would be threatened. Now that China had proved its aggressive nature, it became essential to apply the same kind of containment policy as had been applied to Soviet Communism. More specifically, the United States was now resolved to defend Taiwan. Initially, the American policy had been to localize the Korean conflict by means of policing the Taiwan Strait, to prevent extension of hostilities to the area. Now the division of Taiwan from China was to be upheld by force; a mutual security pact was signed with the National government to render assistance in case of enemy attack. In addition, it became a set American policy not to recognize the Peking regime as the government of China. As Dean Rusk, assistant secretary of state for Far Eastern affairs, said in May 1951, "We do not recognize the authorities in Peiping for what they pretend to be. The Peiping regime may be a colonial Russian government—a Slavic Manchukuo on a larger scale. It is not the Government of China. It does not pass the first test. It is not Chinese. It is not entitled to speak for China in the community of nations." The Chinese Communists from now on became merely "authorities in Peiping"—not even the term "Peking" was used in official American statements, although the Communists had reverted to the ancient title of the capital, dropping the name "Peiping," the term the Nationalists had given the city in 1928 when they moved the capital to Nanking.

Thus an important shift in America's China policy occurred during President Truman's and Secretary Acheson's tenure of office. Although before 1950 they had been willing to consider *de facto* recognition of Communist China and to refrain from giving aid to the Nationalists in Taiwan, things were entirely changed after the Chinese participation in the Korean War. There might have been a more moderate response, even if the policy of containment was applied to Asia as to Europe. For instance, American policy toward the Eastern European countries, Soviet satellites, was less extreme than the policy toward Communist China, a Soviet satellite. But the fact of fighting a war with the Chinese made it impossible to evolve a more flexible policy at the time. The idea expressed by the phrase "after what they have done to us" became the point of departure in any discussion of China. Not only ideologically but militarily American interests were seen to be deeply involved. The United States must now resist any further alteration of the status quo by force. The loss of Taiwan, as MacArthur reminded the Congress in 1951, "might well force our western frontiers back to the coasts of California, Oregon, and Washington." Similar considerations motivated a departure in policy toward Indochina. America's involvement in Vietnam began in 1950, with the initial aid to the French of $150,000,000.

American Policy and Attitudes in the 1950's

After the Sino-American embroilment in Korea, propaganda came to play a major role in relations between the two countries. In the absence of direct contact, policy was literally made on the basis of images, and people's understanding of issues was related to these images. This does not mean, however, that propaganda was entirely false. As hinted at already, an image of Sino-American conflict had as much plausibility and perhaps more reality than the old cliché about friendship between the two. In military terms, the two countries did in fact exist in direct confrontation and struggled for greater influence in Asia. There was nothing fantastic about the image of an impending crisis because of fundamental contradictions between the two countries. At the same time, the American people tended to confuse the nature of the conflict by continuing to view China as primarily a Soviet satellite. Instead of looking at Sino-American relations as those between the two countries, Americans entertained an image of global confrontation with the Soviet-directed Communist movement, of which China was a part. It was only late in the decade of the 1950's that some began to see China as a distinctive problem.

The basic language of confrontation with Communist China had been formulated during the last years of the Truman administration. The new Peking regime was viewed as an alien establishment, not representative of the Chinese people. Instead, Taiwan was pictured as more Chinese than mainland China; the island province was the true China, the free China, more representative of the Chinese people than their Red masters. There was, of course, a rising criticism of the State Department's handling of the China question, culminating in the series of Senate hearings; but such criticisms should not be made to obscure the fact that the American government shared essentially the same image of Chinese affairs as those held by the critics. At bottom was the notion that somehow the recent happenings in China were un-Chinese. Only a few years earlier, the Chinese people had been seen as a heroic people, persevering against odds and patiently struggling against a mighty Japanese army. More recently, they had appeared as internally split, unable to organize a unified government, endlessly engaged in factional strife. The Korean War had revealed, however, that a massive Chinese army could more than withstand the better equipped American force. A Chinese mass with the same traits of diligence and perseverance, but armed with modern weapons and imbued with the Communist ideology—this was a formidable spectacle. The Chinese army could no longer be equated with inefficiency and corruption. Just like the Japanese army several decades earlier, the Chinese masses were evolving a highly trained and efficiently organized modern army.

The potential danger of the existence of such a fighting force was well recognized by the American government as well as by public opinion. However, initially they both tended to view the situation as somehow unnatural and transitory. Segments of public opinion responded to it by conjuring up an idea of massive Soviet and even American conspiracy against freedom in China. Since the emergence of a powerful China was such a sudden event, many wondered why it had been possible and jumped to the conclusion that the Chinese themselves could not have brought it about. They must have been assisted by the Russians and by left-wing sympathizers within the United States. The idea that the "errors which brought on [Chiang's] defeat were not Chiang's; they were Marshall's. They were not China's; they were America's," as George Sokolsky expressed it in 1951, seemed plausible. From the perspective of today, it is evident that the critics of the Truman-

Marshall-Acheson policy seriously underestimated the forces indigenous to China. They ignored the likelihood that with or without outside help, in fact with or without Communism, the Chinese people would eventually have developed a strong, unified country, and that a unified China would not necessarily be pro-American. Nevertheless, Congressional and public denunciations of policy makers did not really contribute to the exacerbation of relations between the two countries. They were the product, not a cause, of the deterioration in Sino-American relations, and a manifestation of, not an antecedent to, the critical confrontation in East Asia. The Democratic administration had played a crucial role in bringing about the crisis.

Given the precedents set by the policy makers in 1950–1953, it is not surprising that the administration of Dwight D. Eisenhower should have continued to view Communist China as a Soviet satellite, bent upon joint aggression and expansionism; hence the need to apply the containment policy to China as well as to Russia. Already the Democratic administration had taken a step in that direction by concluding a peace treaty with Japan without the participation of the Soviet Union and Communist China. The fact that Dulles, a Republican, co-operated with Secretary of State Acheson in the matter and that the peace treaty enjoyed bipartisan support in Congress indicates basic agreement among American leaders that their debate on the China question should not be allowed to affect the new policy toward Japan. That policy was to make Japan an American ally in the Asian struggle against the forces of Communism. Thus, in return for restoration of normal relations, the United States obtained the right to retain military bases in Japan and use the entire archipelago of the Ryukyus as an Asian military bastion. The coupling of rapprochement with Japan and hostility toward Communist China was also evident in the pressure exerted on the Japanese government to conclude a peace treaty only with the National government in Taiwan. Once the government of Yoshida Shigeru gave the needed pledge, there was no opposition within the United States to the peace treaty. By 1951 opinion polls indicated that a majority of Americans expressed friendly sentiments to Japan, a country that only a few years earlier they had considered very likely to start another aggression. It was especially noticeable that the most friendly sentiments toward Japan were found in the western states, probably indicating that part at least of the pro-Japanese feeling was attributable to the inversely growing fear of China.

Dulles' assumption of office as secretary of state ensured that there would be no change in American policy toward East Asia. The Eisenhower-Dulles diplomacy may be characterized as an attempt to perpetuate the status quo that existed at the end of the Korean War. Alliances with Japan, South Korea, and Taiwan were designed for this purpose, as was the Southeast Asia Treaty Organization. The defense of Taiwan and the offshore islands, in particular, meant determination to prevent Chinese Communist seizure of these territories. As such it had a symbolic significance, expressing America's commitment to the status quo and resistance to further change in the balance of power.

It is equally clear that the containment policy never implied a "liberation" of lands that had fallen into Communist hands. Despite much talk of rolling back the tide of Communism, there was really little intention in Washington of a massive counteroffensive against the Communists. If proof were needed, the episodes in Hungary and Poland in the autumn of 1956 supplied it. In East Asia, there was no thought of encouraging the Nationalist regime in Taiwan to stage a counterattack on the mainland. Except briefly in 1953–1954, when the Eisenhower administration "unleashed" the Nationalist forces without result, the United States sought to restrain them from resorting to force to reconquer China. This was because the United States feared involvement in further land warfare in Asia. What America sought, as Secretary of State Dulles pointed out, was to prevent the Chinese Communists from trying to drive the United States out of the western Pacific. The presence of American power in that region was axiomatic; its existence was the basis of foreign policy. To check Chinese Communist expansionism in Asia, therefore, implied an image of Asia as a condominium of various forces, the most important being American power. This did not imply, however, that the United States would seek domination. Dulles had no idea of crushing the Chinese Communist regime by using American power.

Such a policy inevitably implied a two-Chinas approach. Though the State Department never acknowledged it, what in fact it was doing was to postulate two Chinas, one in China and the other in

Taiwan. American policy makers morally disapproved of the regime in China, considered Communist rule as transitory, and refused to regard it as the government of the Chinese people. But at the same time they restrained the lawful government of China, in exile in Taiwan, from staging a counterattack so that it could become the legitimate government of China in fact as well as in name. The United States, in short, was supporting a regime as the government of China but refusing to let it extend its authority to the Chinese people. This was tantamount to assuring the Communist regime in China that while it could not be regarded as the government of China it would not be attacked by force.

Whether this was the best policy under the existing conditions of international politics is open to question. It should be recalled that the Eisenhower-Dulles policy of containment coincided with the emergence of a new policy in the Kremlin. Even before Stalin's death, from around 1952, the Soviet Union had begun pursuing a policy of peaceful coexistence. This, as is well known, was a policy of taking advantage of internal contradictions within the capitalist camp, rather than of outright confrontation with it. The fundamental fact was that the Soviet Union did not want a global war; it was satisfied with its own power and relative position in world politics. Henceforth it would seek to undermine capitalist strength by non-military means. The Soviet Union would not tolerate revisionist moves within its own camp, but it would be willing to abide by the status quo that had been reached after the Korean War.

In retrospect, it seems evident that the Dulles strategy of containment was the obverse of the Soviet policy of peaceful coexistence. In essence both presupposed a definable status quo and willingness to abide by the status quo. This is one reason why there was no overt crisis at this time; so long as both sides tacitly acknowledged the policy of coexistence, there was unlikely to develop any military confrontation. At the same time, there is no question that American policy failed to evolve any positive response to world conditions. It was satisfied with maintaining the status quo, defined in military terms. Given the Soviet policy of peaceful coexistence, the United States might have taken some bold initiatives to alter the mechanism of international relations. For instance, a great deal might have been done through America's economic resources. The United States might have resorted to an aggressive economic policy to bring the nations of Eastern Europe and Asia closer to the capitalist camp. In fact, Dulles seems to have feared the new Soviet policy of peaceful coexistence, assuming that this was a disguise for Russian economic offensive. He remarked once that he much preferred Stalin's simple, militaristic policy to Khrushchev's economically oriented policy. This would have been all the more reason why Dulles might have resorted to a bold nonmilitary initiative, but in fact he did little to transcend the strategy of massive retaliation. Even while the gap between power and diplomacy widened, as nuclear weapons corresponded less and less to specific policy objectives, there was little effort to bridge the gap and somehow devise a new strategy for the new age.

Such observations become even more pertinent when one turns to America's Asian policy under Eisenhower and Dulles. The policy of the status quo might have been clearly definable and workable in an area such as Europe with a history of international power politics, where it was not very difficult to visualize a status quo as a basis for peace. Asian states, however, cannot be equated with the nation-states of the modern West. Asian nationalism is different from Western nationalism. In the absence of sovereign nation-states, the balance of power must inevitably mean something quite different from what it implies in Europe. China and Korea, two of the more highly integrated and therefore nationalistic states in Asia, moreover, were subdivided; there were two Chinas and two Koreas. The idea of the status quo, furthermore, might not be workable in an area where potentials for economic and social change were far greater than in the industrial states that had already passed the "take-off" stage. Social and economic change might be accompanied by a political revolution, obliterating any temporary modus vivendi based on the status quo. Finally, the maintenance of the peace based on Soviet-American tacit understanding might not be acceptable to Asians, who might regard such understanding as a collusion by the two Western superpowers. Given the tradition of Western colonialism and the subsequent mistrust by Asians of the West, the Asians might decide to follow their own course, without becoming involved in the cold war or in any scheme of American-Russian agreement. In other words, there would always be a potential for neutralism in Asia.

If this was the reality of Asian politics, American policy makers did not respond to it. Their basic orientation was dualistic, aimed at containing Communist power and showing little sympathy for the neutralist sentiment. Dulles at one point called the idea of neutrality "immoral." American policy tended to link the forces of anti-colonialism in Asia to Communist expansionism. The United States instead stressed "orderly change" in international affairs. Ironically, this took the form of supporting the existing governments in Korea and Taiwan, but of ignoring the established authorities in China. While the American support of Syngman Rhee did not prevent his downfall in 1960, the official American view that "Communism's rule in China is not permanent" failed to bring about any "orderly change" in the mainland favorable to the United States. At bottom was a reluctance to recognize the peculiarities of East Asia to which the universal yardstick of anti-communism might not be applicable. By assuming that the Chinese people, once they got rid of the Communist masters, would resume friendship with the United States, American officials were indulging in the illusion that the Chinese would behave like the Germans.

It is frequently argued that the state of American public opinion was such that the administration had no choice but to maintain its rigid stand toward China. Dulles was extremely sensitive to public opinion, in particular Congressional opinion. It seems doubtful, however, that the opinions of influential groups in America were as rigid as Dulles thought. If perennial opinion polls and sensational propaganda activities by some pressure groups were the equivalent of public opinion, then the evidence is almost totally one-sidedly anti-Chinese. In any opinion poll, there could be found at least 60 per cent of respondents who expressed themselves against recognition of the Communist regime in China. In February 1954, as many as 60 per cent of those polled answered in favor of leaving China out of any discussion of peace in Asia. Next year over 50 per cent of respondents favored the use of atomic bombs in China should the Chinese attack the offshore islands. The "committee of one million" was organized in 1953, devoted to the cause of opposing the seating of Red China in the United Nations as the representative of the Chinese people. The McCarthy hearings had the effect of silencing writers hitherto friendly to the Communist regime. Americans read less and less of their writings, and more and more about Chinese cruelty and terrorism, such as that experienced by American soldiers in the Korean War. Anti-communist writers sought to perpetuate the image of Communist China as not Chinese. Once this premise was accepted, it logically followed that the United States should oppose its seating in the United Nations and its recognition as the government of the Chinese people.

Given the anti-communism of the American people, the image of Communist China as Communist and non-Chinese fitted a psychological need to explain away what had happened in that country and to justify the policy of passivity toward it. It did not follow, however, that the majority of the American people accepted the government of Chiang Kai-shek as the government of China. During the Korean War, a majority of them supported the Nationalists' aspirations to go back to the mainland by force. But after the war few retained the illusion that the island of Taiwan was China. In fact, more and more Americans came to view with uneasiness the obligation to defend by force the island of Taiwan and its vicinity. By 1957 at least an equal number of those polled opposed rather than supported the defense of Taiwan and the Pescadores by American military power. Those who opposed it came to support the defense of these islands through their neutrality and under United Nations mandate. Practically no one called for return of Taiwan to China and reunification with the mainland under the Communists. Nevertheless, such changing attitudes toward the Nationalist regime were indicative of an undercurrent of American thinking that refused to support the claims of a government in exile simply because it was anti-communist.

From such a "realistic" estimate of the Taiwan situation, a similarly realistic appraisal of the China question could also be expected to emerge. For, if Taiwan was not Chinese, the real China must really be on the mainland, where China had always been. And there was no mistaking the fact that a government existed that spoke in the name of the Chinese people and that had fought fiercely against American troops in Korea. If one were to dismiss the government as a Soviet puppet, one still had to account for the existence of China. One could underplay the Communist side of the new China and try to deal with China as China. Such an attitude, while not yet clearly defined, was emerging in the late 1950's as a powerful countercurrent to the moralistic anti-communism of the administration and the extremist groups.

Chinese Interpretations of America

Compared with American views of China in the 1950's, China's attitude toward the United States may be said to have been more realistic. While Marxism-Leninism-Maoism was the language of Chinese foreign relations, the Chinese were more ready than Americans to think in terms of military considerations. Although the United States was still the ideological enemy, it was fundamentally viewed as a threat to China's national security. "Today American imperialism has become the greatest enemy, threatening our survival," said one writer early in 1951. Having tried to conquer Korea, the United States was pictured as being intent on thrusting at the heart of China. American military power, it appeared, was rearming Japan and using Japan's resources to plan attacks on the mainland of Asia. The Chinese people were told by their leaders to prepare for war with the United States; they were told of the ineffectiveness of America's nuclear weapons in the Chinese villages and of the need to have faith in China's ultimate victory.

At the same time, the 1950's saw an attempt by the Communist leaders at massive indoctrination of the Chinese people, both to ensure stability of the Communist regime and to prepare the nation ideologically for a showdown with the United States. Hate-America campaigns were organized, intellectuals underwent hours of study sessions to re-form their ideas, exhibitions were held showing the alleged use by the United States of germ warfare techniques during the Korean War, and history books were rewritten to show how America had consistently exploited the Chinese. Taking up a theme that had already been developed before 1950, Chinese writers spoke with one voice of the evil record of American imperialism in China during the last century and a half. They took pains to prove that of all the imperialist powers that had preyed upon China's weakness, none was more sinister and cunning than the United States. As one writer put it, Britain and Japan were "wicked in the extreme," while America "smiled on the surface and hid a sword inside." People all say, the author continued, that a smiling tiger was the most dangerous enemy. Another author noted, "Americans are very proud of the fact that they are number-one in everything. It is very true; it was Americans who first signed a most-favored-nation agreement with China, first excluded overseas Chinese and mistreated Chinese laborers, most eagerly sought to assist the reactionary Manchu regime to suppress the Chinese people's revolutionary movement, and carried out the most sinister policy of cultural invasion." Through sending out missionaries and receiving Chinese students for education, the United States had endeavored to establish political and economic hegemony over China. After all, wrote one author, the schools Americans founded in China were American schools, not Chinese schools, and they were designed to undermine Chinese youth's national consciousness.

Recent history was presented in equally simplistic terms. Once the nature of consistent American expansionism was accepted, even the fact of American opposition to Japan could be comprehended as but a minor variation in the over-all theme. The Washington Conference, for instance, was seen as nothing more than a stage in the imperialist aggression; for one author the Nine Power Treaty perpetuated the imperialists' united front in China to preserve intact the latter's status as a semi-colony; for another author the Washington treaties merely endorsed the United States instead of Japan in the monopolistic position in China.

The American policy of "non-recognition," which had defined America's approach to Japan in the 1930's, was now called a deceptive device to fool the Chinese; it was in fact designed to encourage Japanese aggression and had nothing to do with American friendship. When the United States did come to take an anti-Japanese stand, this was not because America was concerned with China's interests but because it wanted to deprive Japan of its predominant position in the China market. During the Pacific war, it was alleged, the United States sought to implant its influence in China by supporting the Chiang regime. Though for a while after 1944 there was some official contact between the United States and the Chinese Communists in Yenan, this was simply in order to placate the sensibilities of the Chinese people. After Stilwell was replaced by the Hurley-Wedemeyer team, the policy of utilizing Chiang Kai-shek to dominate in China became the basic policy. The Marshall mission was really a smoke screen, designed to conceal assistance to the Kuomintang. One author called Marshall an obedient executor of Wall Street policies. After the Chinese Communist victory, the United States engaged in a conspiracy to seek Taiwan's independence and separate China and the Soviet Union. Now the war in Korea indicated America's final attempt to intrude into the Asian continent and establish an anti-Soviet, anticommunist stronghold.

Obviously, there was some psychological need for the Chinese intellectuals and people in general to believe in these distortions. The very extremity of language may imply skepticism, since it may have been intended to overcome reluctance to believe in an American plot consistently to subjugate the Chinese people. In view of the prevalence of American-educated intellectuals and the influence of American missionaries, schools, and hospitals in China, it must have been considered imperative to convince the populace that all these were expressions of American imperialism. "From the visit to Canton of the *Empress of China* in 1784 down to the present day, America's China policy has always consisted in a policy of attacking, exploiting, and opposing the Chinese people." Such a statement had to be believed in before one could clearly see a link between the Korean War and the past relations between the two countries. Thus the rewriting of history became an integral part of the nationwide campaign to excoriate the United States and turn national energy to fighting the anti-imperialistic struggle.

Professional historians contributed greatly to producing fixed images of Sino-American relations. Monograph after monograph was published on the same theme, America's persistent design to establish control over China. Probably the most systematic and ambitious writing on the subject in the 1950's was Ch'ing Ju-ch'i's *History of American Aggression on China,* of which Volume One was published in 1952 and Volume Two in 1956. In these volumes the author starts out by attacking American writers on the subject as bourgeois historians intent upon intoxicating the Chinese reader with their talk of friendship between the two peoples. Actually, he says, the history of American policy in China is nothing more than the history of United States capitalist aggression on China. Relations between the two countries were determined, first, by a particular stage in the development of American capitalism, and, second, by the relative strength of American capitalism in the world.

Thus between 1784 and 1844 America's "predatory commercial capitalism" exploited the Chinese; after the Opium War, the policy of equal opportunity served as means of capitalist aggression on China; after 1861 United States imperialism prepared for monopolizing the China market; between 1900 and 1946 American imperialism in fact had a monopolistic control over China through the Open Door policy. After 1946 the United States waged aggression over the Chinese people. Although, the author says, statistically speaking American trade with China was almost minimal in the nineteenth century, this does not cloak the fact that the United States was always preparing for monopolistic control of the China market. This was inevitable, given the fact that American capitalism reached the stage of "finance capitalism" in the second half of the century, thus making it imperative to establish control over China. In fact, because trade with China was small, Americans had all the more reason to clamor for further opening of China. Moreover, all aspects of American activities—commercial, cultural, political—were interrelated. Thus missionary activities were instruments of American imperialism, designed to weaken Chinese morale and denationalize the Chinese mind.

Given such trends in Chinese writing, there was little hope that Chinese and American intellectuals would be able to comprehend each other in a mutually recognizable language. American publications, it is true, continued to find their way into China and they were utilized by Chinese writers. The above work by Ch'ing, for instance, makes substantial use of findings by "bourgeois historians." As mentioned earlier, the author condemns them as opium intended to numb the minds of the Chinese by talking about America's friendly policy toward them. At the same time, these American historians unwittingly supplied documentation that revealed the true intentions of the imperialists. Thus their work could be of use if read with caution. Even such a narrowly defined interchange between Chinese and American writers was extremely risky, as proved when Ch'ing Ju-ch'i was accused by one reviewer of his uncritical reliance on bourgeois writers. In such an atmosphere, it was hopeless to expect any kind of intellectual communication between the two peoples.

On the other hand, official Chinese policy did reveal a greater degree of flexibility. For a few years after the Korean War, the

Chinese leadership sought to follow a less rigid pattern of foreign policy. Very likely this was a result of a conscious decision to avoid another major war and concentrate on national economic development. The Soviet shift to a peaceful coexistence policy added weight to the new Chinese stand; very probably there was unity in Soviet and Chinese approaches. The leaders in Peking were now more willing to recognize neutralism as a possible alternative, whereas earlier they had declared that there was no third choice between progress and reaction. The Bandung conference of 1955 was intended to create a new image of China, willing to understand the neutralist sentiment of Asian and African countries and dedicated to the cause of peace. The Chinese Communists defined this period as a transition period, in which their country would take a gradualist road to socialism without rigidifying international bipolarity. They were interested in opening talks with American representatives, and after August 1955 Chinese and American ambassadors met periodically, first in Geneva and later, after 1958, at Warsaw. At these meetings China sought to soften America's embargo on trade with Communist China.

In terms of conceptual development, Chinese diplomacy of this period was notable for its attempt to appeal to the self-consciousness of Asians and Africans. China was trying to identify itself with the aspirations of these nations, in order to increase its influence among them and emerge as their leader in the anti-Western, anti-colonialist struggle. Thus invitations were issued to an increasing number of Japanese, who would travel to China and be reminded of the cultural affinity and historical ties between the two peoples. Through such means it was hoped that the Japanese people would detach themselves from the American policy and ultimately reduce Japan's value in the American security system.

It belongs to the realm of conjecture whether a sufficiently modified policy on the part of the United States might have brought about an improvement in Sino-American relations—for instance, whether America's withdrawal of the trade embargo and the resulting resumption of trade might have altered Chinese economic planning and foreign policy. Sooner or later, however, the thorny question of Taiwan was bound to arise. The only way to settle it might have been by avoiding it. This would have been the case only if the two sides had been sufficiently interested in rapprochement.

From the Chinese point of view, however, such rapprochement was not imperative; so long as they were sure that the United States would not resort to force, they could remain content with the existing tension and meanwhile cultivate the friendship of Afro-Asian nations. They were even willing to negotiate trade agreements with Japan. Though they believed Japan remained a satellite of the United States, Sino-Japanese trade might encourage latent pro-Chinese elements within Japan to assert their initiative and weaken the American orientation of the Tokyo government.

More fundamentally, anti-Americanism as a basic orientation of the new Chinese state had never been altered even during the period of relative moderation. Tactically, the Chinese might resort to flexible policies, but the ideology itself could not have been changed without profound repercussions on the rationale of the Communist state itself. In the mid-fifties, the Communist leaders in China explored possibilities of tactical change with respect to the United States, but their experience was such as to convince them of the undeniable existence of American power in Asia. Consequently, their language of diplomacy was steadily stiffened until, by 1957, they were confidently speaking of the superiority of the "eastern wind" over the "western wind." They were heartened by the Soviet success in missile strategy and saw it as the turning of the tide against the United States. It is from about this time that one senses in the Chinese leaders' expressions an idea of China as a power, not only as an ideologically committed nation. Given this fact, it would seem extremely unlikely that a softening in the American stand would have caused any improvement in Sino-American relations.

The Sino-Soviet Split

The Sino-Soviet dispute since the late 1950's definitely brought about the awareness that the Sino-American crisis was indeed a crisis between the two countries, not simply part of a wider, global confrontation between Communism and anti-communism. As Sino-Soviet ties deteriorated, the Chinese realized that they might have to assume the leading role in the struggle against imperialism. It is well to remember that the dispute between the Chinese and Russian Communists concerned the question of tactics toward the United

States. In the Chinese view, to cope with the threat of American imperialism by a policy of peaceful coexistence, as the Russians seemed to be doing, was unrealistic. Compromise with imperialism would only perpetuate it. As the Chinese saw the world situation, anti-imperialist forces were steadily expanding, and there was every possibility that these forces would in the end triumph over the forces of imperialism. If the Soviet Union was unwilling to lead the struggle, then China must do so. Keeping up spirited resistance to the United States was the only way to reduce its influence in Asia and elsewhere. The Chinese considered the nature of imperialism unchanged and still predatory and aggressive. So long as it existed there could be no real peace in the world. "The true nature of imperialism has not changed, and can never be changed." There was no possibility of peaceful coexistence with such a force. The easing of international tension could be brought about, not by softening one's stand against imperialism, but by persisting in the struggle. Whereas the Soviet leaders insisted that ways must be sought to avoid nuclear warfare, the Chinese countered, saying that not nuclear weapons but people were the decisive force in history and that in case of a nuclear war the United States would have committed suicide, leaving mankind surviving the war and enjoying peace afterwards. Upon the ruins of imperialism, the people of the world would build a civilization a thousand times higher than the capitalist civilization they would replace.

Naturally, the Chinese leaders were sensitive to the danger of an American nuclear attack on China, and they took steps to protect factories and military installations. Besides, they themselves began developing nuclear capabilities, first by turning to Soviet help and then, after Soviet technicians were withdrawn in 1960, by their own effort. But this simply proves their determination to fight American imperialism and their conviction about the incompatibility of China and the United States. Thus while Russia was willing to accept the status quo on the basis of the clear superiority of Soviet-American nuclear parity, the Chinese refused to admit the possibility of peaceful coexistence. Since continued struggle and ultimate confrontation were unavoidable, China must take constant steps to weaken the relative power of the United States. This was the rationale behind their advocacy of the "wars of liberation," even at the expense of perpetuating international tension. Actually, international tension would never be eased until American power was decisively weakened.

A few specific examples will further illustrate the Chinese attitude at this time. Communist China was definitely opposed to the 1963 treaty partially banning nuclear testing. This appeared to epitomize Soviet-American collaboration. The nuclear powers were pictured as entering into a monopolistic club, blackmailing all others by freezing the nuclear status quo, so that they alone would be in a position to dictate world order. To accept the definition of the status quo by the Big Three was tantamount to condemning China to a subordinate position, whose security was placed at the mercy of the nuclear powers. Since the existing distribution of power in the world itself was the same thing as American aggression, it was natural that China should oppose the existing status quo. Moreover, the test-ban agreement would perpetuate China's dependence on the Soviet Union for its protection, with the consequent possibility that China would have to accept whatever was agreed upon by the Russians in collaboration with Americans. In fact, Soviet participation in the test-ban treaty gave final proof that Russia had defected from the ranks of anti-imperialists. The Chinese people would never go along with such a disgraceful betrayal of the world's progressive forces. From then on, China would have to replace Russia as the leader of these forces. The American leaders would never succeed in their plot to isolate China by collaborating with the Soviets. The more these two countries conspired together, the stronger China's will would be to challenge the arbitrary status quo and persist in anti-imperialist struggle.

There was thus little difference in China's view of America under Eisenhower and under Kennedy. If anything, the Kennedy administration seemed the more sinister of the two because of the way it was effecting rapprochement with Russia. Such impressions seemed confirmed by the continued policy of separating Taiwan from China. As will be noted below, the Kennedy administration was willing to talk frankly about the possibility of dealing with two Chinas. From the Chinese point of view, however, the continued separation of Taiwan from China was nothing but an expression of America's aggressive designs. The Chinese Communists never deviated from their view that there was only one China and that Taiwan was a province of China, not a separate national entity. American endorsement of Taiwan as distinct from the mainland was regarded as a direct threat to the security of China. When, in 1961, the Chinese and the American ambassadors in Warsaw explored the possibility of exchanging newsmen, the Chinese made known their stand that only those Americans would be admitted to China who supported the withdrawal of American forces from Taiwan. Since the American government did not alter its opposition to the replacement of the Nationalist representatives at the United Nations by Communist delegates, the Chinese continued to consider the Taiwan question as a test of American policy toward China.

It does not seem that the Eisenhower administration consciously sought to take advantage of the Sino-Soviet rift. As Secretary of State Dulles said on numerous occasions before his resignation in 1959, "International communism is in effect a single party." China's Communist regime was still considered to be dependent on Soviet Russia, if for no other reason than that it was imperative to continue the policy of non-recognition. There was no departure from the policy of containment of China through multilateral treaty agreements and military assistance to the Nationalist regime in Taiwan. In addition, there was no visible interest in utilizing the Sino-Soviet dispute to America's advantage in Asia. Despite the implied nationalism in the dispute and the fact that countries within the Soviet bloc were exhibiting restlessness, there was no change in the American policy of dualism, looking with suspicion at movements toward neutralism and independence. In southeast Asia, for instance, the United States was reluctant to endorse a neutralist Laos although it might be just as opposed to Communism as to anti-communism.

There were signs, however, that outside the narrow circle of policy makers, ideas were gaining currency looking toward some change in the basic orientation of United States dealings with the Communist nations. "Polycentrism" became as familiar a word in the discussion of foreign affairs as "containment" and "massive retaliation." The idea connoted the image of a world divided, not between two poles but in several groupings of nations, with power centers no longer locatable only in Moscow and Washington. International Communism, in particular, was clearly seen as undergoing change. If ever there was such a thing as monolithic unity in the

Communist camp, the very existence of the Sino-Soviet dispute seemed to provide undeniable evidence of diversity and nationalism within the camp.

Opinions differed as to how the United States should chart its course in a polycentric world. Some were inclined to the view that no matter how seriously China and Russia differed, their differences did not divide them on the proposition that a weak America served their interests better than a strong one. Consequently, the Sino-Soviet dispute was far from a welcome phenomenon. In fact, the loss of Soviet control over Chinese policy might make for more intransigence on the part of the Chinese. Others argued that although the Communists disputed among themselves on their tactics toward the anti-communist camp, diversity itself was to be welcomed since it might undermine the myth of a Communist monolith. The United States, it was held, should base its policy on the recognition of the emergent nationalism in the Communist camp so that the ideological content in Soviet-American relations might be replaced by the more obvious concerns of national interest.

Regardless of how one viewed the Sino-Soviet dispute, it is noticeable that prominent voices began reasserting themselves, calling for modification of American policy toward China. One milestone was reached by the publication of the "Conlon Report" in 1959. A result of policy studies commissioned by the Senate Foreign Relations Committee, the report—by Robert Scalapino —contained a realistic appraisal of the China question. His view was that Communist China was a reality; the Chinese Communists, whatever their motivation and source of their inspiration, had succeeded in establishing a powerful and centralized government in a country that had been lacking such an institution throughout recent history. Since this was the case, realism called for some kind of association with it. Thus Scalapino advocated resumption of *de facto* relations with the Chinese regime, leaving aside the question of Taiwan. In his view there was no need to alter America's commitment to the Nationalist regime. The essential thing was to recognize the reality of Communist power on the mainland of China and to deal with it on that basis. Such views seem to have represented the thinking of most experts in the late 1950's. Here the Sino-Soviet dispute was not of direct relevance. But it showed how far China had traveled in a little over a decade since the end of the war. Now the Communist leadership seemed solidly established and even claiming a leading role in the international Communist movement. This situation could not be adequately dealt with from Washington without at least making some attempt at coming to terms with the facts.

Friction in American-Japanese Relations

Perhaps an unexpected by-product of the Sino-Soviet dispute was a strain in Japanese-American relations that marked the coming of age of the new, reconstructed Japan. The strain was ultimately attributable to the Sino-Soviet dispute since it was produced by the new, aggressive Chinese policy toward Japan. The Chinese sought to maintain influence over the Japanese Communist Party and to work through the Japanese Socialist Party to undermine the Kishi government. Toward Kishi Nobusuke, who came to power in 1957, the Peking government was noticeably cooler than toward his predecessors. China abruptly called off trade agreements and overtly encouraged opposition forces in Japan to strike a blow at the pro-American foreign policy of the government. As an alternative to the Japanese-American mutual security pact, China proposed that Japanese security might be jointly guaranteed by China, the Soviet Union, and the United States. This would be the first step toward detaching Japan from the United States. The Chinese gained a considerable victory in this tactic when Asanuma Inejirō, secretary general of the Socialist Party, openly endorsed the statement, in 1959, that United States imperialism was the common enemy of the Chinese and Japanese peoples. The Peking policy makers envisaged Japanese-American relations as in a state of change and sought to encourage the trend by explicit support of anti-American movements within Japan.

Russia's policy of peaceful coexistence, moreover, took the form in Asia of encouraging Japan's neutralist sentiment. Though the Soviet Union sought to perpetuate the status quo in Europe, it feared that the status quo in Asia would only prolong Japanese-American ties. Thus the strategy was to wean Japan away from America by promising the guarantee of Japanese security by agreement among the big powers—quite the same idea as the Chinese proposal. The Soviet government tried to appeal to Japan's pacifist and neutralist sentiment and draw Japan away from the United States and, subsequently, from China.

Under the circumstances, it is easy to see why Japanese-American relations went through a moment of strain and crisis. Japanese opinion was divided between those who sought understanding with both the Soviet Union and China, and those who continued to view the American alliance as basic to national security. Since peaceful coexistence appeared to many to be the trend in the world, they questioned the need to maintain the American security treaty, which would have the effect of prolonging Japanese identification with the capitalist camp, at a time when a thaw was developing in international affairs. Also, China would continue to be antagonized so long as Japanese policy followed American policy. The only way out of the difficulties seemed to be to accept some idea of neutrality and renounce sole dependence on American protection.

Japanese government leaders, however, were seeking ways of modifying but not abrogating the arrangements with the United States. The existing security pact was considered inadequate as it had been adopted shortly after Japan regained independence. In the old provisions, America's obligation to defend Japan was not explicitly stated; rather, the stress had been on Japan's obligation to supply the United States with bases and facilities. In addition, no clear provision had been made about "prior consultation" between the two governments in case the United States decided to employ its men in Japan for action elsewhere, and in case it planned to bring nuclear and other weapons into Japan that might conflict with the provisions of the Japanese constitution. To remedy these defects, the Kishi government sought revision of the security treaty, and its efforts were favorably received by officials in Washington. The new security treaty that was worked out and ratified in 1960 was, therefore, a step forward from the official Japanese point of view; instead of a one-sided arrangement, it specified the obligations of the United States to defend Japan and also to consult Japan prior to important changes in the disposition of its forces.

The climax in the Japanese opposition movement was reached in the summer of 1960, when street demonstrations and study groups were organized to protest against the Kishi cabinet's handling of the treaty issue and against the prospective visit of President Eisenhower to Japan. Since the date set for the visit, June 19, coincided with the date beyond which the new security treaty would automatically come into effect, the fears of many Japanese seemed confirmed; the anti-democratic forces in Japan were staking their survival on alliance with America. President Eisenhower, it has since become known, was unhappy over such a chronological coincidence and sought to view his trip as merely a good-will mission. Most Japanese agitators and organizers of the nationwide protest movement seem to have sensed the distinction, for they took pains to dissociate themselves from rabid anti-Americanism and to concentrate on attack upon Kishi. Fundamentally, however, the movement had its roots in the Japanese image of the postwar world, an image in which Japan seemed reborn as a peace-loving, democratic nation, in a world moving toward peace and democracy. Kishi represented a force to reverse the tide of history; his wartime and prewar career evoked memories of the past. Since he seemed to be tying his own fortune to the American alliance, the United States was guilty at least by association. Moreover, the basic conception of a bilateral military treaty, at a time when peaceful coexistence was the ringing demand of humanity, seemed anachronistic. In this sense, condemnation of American strategy could not be avoided. The 1960 riots were thus a climax of postwar thinking and psychology in Japan that postulated a new era in world politics and Japanese history and held the United States partly to blame for the cold war.

In the end, the security treaty stayed but Kishi left. As soon as the prime minister stepped down, after requesting cancellation of Eisenhower's trip for fear of unforeseeable incidents, the popular movement subsided, and the Liberal Democratic Party, which was now headed by Kishi's successor, Ikeda Hayato, went on to collect an overwhelming majority of votes in subsequent elections. This goes to show that the Japanese people had been concerned over the possible resurgence of militarism and dictatorship in alliance with American power, but that once the two were separated in their perception, they could accept the fact of American protection with equanimity. Undoubtedly, such an attitude was encouraged by the expectation that the Democratic administration in Washington would be more receptive to Japanese opinion than the Eisenhower administration. It is difficult to say how the Japanese might have responded to a Republican victory in the presidential election of 1960. It does not seem inconceivable, however, that even in that event much of the nationwide protest movement would have been dissipated, as the Ikeda government took pains to play down the American aspect of his policy and tried to create new symbols and slogans for Japan's future course. More basically, there was the awareness that the Japanese had now re-entered the international arena and that, instead of blindly following the American lead, they would make their views known. For Japan, too, one era was passing.

Peaceful Coexistence in American Policy

John F. Kennedy showed greater interest than his predecessor in adopting peaceful coexistence as a basic framework of American foreign policy. To what extent his policy was merely acknowledging a *fait accompli* is open to question. Certainly, there were few innovations in the basic Kennedy approach to the Soviet Union. At bottom was the same determination to maintain and even to freeze the military status quo that had moved the Eisenhower administration. At any rate, a recognition of the Soviet-American community of interest in maintaining nuclear supremacy enabled the new Democratic regime to concentrate its efforts on non-military matters, such as tariffs and cultural exchange, as areas in which an American initiative could be undertaken. The idea was that once the two superpowers recognized frankly their commitment to the status quo and the peace based on it, they could develop economic and cultural ties that might strengthen the commitment.

It was primarily in Asia that the new emphasis on peaceful coexistence blossomed into some new policies. There was more willingness to take advantage of the Sino-Soviet rift to encourage third-force movements in Asia. This was a reflection of the view that not all Communist nations were equally aggressive; there were at least two patterns in Communist foreign policy, the Russian and the Chinese. Asian countries might be induced to see the difference. Moreover, if they chose to remain outside the big power blocs, they should be encouraged to do so, inasmuch as such a decision would exhibit their independence of Communist China. Finally, if they sought to effect modernization through socialist, collectivist methods, they should not be denied their chance but should be induced to follow the Soviet rather than the Chinese pattern of development and foreign policy.

The way American leaders gradually came to differentiate between the Soviet Union and China closely parallels the way they came to view China in power terms, rather than purely in ideological terms. Communism as such was not the unmitigated evil against which America must always be prepared to fight. It was a particular brand of Communism, the Chinese brand, that was the greatest enemy. This is little different from saying that China as a nation was a military antagonist; it was not simply the Communism of its leaders, but the whole complex of the new Chinese state that posed a threat to the peace and security of Asia. President Kennedy, for instance, characterized China in terms of its "700,000,000 people, Stalinist Government . . . nuclear power . . . Government determined on war as a means of bringing about its ultimate success." Here was a clear recognition of Communist China as a power and therefore as a potential threat to the United States.

The isolation and containment of China, then, became a cardinal doctrine of American foreign policy under the Kennedy administration, a policy that was pursued by the succeeding Johnson administration. In Laos, for instance, the Department of State departed from the policy under Dulles of refusing to deal with, and even of taking a hand in overthrowing, the neutralist government under Prince Souvanna Phouma. Now he was eagerly sought after as the man who would hold the southeast Asian kingdom together, albeit in strict neutrality. A neutral Laos was obviously much more desirable than a pro-Chinese Laos; it might even be more desirable than an obviously pro-American regime, which might be a regime that could well divide the country and weaken its potential as a shield against China. Similarly, the United States was much more forceful than earlier in giving military assistance to neutralist India. Despite the fact that India already recognized Communist China and collided with America on that question in the United Nations, there was the belief that a strong India, no matter what its diplomatic orientation, could not but be a check to Chinese expansionism. Likewise, the United States took steps to encourage rapprochement between Japan and South Korea as well as moves toward a Pacific economic union. Administration spokesmen deliberately spoke of Japan as a partner in the undertaking. No longer a ward or a mere base for American forces, Japan was to be encouraged to play a major role in the development of a more integrated Pacific and Asian community of nations. Though such a conception hardly went beyond vague generalities, it was a step in a direction different from that of the old multilateral security arrangements. The United States would continue to supply military power, but if it were coupled with Japan's industrial power, other lands' natural resources, and above all the Asian peoples' determination to modernize themselves within free societies, such a community of nations should bring about a new era of peace and prosperity in Asia and provide the best guarantee against aggression.

Basic to such a notion is the idea of "development," a word used on numerous occasions by President Kennedy as well as by Secretary of State Dean Rusk. History is viewed as a steady realization of man's aspirations for economic security and political freedom. Events in the Soviet Union seemed to prove that even in a totalitarian regime, these aspirations could never be extinguished but rather drove the leaders to adjust themselves to them. As a result of economic development, there had emerged a more mature attitude toward international affairs, and now the Soviet leaders seemed eager to maintain world peace and work toward the betterment of their people's standard of life. The same could be said of most other socialist countries. In Asia, where the majority of people were undergoing stages of modernization, the cardinal fact appeared to be that of their yearning for peace, prosperity, and dignity. Their aspirations could never be crushed by arbitrary power from outside. The United States must identify itself with these forces and help the process of development in these lands. The "winds of freedom" in Rusk's words were blowing everywhere; America must recognize this and help the trend, no matter where these winds were.

When applied to the China question, such a belief calls for two different sets of policy. On the one hand, it leads to the idea that the Chinese people, too, would want change and freedom, that they, too, aspire to better life. At the least it might be recognized that some time in the future winds of freedom would visit China and the people would be more receptive to reasoning. On the other hand, insofar as the present leadership in China was impervious to these trends, they must be resisted with all available means lest they should violate basic human freedoms elsewhere. Until the winds of freedom enveloped China, it was best to isolate that nation and show it the untenability of forcing violent change upon other peoples.

The famous "open door" speech by Roger Hilsman, assistant secretary of state for Far Eastern affairs, shortly after President Kennedy's assassination, reveals the same duality. He stated, "We find important differences in the willingness and ability of the Soviet Union and Communist China, at the present stage of their respective development, to reach limited agreements which can bring some reduction of the terrible dangers and tensions of our present-day world." Because the Communist leaders in China were wedded to "a fundamentalist form of Communism which emphasizes violent revolution, even if it threatens the physical ruin of the civilized world," they must be met by firmness and strength, so that they would not "subvert or commit aggression" against China's "free world neighbors." Yet at the same time Hilsman recognized the possibility of change in China, especially as the second-echelon leaders reached positions of power and realized the gap between reality and the grandiose theories of the top leaders. "We are determined to keep the door open to the possibility of change, and not to slam it shut against any developments which might advance our national good, serve the free world, and benefit the people of China." The speaker was extremely vague as to how change would come about in China, but he mentioned the Chinese tradition of patience, tolerance, and diversity. This, coupled with the coming into being of hopefully pragmatic second-generation leaders, would in time transform Chinese society.

Despite such an "open door" approach, basic American policies toward specific questions of China were unchanged. For instance, no new policy on Taiwan was suggested in the Hilsman speech. He reiterated America's commitment to protect Taiwan and declared, "So long as Peking insists on the destruction of this relationship as the sine qua non for any basic improvement in relations between ourselves and Communist China, there can be no prospect for such an improvement." In the American view Nationalist China was a sovereign state, with which the United States had entered into a binding compact. To concede, as the Peking government insisted, that Peking had legitimate authority over Taiwan, was to condone aggression. In fact, it seems clear that from about 1961 Washington's main concern was with keeping Taiwan in the United Nations and preventing its seat from being taken away to make room for Communist Chinese representation. Taiwan, said many officials, was a model for underdeveloped countries; it had achieved an enormous success in economic development and political modernization, within the framework of a non-communist system. It was unthinkable to give up such a country to the Communists. Taiwan was a developing nation, a member of the peace-loving community of Asian countries, while Communist China was still in its aggressive stage. Until it changed its outlook, a possibility which was not entirely out of the question, China's expansive tendencies must be resisted with force and determination.

What the United States was attempting, then, was to define a military status quo in Asia and promote greater economic interdependence and regional integration, to promote the welfare of the inhabitants. Both of these objectives would in effect isolate China, but they held out the prospect of some day dealing with the new China as a nation. If the Chinese on the mainland refrained from aggression, and if they sought instead to concentrate on the economic development of their country, some basis might be found for resumption of contact between China and the United States. Here was a definition of international relations by a nation at a higher stage of modernization, at a time when the majority of nations were still either underdeveloped or only partially modernized. Such a definition from the Chinese point of view was tantamount to perpetuating American ascendance in the world. Nevertheless, it is to be noted that by the 1960's American officials were willing to depart from the old dualism of Communism and anti-communism and think of China as a nation with whose problems and policies the United States would have to cope realistically.

All indications are that such an attitude was shared by a majority of informed Americans. Surveys made in this period were unanimous in concluding that while there remained a sizable undercurrent of anti-Chinese views, at least half of those with any ideas about China were ready to approve of steps to improve relations between the two countries—sending surplus food to the Chinese, seating Communist Chinese representatives in the United Nations, and taking similar steps to increase contact between the two peoples. Given strong presidential leadership, a study concluded, most Americans would not object to the seating of Chinese Communists in the United Nations; only 30 per cent or less would favor American withdrawal from the international body if China were admitted. All of this indicates that American opinion paralleled American official thinking in its evaluation of the China problem. Instead of treating it as a moral question, there had developed a more prudential attitude, a willingness to view China in power terms.

The fact that in the early 1960's Japan consciously pursued an economically oriented foreign policy added another dimension to American-Asian relations. So far as the United States was concerned, Japan was a key "partner" in East Asia and it gave official endorsement to any moves on the part of Japan to emerge as an independent, self-assertive nation. Ambassador Edwin O. Reischauer, serving in Tokyo during 1961–1966, expanded the idea of partnership and encouraged the notion that Japan was a country endowed with all the attributes, save military, of a great power, at a much higher stage of modernization than China or any other country in Asia. The United States and Japan, in this view, were two advanced states with many common interests, and their differences could be resolved through "dialogues" as between equals. Such ideas began to appear less and less extraordinary to a people who, sixteen years after the war, were regaining their self-confidence. In a sense the ideals of the Japanese of Prime Minister Ikeda's generation, born at the turn of the century and educated in the Western-dominated atmosphere of the 1910's and the 1920's, came to a fruition in the 1960's. Unencumbered by costly military expenditures or by big-power status, Japan could take a single-minded road to economic advancement. The country would then equal the West in material terms, and on that basis it would be able to make a contribution to world peace. Japan would be one of the three "pillars" of the free world, the other two being the United States and Europe. But it would also trade with the Communist countries under the principle of the "separation of politics and economics." Politically, Japan would remain allied to the United

States and tied to the free world, but economically it would cultivate overseas markets wherever possible.

In a way it was ironical that a new "realism" in Japanese intellectual thinking followed, rather than preceded, such an orientation in foreign policy. Ordinarily, a great intellectual debate would have ushered in a new policy orientation instead of concerning itself with the pros and cons of actual policy. However, Japanese writers and specialists on world affairs who espoused realism were conspicuous for their support of the basic framework of Japanese foreign policy and thus gave an intellectual endorsement to Ikeda's approach. What is more striking, they sanctioned the whole course of postwar Japanese history as generally good, whereas their opponents were unhappy about the basic trends in Japanese foreign affairs after the Korean War. While the predominant line of intellectual thinking before the 1960's had been to favor pacifism, disarmament, and often neutralism as a way to peace, there now emerged a school of thought that frankly espoused realism in international politics. As one of its champions said, "I am a realist in the sense that I comprehend international politics primarily within the framework of the struggle for power and emphasize the role of power in international affairs." Such an attitude was consciously opposed to the more pervasive view that gave precedence to moral and ideological concerns. The postwar military alliance with the United States, for instance, would be condemned by the idealists as having contributed to tension in East Asia and delimited freedom of action for Japan. The realists, on the other hand, argued that the American alliance had actually created a balance of power in East Asia that had prevented a major crisis after the Korean War. Those who called for Japan's neutrality were thus not only ignorant but irresponsible; they did not seem to consider realistically the consequences of Japan's neutrality for the balance of power or for peace in East Asia. There was really no connection between neutrality and peace.

Although there was really little that was new in the "realism" thus developed, it found Japanese opinion receptive. While the impression of anti-Americanism that the Japanese intellectuals had given was not wholly accurate, it had also been true that the opponents of anti-American thought had not found a cogent theory. Now, however, realism supplied an intelligible framework. Because of the very strength of this position, it evoked heated discussion. The realists were accused of being in fact unrealistic in trying to perpetuate the status quo, or of having betrayed the postwar democratic revolution in Japan. Nevertheless, realism as a framework of thought stayed with Japanese consciousness and legitimized the government's commitment to the American alliance as well as to its economically oriented foreign policy. Thus in Japan, too, a current of intellectual opinion was approximating perception with reality. The United States came to be viewed by some not as the epitome of capitalism or the culprit in perpetuating the international tension, but as a power, one of the two great powers, whose policy Japan might manipulate in order to safeguard its own interests. There was, moreover, an implicit assumption that only the coincidence of interests, not any sentimental ties, bound the two countries together. By the same token, the realists looked at China as a power of formidable potentialities. Thus the realists had to devise an equation in which Japan between America and China might somehow maximize its interests.

12
Epilogue: Toward a More Peaceful Pacific

After nearly two centuries of forming images of each other, Americans and Chinese seem only to have reached the point where any two nation-states would be at the initial stage of confrontation; each is fundamentally concerned with the threat that the other presents to its security, whether actual or potential. Japanese and Americans have gone through this stage once, but after twenty years of necessarily discreet silence the Japanese are again showing renewed concern with national security problems. It is as though American-Chinese-Japanese relations had been reduced to the most elementary level of military and power equations. Paradoxically, such a situation serves to highlight the crucial importance of ideas in the tripartite crisis.

Concern with the military aspect of Sino-American relations has increased as a result of the war in Vietnam and China's nuclear tests. The question most seriously asked, accordingly, is not whether Communist China should be recognized or allowed to trade with the United States, but whether there will be war between the two countries. The emergence of China as a nuclear power has produced many gloomy forecasts. Journalists have declared that China has become the most dangerous country in the world, the greatest threat to peace; specialists have analyzed the impact of China's nuclear armament on United States security and interests with varying degrees of pessimism but with equal seriousness; and officials have quietly taken steps to reassess strategy in the Pacific and prepare for a possible nuclear war with China, while at the same time reassuring Asian countries that there would be no change in the policy of containment. The Chinese, on their part, have developed new security problems for themselves as a result of cultivating nuclear capabilities. Although they have started on this course to break the American-Soviet nuclear monopoly, which was considered inimical to Chinese security, they would now have to consider the possibility that other powers would adjust their strategies toward China and even try to destroy its military installations before they grew into menacing proportions.

The war in Vietnam, too, has been basically a military question involving China and the United States. The question has been phrased in the form of "where to draw the line." Because southeast Asia has not been a clearly delimited sphere of influence of either China or America, both powers have quite naturally tried to establish a power equilibrium, each to its own advantage. Vietnam functions as a contested buffer between the two powers. However, the Vietnamese situation is satisfactory to neither country, since instability and uncertainty could lead to a shift in the balance of power. At the same time, the United States has made it clear that it will not extend the war into Chinese territory and that it will not take steps that might invite direct Chinese participation in the Vietnam conflict. The underlying policy assumption for the American government has been that the forceful reunification of Vietnam by the Communists would be a threat to the peace and security of Asia, since such a Vietnam would be closely tied to Communist China, whether voluntarily or involuntarily. An independent Vietnam, at least an independent South Vietnam, would be a symbol of southeast Asia's independence of Chinese control. Otherwise, the whole of Asia would fall to Chinese hegemony. Chinese reasoning is quite similar. Peking sees a threat to its national existence if the United States came to control the whole of Vietnam. Short of that, China would not directly intervene in the hostilities. Chinese security would not be menaced so long as American power were kept away from the Chinese border areas. At the same time, prolongation of the Vietnam conflict would wear out American resources, physical and spiritual, and tend to reduce the influence of the United States in southeast Asia. This, of course, would serve to mitigate American power vis-à-vis China. For this reason, it is considered essential to aid the anti-American groups in Vietnam short of war.

An index of the way China and the United States have come to grapple realistically and coherently with their military relations has been the growing national debate in each country on the subject. Given the fact of military confrontation and the policy of avoiding war, the leaders in the two countries have had to reconsider basic approaches to each other and reassess their respective capabilities. The growing interest in certain American circles in establishing contact with Communist China indicates the frankness with which they now view that country. It is an index, not of improvement but of increasing seriousness in the relations between the two powers. The more serious the relationship and the more threatening the prospect of conflict, the greater would be the need to shed time-worn clichés and self-centered images and grapple the reality of power. No friendly gesture on the part of America would reduce China to the status of a small power; on the contrary, China will continue to grow militarily and otherwise regardless of the attitude of the American people. For this very reason, many have felt the necessity to view China as China now is and explore areas where compromise could be possible. Thus, for instance, many have stressed the need to seek China's participation in any discussion of disarmament. It would be useless to enter into a nuclear disarmament agreement from which a major nuclear power was excluded. The fact that the government in Washington generally takes the same view indicates the growing realism in American policy as a by-product of the military confrontation.

The hearings on China in the Senate Foreign Relations Committee, held in March 1966, were a landmark in that they raised questions of tactics on the assumption that Sino-American relations were entering a moment of serious crisis. The policy of "containment without isolation," which various experts suggested, had a symbolic meaning; the time had come when China as a power could no longer be treated as a non-nation, a non-government. The American people must shed the myth that China was not really China, and try to cope with the China question realistically and prudently. Containment would be a valid strategy militarily; but if it were to work, the strategy should not be cluttered with the intellectually dubious assumption of China's non-existence or impermanence. Even those who insisted on the isolation of China gave the policy a military rather than a moral meaning. The continued non-recognition of the Communist regime, for instance, was defended as the best way to counter China's military threat. Recognition, in this view, would only embolden the Chinese to undertake further aggressive acts. In this way, the hearings and the national debate they generated served to mark the coming of a new era in the American view of Sino-American relations.

In China, too, the leaders have seriously debated tactical questions vis-à-vis the United States. While the basic axiom of confrontation with imperialism is accepted by all, there remain specific problems of dealing with the United States. Whether to accept the American challenge and engage in an all-out effort short of war to counter American military force in Asia, or whether to concentrate on industrialization and the strengthening of the social structure, postponing as much as possible a showdown with imperialism, is the central dilemma of Chinese policy. While there are other questions involved in the recent Great Proletarian Cultural Revolution, there is little doubt that foreign policy has been one of the most difficult issues faced by the Chinese leaders. Because it is recognized that a wrong step on their part could bring about foreign—in particular American and/or Soviet—intervention, the development of national unity and coherent policy is of utmost importance.

In Japan, meanwhile, the possibility of Chinese-American war has served to focus national attention on the question of security. Whether to continue to depend on the American "nuclear umbrella" for protection, to develop Japan's own nuclear capabilities, or to renounce force and military alliances as safeguards and instead work for a neutralized East Asia—through such questions the Japanese have tried to clarify their country's power position vis-à-vis China and the United States. Here, too, the debate has been reduced to purely military calculations. For the first time since the end of the war, realistic evaluations of Japanese security problems have been attempted by those in and out of the government. How to protect the country, sandwiched between two, indeed three, nuclear powers, is the question that fascinates where it does not obsess the people. Dependence on American military force, the necessity for which is recognized by a majority of writers, is viewed as having certain risks. Japan's identification with American strategy might provoke China; and, conversely, America in its anxiety to avoid war with China might decide to withdraw protection from Japan. Thus ultimately the question of Japan's own armament is bound to arise.

In viewing Sino-American relations as in a state of crisis, the Chinese and Americans may be said to have finally accepted the reality of their military confrontation. If idealism and ideology have in the past led to misunderstanding, the new realism may be expected to pave the way toward some kind of mutual accommodation in the future. Because the two countries have never before viewed each other in purely military terms, the new phase in their relations may lead to a saner approach to Asian problems. Viewed from such a perspective, the prophets of doom in China and America, who paint gloomy pictures of ultimate conflagration, are really prophets of hope, demonstrating that the common language of confrontation has been accepted by both sides. By the same token, the two countries might now be better prepared to adjust themselves to changing balances of power. For instance, if there occurred a relative increase in the military power of Japan or India, China and the United States might be more ready to consider rapprochement. If, decades hence, Chinese and Americans were to enter a new epoch of mutual understanding, they would find that such understanding was possible only after the critical period of the 1950's and the 1960's, in which they sought to penetrate rhetoric and consider factors that produced the state of near belligerency.

And yet, Chinese, Americans, and Japanese will never be able to escape the need for ideas. It is not simply that Communist ideology is inseparable from Chinese foreign policy, or that the dogma of anti-communism is intertwined with American strategy. Every policy and every strategy are by definition dependent on antecedent events and their evaluations through the medium of ideas. The point, rather, is that even if it were possible to strip the Chinese state of its doctrine, and the American nation of its beliefs, their encounter as two military powers would define only the outline of their relations. After all, national security is an idea. By talking about the nation's survival, one is talking not only of its physical existence but also of what it stands for. The Japanese, for instance, may argue for or against nuclear armament, but even if this question were settled there would remain the far more difficult problem of what it was that had to be protected. The search for national purpose and cultural identity would continue.

All international relations, in this sense, are relations among ideas, among images people and nations have of themselves and each other. The human mind must always intervene between the world and a given policy. The role of ideas and their images, however, seems particularly significant in American-Asian relations. To state reasons for this fact is to summarize this book.

First of all, American–East Asian relations started primarily in the realm of ideas rather than of deeds. China, for instance, was more an idea in the American mind than a physical reality. It stood for something, just as Japan would in time come to symbolize Asia's "awakening." China and Japan, in fact, "awakened" in American imagination on quite a number of occasions, reflecting the fact that on these occasions it was the Americans who reached out to Asia.

Second, it was through some framework of thought that rapidly changing conditions of life in East Asia could be comprehended. For instance, Japan's emergence as a modern state and eventually as an imperial naval power had to be fitted into American consciousness in some intelligible manner. The initial framework of Westernization, which enabled Americans to view Japanese progress complacently if not condescendingly, would no longer suffice when Japan began menacing Western interests in Asia. Some idea had to be found to account for such a development. Similarly, the growing importance of Asia in world politics would need a new vocabulary if the phenomenon were to be related to more familiar conceptions of international relations. Not only Americans, but Japanese and Chinese tried to devise systems of thought which would enable them to relate the particular to the universal, the unfamiliar to the familiar. Whether Asia in world politics was fundamentally different from Western-centered international affairs was a question that fascinated generations of writers and officials in these countries. Initially, Asia was seen merely as an object of Westernization or of Western power politics. The rise of Japanese power and of Chinese nationalism then called for typologies of the East-West relationship. The United States as the strongest Western country, Japan as the strongest Asian country, and China as an arena of American-Japanese contention; or China as the Asian power and Japan as looking both toward America and toward China; such phenomena called for subtle generalizations and comprehensive ideas.

Third, the self-conscious formulation of American foreign policy in terms of certain ideas, under Presidents Taft and Wilson, had a profound impact on American–East Asian relations. From then on, official relations between the three countries came to depend as much on "idealism" as on "realism." In addition to naval rivalry in the Pacific or economic competition in Asia, ideas such as self-determination of peoples and helping a weak country became associated with American policy in East Asia. These ideas, and what followed from their dissemination, played crucial roles in the 1930's and afterwards.

Fourth, not only in America but elsewhere, the twentieth century saw an expanded interest on the part of ordinary men in foreign affairs. In an age of mass media and public opinion, people's conceptions of the world and attitudes toward international problems became an important determinant of foreign policy. Although "people's diplomacy" is an elusive phrase, the fact remains that in China and Japan as well as in America such a term was used to describe the growing concern of the people with external issues and their demand to have a greater say in decision making. Their prejudices and misconceptions thus inevitably found their way into official policy. Because the three peoples had had little international experience and shared few common assumptions, their ideas and emotions served to magnify their differences or exaggerate areas of agreement. It should be kept in mind, however, that the increased role of public opinion in international relations was a world-wide phenomenon in the twentieth century. Because the United States and East Asia came into direct contact only in the present century, their mutual relations became part of the global picture of increasing interregional communication and the expanding importance of popular ideas and attitudes.

Fifth, related to the above phenomenon, is the role of the government in creating, controlling, and manipulating public opinion. This is especially notable in times of war or in a totalitarian setting. The last several decades have seen the governments of Japan, China, and the United States controlling popular knowledge of and attitudes toward the world by monopolizing information, misinterpreting data, publishing propaganda materials, and directly or indirectly interfering with education. People have believed in the particular view of American–East Asian relations that their leaders have imparted to them. In this sense, Sino-American relations have been little more than what the two governments say they are. Because the Chinese Communists have monopolized all political and educational channels in the country, the role of propaganda in China has been overwhelming; it would seem that the mass of people have no way to distinguish between propaganda and facts.

Sixth, military and economic aspects of foreign relations are much easier to define than the cultural, psychological, emotional aspects; and yet these latter are the key to cross-cultural understanding. Militarily, China and the United States might today "understand" each other as potential enemies, but their psychological and ideological incompatibility remains. Japan and the United States, on the other hand, have learned to look at one another as partners in trade and in mutual security arrangements. How far the two peoples "understand" each other, however, is open to question. As a writer in a recent issue of the *Atlantic* put it, "Japan, today the world's third largest industrial power, looms above Asia as does Fujiyama over the plains of Tokyo, yet as far as most Americans are concerned, their major Pacific ally is all but unknown." James W. Morley has written that the American people seem "abysmally uninformed and unprepared" for the rise of Japan as the power in Asia and as one of the three great industrial countries in the world. The Japanese, in contrast, may factually know more about the United States. But their study of American history, culture, and institutions is still at a primitive stage of development, compared with the study of Europe. Titles such as *America and I, My Amer-*

ica, and *This Is America* easily become best sellers, but few Japanese writers have done more than report on their personal experiences in the United States. Obviously, cultural interdependence between the two countries has lagged far behind military and economic ties. It remains to be seen whether the Japanese, Americans, and also Chinese might yet succeed in developing ideas and assumptions that could contribute to reducing misunderstanding.

Seventh, ideas about the past necessarily derive from particular experiences, whether personal, national, or international. Although there is no logical connection between a specific experience and an idea about that experience, there is no question but that images about the past constitute part of one's vocabulary and mental equipment; indeed "lessons" derived from the past are often an important part of the language of international affairs. Because of the very paucity of their experience in the world scene and the rapidly changing patterns of their mutual relations, the United States, China, and Japan have given undue importance to the past as they each see it. For instance, the Chinese attitude toward the United States is a product of the postwar experience, itself a creature of abnormal circumstances, and is shaped by the image of the Western imperialist aggression after the Opium War. Likewise, America looks at China on the basis of the limited contact before and after the war and especially the unusual episodes of the postwar years. There seems little in the past from which a new vision of more peaceful relations could be derived. What these three nations have experienced of each other in the past does not automatically provide a language for tomorrow.

That fact more than any other is why the future relations between Asia and the United States depend so much on genuine intellectual communication. Only when American–East Asian relations are seen as an intellectual problem, and only when efforts are made to overcome propaganda, emotionalism, and excessive empiricism, will it become possible to transcend the past and look toward a more peaceful Pacific. If Chinese, Japanese, and Americans could develop a new vocabulary to facilitate mutual association, if they could liberate themselves from the burden of the past—if someday that were brought to pass, then the trans-Pacific community of peoples would in fact emerge and make its unique contribution to the development of human understanding.

V
Developments Since the 1960's

13
The End of an Era

Changes in the San Francisco System

The preceding chapters were written in the mid-1960's. Now, nearly thirty years later, it is clear that many observations contained there, especially toward the end, reflected the then widespread feeling of pessimism if not despair about the state of U.S.-Chinese relations. From the vantage point of 1965–1966 when the book was first written, it appeared as if the two countries were, and would remain, adamantly opposed to each other militarily and ideologically. The sense of crisis was heightened by the escalating war in Vietnam and by the Great Proletarian Cultural Revolution, two major events that were still under way when this book was published (1967). The United States government justified its deepening military involvement by citing the need to contain Communist China, while the People's Republic intensified its ideological campaign to mobilize the masses against foreign imperialists and their domestic "lackeys." Japan, in the meantime, was hardly noticed. It did not play a role in the Southeast Asian conflict, and its policy toward China meekly followed—or so it seemed—America's. The future of American-Asian relations for the foreseeable future seemed to depend on the outcome of the apparently interminable Cold War confrontation between the United States and the People's Republic of China (PRC).

Within a few years, all this was to change. Indeed, between 1968 and 1973 international affairs developed with such breathtaking speed and in such unpredictable ways that soon commentators were talking of the passing of an era, even the end of the Cold War. The United States began to wind down its war, negotiated nuclear non-proliferation and arms control agreements with the Soviet Union, and took steps to recognize the People's Republic of China. The latter, in turn, experienced a leadership crisis, with a handful of top leaders deciding to break with the anti-U.S. stance and to reciprocate Washington's overtures for a rapprochement, in the meantime maintaining a hostile attitude toward Moscow. Japan followed America's lead in reorienting its policy toward Peking, but at the same time achieved spectacular successes in its trade and industrialization programs. As America's economic supremacy began to be challenged by Western Europe and Japan, inter-Allied friction on trade and monetary issues grew, and the postwar system of international economic relations collapsed. At home, Americans of all ages and circumstances came to question some of the premises of Cold War diplomacy. By 1973, the images and vocabulary in which one used to comprehend world affairs had been significantly altered; in fact, images and words describing American relations with China, and even Japan, in the 1970's would have been unimaginable a decade earlier.

One good way to understand this sea change is to go back to the Japanese peace treaty of 1951 (see p. 294). Although some fifty countries signed the treaty at the peace conference held in San Francisco in September of that year, it was the United States that had taken the lead to end the occupation of Japan and to reintegrate that country into the community of nations. The community of nations, however, meant at least two different things. First there was the United Nations, founded in 1945 as the successor to the prewar League of Nations and as the embodiment of the world's determination to prevent another war. Perhaps its most important principles were written into chapter two of the United Nations charter: "All members shall settle their international disputes by peaceful means . . . and give the United Nations every assistance in any action it takes in accordance with the provisions of the Charter.'' The ideas of international cooperation and collective security were to have provided the basis of the postwar international order. But this world organization proved ineffectual in the absence of solid cooperation between the United States and the Soviet Union, and in the absence of PRC participation. (China was represented in the U.N. by the Nationalist regime in Taiwan.) So, while Japan duly became a member of the United Nations in 1956, neither U.S.-Asian affairs nor international relations on the whole were significantly affected by it. Rather, the San Francisco peace treaty, which did specify that Japan would abide by the policies and principles contained in the United Nations charter, tended to confirm the second definition of international relations, a world divided by Cold War antagonisms. Neither the Soviet Union nor the People's Republic of China signed the peace treaty, whereas Taiwan did, and the United States and Japan coupled it with a security treaty, tying the latter unambiguously to the former in a divided world. During 1951–1954 the United States signed bilateral treaties for mutual defense with the Republic of Korea, the Philippines, and the Republic of China, while also entering into two regional pacts: the Southeast Asia Treaty Organization and the ANZUS. The former established a system of collective security to defend the status quo in Indochina, while the latter brought Australia and New Zealand into the American security arrangements for the Pacific.

We may call these arrangements ''the San Francisco system.'' It was, to be sure, not as systematically developed or regionally as integrated as the North Atlantic Treaty Organization; nevertheless it established a framework for America's Asian-Pacific strategy. That strategy was essentially part of the global Cold War. As noted in chapter 11 (pp. 305–308), the split between China and the Soviet which began to be noticeable by 1960 indicated that the world was not exactly divided into two hostile camps. Both the U.S.-Soviet agreement on banning atmospheric nuclear testing (1963) and the growing self-assertiveness on the part of some Third World countries showed that the world was divided into more than just the Soviet bloc and the U.S. allies. Nevertheless, throughout the 1950's and most of the 1960's, the antagonism between the United States and the Communist powers provided the basic framework for Asian regional affairs. Despite the Sino-Soviet split, the two countries' thirty-year alliance (concluded in 1950) remained in effect, the United States and Japan renewed its security treaty in 1960, and even India, which had spearheaded the movement for Asian and African neutralism, turned to the United States as well as to the Soviet Union for help when it clashed with China over a border dispute in 1962.

The San Francisco system gave the Asian-Pacific region a degree of stability in that the foreign affairs of most countries in the area were defined in terms of the Cold War. Moreover, given America's commitment to the status quo, and to its willingness to use military force to uphold the regional balance of power, countries such as Japan, Taiwan, and South Korea were able to spend much less than they might otherwise have done on defense, and so to divert more and more of their resources to economic development and growth. This was particularly true of Japan, where a determined political leadership (exemplified by Prime Ministers Yoshida Shigeru in the 1950's and Ikeda Hayato in the 1960's) followed a policy of giving primacy to economics; only a minimal amount was spent each year on defense, and the amount steadily declined as a percentage of the national income so that by the mid-1960's it fell to about one percent. This was rather an exceptional case, and neither Taiwan nor South Korea—nor any other country tied to the United States—could afford such luxury. Even they, however, began turning their attention to economic tasks, laying the groundwork for their impressive performances in the subsequent decades. Stability in the domestic political context, on the other hand, frequently meant domination by those committed to the U.S. alliance and to the policy of combating Communist power, whether Soviet or Chinese. The Liberal Democratic Party in Japan, which was formed out of conservative parties in 1955 and never relinquished its hold on national politics thereafter; the presidency of Syngman Rhee and, after a brief period of turmoil following his resignation in 1960, that of Park Chung Hee in the Republic of Korea; and the Nationalist regime in Taiwan under Chiang Kai-shek—these were examples in which domestic political order and foreign affairs were two sides of the same coin.

American approaches to Asia during this period, as outlined in chapters 11 and 12, were defined within the same framework, thus further confirming it. Recent scholarship reaffirms that both the

Eisenhower and the Kennedy administrations adhered to the basic view of the Sino-Soviet bloc as a threat to the security of the area. The United States still viewed itself as engaged in a Cold War contest with the Communists, and so it was considered incumbent upon itself to uphold the status quo, in other words, the San Francisco system.

The Vietnam War

Nowhere was this commitment more clearly revealed than in the Indochina peninsula. Both the Eisenhower and the Kennedy administrations took it for granted that Southeast Asia constituted part of the San Francisco system. The much discussed and criticized "domino theory," that if Vietnam fell other countries in the region would fall one after another, in turn threatening the security of the rest of Asia and indeed of the whole world, was at least logically consistent with an image of the world in which forces of order were struggling to maintain stability against forces of disorder, whether led by Moscow or by Peking or by both. The vocabulary of the American involvement in Vietnam which stressed "nation-building," economic development, and U.S. "credibility" all fitted into the picture. South Vietnam was viewed as a small, young country trying to preserve its independence; it deserved support so that it could concentrate on economic development like other Asian countries; and if South Vietnam fell to the Communists, one corner of the alliance system would have been destroyed, bringing to question American power and determination to uphold the rest.

The intensified U.S. involvement in Vietnam under President Kennedy paralleled the emerging American perception of China as the most dangerous threat to the Asian regional order. In 1956, the National Security Council had determined (in a memorandum known as NSC 5612/1) that Vietnam was an arena for Communist expansionism, a test ground for the functioning of the Soviet system of alliance. By the early 1960's, however, as the United States and the Soviet Union took tentative steps toward accommodation on nuclear issues, and as the Sino-Soviet split became more and more apparent, China came to be seen as the major antagonist in Southeast Asia. In other words, Vietnam provided the setting for the United States to confront Chinese power. Events in the peninsula were put in that framework. Although the turmoil in South Vietnam had much more to do with the inability of its leadership to maintain order and to obtain public support, weaknesses that were incessantly taken advantage of by both the Vietcong (Communists in the country) and by North Vietnam for extending their influence, Washington leaders and observers saw China's hand behind them, giving support to and manipulating them in its own interest. Indeed, even those in America who, from around 1965, began criticizing the war effort, often argued that by fighting them the United States was pushing the Vietnamese to the support of China, whereas they should be encouraged to remain independent of China, a situation that would be advantageous from the American point of view.

Although President Kennedy was assassinated in November 1963—ironically, the same month saw the assassination of Ngo Dinh Diem, the unpopular leader of South Vietnam—his policy was continued under his successor, Lyndon B. Johnson. In fact, both of these assassinations can be said to have led to an escalation of the war. President Johnson felt to "win" in Vietnam was a mandate he had inherited from Kennedy, and believed to retreat there would be much less acceptable to him as he lacked his predecessor's popularity to begin with. The end of the oppressive Diem regime in Saigon, on its part, created a situation where no one person or party emerged that was capable of maintaining any degree of unity and order in South Vietnam. Politicians and generals came and went, claiming to represent the Vietnamese people, and the United States hopefully looked to them as the new leaders to coalesce anti-Communist forces in the country. No such coalescing was forthcoming, however, and Johnson felt obliged to send in more and more American troops to combat the Communists. The war clearly became an American war. Unlike the Korean War, U.S. allies did not help out, except for South Korea which sent 143,000 troops in 1966 alone. This, however, was a significantly smaller number than the nearly 500,000 American men, or than the 320,000 China sent during 1965–1970. The fact remains that during 1965–1967 the Vietnam War continued to escalate, and with it the sense of mutual hostility not just between the United States and North Vietnam, but ultimately between the United States and the People's Republic, intensified.

The Cultural Revolution in China

That the escalating Vietnam War coincided with the launching of the Cultural Revolution in China was no accident, although the two had different origins. For the Chinese leadership had become seriously divided over the direction of the socialist state, both domestically and in its international setting. The so-called "great leap forward" of the late 1950's and the early 1960's, aimed at rapid industrialization through agricultural collectivization, had proven disastrous. (Food production fell from 200 million tons in 1957 to 143 million tons three years later.) There was much questioning of the economic policy, but it inevitably produced debate on the nature of the type of society and state China was to have. The issue had implications for foreign relations insofar as the stress during the "great leap forward" period had been on "self-help," to increase industrial and agricultural production through China's own efforts, rather than through imported capital and technology, or through a heavy dependence on foreign trade. Although Soviet scientists and technicians had been active in China after 1950, their main contribution had been to help China's nuclear development, and moreover, they began leaving the country after 1959, reflecting the Kremlin's unhappiness with China's belligerent stance toward the United States. The Soviet Union had also extended credits to China, totalling some $400 million, but interest payments on the loans were considered excessive by the Chinese. For all these reasons, the stress on "self-help" expressed their determination to develop their society as the more perfect socialist utopia, no matter what was happening elsewhere in the world. At the same time, their achievements would, it was believed, inspire other Third World countries to emulate them and assert their independence of the superpowers. At the same time, however, it could not be denied that China was becoming isolated in international affairs. The United States and the Soviet Union were engaged in ongoing negotiation on nuclear issues, and the Third World, far from being united in opposition to the superpowers, was going through domestic turmoil and internecine warfare (for instance, the India-Pakistan war of 1965).

The apparent rapprochement between the United States and the Soviet Union, coupled with the escalation of the Vietnam War, in the mid-1960's, compelled the Chinese leaders to clarify their stance on foreign affairs, even as they had to grope for a way out of the economic crisis in the wake of the failure of the "great leap forward." Some argued for a more moderate pace of social and economic change, less emphasis on ideological purity and more on political stability, and a pragmatic foreign policy so as to avoid China's isolation. Others, however, denounced such pragmatism and moderation as stifling revolutionary enthusiasm and paving the way to bureaucratization. Mao Tse-tung represented this latter view. He was unhappy with what he took to be the growing influence of technocrats and bureaucrats in the country who appeared intent on stabilization and routinization at the expense of keeping alive the revolutionary heritage. Now, more than ever, there was a need to preserve and strengthen that heritage; in a world in which the superpowers appeared to be ganging up on the rest, when one of them was stepping up its military assault on China's southern neighbor, this was no time to talk of stability and pragmatism. Rather, only by combating all tendencies toward relaxation and complacency, and by perpetuating the movement for a radical transformation of society, could the Chinese be certain of their security and independence.

Mao's doctrinaire rigidity might not have prevailed if it had been discussed only among the top ranks of the party and the government. But he shrewdly saw the possibility of appealing to the masses for support. Those who had not been satisfied with the achievements of the revolution up to that point, those who still felt disadvantaged and resented the privileges accorded high officials, well-to-do businessmen, farmers, and professional people, and those who had been indoctrinated by years of anti-foreign chauvinism—these people could be turned loose to revitalize the political affairs of the nation, to block the tendency toward bureaucratization, and to keep the society in a constant state of fervor which alone ensured the success of the revolution. Mao's instincts in turning to them proved correct, and during 1966–1969 (and, to a lesser extent, during the early 1970's as well), waves of demonstrations by millions of Chinese filled the streets and disrupted the countryside. Their idealism was misguided but genuine; they sincerely believed the country was in danger because of foreign imperialism and domestic enemies ("capitalist-roaders"). Unless they were eradicated, the revolution could not survive. They must be prepared to wage war against both. Thus they attacked, often murdering, those at home who were considered traitors to the revolution, while they earnestly prepared for certain war with foreign aggressors—most likely the United States but also including the Soviet "revisionists."

Even then, mass enthusiasm under Mao's inspiration would not have been successful against the entrenched authority of the state and against the continued influence of pragmatists without the backing of the army, or the People's Liberation Army. In the Cultural Revolution's first stages, the army played a decisive role in supporting the masses against the political and educational elites. It saw its role as that of furthering the cause of the revolution in competition with party and government functionaries, and it saw Maoism as the instrument for enhancing its own influence. Most crucial was the emergence of Lin Piao as the PLA's top leader with the blessing of Mao. Lin had to struggle with other army leaders who were more cautious about involving the armed force in domestic politics and about an ideologically driven foreign policy. But Mao chose Lin over others not only as head of the army but also as heir designate; in a constitution rewritten during the Cultural Revolution, Lin Piao's name was specifically mentioned as the heir to Mao Tse-tung. Lin won Mao's support by developing a vision of a global conflict in which the power centers ("cities") like America and Russia would be surrounded by the rest ("the countryside") and ultimately defeated. China was to be the spokesman and leader of the global village, encouraging others to strengthen themselves to carry out the task.

A Cultural Revolution in America

Thus it was that the United States and China developed their most hostile views of one another during the second half of the 1960's. The Vietnam War exemplified their perceptual confrontation. America was in Indochina to prevent Chinese takeover, so it was said in Washington. The Chinese were helping the Vietnamese to frustrate America's global ambitions, they were told in Peking and elsewhere. There was a symmetry of images. As noted in the preceding chapter, the two countries had reached perhaps the most serious state in the history of their bilateral relationship. It is also interesting to note, however, that the Vietnam War was giving rise to some radical critique in the United States, part of which took the form of embracing Maoism, either totally or partially. For those Americans, especially at colleges and universities, who were increasingly critical of the war, it did not seem enough merely to question its costs or tactics. As more and more young men were drafted into the armed forces, some took the drastic step of moving to Canada and elsewhere to escape the draft, others ended up in prison failing to be inducted into the army, while still others organized movements to protest, not just the practical wisdom of fighting such a war, but the very nature of America's Cold War policy of which the war was an inevitable product. In reaching such a point of view, this last group often spoke the language of Maoism: American "imperialism," "people's revolutionary victory," and the like. From their point of view, their country had been engaging in imperialistic warfare for generations, but the Vietnam War was particularly heinous as it was a counter-revolutionary war against the nationalistic aspirations of the people. China supported the revolution, and so to persist in an anti-Chinese rhetoric while engaging in suppressing the Vietnamese revolutionary nationalism was a double crime. So reasoning, some of the more radical opponents of the Vietnam War turned themselves into American revolutionaries, verbally and sometimes physically assaulting "the power structure"—those who allegedly monopolized political and economic power in the country and who had masterminded the Cold War strategy.

It may be noted that the late 1960's were thus characterized by rhetorical excesses in both China and the United States, which were vastly out of proportion to the actual involvement of the two countries in the Vietnam War. Washington made sure that the escalating war would not extend itself to China, while the latter had no desire to repeat the costly experiences of the Korean War when Chinese had suffered huge casualties. But both needed conspiracy theories to justify their limited involvement. For the American supporters of the Vietnam War, the ultimate target was the Chinese conspiracy to overturn the whole of Southeast Asia, and for the Chinese during the Cultural Revolution, the American conspiracy to entrench itself in the area would, if successful, lead to the demise of their own revolution. American opponents of the war had their own conspiracy theories, linking foreign policy with domestic affairs in the framework of the "power structure" or the "establishment," perceived to be in control of national and international affairs for their own interests.

These were clearly exaggerated notions, but they should be understood in the context of domestic developments in both countries. For the United States, too, like China, a cultural revolution was erupting. The "American way of life" was increasingly coming to be seen as a half-truth; the much vaunted material well-being and social comfort of middle-class Americans had hidden "the other America," it came to be pointed out: the America of poverty, racial discrimination, and male domination. Observers began pointing to those in society who had not belonged to the white, Anglo-Saxon, male majority. The complacency of earlier writers about the unity and uniqueness of American civilization gave way to self-criticism about the history of social conflict and violence in the country, and to the view that the nation had never been as exceptional as it had led its people to believe. On the contrary, the country had been deeply divided along racial and class lines, and it had not been free from the sort of tensions and violence that had been characteristic of other societies.

Such a view, an anti-exceptionalist formulation of American identity, was typical of the turmoil of the late 1960's when familiar categories and boundaries that constituted the vocabulary of discourse became blurred, if not disappearing altogether from American discussions of national and international affairs. America was no less imperialistic than others, it was maintained by many, and to claim its moral superiority was a self-delusion. To take away the air of superiority and the rhetoric of exceptionalism from discussions of public issues had the effect of encouraging a more "realistic" appraisal of foreign and domestic affairs; it relativized America and enabled one to compare the United States to other countries in terms of the same indicators (power, ambition, capabilities) as would apply to all of them. But because this stress on the unexceptional character of America was so different from the earlier images prevalent in the country, it compelled much soul-searching. For if the nation was not that different from others, why had this not been stressed earlier? If the United States was no better or worse than, say, the Soviet Union or China, how could it justify its policies designed to check their aggressive tendencies? Indeed, some even began to argue that American foreign policy had, if anything, been even more aggressive and expansionist than theirs. Some, though not all, the "revisionist" historians, for instance, became extremely critical of the course of United States foreign relations. To read their works published in the late 1960's and the early 1970's is to realize how pervasive these self-critical tendencies had become. Thus it was argued that the United States had been as responsible as the Soviet Union for the origins of the Cold War, that expansionism had been an inevitable consequence of economic interests determining policy so that the nation would aim at opening up and expanding foreign markets, that Wilsonian and other idealistic language had been an instrument of American capitalism, that such rhetoric had at bottom been counter-revolutionary, and that, most fundamentally, the United States had sought to create a world after its own image and denounced those who dared to question its superiority.

The highly critical tone of scholarly revisionism was combined with movements for civil rights, women's rights, sexual freedom, community living, and free artistic expression to create a new cultural agenda, a cultural revolution in which tradition, discipline, and order were replaced by innovation, experimentation, and lack of respect for authority. No wonder, then, that China, whose revolution seemed to exemplify these new forces, appealed to an increasing number of Americans, especially its youth. There developed some sort of a psychological rapport between Chinese and Americans even while the respective governments maintained no official relations and engaged in mutual recrimination. Ironically, as will be noted, it would be the government authorities, not the people themselves, that would initiate steps toward a Sino-American reconciliation.

Amid such conceptual excesses, efforts were made to retain a sense of balance in discussions of Sino-American relations. Those in the United States who were dissatisfied with the government's ostracization of the People's Republic of China but who did not embrace the cult of Maoism, were anxious to find a middle course, what some called the "containment without isolation" of China. At the Senate hearings on China held in 1966—in themselves a landmark, reflecting the sentiment that a new approach to the PRC was overdue—prominent scholars such as John K. Fairbank, Lucian Pye, Robert A. Scalapino, and Allen Whiting agreed upon the need to end China's ostracization without, however, changing America's commitment to defend Taiwan. They were confident that trade and cultural ties with Peking could be initiated without jeopardizing the security of the Republic of China or undermining the framework of the containment strategy. Even such modest proposals bore no immediate fruit, and the start of the Cultural Revolution just after the hearings were concluded seemed to deride any attempt at revising current policy. Nevertheless, the more serious the situation in China and Vietnam became, the more determined grew the advocates of a new approach.

Fairbank, perhaps the most visible of China specialists in the United States, served as president of the American Historical Association in 1968, the year when its annual convention was moved from Chicago to New York at the last moment because of the members' anger at the Chicago police handling of demonstrators during the Democratic Party convention in the city that summer. The AHA business meeting went on into early morning hours discussing whether the scholarly association should take a stand on public issues like the Vietnam War. (No action was taken then; even some of the most radical opponents of the war did not wish to "politicize" the AHA.) In his presidential address, Fairbank took note of "our inadvertent war in Vietnam" and implicitly condemned it when he asserted, "Today the greatest menace to mankind may well be the American tendency to overrespond to heathen evils abroad, either by attacking them or by condemning them to outer darkness." But he also observed that the Chinese had the same proclivity to believe that "morality sanctions violence." In such a dangerous situation, what was needed was "a truer and multivalued, because multicultural, perspective on the world crisis." More specifically, Fairbank called for an intensive study of the history of American–East Asian relations, to comprehend why things had gotten to where they were, and to develop the perspective necessary for understanding the intertwined fates of America and Asia. Above all, it "is peace with China that must be struggled for and won." That struggle Fairbank saw as primarily intellectual. The establishment, under his inspiration and with the support of other prominent historians, of a Committee on American–East Asian Relations in 1968 reflected the same ideas. The Committee, which still exists, exemplified the scholarly community's concern to go beyond traditional frameworks such as American history and Chinese history, and thus in its blurring of boundaries it, too, may be said to have been a product of the times.

Japan's Economic Success

While the United States and China were engaging in mutual recrimination and undergoing profound social and political turmoil at home, Japan was quietly developing itself as an economic power of major proportions. This was one of the significant anomalies in American–East Asian relations. Only a little more than twenty years after the end of the war, the defeated nation was emerging as one of the fastest growing economies in the world, while the two key victors were experiencing difficulties. In China, for instance, food production diminished during the Cultural Revolution, and its factories and stores were in disarray. The United States, on the other hand, continued to grow economically, but not fast enough to keep up with the spiralling costs of the Vietnam War (amounting to as much as $100 million a day during its heights). The war was financed through inflation (printing of more money) and borrowing (government deficits) rather than through taxes, although toward the end of his presidency Lyndon Johnson did institute a modest tax increase. The rate of inflation reached six percent by the late 1960's, and government deficits exceeded $10 billion. These were ominous signs, indicating that the war could have severe repercussions on the economy. Among other things, it would cut into domestic industrial development and make American products less competitive. The value of the dollar would begin to decline relative to the currencies of faster growing economies, European and Japanese. The diminished value of the dollar in turn would drain gold out of the country as foreign governments holding dollars would be eager to exchange them for gold. The dwindling gold reserve—which fell below $10 billion in 1971 for the first time since the 1930's—would further erode confidence in the strength of the American economy.

These signs of trouble were becoming visible only at the end of the decade, and, as will be seen, no decisive measures would be taken to deal with them until 1971. In the meantime, the contrast between America's economic difficulties and Japan's spectacular performance could not be ignored. Perhaps for the first time since 1945, the Japanese public and leaders regained confidence and became less defensive about themselves. To be sure, many of them were deeply affected by events in China and the United States. Left-wing intellectuals and student radicals idolized Mao and the Cultural Revolution, some of whom resorted to violence to wrest power from the "power structure" in the government, universities, and publishing houses. Others founded anti-Vietnam War organizations to act in coordination with similar bodies in the United States, while still others emulated the life-styles of the American "counter-culture." The impact of these activities on life in Japan, however, appears to have been much less severe than in China or the United States. For the majority of the population, increasing productivity, raising the standard of living, and then spending some of the earnings were the principal preoccupations. As national income increased six-fold during the 1960's, and as restrictions on foreign exchange were removed in 1965, the Japanese began traveling abroad in large numbers for the first time in their nation's history. Not just intellectuals and businessmen, but students, office workers, and house-wives began joining package tours to spend a few days and many more dollars in America, Europe, and elsewhere. The contrast of the enjoyment of material comfort and leisure in a politically stable Japan and the turmoil of American society could not have been sharper. Officially, too, the government in Tokyo did little more than give rhetorical support to America's war in Southeast Asia. Indeed, the Foreign Ministry's annual reports (so-called Blue Books) described the war as unpopular at home and abroad, one in which Japan itself would remain uninvolved. It is revealing that while maintaining such a stance, Japanese officials were eager for trading opportunities in Vietnam, expecting that once the war ended, in whatever fashion, there would be a huge need for capital, technology, and goods which Japan would be able to provide. At the same time, the cabinet of Satō Eisaku (whose long tenure, between 1964 and 1971, has been unprecedented in modern Japanese history) took steps to persuade the United States to return Okinawa to Japan—this at the very moment when the island, under U.S. occupation even after the San Francisco peace treaty, was being used as a base of operation for the Vietnam War. It is a sign of the essentially solid relationship between the two countries that Washington responded favorably to Japanese wishes and began the process for an eventual retrocession of Okinawa, which materialized in 1972, even when Japan was almost totally uncooperative in the Vietnam War.

The fact that the United States was becoming bogged down in an apparently endless, frustrating war in the Vietnam jungles, while Japan was persisting in its non-militaristic policy, a "high road" with regard to international conflicts, may have served to equalize, psychologically, the two peoples' self-perceptions. In other words, just as Americans were feeling frustrated, losing self-confidence, and becoming self-critical because of the war, Japanese were recovering from the trauma of the earlier war, regaining a sense of national pride and achievement, and reaffirming the postwar commitment to peace and prosperity. It was no accident, perhaps, that when several leading historians from the two countries met in Hakone, west of Tokyo, in the summer of 1969 to review the road to Pearl Harbor, the origins of the Pacific war appeared much more ambiguous than had earlier been supposed. In comparing notes about the respective decision-making systems and discussing how the Japanese-American war might have been avoided, the conference participants tended to see the two nations as having been equally responsible for the coming of the war. If Japan's cumbersome decision-making process had been unable to check the military's often unilateral acts on the Asian continent, the indecisiveness and lack of clear definition of policy on the American side had not helped. Somehow the two sides should have made a more serious attempt at finding areas of compromise and sought to understand each other's perspectives better. The implication was that war could have been avoided if there had been better communication and understanding across the Pacific.

In retrospect, this and similar instances in the late 1960's and the early 1970's are notable not so much for their complacent tone about U.S.-Japanese relations, past and present, as for the tendency to treat these relations in isolation. It was as if the two countries had developed a close association after the war so that even the prewar history could be treated as if it had been a family quarrel. Perhaps this was inevitable, given the state of hostility between China and the United States, the still accepted framework of the Cold War in American and Japanese policies, and the challenge to U.S. power being presented by the Vietnamese. In such a situation, Japanese and American images could overlap and present a picture of shared interests and perspectives. In a world undergoing chaos and uncertainty, the seemingly solid partnership across the Pacific must have been a source of satisfaction to both countries. All this, however, was about to change.

A Geopolitical Revolution

On July 15, 1971, President Richard Nixon astounded the world by announcing that Henry Kissinger, his national security advisor, had undertaken a secret mission to Peking and conferred with Chinese leaders to arrange for the president's trip to China the following February. The announcement was so unexpected that the Japanese immediately referred to it as a "Nixon shock." They had to accommodate the new development into their thinking and reorient their approach to the People's Republic, as did virtually all other countries. Within a few years, both the United States and Japan would be extending their recognition to Peking, thereby putting an end to the San Francisco system. The Vietnam War would end with America's withdrawal. Equally significant, U.S.-Japanese relations would show signs of a serious strain reminding some of the pre-Pearl Harbor days.

"Geopolitics" was the term used most frequently by both Nixon and Kissinger in explaining the decision to reverse America's longstanding policy to contain, and not to recognize, the People's Republic. The term implied recognition of the power realities in the world, that is, that China was a power, whether or not one liked the fact. A country of eight hundred million, now possessing nuclear weapons, politically unified (though of late going through the trauma of a Cultural Revolution) simply could not be ignored. "We must live with Communist powers . . . we must accept the realities," President Nixon said. Kissinger, a scholar of nineteenth-century European diplomacy, readily agreed. Of European background, he had often felt that the American people were almost congenitally incapable of viewing world affairs in geopolitical terms, instead infusing them with moral meaning or treating them emotionally. In thus considering the realities of power the key to international relations, Kissinger was, of course, not exceptional. He was in the same intellectual tradition as George Kennan, Hans Morgenthau, and others of the school of "realism" whose ideas had emerged as an important strain in American thought during the 1940's. Some, if not all, of these realists had advocated a flexible approach to the PRC, but they had been unable to have the United States government accept the suggestion. It had appeared politically too sensitive a change of policy. After all, the debate on "the loss of China" was only twenty years old, and the two Democratic presidents, Kennedy and Johnson, had been motivated to escalate their involvement in Southeast Asia in part because they did not want to be accused of having "lost" Vietnam. Now, however, Richard Nixon, whose political career had been closely identified with the anti-Communist crusade and who had actively pursued the "loss of China" issue in national politics, was in the White House, so that he would be free from a dangerous political fallout of the sort that had visited his Democratic predecessors if he were to reorient policy toward Peking. He could engage in realpolitik because his past record of anti-Communism was clean, as it were.

It would be wrong to conclude, however, that the embracing of geopolitics was all there was to the new Nixon-Kissinger initiative. After all, the Cold War strategy of containment had been a response to the perceived threat of Soviet and Chinese power, as had the policy of seeking nuclear non-proliferation. Balance of power considerations had not only not been absent in postwar U.S. foreign policy, they could even be said to have been at its foundation. What the Nixon policy suggested was that power calculations could produce more than one policy option, that ultimately even geopolitics was a matter of perception. For there was as much geopolitical logic to continuing the isolation of China through some sort of collaboration with the Soviet Union, as Kennedy and Johnson had tried, as to bringing China into the picture as a third factor in the game of power politics, as Nixon and Kissinger were now doing. So it was not just the primacy of realpolitik over other considerations, but more importantly a reinterpretation of the power situation that produced the Sino-American rapprochement.

That reinterpretation was no less than a reconsideration of the existing structure of Asian-Pacific regional relations, namely the San Francisco system. As seen above, that system had presupposed a division of the whole region into two camps and thus justified both the containment of China and the war in Vietnam to preserve the status quo. What was now being proposed was to loosen this structure, if not to alter it entirely, by obliterating the rigid line separating the two sides. Not that China would now come into the U.S. alliance system, but that it would be recognized as the third major power in Asia, and indeed in the world so as to make use of it in global geopolitics. The new policy would also mean reconsidering the role of American military strength as the key factor in upholding the regional balance of power. U.S. military presence might be reduced, and Asian countries would be expected to do their share in their own defense. In the process, some of the existing alliance and security treaties the United States had entered into with Asian and Pacific countries would be modified, even abrogated in certain cases.

Part of the new thought was evident already in 1969 when President Nixon went to Guam as part of his Pacific trip and enunciated a policy (the so-called "Guam doctrine") that stressed the importance of Asians contributing to their own security. American nuclear and naval force would still be available to preserve the status quo, but U.S. ground forces would be gradually reduced. This was a clear signal for an ultimate withdrawal from Vietnam. By 1969 Washington's leaders had come to believe that, even though the Vietnam War might yet be won, the financial and political costs would not be worth the effort. Nixon had become president by pledging to end the war in an honorable fashion, but the only way this could be done was to reestablish some sense of regional order so that American withdrawal from Indochina would be seen as part of this development. Thus, while the Guam doctrine was silent on China, a new approach toward that country was clearly a necessary part of the package. Between 1969 and 1971 the United States government sent out signals, for instance lifting the long-standing ban on travel to China and ending naval patrols of the Taiwan Straits to indicate an interest in redefining its Asian policy. The wholesale rejection of the San Francisco system was never contemplated. Nevertheless, such overtures implied that all aspects of American policy in the region would be affected, for, after all, the policy had been designed to keep the PRC isolated.

And the Chinese leadership, too, was ready to end diplomatic isolation, self-imposed or not. They were consummate geopoliticians, according to Kissinger who records in his personal memoirs that geopolitics was what linked him with Chou En-lai, the one pragmatist among Chinese leaders who had managed to survive the Cultural Revolution. Chou persuaded Mao that China needed to reorient its foreign policy away from its excessive ideological definition which had necessitated a hostile stance against both American imperialism and Soviet "social imperialism." When Soviet troops invaded Czechoslovakia to suppress its more liberal leaders and announced the "Brezhnev doctrine" that it was incumbent upon the Soviet Union to preserve friendly Communist regimes in other countries even through the use of its military force, Chou and several of his close associates concluded that the Russians might act likewise against China. Should that happen—and indeed in 1969 there was a series of border clashes between Chinese and Soviet troops along the Manchurian-Siberian frontier—could China afford to be involved in an anti-U.S. campaign? By coincidence, in May 1968 American and Vietnamese representatives began their talks in Paris to try to scale down the conflict in Southeast Asia. Although the talks—which President Johnson authorized to placate public opinion, while the Vietnamese also welcomed the respite from vicious fighting—remained inconclusive, they impressed the Chinese leadership as evidence that U.S. imperialism was unlikely to be completely defeated. So, when in August Soviet forces occupied Prague, the Chinese were forced to take a more pragmatic view of the surrounding power realities.

There was a domestic implication to this reassessment. Lin Piao had advocated a global anti-U.S. and anti-USSR strategy in which China, cleansed of internal enemies, would take the leading position. Chou opposed such a stance, and after 1969 came to call for a modification of China's policy toward the United States so as to focus on the immediate Soviet threat. This did not mean that China would completely reverse itself and embrace America as a potential ally against Russia; rather, China would be less strident in denouncing the United States and its security system in Asia in order to concentrate on the Soviet Union for the time being. Lin, on his part, continued to insist that the anti-U.S. campaign be maintained even as the anti-Soviet Union struggle was stepped up. (In fact, he would soon have second thoughts about the latter and presumably seek asylum in the Soviet Union when he lost the power struggle among Mao's followers.) By 1969, however, the Chinese-Soviet crisis appeared to have reached such a state that this type of an all-front conflict against both nuclear giants became more and more frightening to contemplate. By then, too, the economic consequences of several years' domestic turmoil were becoming all too apparent. Chinese leaders despaired of trying to restabilize social and economic conditions while at the same time engaging in an ideological warfare overseas. The moment had come, they judged, to restabilize both domestic and foreign affairs.

Stability had been equated with the status quo and counter-revolution during the initial phase of the Cultural Revolution, and the Chinese people had been exhorted to dedicate themselves to perpetual revolution. Now, however, some at least of thc leaders concluded that things could not go on in this manner forever. Unless checked, revolutionary fervor would lead to complete chaos, a situation that could invite foreign intervention or attempts at counter-revolution. Some wcnt farther and began to argue that in order to resume programs of economic modernization and military strengthening, even the revolutionary doctrine of "self-help" might have to be modified. Trade with Japan, in fact, had not diminished during the Cultural Revolution. As economic dependence on the Soviet Union and Eastern Europe steadily abated, Japan was emerging as China's main supplier of consumer goods as well as industrial machinery. Amounts were still small, of course, because of the political turmoil, but the connection had proved useful. There was little doubt that European and American capital and technology would prove to be even more so. It was conceptually not very easy to turn away from "self-help" to importation of Western capital and goods, but at least this fitted in with the existing image of the Western countries as hungry for Chinese markets. The United

States, in particular, could be expected to crave for the China market in order to rebuild its own economy after the costly war in Vietnam.

Even though the factors that produced the Sino-American rapprochement thus appear clear, and one tends to assume there was a logic behind the phenomenon, we should not underestimate the perceptual revolution that was required both in China and the United States to bring it about. Just as Americans had to reverse familiar images of Chinese totalitarianism, aggression, and expansionism to accept an accommodation with the PRC—not in the name of waging the Cold War or in response to any change in Chinese politics or foreign policy, but in terms of power politics—so did the Chinese have to suspend their revolutionary rhetoric and anti-American ideological campaign which had been waged for two decades—again, not because they were persuaded that the nature of U.S. imperialism had changed but because of the need to focus on the greater threat of Soviet imperialism. The months between February 1969, when President Nixon approached President Charles DeGaulle to seek his intercession in establishing connections with Peking, and the trip to China in February 1971, were in a sense a preparatory period in which leaders in both countries tried to find some common vocabulary in which their rapprochement could be couched. Of course, geopolitics lay at the basis but, as already noted, geopolitics by its own nature is volatile and can never serve as the sole linchpin of any solid, stable relationship among nations. During those three years, Chou wrote a letter to Nixon, Mao met with the American journalist Edgar Snow, another, James Reston, followed Kissinger in visiting Peking, and scholars and publicists in the United States and elsewhere tried to make sense of the rapidly changing course of events in Asia. In the meantime, China withdrew its forces from Vietnam, the U.S. Congress repealed the Tonkin Gulf resolution of 1964 that had authorized the bombing of North Vietnam, the leaking of the "Pentagon Papers" revealed the degree to which the American public had been kept ignorant of secret missions and clandestine operations in Vietnam, Chinese and American ping-pong players met in Nagoya and competed again in Chinese cities, and several Western countries extended their diplomatic recognition to the People's Republic. Most significantly, the United States did not oppose the PRC replacing the Republic of China in the United Nations Security Council. This action, taken in the fall of 1971 without too much outcry in America, was a clear sign that the time was ripe for a mutual accommodation. As if to put finishing touches to the story, Lin Piao fled Peking, presumably for the Soviet Union, at about the same time, thus removing himself and his followers (later identified as "the gang of four") as obstacles in the way of a Chinese-American detente. China was slowly but steadily becoming reincorporated into the international community.

After such preparatory work, it is not surprising that President Nixon and Premier Chou En-lai were able to agree on a mutually acceptable text, the so-called Shanghai communiqué, issued on February 28, 1972, at the conclusion of the American leader's historic trip to China. The communiqué is such a crucial document, one that in effect defined yet another pattern of U.S.-Asian relations to supplement, if not replace, the San Francisco system, that it deserves to be cited at length. After an introductory passage, the communiqué stated:

> First, the two leaders expressed basic agreement that: countries, regardless of their social systems, should conduct their relations on the principles of respect for the sovereignty and territorial integrity of all states, non-aggression against other states, non-interference in the internal affairs of other states, equality and mutual benefit, and peaceful coexistence.

These were exactly the five principles first enunciated in 1954 at a meeting of Chou En-lai and Jawaharlal Nehru and later incorporated into the "ten principles of peace" adopted at the Bandung conference of 1955. By agreeing to them, the United States government was identifying its position with that of the People's Republic of China, while the latter in turn was acknowledging that it was possible even for an "imperialist" nation to accept and abide by the same principles. This statement was then followed by their further agreement on three specific propositions:

> Progress toward the normalization of relations between China and the United States is in the interest of all countries; both wish to reduce the danger of international military conflict; neither should seek hegemony in the Asia-Pacific region and each is opposed to

> efforts by any other country or group of countries to establish such hegemony.

Here, clearly stated, was the decision by Peking and Washington to establish normal diplomatic relations. Although it would take another seven years before such relations were formally established, this statement of intentions was enough to indicate the revolutionary character of the communiqué, for it amounted to nothing less than a complete shift away from the self-imposed policy of mutual exclusion that the two governments had pursued since the Korean War. When combined with the third sentence, that they opposed "hegemony" by any power in the "Asia-Pacific region," Sino-American relations could truly be said to have entered a new epoch. Both countries had accused each other precisely of seeking "hegemony," and so to renounce it, however rhetorically, was a major step. Of course, the term also implied that they would resist Soviet domination of the region, but there was little new in that formulation. What was envisaged was some sort of balance among the three powers so that the Asian-Pacific arena of world affairs would be altered from the previous pattern of U.S.-Chinese confrontation in a divided region to that of coexistence and accommodation. The "Asia-Pacific region," an expression that was rather new in international agreements, was significant because it conceptualized some sort of regional order embracing both Asia and the Pacific. That was the same arena for which the Yalta conference had defined some order and, after its demise, the San Francisco system had proposed a framework for international relations. The Shanghai communiqué would modify this latter arrangement by bringing China into it. Although it was not clear whether the San Francisco system would be totally destroyed, its significant transformation was obvious in view of the fact that the San Francisco arrangements had been devised in large part to keep China isolated and contained. The new structure of Sino-American relations contradicted that rationale, and so in that sense the basic structure of American–East Asian relations defined in 1951 may be said to have come to an end.

There was one other important element in the Nixon-Chou statement. That concerned the Taiwan question, the fundamental point of dispute between the two countries inasmuch as the PRC had never recognized the separate existence of Taiwan, whereas the United States had dealt with the island's Nationalist authorities as the legitimate representatives of China. Their positions did not change overnight, but the two sides agreed on a compromise formula:

> The U.S. side acknowledges that all Chinese on either side of the Taiwan Straits maintain there is but one China and that Taiwan is a part of China. The United States Government does not challenge that position. It reaffirms its interest in a peaceful settlement of the Taiwan question by the Chinese themselves.

This was an ingenious way of solving the impasse; both sides stated their positions, and while no immediate agreement could be achieved, the mere fact that such a statement was included in the communiqué implied that they would be willing to set aside the thorny question and focus on other areas where their relations could be built up, such as trade.

The Sino-American rapprochement was enormously popular in the United States and, so far as can be determined, in China. To be sure, those in America who had developed close ties with the Chinese in Taiwan—including apparently the bulk of Chinese living in the United States—were dismayed by the Nixon administration's about-face, considering it a betrayal of the Nationalist authorities who had loyally stood with the nation during the Cold War. But the bulk of editorial opinion in the major newspapers, journals, and television/radio stations welcomed the Nixon initiative. The belief that the rapprochement with Peking would lead to the ending of the war in Vietnam was one obvious reason. Since China's alleged expansionism had been given as a principal justification for the war, the Sino-American detente on the basis of the non-hegemony principle could only mean that rationale was no longer valid. It would be possible for Americans to persuade themselves that they had done the best they could to maintain stability in Southeast Asia, but that now the task must be carried out in the larger context of the developing U.S.-PRC relations. Such a view, of course, implied that the long-standing image of the Chinese Communists as aggressive expansionists had to be modified. To reverse such an image and to embrace an alternative one, depicting them as peace-loving, would probably have been difficult, but at least one could take comfort in the fact that the Chinese were renouncing hegemonic ambitions and accepting, at least as part of the new agreement, America's interest in a peaceful settlement of the Taiwan question.

Does the fact that American images of China dramatically shifted virtually overnight, and this not as a result of a groundswell of public opinion but in response to some high-level geopolitical maneuverings, mean that these images had been terribly superficial to begin with, easily manipulable by dictates of official policy? As the preceding chapters have argued, images *had* changed from time to time irrespective of shifts in "objective" conditions and with little relationship to hard "realities." But to observe the superficial nature of cross-national images is not the same thing as saying that they are empty words or irrelevant clichés that are made and unmade with no significant impact on international relations. What is striking about the sudden reconciliation between Americans and Chinese is the very fact that their mutual perceptions shifted with relative ease. This was so, it would seem, because even the most extreme rhetoric of Cold War anti-Communism in America or the Cultural Revolution in China had not obliterated another set of images, those linked to periods in the past when the two countries had viewed each other favorably. They had been "sister republics," then wartime allies, and developed close connections through missionaries and educators. Images produced by such experiences had not totally disappeared and could be resurrected, made once again more authentic now that reconciliation was in effect. Thus within days of the Nixon trip to China, American television stations began showing films of the Asian war in which the two countries had fought together against the Japanese enemy, and China specialists who had advocated a change in official policy were once again sought after as luncheon speakers to talk about the great Chinese civilization. In China, too, books and articles began appearing that talked of the two countries' "traditional friendship." Instances of American policy toward China that had hitherto been cited as examples of U.S. imperialism—such as the Open Door and Wilsonianism—could now be presented as evidence of American friendship and support for China. A historian asserted in a book published in 1973, "the American people are a great people with a revolutionary tradition who can be expected to make a contribution to the progress of mankind."[1] Such a book would not have been publishable before 1972, but the theme was one that had been commonplace before 1949. In other words, what was happening was the overcoming of the recent images and the return of earlier, more familiar ones.

The Nixon Shock in Japan

Earlier in the history of American–East Asian relations, favorable American images of China had almost invariably been combined with unfavorable views of Japan, and vice versa. It had been rare for Americans to entertain positive images both of China and Japan. This was often a reflection of the fact these two Asian countries had been in conflict much of the time, but even when they were not, such as the years around 1905 or during the 1920's, Americans had tended to opt for either one of them as their favorite Asian country. One interesting phenomenon of the early 1970's was that the Sino-American rapprochement as such did not recreate negative perceptions of Japan. Rather, officials and publicists alike emphasized that the new approach to China not only did not mean a shift in U.S. policy toward Japan but that it could even strengthen the bilateral alliance. Henry Kissinger spoke of the "new structure of international relations" that was being defined as a result of the American initiative, a structure that accommodated Chinese power but also assigned a role to Japan as America's partner in Asia and the Pacific. The security pact between the two countries would not be altered—indeed, it was renewed for the second time in 1970 without much fanfare, and there was no strong protest movement in Japan comparable to the disturbances of 1960—and it was expected to become even more solidified now that China would cease to denounce it. The improvement in U.S.-Chinese relations should thus help stabilize Chinese-Japanese relations as well.

The Japanese were at first not so sure. Prime Minister Satō is

[1] Cited in Warren I. Cohen, ed. *New Frontiers in American-East Asian Relations* (New York, 1983), p. 69.

said to have told the Australian prime minister that the Americans had "let me down."[2] He was given only a few minutes' advance warning of the initial Nixon statement on China in July 1971, and had clearly failed to anticipate a major shift in America's China policy. Not that the Japanese government had meekly followed Washington's lead in isolating the PRC. As noted above, even during the Cultural Revolution, Japanese trade with China had continued, and private semi-official delegations had never stopped going to Peking to negotiate trade and other arrangements. Nevertheless, Tokyo had loyally stood by America's policy of not recognizing the PRC and not supporting its claim to the seat occupied by Taiwan in the Security Council of the United Nations. So there was a sense of shock at having been kept completely in the dark by Japan's only ally in the world. If the Americans could thus deal with the Chinese over the heads of Japanese, what would they not be capable of doing? What was the meaning of a partnership when the junior partner's sensitivities had apparently not been taken seriously by the senior partner?

If such sentiments emerged among the Japanese in response to the Nixon initiative, however, they were mostly kept to themselves, for they really had no choice but to accept the fait accompli and, instead of grumbling publicly, try to do what they could to accommodate the profound transformation in Asian-Pacific relations into their sense of the regional system. Given their postwar habit of accepting the American lead in security issues, and given the pragmatism (some would characterize it as opportunism) that had been a main feature of Japanese foreign relations since the nineteenth century, it is not surprising that Tokyo's leaders soon began preparing for their own rapprochement with the PRC. Their task was easier, at least mentally and psychologically, in that Chinese-Japanese ties had never been cut off entirely but on the contrary maintained through their increasing trade and other types of contact. Moreover, China had not insisted on any modification of the U.S. security arrangements with Japan as a precondition for the Nixon trip. On the contrary, Chinese leaders may already have begun thinking that the U.S.-Japanese alliance was a good way to

[2] John Welfield, *An Empire in Eclipse: Japan in the Postwar American Alliance System* (London, 1988), p. 295.

prevent the resurgence of aggressive Japanese militarism, in addition to being useful as a check on Soviet ambitions. Although there were more complicated issues in Chinese-Japanese relations that might, ordinarily, have created obstacles in the way of a speedy rapprochement—especially Japan's fourteen-year aggression in China and the atrocities committed against the Chinese—the leaders in China chose not to press on Japan's war guilt question or to demand huge reparation payments. Instead, they judged, so it would appear from circumstantial evidence, that these issues could be raised in the future but that for the moment the crucial thing was to build on the momentum of the Sino-U.S. detente and to consolidate it by adding Japan to the picture.

It was fortunate for Japan that the Chinese leaders at that time were in the mood to accommodate Japan as well as the United States. This may have reflected Peking's urgent need for Japanese as well as American goods and capital in order to reconstruct the economy after the devastations brought about by the Cultural Revolution. Chou and the "moderates" may have also wanted to establish their legitimacy domestically through a bold new initiative in foreign policy, to differentiate themselves from those identified with an anti-U.S. and anti-Japanese posture. Even they, however, could not have easily explained their shift of policy toward Japan to a populace who had experienced its aggression and who had been taught to view the U.S.-Japanese alliance as designed to help revive Japanese militarism. It was important, therefore, that Japan reassure them of its peaceful intensions and somehow take note of its aggressive behavior during the war. So, when Tanaka Kakuei, who had succeeded Satō as prime minister, visited Peking five months after President Nixon had made his trip, he expressed Japan's regrets "for causing enormous damages in the past to the Chinese people through war," and reaffirmed that postwar Japanese foreign policy was committed to peaceful and friendly relations with all nations. That the Chinese did not really consider such an expression sufficient to atone for Japan's war guilt would become clear in the years to come. For the present, in any event, they chose to be satisfied with it and focused their energies on getting Tanaka to accept the same phraseology as had been contained in the Shanghai communiqué as the basis for Sino-Japanese reconciliation. Thus the new Chinese-Japanese communiqué reiterated the "five principles of peace'' as well as the ''anti-hegemonic'' clause in the Nixon-Chou statement. Here was another indication that China, Japan, and the United States had now come to accept the same vocabulary of international relations in the Asia-Pacific region.

To many Japanese, that vocabulary suggested geopolitics, something they had not been accustomed to in the quarter century after their defeat. Was Japan about to join the game of power politics and be ready to play it the way the United States and the People's Republic were apparently doing? That sounded like losing Japan's postwar innocence, going against the idealistic principles written in the constitution. What would such a change do to the essentially peaceful orientation of Japanese foreign policy? More critically, was the bilateral partnership with the United States about to be replaced by something different? Having been accustomed to seeking its peace and security within the framework of the American treaty and the ''nuclear umbrella,'' these were disturbing questions that suggested that for Japan, too, an era was passing.

The Crisis of the Bretton Woods System

If the Sino-American rapprochement had been the only significant development in international affairs at that time, the world, and Asia and the Pacific in particular, might sooner or later have adjusted itself to the picture and developed a new framework of stability. Only a partial reorientation of thinking and conceptualization might have been needed to cope with the change. In the event, however, the early 1970's witnessed another, no less cataclysmic, change on the global scale: a serious economic disequilibrium brought about by a weakened value of the dollar and precipitous increases in the price of petroleum. Together, they threatened to undermine the system of global economic development that had been as much part of postwar international relations as the Cold War.

Throughout the 1960's, the global economy had steadily expanded, fueled by a spectacular growth in international trade. Thanks to relatively cheap and abundant petroleum resources, mostly from the Middle East, European and Japanese economic recovery and reindustrialization, and America's initiative in removing trade barriers (the so-called Kennedy round was the first of its kind, designed to promote freer flows of goods among nations), global commercial transactions more than doubled in the decade. Although developing countries lagged behind the more advanced countries of Europe, North America, and Japan, at least as far as the latter were concerned, there was little doubt that they were developing closer economic relations than ever and that their growing commercial interdependence sustained their more formal military partnership. All this, however, had been based on the strength of the dollar as the key medium of exchange. International commercial transactions were mostly conducted in terms of the U.S. currency, the only really "hard" currency in that dollars could be exchanged, in the international market, for gold at a fixed rate. (This had been set to $35.00 per ounce of gold.) Other currencies were valued in terms of their relations to the dollar, and thus on the whole there developed stable rates of exchange among the major currencies, an important condition for maintaining international trade. Moreover, when a country experienced temporary exchange difficulties due to sluggish trade or other reasons, it could be given a respite through the International Monetary Fund which would give it emergency credits so that the country would not resort to devaluation, as happened so often during the 1930's. There were many other aspects to this scheme, the so-called Bretton Woods system (named after the meeting at Bretton Woods, New Hampshire, in 1944, which established it as the framework for postwar international economic transactions), but for our purposes it is enough to note that the United States, with the largest gold reserve of all, was the mainstay of the system and that for other countries to join the International Monetary Fund symbolized their status as major actors in the economic sphere. (Japan did so in 1952, but the PRC would not till 1980, an indication of their different economic systems as well as levels of trade.) The United States was the world's leading trading nation, invariably exporting more than importing, and using the trade surpluses for investments and loans overseas as well as for paying for its forces stationed throughout the world.

Around 1970, however, both America's superior position in world trade and the strength of the dollar became threatened. In 1971, for the first time since 1894, the United States recorded a trade deficit, its gold reserve dwindled to a level considered to be dangerously low, and the real value of the dollar vis-à-vis some other currencies such as the franc and the mark weakened to such an extent that, had the French and German governments decided to exchange their dollar holdings for gold, America's gold reserve would have further eroded, severely straining the Bretton Woods system. These developments were in part related to the war in Vietnam; the costs of the war had been staggering and were causing inflation, making goods produced in the United States that much more expensive, while at the same time the inflated economy attracted vast quantities of foreign goods. The war was also causing governmental deficits, with the result that confidence in the continued strength of the currency also began to diminish. As if this were not enough, in 1973 the Organization of Petroleum Exporting Countries (OPEC) announced steep price increases, virtually quadrupling the price of "crude" oil. The effect was instantaneous: the rising cost of imported oil for all industrializing countries, their consequent trade deficits, and their domestic inflation. The United States, which produced three-quarters of the petroleum it used, was less severely hit than Japan or the European countries, but it was likewise affected by double-digit inflation. All of a sudden, it seemed as though the economic underpinnings of the postwar world were being undermined. If the early 1970's marked the end of an era geopolitically, this phenomenon was also confirmed in the economic sphere.

The implications of these momentous changes in international economic affairs for U.S.-Chinese relations were perhaps slight, given that China was not a major trading nation. It is true that after 1971 the two countries resumed their trade for the first time since the Korean War, but the initial amounts were minimal. (For instance, in 1975 the bilateral trade amounted to less than one-seventh of that between the United States and Taiwan, and less than three percent of that between America and Japan.) For U.S.-Japanese relations, however, the effect was enormous. It was not simply that major readjustments became necessary in their monetary transactions; the value of the yen had risen against the dollar, and so, at a meeting of the finance ministers of the major economic powers held in Washington in 1971, it was decided to revalue the yen by nearly twenty percent against the dollar as part of a comprehensive arrangement for readjusting rates of exchange.

The agreement did not last long, however, and after 1974 the nations scrapped it for a system of "floating" rates, in other words, constant fluctuations in rates of exchange. Moreover, in 1971 the dollar was "decoupled" from gold, no longer exchangeable into the metal so that even a country's gold reserve would now mean little. What was even more shocking was President Nixon's unilateral announcement in the summer of 1971—exactly a month after revealing the Kissinger trip to China—that the United States was imposing a temporary surcharge on all imports and also instituting a freeze on wages and prices. Such unprecedented steps, reminiscent of economic policies of socialist or fascist countries, were clearly understood to be an emergency measure, but precisely for this reason they created the impression of the American economy in deep trouble, for the first time since the war.

Equally important was the beginning of U.S.-Japanese (as well as U.S.-European) tensions over trade matters. The "trade friction," as it came to be called, between the world's (still) leading economic power and its trading partners arose out of the crisis of the Bretton Woods system. There was serious disagreement over such matters as the extent to which the dollar should be devalued vis-à-vis other currencies and measures to rectify trade imbalances which had developed among them. Japan had begun exporting more to America than importing from it, as did most of the European countries, some of which had come together to form a European Economic Community. From the American point of view, the time had come to put an end to what was believed to have been the postwar pattern of Japanese and European dependence on the American market. Officials and significant segments of public opinion began developing an image of these countries as "rivals" rather than partners. It followed that they were all engaged in serious competition, and that the United States could no longer afford to look upon them complacently or benevolently. Instead, America must protect its own interests, and if the Europeans and Japanese refused to relent their aggressive trade offensive, the United States would be justified in taking necessary counter-measures.

These were serious developments for Japan, as its political and business leaders had taken for granted the virtually unlimited access to the American market, while they themselves had carried out a protectionist policy in order to encourage the growth of those industries that were "targeted" or deemed worthy of official support in order to make their products competitive in the world market. Gone were the days when, as John Foster Dulles had said in the early 1950's, Japan would have little else to export than toys and foodstuff. By the late 1960's, its export to the United States consisted of steel, television sets, and automobiles as well as cotton textiles, cameras, and tape-recorders. The traditional image of Japan as a seller of flimsy trinkets made by low-paid laborers was giving way to that of a modern, technologically rapidly advancing nation that could develop into America's serious competitor. Although there was little sense of urgent crisis, the Nixon administration was aware of these changing currents of thought and sought a series of agreements with Japan in which the latter would "voluntarily" restrict the shipment of certain items (initially textiles) to the United States. That the world's leading champion of free multilateral trade should begin to resort to such policies created in Japan the feeling that here, too, the familiar framework of international relations was disappearing. It was, to be sure, very difficult for the Japanese to view themselves as an economic giant. Although in terms of national income Japan had come to surpass most European nations, it was still far behind America; Japan's per capita income in 1970, for instance, was $4,622, whereas America's was $7,428. Still, it had to be admitted that the pace of growth was much faster in Japan than in most other countries, including the United States. The fact that much of the phenomenal growth took place while America was mired down in a costly war in Southeast Asia gave rise to the view that Japan had been selfishly seeking to enrich itself while America was committing its resources to the defense of Asian security from which the former benefited.

All this was appreciated by Japanese officials and publicists, some of whom began arguing that the nation must reconsider the basis of its postwar foreign policy. Some even spoke of America's "disintegration," as a consequence of the domestic turmoil, economic crisis, and foreign war. Yet few advocated a complete overhaul of Japanese policy. The rapprochement with China did give the country some flexibility, but that, as noted above, had been achieved by following the American lead and within the framework of the security treaty. There was no inclination to change the dependence on it and on the American "nuclear umbrella." Opinion polls almost always found a majority of Japanese expressing friendly sentiments toward the United States, considering it the country they "liked" best (or second best, after Switzerland, as happened sometimes in such polls). This did not mean, however, that, as the United States appeared to falter in its leadership role in world affairs, Japan would be willing to offer help, much less entertain the thought of more actively cooperating with the Americans, whereas an increasing number of Americans thought the Japanese should overcome their "nuclear allergy" and other symptoms of a defeated and weak nation and begin to play a role in world politics. But what that role should be was not very clear, either to Americans or to the Japanese. At a time when the world was going through a profound transformation, few innovative ideas emanated from Japan. The bulk of its people were still comfortable with their postwar constitution and the primacy of economics to which they and their leaders had committed themselves domestically and internationally.

14
Toward a Post–Cold War Order

The 1970's and the 1930's

In many ways the economic crisis of the 1970's evoked memories of the 1930's. Like the earlier decade, the 1970's saw the international economic system in disarray, with nothing to take the place of the Bretton Woods system and with nations resorting to protectionism and unilateral measures to promote their respective interests. There was talk of trade friction, tariff barriers dividing up the world into economic cocoons. The United States, the European nations, and Japan often accused each other of selfishness. Henry Kissinger, secretary of state after 1972, engaged in a "linkage" diplomacy, connecting American support for European security to the latter's concessions in trade matters. Americans accused Japanese of taking for granted their "free ride" on defense, implying that their alliance, too, was not irrevocable. When, in 1979, the second "oil shock" came, with yet another doubling of the price of crude oil produced by the OPEC countries, the world appeared condemned to a long period of economic stagnation as well as fierce commercial competition to produce tariff revenue with which to pay for imported oil. Domestic economies of the advanced countries registered minus growth rates from time to time, while recording continuously high rates of inflation. "Stagflation"—a state of stagnation combined with inflation—seemed to be their fate. The situation was so serious that a high American official said that even the survival of Western civilization was at stake. Also in 1979, Soviet troops marched into and occupied Afghanistan, as if to take advantage of the disarray among the Western allies and to extend its own sway over border areas. Soviet action belied the spirit of the detente that had been carefully worked out since the 1960's. A new Cold War—possibly even more ominous than the earlier one—appeared to be just around the corner. All negotiations on arms control agreements were halted, President Jimmy Carter (1977–1981) stopped grain shipments to the Soviet Union, and the United States and some of its allies (including Britain and Japan, but not France and Italy) boycotted the 1980 summer Olympic games in Moscow. Comparing world conditions in 1980 with those of only four years earlier, one might have felt that peace and prosperity were once again in great danger, that the combination of a security with an economic crisis made the decade look very much like the 1930's.

And yet, mercifully, the 1970's proved to be quite different from the disastrous 1930's. For one thing, world trade, in sharp contrast to the 1930's, did not diminish in the 1970's. Each nation was eager to expand its export trade in order to finance the cost of more expensive petroleum imports and also sought to make its domestic industry more efficient and cost-effective in order to produce goods more competitively. Moreover, although one corner of the Bretton Woods system—dollar convertibility into gold, and fixed rates of exchange—had disappeared, the International Monetary Fund remained, as did such other mechanisms for ensuring the smooth growth of international trade as the General Agreement on Tariffs and Trade (GATT) and the Organization for Economic Cooperation and Development (OECD) of which the advanced countries of the West and Japan were members. None of them chose to repudiate such membership, and all at least paid lip service to the principle of economic multilateralism. In 1975, indeed, the leaders of the principal industrial nations (the United States, Japan, Britain, France, West Germany, and Italy) met in Rambouillet, outside

Paris, to confer on ways to prevent the world economic crisis from eroding the postwar system of commercial and financial exchanges. They pledged to continue to work together for coping with energy, currency, and other issues. They would henceforth meet once a year, a symbol of cooperation among the economic powers. Although these conferences were not immediately reflected in improved economic conditions, at least they expressed the governments' determination never to allow the crisis to degenerate into the type of chaos that prevailed on the eve of the Second World War.

It is also significant that, unlike the 1930's, economic crisis did not result in military strengthening and confrontation. The United States took the lead in cutting its defense budget, so that its share of the national income fell from over eight percent in 1970 to about five percent ten years later. The implications were obvious; the nation would not resort to increased military spending to get the economy out of the stagnated state. Until the Soviet invasion of Afghanistan, moreover, Washington continued to seek a nuclear arms reduction agreement with Moscow. The United States reduced its military personnel in Taiwan from 8,000 in 1972 to virtually zero by 1979, and President Carter had plans to remove more than half of the 40,000 U.S. forces stationed in Korea. (This last step was not taken because of political turmoil in Korea following the assassination of President Park Chung Hee in 1979.) Japan, although it was under some pressure from America to increase its defense commitments, adhered to its "three non-nuclear principles" first adopted under Prime Minister Satō (not to produce, use, or "introduce" into its territory nuclear weapons). The cabinet of Miki Takeshi adopted a defense policy ("the basic guidelines for national defense") in 1976, reiterating Japan's purely defensive posture, and thus confirming its primary dependence on the United States for its security. Miki also endorsed the policy of limiting annual military budgets to within one percent of the country's GNP.

Most important, American-Asian relations during the 1970's continued the momentum begun under President Nixon and Henry Kissinger during 1969–1972. The United States and the People's Republic of China established normal diplomatic relations in 1979; Japan and China did so in 1978; and China abrogated its treaty of alliance with the Soviet Union in 1980, on the expiration of the thirty-year term. The United States steadily wound down its war in Southeast Asia, the last American troops evacuating Saigon in April 1975. Vietnam became unified in 1976—and promptly invaded the neighboring country, Cambodia. This brought about a Chinese incursion into Vietnam in support of the ousted Pol Pot regime in Cambodia. The United States took no official position on these new developments in Southeast Asia. Although the atrocities by the Pol Pot authorities were well known, there was little inclination to applaud Vietnam's action in driving them out of Pnom Penh, or to quarrel with China for its support of the latter, even its invasion of Vietnam. In the meantime, the Southeast Asia Treaty Organization, the legal framework for America's war in Indochina, was quietly dissolved (in 1977). So, within but a few years after the devastating and frustrating war, the United States virtually removed itself as a factor in Southeast Asia, letting indigenous forces and the Chinese determine its future course.

How would a new stability in Asia be defined? That was a key issue in the wake of the U.S.-Chinese rapprochement and the end of the Vietnam hostilities. Kissinger had spoken of a new structure of international relations in which the United States, the Soviet Union, and China would maintain some sort of balance. But this conception was very vague regarding other countries, particularly the Third World. Teng Hsiao-ping, one of the Chinese leaders who would inherit the mantle of Mao and Chou after their deaths, both taking place in 1976, rejected the view that China was one of the great powers; instead, he told the United Nations assembly in 1974, his country would continue to identify itself with, and speak for, the Third World. Even this, however, was not a clearcut proposition, for by then it was becoming all too clear that the developing nations were becoming seriously divided between oil producers and the rest, their economic gaps widening steadily. Moreover, Third World countries were never politically unified, as China itself was demonstrating by invading Vietnam. So, if the San Francisco system had been undermined by the Sino-American detente and the American withdrawal from Southeast Asia, little had taken its place as a new framework for regional order. This was in sharp contrast to Europe where, in 1972, a new framework, the Conference on Security and Cooperation in Europe (CSCE), was established, drawing participation from both the NATO and Warsaw Pact nations. Most European countries as well as the United States and Canada now took part in CSCE meetings, and, if nothing else, the institution served as a setting for discussion of security, trade, and other issues of concern to most Western nations. Nothing like the CSCE was ever developed for Asia. America's bilateral security ties with Asian countries remained, and, although the now defunct Southeast Asia Treaty Organization was in part being replaced by the Association of Southeast Asian Nations (ASEAN), formed in 1967 by some countries in the region (not including Vietnam), the ASEAN was initially seen as an economic association to promote mutual trade, and in any event it did not include the rest of Asia.

It may well be that in such a situation Japanese proposals for a "Pacific basin" had some significance. The idea was promoted actively by Prime Minister Ōhira Masayoshi (who occupied the office during 1978–1980) and was little more than an expression of his aspirations. Still, the idea was significant because it went beyond the framework of the bilateral security alliance with the United States as the key to the country's foreign affairs. Instead of linking itself to America, and now to China, through separate arrangements, the Pacific Basin conception indicated the need for a regional approach. It so happened that in the 1970's Japan's ties to Southeast Asia visibly deepened. Most of this was in the economic realm. Having by then completed all reparations payments to the countries in the areas which Japanese forces had occupied, the time seemed opportune to expand Japanese trade and, increasingly, investment activities there. That would have the effect of diversifying Japanese economic activities at a time when there were emerging pressures in the United States to check the growth of Japanese exports. Moreover, Japan, having reached the status of a principal economic power, now began extending aid (the so-called ODA, or official developmental aid) to countries such as Indonesia, the Philippines, Thailand, Burma, and Malaysia. All this may be seen as indicating an attempt to define a new framework for Asian-Pacific international relations in the wake of the erosion of the San Francisco system.

The Emergence of Cultural Diplomacy

By far the most interesting development of the 1970's, however, was the growing significance of cultural issues in international relations. Besides the geopolitical dimension—characterized by the Sino-American detente and U.S.-Soviet arms control negotiations—and the economic dimension—represented by the global disequilibria—some other significant themes emerged to affect the course of international relations. One was a concern for human rights. The Helsinki meeting of CSCE members in 1975 adopted a declaration with a ringing endorsement of human rights: freedom of expression, freedom of the press, and so forth. Not that these freedoms were going to be practiced right away in the Soviet Union or Eastern European countries, but the mere fact that they endorsed the principle was important. It was as if the principles first clearly articulated in the United Nations charter and the U.N. "declaration on human rights" were now once again being taken seriously as an integral part of a stable international order. Another was the growing awareness of environmental issues, such as industrial waste, pollution, soil erosion, and deforestation as a result of economic change. Step by step, industrial countries began taking measures to clear up rivers, fight smog, and restrict uncontrolled damages to nature and its species (some of which were now defined as "endangered"). And then there were also religious movements that cut across national boundaries and united people through their shared search for an alternative way of life. Mostly fundamentalist, these movements (notably Catholic and Islamic) surfaced toward the end of the 1970's to challenge secular authorities. All these were cultural phenomena in that they could not be readily subsumed under more conventional categories of security, trade, and related questions. For our purposes, however, their emergence is particularly interesting as they add to, and further complicate the discussion of mutual perceptions.

In a way it was symptomatic of the age that Japan under Prime Minister Ōhira began talking of a "comprehensive security," embracing strategic, economic, and cultural aspects of the country's foreign policy. Japan's security, he reasoned, depended not just on the military arrangements with the United States or the new relationship with China, or on trade and investment abroad, but also on establishing close cultural ties with other countries. Already under Prime Minister Tanaka, steps had been initiated to promote a cultural diplomacy, most visibly through the establishment of the Japan Foundation in 1972. In Japan this organization was called "the foundation for (the promotion of) international exchange," which better expressed what the semi-official organization (funded both by tax money and private contributions) aimed to do. The idea was to promote international understanding through assisting Japanese studies programs, language training, artistic exhibits, and the like in other countries. While the stress was almost wholly on Japanese culture, at least here was recognition that the government must begin to take a more serious interest in this aspect of international affairs. Then a few years later, when Prime Minister Fukuda Takeo visited Southeast Asia, he enunciated the so-called Fukuda doctrine which read very much like a Wilsonian statement; it stressed the need for cultural, intellectual, and psychological rapport between Japanese and other Asians in order to create a more solid basis for their interrelationship. The idea was that what Fukuda termed "heart-to-heart" diplomacy was the key to better relations among nations.

It might have seemed that there was little need to stress such a theme in U.S.-Japanese relations, for the two countries had, after all, been interacting at all levels since the war. Certainly, more Japanese had visited the United States after 1945 than any other country, and Americans usually comprised the largest group of foreign visitors to Japan. American studies of Japan, and Japanese studies of America, had made vast strides, and many Japanese leaders in government, business, journalism, scholarship, and the arts who were in their fifties or younger, had studied in American colleges and universities. The fact that nevertheless the Japan Foundation targeted the United States as the major arena for its initial activities—through the foundation, ten American universities were granted one million dollars each to endow a professorship in Japanese studies—indicated the realization that much more needed to be done. Indeed, the closer the two countries had become in security and economic affairs, the more serious the seeming gap remained in their mutual knowledge. The Japanese began talking of "perception gaps," believing that they knew far more about America than Americans knew about Japan. It would be difficult to evaluate such impressions, but at least it was true that far more American books had been translated into Japanese than vice versa, and far more Japanese understood (if they did not speak) English than Americans did Japanese. The Japanese government itself now recognized the need to do something about the situation. Soon business organizations became interested in likewise funding Japanese studies programs abroad, not only in the United States but also in Europe and Asia. China, too, became an object of Japanese cultural diplomacy, although it would be several years before a sizeable number of students were exchanged between the two countries.

The point is that these cultural initiatives were not an isolated phenomenon but fitted into one emerging theme in international relations during the 1970's, the importance of cultural issues. Even in U.S.-Chinese relations in which, as noted in the preceding chapter, geopolitical calculations were the key to the two countries' reconciliation, from early on there was strong interest in the United States in cementing the new ties through scholarly, educational, and journalistic connections. The National Science Foundation established a special office to deal with the exchange of scientific information between the two countries, and a Committee on Scholarly Cooperation with the People's Republic of China was organized as the framework for promoting student and scholarly exchanges. This was a nationwide endeavor in that leading academic figures in all fields (not just specialists in Chinese studies) were recruited to serve under its auspices, and through it and the Fulbright program which now extended its activities to the People's Republic of China, Chinese scholars and graduate students began to be invited to American universities and research institutions, and their American counterparts visited China in return. Soon Chinese academic visitors became a familiar sight across America. Although the same could not be said of Americans in China, whose number was smaller and whose movement was much more restricted, the mere fact that Americans began appearing in Chinese cities for the first time since the Korean War was as much a cultural as a geopolitical phenomenon.

The large number of publications in both countries on Chinese-American relations that appeared after the Nixon trip of 1972 attest to the fascination with the cultural, as well as foreign policy, implications of the new development. On the American side, what is impressive is the generally high quality of the writings as well as a large number of specialists equipped to offer sophisticated analyses of China. During the twenty-year period of diplomatic isolation of the PRC, American academic institutions had trained hundreds of historians, political scientists, economists, and others specializing in China, particularly postwar China. Now their training was put to use, not only to further their own scholarly activities through direct contact with their Chinese counterparts but also through communicating their findings and their perspectives to the larger reading public. Thus many publications at this time were collections of essays by these specialists: for instance, William Barnds, *China and American,* Michel Oxenberg, *The Dragon and the Eagle;* and John K. Fairbank, *Our China Prospect*—all published in the late 1970's—sought to examine various aspects of the bilateral relationship but put particular stress on the cultural dimension. Unlike many earlier accounts, written by missionaries and journalists, which had tended to draw rather romantic images of the Chinese and of U.S.-Chinese relations, publications in the 1970's were less melodramatic or sentimental, perhaps reflecting the geopolitical road to the reconciliation. For this very reason, interesting questions were already being raised about the compatibility of China and America, the question of whether the two peoples could readily "understand" one another being the central one. Scholarly opinion was much more restrained about such a possibility than would have been the case several decades earlier, but this all the more impelled American writers to inquire into the social and cultural differences between the two peoples. As the title of a book, *The China Difference,* by Ross Terrill revealed, there was ready acceptance of the view that in politics, social organizations, cultural activities, and interpersonal relations, the differences between Chinese and Americans appear to be even greater than had been imagined before direct observation became possible. Intercultural relations must, therefore, be built on the recognition of such differences. Before the war it had been popular to think of the two countries somehow sharing many characteristics and common destinies; now their sharp distinctions were being taken for granted so that cultural communication and interchange would not necessarily mean China was going to be transformed in the American way but rather signify that Americans were going to rediscover China as a great civilization in its own terms. In any event the opening of direct contact was the crucial step for mutual understanding.

The Chinese, too, were keen on understanding American society and culture, about which most of them had only developed stereotypical notions through indoctrination. The resumption of contact gave rise to some serious questioning about them. To be sure, it appears that the first groups of Chinese journalists and intellectuals who visited the United States looked for, and found, evidence confirming the accepted images of American capitalism in crisis or American society in disarray by crime, unemployment, and excessive liberties. Writings on America continued to be couched in Marxist frameworks of class divisions, revolutionary struggles, imperialism, and the like. But it is interesting to note, as David Shambaugh has shown, that from early on Chinese intellectuals began to take seriously some seeming gaps between Marxist presuppositions and the actual situation directly observed in America. Thus, instead of America being divided into the capitalist and proletarian classes, Chinese writers recognized the existence of the middle class comprising, as they realized, as much as three-quarters of the population. The proletariat, too, did not appear to be steadily becoming impoverished and driven to revolution. Rather, American workers could be seen as only "relatively" impoverished and were not necessarily poised to start a revolution.[1] Regardless of differences of opinion on such matters, however, Chinese authors had to incorporate the Sino-American detente into their writings. As noted in the preceding chapter, there was readiness to revert to the theme of the "traditional friendship" between the two peoples. Many writers had grown up during the 1930's and the 1940's and so remembered such rhetoric from the period of the Second World War. Hundreds had studied in the United States before 1949; some had even taught in America before returning home. It was not difficult for them to recall that earlier phase of U.S.-Chinese cooperation and characterize the developments after 1971 as resuming that pattern of relations. To rewrite the history of the bilateral relationship, where for over twenty years the main theme had been America's imperialistic designs to subjugate China, would be more difficult, but even here there were signs already at the end of the 1970's that some were willing once again to differentiate the United States from other imperialist powers and to reinterpret American policy so as to stress its less aggressive nature than the rest.

The opening up of China and the resumption of intellectual communication, however limited, between Americans and Chinese took place in a world environment in which themes like human rights

[1] David L. Shambaugh, *Beautiful Imperialist: China Perceives America, 1972–1990* (Princeton, 1991), pp. 141, 148–49.

and the protection of the natural environment were growing in importance. In time, therefore, U.S.-Chinese relations would also come to be affected by the same issues. For the time being, it was significant that, while geopolitics provided the basis for their rapprochement, their cultural contact fitted into the global scene in which communication across national boundaries on the part of individuals, ethnic and religious groups, and ideological movements was beginning to pose a serious challenge to the existing framework of international affairs.

The Asian Economic Miracle

The whole world came out of the decade of the 1970's in a state of crisis. Not only did it appear that the international economic disorder that had been exacerbated by the second oil shock of 1979 was going to stay, but something had also gone wrong with the U.S.-Soviet detente. Soviet troops remained in Afghanistan and SALT II (limiting anti-ballistic missiles) remained unratified. The globe seemed to be once again entering a period of turmoil, some calling it the second Cold War.

Within a few years, the atmosphere was to change, almost completely. To compare international events in 1990 with those in 1980 is to realize what a watershed in modern history the 1980's proved to be. By the end of the decade the United States and the Soviet Union had resumed and successfully completed a series of arms limitation negotiations; the latter under the leadership of Mikhail Gorbachev undertook sweeping democratization programs; similarly reformist movements spread all over Eastern Europe; ethnic self-consciousness and religious fundamentalism further became intensified, threatening secular state authorities in the Middle East and parts of Asia; China, on its part, withdrew troops from Vietnam and took steps to effect a rapprochement with the Soviet Union and in the meantime experienced one of the most massive democratization movements—as well as the brutal suppression of them. By the end of the 1980's commentators in the United States and elsewhere were talking of the end of the Cold War. Even the Cold War was now credited by some writers with having saved the world from self-destruction; the superpowers' nuclear balance, they argued, had preserved the "long peace" so that now they were ready to cooperate with each another and with other nations in establishing a new world order. And indeed in 1990 the world witnessed an unprecedented phenomenon: the United States and the Soviet Union joining together with other members of the United Nations in rebuking Iraq for invading Kuwait and endorsing U.N. sanctions against the aggressor.

In the economic sphere, changes were no less momentous. The leading capitalist countries managed to put an end to inflation; petroleum prices eased considerably; world trade continued to expand; and there were stock-market and real estate booms in all capitalist countries, adding to the ranks of the super-rich who enjoyed extravagant styles of living. At the same time, in part reflecting worldwide trade expansion and also the American government's low-tax policy under President Ronald Reagan, the United States began recording what came to be known as "triple deficits," in trade, balance of payments, and government finances. Trade deficits, which had appeared in the early 1970's for the first time since the 1890's, continued to grow. In 1987, for instance, the total American exports were $252.9 billion, but imports amounted to $424.1 billion. These trends exacerbated the balance of payments picture, as the trade deficits were not made up for by other kinds of foreign exchange earnings such as returns on investment and loans overseas or net tourist revenue. On the contrary, foreign investments and loans in the United States grew to such an extent that they came to exceed American capital export abroad. In other words, for the first time since the First World War, America became a net capital importer. Some of the capital imported was invested in factories and real estate, but a growing portion consisted of foreign purchases of governmental bonds. This in turn reflected a notable phenomenon of the 1980's, continued fiscal deficits and governmental debt. The budgetary deficit totalled $212 billion in 1985, almost equal to the amount spent on defense ($253 billion). In that year the federal debt outstanding was $1,827 billion. About one-fifth of these balances was accounted for by foreign borrowing. Here was another momentous development of the 1980's; the United States, still the world's leading economic power in terms of production and income, was having to depend more and more on imported goods and capital to sustain its level of living and its governmental operations.

American–East Asian relations were bound to change under those circumstances. Indeed, the economic aspect of the change was nothing short of being phenomenal. For the 1980's were a decade of impressive economic growth for Asian countries on the whole. Hitherto only Japan could be said to have reached the status of a fully developed economic power rich in income, if not in land or resources. By the end of the decade, South Korea, Taiwan, Hong Kong, and Singapore—the so-called "newly industrializing economies" or "little dragons"—were fast moving in the same direction, and the countries of Southeast Asia, too, did not lag far behind. The People's Republic of China achieved significant successes in its own way, its national income (to the extent that one can determine it) often increasing at an annual rate of more than ten percent. Thus throughout most of the 1980's, the whole of Asia (with the single exception of the Philippines) registered higher rates of growth than any other part of the globe. The phenomenon was so striking that a study undertaken for the U.S. Congress even observed that by the end of the century some Asian countries would come to enjoy a standard of living higher than that of less advanced economies of Europe. (In terms of "purchasing-power adjusted per capita income," Singapore and Hong Kong were already ahead of Austria and Italy in 1985, while Taiwan, Malaysia, and South Korea were just below Portugal.)

The spectacular Asian economic "miracle" owed much to the United States. First of all, the latter continued to provide a military presence through its bases and fleet in the region. Although it might be questioned (as it was in various parts of Asia) whether such a presence was really needed, especially in the second half of the decade when the ending of the Cold War appeared to be in sight, at least America's willingness to continue to be the major military power meant that other countries could afford to spend less on defense, thus diverting more of their resources to economic ends. China was the most spectacular example of this; its defense spending fell from roughly $23 billion in 1980 to one-fourth that amount by mid-decade, while its GNP more than doubled. (One consequence of this was that for the first time since the war Japanese defense spending came to exceed China's, but even so Japan's military budgets were barely one-tenth of the total U.S. defense expenditures.) There seems little doubt that the "long peace," whether one is to attribute it to the U.S.-USSR nuclear balance, to the Cold War strategy of containment, or to other geopolitical causes, provided an opportunity for Asian countries to concentrate their energies on industrialization and foreign trade, two keys to their economic successes. They followed "the Japanese model" of maximizing exports as the secret of economic growth and, in order to do so, targeting certain manufacturing industries for special support and official guidance. Of course, there were many other factors involved, especially these countries' high rates of saving (often exceeding twenty percent of personal income) so as to provide capital for investment, low interest rates (making it easier for businesses to borrow money), more efficient food production (so as to reduce the need for imports), and a high level of literacy and education. All these, however, would have meant less if the Asian countries had had to spend more on defense. In that sense, the generally stable international environment in the region which the United States sought to sustain was a crucial factor behind the story.

Secondly, the United States more directly helped the Asian countries' economic growth through purchasing large quantities of their goods. This is graphically demonstrated by the fact that these countries almost always exported more to America than importing from it. In 1988, for instance, Asia accounted for 24.2 percent of total U.S. exports, but 39.5 percent of its imports. Altogether Asian countries sold $106.8 billion dollars more than they purchased from the United States. Since in that year the trade deficit came to $171.2 billion, this meant that over sixty percent of America's unfavorable balance of trade was accounted for by huge Asian exports to the U.S. market. Japan, of course, was the most important in the picture; more than one-half of Asian exports to America originated there, and Japan's favorable balance of trade with the United States approximated $60 billion, or about 35 percent of the total U.S. trade deficit. But other countries, especially Taiwan, South Korea, and the members of the ASEAN were doing their share, so that it may be said without exaggeration that the accessibility of American markets to Asian goods was a principal cause of the expansion of Asian export trade in the 1980's which in turn fueled its growth. Not only in merchandise, however, but also in services and in capital, the United States was quite open—if not completely, then at least more so than the Asian countries themselves—so that by the end of the decade Asian banks and Asian-owned real estate properties were becoming familiar sights in all sections of the country.

No less important was the continued openness of American society in the wake of the Vietnam War and the Vietnam-Cambodian conflict. "Boat people," adrift in Southeast Asian waters, were often given temporary shelter in Hong Kong and Japan, but ultimately most reached the United States. But there were less dramatic but equally significant waves of Asians coming to America as immigrants, many of them businessmen, engineers, and other professionals. Their number increased so rapidly that in certain parts of the country, especially California, they came to constitute a highly visible minority. Indeed, in a state like California, Asians and Mexicans were coming to equal Americans of European origin in number. Although in the United States on the whole, Asians comprised less than three percent of the total population, even that was a phenomenal growth considering the fact that before the immigration revision of 1965 they had barely accounted for one percent. By the end of the 1980's, not only Americans of Chinese, Korean, or Japanese background, but also those of Southeast Asian origin were rapidly making their mark on American education, where they did especially well in mathematics, the sciences, and engineering; in colleges and universities their number was far in excess of their relative numerical status in the whole nation. And these Asian-Americans, too, played a role in the Asian economic miracle because they brought with them, and spread, their food and ways of life, possessed much capital, and patronized products of their countries of origin.

For all these reasons, Asia and America became more closely connected economically than ever before, and this connection was essential for the economic miracle taking place throughout the region. The phenomenon, however, was not without its problems, especially when it was seen from the American perspective. Somehow it seemed as if America's "triple deficits," with all the problems the term implied, and Asian economic successes were two sides of the same coin. At least many Americans were convinced that if they were to put an end to the situation, they would have to do something about what they considered Asia's excessive tendency to expand their trade and investment activities in the United States. Toward Japan there had already been "trade friction," as noted above, and this did not go away in the 1980's; it developed into a serious trade rivalry, even a "trade war," as some called it. There was no denying that trade had been growing more and more asymmetrical, with Japan continuing to accumulate trade surpluses vis-à-vis the United States. Even after a significant dollar devaluation toward the yen in 1985 (when the value of a dollar dropped more than twenty percent, to around 180 yen, and within a few years it was to go down even further), there was little change in the picture, as Japanese manufacturers began focusing on high value–added items for export, away from goods that depended on cheap labor (in fact, Japanese wages were increasing so rapidly that, in terms of the appreciating value of the yen, they were coming to approximate America's) toward goods that required high technological input. Besides, the enhanced value of the yen enabled the Japanese to invest in American factories and real estate, making Japan's economic presence more visible, another source of American irritation with and images of Japan's "economic invasion."

From the turn of the century, Japan had often been pictured as a "competitor" by the United States. But that had been primarily in terms of Japan's low wages and of its control over its empire from which foreign goods were shut out. Now, however, the image was one of Japan having become an economic superpower and still refusing to act more responsibly and with greater self-confidence. Instead, the country was pictured as being aggressively self-centered, intent on expanding into American and other markets with a single-minded determination without regard to the impact this would have on foreign countries. Japan, in other words, was being "unfair." The complaints about Japanese unfairness in trade practices had been heard before the war, but this time they took on ominous overtones because Japan was no longer perceived to be a poor country, as before the war. If it were poor, its selfish behavior might be excusable, but now that Japan had reached the levels of other leading economic powers, it must be held to higher standards of conduct. If Japan still refused to stop unfair practices, other nations were justified in retaliating in kind. So it came to be argued in increasing frequency in the United States.

That U.S.-Japanese trade continued to expand throughout the 1980's suggests that despite such rhetoric the bulk of American consumers were not deterred by images of an aggressive and unfair

Japan from purchasing its products when they were perceived to be more satisfactory at certain prices than domestic goods. Still, voices calling for protection and even retaliation could not be ignored by officials in Washington and Tokyo, and they took a number of steps to alleviate tensions. One device was called "voluntary restraints." These amounted to violating the very principle of open, free trade which both governments had professed to support, the justification being that no completely free trade would work when business organizations and practices were so different between countries. In order not to jeopardize its trade with the United States, Japan would agree to limit the sale of certain items, most notably automobiles, to a specified number per year. Washington and Tokyo also began talking of "structural impediments" that allegedly prevented Japan from importing more American and other foreign goods. To couch the trade dispute that way was clearly to introduce a cultural factor, to discuss commercial relations in terms of certain assumptions about one another. Japan, in such a framework, was a much more "closed" society than America because of complex interpersonal and inter-group linkages, making it all but impossible for outsiders to penetrate. "Structural impediments" referred to these inter-linkages. For instance, it was suggested that a product took many more layers of intermediaries before it reached the consumer in Japan than in America. The system was designed to preserve close personal relations. But such a formula also implied a view of the Japanese consumer as a passive recipient of the complicated and irrational market mechanism, in contrast to the American consumer who was more aware of his or her rights and would not tolerate such a cumbersome system. From such a perception, one could go on and make all kinds of generalizations about the differences between the two societies, indeed two cultures. James Fallows, for instance, argued that Japan was a country where production was given top priority, whereas in the United States consumption was considered more important. If true, these differences would also be reflections of some deeper cultural traits of the two peoples. It was not surprising, then, that so much was being said about the underlying cultural differences that made any stable relationship across the Pacific very difficult.

The so-called "Japan bashing," a phenomenon that became noticeable in American commentaries on Japan in the late 1980's, fitted into such developing perspectives on that country. Going much beyond stating grievances about Japan's ambitious designs to penetrate the American market or demanding temporary restraints on Japanese exports, the critics considered the two societies—their systems of defining rights and duties, their policy-making apparatus, their work (and leisure) habits, their day-to-day styles of living—so different that it would be futile to try to deal with Japan as if it were just another country, like France or Germany. Instead, it would have to be assumed that the Japanese would continue to operate in their own fashion so that, if America were to get anywhere in trade and other negotiations, only a tough stand would work. Not because such a stand would bring about lasting changes in Japanese behavior patterns, but simply because "external pressure" was the only effective instrument for forcing concessions from a reluctant Japan, it was imperative to employ this means. This argument was seemingly in contradiction with official negotiations on removing "structural impediments," which implied that it was possible to transform at least the Japanese system of distribution, with all the cultural consequences such action entailed. In a sense these negotiations were a test of whether Japan would indeed change significantly or, as the "bashers" were arguing, the two countries would remain as sharply divergent as ever. At the end of the decade no clear answer was forthcoming.

America in Decline?

Another interesting aspect of the U.S.-Japan trade dispute was the emergence of the idea that it was not so much Japan as America that needed to change if it were to remain competitive in the international market. The economic turmoil of the 1970's that had generated some dire forebodings about the future of Western civilization was followed, in the 1980's, by a more self-confident outlook at one level, especially as the United States and other countries managed to contain inflation and began recording respectable rates of growth once again. At the same time, however, America's "triple deficits," especially the chronic trade imbalance, deeply troubled many who began to think this was not a temporary phenomenon but expressed an overall crisis in American society. The nation's competitiveness could not be restored, they argued, simply by forcing other countries to accept voluntary trade restraint agreements. The problem was more fundamentally rooted in America, where rates of savings were lower than in most other countries, where pupils' comparative test scores lagged behind those elsewhere, and where violent crime appeared more pervasive than in Europe or Asia. Unless something were done in these areas, it was pointed out, the United States might have to "decline" in its relative power and influence in the world.

The "declinist" argument was best presented by Paul Kennedy's *The Rise and Fall of the Great Powers,* published in 1988, although other scholars had written in the same vein earlier. Kennedy's book was a panoramic presentation of the modern great powers since 1500 and traced the reasons for their rise and eventual decline, the key factor for the latter phenomenon being the disparity between resources and costs of maintaining imperial greatness. Transposed onto the American scene, the argument suggested that the United States, once enjoying the hegemonic position in world affairs, had stretched its resources to finance its obligations throughout the globe to such an extent that its "imperial overstretch" was making its relative position weaker. Just as earlier empires had declined for the same causes, America might have to face that fate unless steps were taken to retrench itself from some overseas commitments and refocused national energies on economic issues closer to home. Japan was quite relevant to the picture in that, just as the United States had replaced Britain as the hegemonic power, it was suggested that the next superpower (at least economically speaking) might well be Japan, which had not spent much on overseas security arrangements but had devoted its resources fully to economic expansion. Japan, too, however, might be susceptible to the same laws, and in the twenty-first century its position might be threatened by the fast growing China.

Kennedy's book became a best-seller in America—and in Japan. The two countries' readers may have read the book for different purposes. Certainly, their responses were not the same. Many Americans were irritated by the declinist argument and thought it was wholly unlikely that the United States had begun to, or would ever, decline. A particularly thoughtful critique was contained in Joseph Nye's book, *Bound to Lead,* published in 1990 as a frontal assault on Kennedy's thesis. As the book's subtitle, "the changing nature of power,'' indicated, Nye criticized Kennedy for failing to recognize that power was never a static, unchanging phenomenon but had undergone changes over time. The power Kennedy talked about, in Nye's view, was what the latter called ''hard power''—military hardware as well as economic indicators such as space, population, and production. Increasingly, however, Nye argued, it was important to keep in mind that international relations were being affected by ''soft power''—or ''cooptive power,'' the power to persuade. In other words, a country could have important power resources because of its values and principles, because of traditions of freedom which other nations might wish to emulate, because of the trust others put in its policy, and because of its citizens' quite simply being better liked as individuals than others. All these were equally important indicators of influence, and in a world where nuclear war or any large-scale warfare appeared to be less and less probable, ''soft power'' was likely to be a decisive factor in determining a nation's standing in the world. In this sense, Nye considered the United States to be still the world's leader. While he and many others admitted that the nation needed to undertake major reforms, especially in education, they believed the people were capable of the task. In this regard, it is interesting to note that one issue about which there was some debate was the degree to which the ''Japanese model'' was useful for America. In 1979 Ezra Vogel wrote a book entitled, *Japan As Number One,* which, as the title revealed, portrayed aspects of Japanese life—low crime rates, high literacy, efficient public transportation, and so forth—as things the United States must take seriously instead of remaining complacent about. That, as well as the increasingly more self-confident and even arrogant statements coming out of Japan—where the Kennedy thesis was often accepted without criticism—about its achievements, compelled Americans, perhaps for the first time in the history of American-Japanese relations, to ponder whether the Americans should be ''more like them.'' The overwhelming sentiment, however, was against such an option. As Fallows pointed out in his book, *More Like Us,* the Americans would be better advised not to follow the Japanese example, which would imply regimentation, discipline, and the nearly total submersion of the individual into the collectivity. That image of Japan, of course, had been in existence for decades, but this was the first time that the question was posed as to whether the more individualistic Americans should consider emulating such qualities. The majority of them would have answered in the negative, but the very fact that such a question was posed said something about changing perceptions of U.S.-Asian relations. (It is interesting to note that a best-selling novel published in 1992, Michael Crichton's *Rising Sun,* presented the argument that the United States must be willing to play by Japan's [often unfair] rules if it were to win the "war" in which the two countries were engaged.)

China, too, was forcing itself upon American consciousness. Not that the country of one billion inhabitants was likely soon to transform itself into another Japan, a formidable prospect if ever realized. Such a possibility seemed remote, given the still very low level of per capita income (about one-tenth of Japan's) and the cumbersome bureaucratic system that hindered efficient operations of its modernization programs. Rather, the question was the future of Chinese politics. There, with increasing contact with the outside world, and given technological innovations such as computers, fax machines, and satellite television which linked China with other countries, reformist impulses inevitably challenged the stronghold of Communist leaders, many of them in their seventies and even eighties. Clearly part of the global trend toward democratization, China's reform movements were much more dramatic and massive because of the sheer size of the population. Led by intellectuals who were fully aware of the international attention their activities would attract, the reformers became more and more active till they organized huge demonstrations in Peking and other cities for weeks in the spring of 1989. Their brutal suppression, the so-called Tiananmen Square massacre, on June 4, was in sharp contrast to the successful overthrowing of dictatorships in Eastern Europe, but several activists escaped to Western countries to continue their agitation.

For the American people, these were highly dramatic, and initially very gratifying, developments. Unlike their relations with Japan, they welcomed the events in China as evidence that the Chinese were becoming more democratic, "more like us." Television and newspaper commentators harped on the theme that, as had happened in the past, intellectuals in China had seized the opportunity to bring about needed reforms. The people were finally awake to their rights. The demonstrators spoke the language of democratization that was easily comprehensible in the West. But then, when the movement was crushed, the same commentators had to acknowledge that China had not really had a viable tradition of democratic government or freedom of expression, and therefore that the movement was bound to fail. Thus in a way comparable to discussions of U.S.-Japanese relations, Americans had to ponder the question of whether the Chinese were ever going to approximate American standards of political behavior. Were items like freedom of the press, human rights, and individual liberties "culture bound," as John K. Fairbank noted, so that relations between two such divergent cultures as America and China could never be understood by the use of these concepts? Or were Chinese aspirations just as genuine as those elsewhere? There was no simple answer, but the United States government did accept the view that human rights were universally applicable and therefore that China should be sanctioned for violating them.

It is perhaps not irrelevant to mention in this context that during the 1980's the Chinese themselves renewed their assault on the Japanese aggression and atrocities committed during the 1930's and the 1940's. Although, as noted in the preceding chapter, Peking's leaders had been willing to forego reparations payments from Japan, they began showing signs of irritation at what they took to be the Japanese tendency to whitewash the war guilt. An incident flared up in 1982 when it was reported in the Japanese press—erroneously, as it turned out—that the Ministry of Education in Tokyo was forcing textbook writers to softpedal their references to war. (For instance, the "rape of Nanking" of 1937 was given minor treatment, and the Japanese invasion was called an "advance." These items had been in textbooks prior to 1982 but became a matter of national and international concern that year because of the press reports.) Throughout the rest of the decade, Chinese authorities accused the Japanese of having insufficiently atoned for the war guilt and of taking steps to revive militarism. Just as frequently, Japanese officials denied such allegations. Often they gave in to Chinese pressures and told textbook writers to take heed of China's and other Asian countries' sensitivities. In such instances, the Chinese were clearly speaking the language of human rights, and that was why the masses, even as they followed the intellectuals in demanding more freedom, also supported the government in its denunciation of Japan's past behavior. We can understand the connection by putting it in the larger framework of the growing cross-national consciousness on rights and freedoms. And to the degree that such consciousness became more widely and more intensely held, America was bound to remain a world leader, perhaps the leading spokesman for these principles. There would be no decline of its role in that sense.

An Emerging Asian-Pacific Community?

In the concluding paragraph of the 1967 edition of this book, I noted, "the future relations between Asia and the United States depend so much on genuine intellectual communication. . . . If Chinese, Japanese, and Americans could develop a new vocabulary to facilitate mutual association . . . then the trans-Pacific community of people would in fact emerge and make its unique contribution to the development of human understanding."

Today, a quarter-century after those thoughts were penned, how does the situation look? The brief survey of American–East Asian relations since the 1960's which the last two chapters have attempted indicates that much progress has been made in the direction of facilitating intellectual communication. Not simply the resumption of exchange programs between the United States and the People's Republic of China, or between the latter and Japan, but in many other ways the three peoples—and, equally important, Koreans, Vietnamese, and others in Asia—have come closer through direct contact and shared experiences. Even when they are in serious disagreement, as in the trade dispute between America and Japan, the vocabulary of their disagreement is more sophisticated, much less emotional than before. All these countries have undergone profound transformations since the 1960's, and at least some aspects of the change have been conducive to promoting communication. The steady diversification of American society is one example, as is the development of middle classes in Japan and (if to a much lesser extent) in China. These phenomena do seem to have made the three countries less distinct from each other than earlier; at least, their sense of exceptionalism may be said to be slowly eroding. If so, that should introduce an element of balance in their mutual perceptions.

Some stereotypes remain. In February 1992, to cite one example, Nathan Gardels, a Los Angeles–based editor, noted that a world order that was "made in Japan" and "co-governs a third of humanity with China could pose a more formidable challenge to Western liberalism than did Soviet communism." How, he asked, could "a communitarian Japan . . . possibly share the same level of concern for the rights of individuals as a culture whose mythic emblem is the Lone Ranger?"[2] These ideas, it may be noted, differ little from the language of East-West differences that was fashionable at the turn of the twentieth century. As the world awaits the arrival of the twenty-first century, it would seem that new concepts and new frameworks are needed to comprehend what is happening in American-Asian relations. Fortunately, the extensive contact among these countries in the last quarter-century does seem to have brought about their respective social changes so that there is a greater tolerance for diversity combined with an increasing sense of shared concerns across nations.

One thing is certain. Americans, Chinese, and Japanese, despite their differences, share the same region of the earth, the Asian-Pacific arena, so that their future relations will be bound up with the future of this entire space. That space contains nearly half of humanity; China alone accounts for about twenty-two percent of the total world population, the United States for about five percent, Japan two and one-half percent. It has been estimated that their relative ratios may decline even as the global population is expected to increase by twenty percent by the end of the century. Africa, Latin America, and South Asia will increase in population faster than the Asian-Pacific region. But this will not diminish the fact that the region will, in combination with Europe, be one of the two centers of economic vitality and expansion. Whether or not the Asian-Pacific region will be able to develop a framework for common action, like the European Community, is the key question. Already many plans have been set forth for integrating Asia and the Pacific, but they differ as to which countries are to be included, and which excluded, as well as the nature of such association. Ultimately, the issue is a cultural one in that no such community of nations will be viable without some shared language, some ideas

[2] *International Herald Tribune,* Feb. 3, 1992, p. 1.

and perspectives the participants have in common. Will they be able to develop such a vocabulary? It is difficult to predict, but it will not be premature to observe that no such common vocabulary will be attained unless and until Americans, Chinese, and Japanese, on the basis of their past experiences and recent interactions, somehow cooperate with one another so that, in the words of Sir Isaiah Berlin, they may develop "a world which is a reasonably peaceful coat of many colors, each portion of which develops its own distinct cultural identity and is tolerant of others," but which accepts "a large minimum of common values."[3] Cultural diversity and shared values, that twin theme is nowhere more graphically played out than in the history of American-Asian relations. If the twentieth century has seen that history filled with conflict, aggression, and friction, it may be hoped that at least some of its less tragic aspects may prove to be harbingers of fruitful developments in the coming millennium.

[3] *New York Review of Books*, vol. 38, no. 19 (Nov. 21, 1991), pp. 21–22.

The Literature of American–East Asian Relations: A Short Bibliography

In a very real sense, everything that Americans, Chinese, and Japanese have written about themselves and about each other is a primary source for the study of mutual perception across the Pacific. In this book I have drawn on such conventional primary sources as diplomatic documents, newspapers, and biographical records. My research took me to archives in Washington, London, Tokyo, Taipei, and various depositories of personal papers. Not less valuable have been articles and books on American-Asian relations that have accumulated in the three countries over the last century and a half. Even scholarly monographs cannot completely escape their historical and geographical environment and are equally useful as original documents. This is not to deny, of course, that my study has profited from the writings of pioneering scholars and fellow historians in various parts of the world. The following pages give but an inadequate idea of my indebtedness to their works. I have listed only those that have been of particular use in the preparation of this book. Items in Chinese and Japanese are grouped at the end.

GENERAL

There are many general histories of international relations and of American diplomatic history that provide indispensable factual background. Particularly useful and up to date are: Paul H. Clyde and Burton F. Beers, *The Far East,*

A History of the Western Impact and the Eastern Response, 1830–1965 (Englewood Cliffs, N.J., 1966), Harold H. Vinacke, *A History of the Far East in Modern Times,* 6th ed. (New York, 1959), H. F. MacNair and Donald F. Lach, *Modern Far Eastern International Relations,* 2nd ed. (New York, 1955), F. H. Michael and George E. Taylor, *The Far East in the Modern World,* rev. ed. (New York, 1964), and Richard W. Leopold, *The Growth of American Foreign Policy* (New York, 1962). H. B. Morse, *The International Relations of the Chinese Empire,* 3 vols. (Shanghai, 1910–1918) is a basic reference book; there is none like it for Japanese diplomatic history. Among European writings, of special interest are Pierre Renouvin, *La Question d'Extrême-Orient, 1840–1940* (Paris, 1946), and E. M. Zhukov, *Mezdunarodnye otnosheniia na Dal'nem Vostoke, 1840–1949* (Moscow, 1956).

Brief surveys of American-Chinese and American-Japanese relations in historical perspective are given in John K. Fairbank, *The United States and China,* new ed. (Cambridge, Mass., 1962), and Edwin O. Reischauer, *The United States and Japan,* 3rd ed. (Cambridge, Mass., 1965), respectively. They supplement the earlier and colorful writings by Foster Rhea Dulles, including *Forty Years of American-Japanese Relations* (New York, 1937), and *China and America, The Story of Their Relations Since 1784* (Princeton, 1946). For American policy toward East Asia, it is surprising that historians have allowed A. Whitney Griswold's classic, *The Far Eastern Policy of the United States* (New York, 1938) to reign and dominate the scene for nearly thirty years. This book, however, is subjected to rigorous examination by Dorothy Borg, ed., *Historians and American Far Eastern Policy* (New York, 1966), a pamphlet containing essays by six historians. A very perceptive analysis is William L. Neumann's, "Ambiguity and Ambivalence in Ideas of National Interest in Asia," in Alexander DeConde, ed., *Isolation and Security* (Durham, N.C., 1957).

Only a few writers have tried to penetrate the surface and study the history of American-Asian relations as a cultural and psychological phenomenon. Robert S. Schwantes, *Japanese and Americans: A Century of Cultural Relations* (New York, 1955), William L. Neumann, *America Encounters Japan, From Perry to MacArthur* (Baltimore, 1963), and Clay Lancaster, *The Japanese Influence in America* (New York, 1963) are pioneering works. Unfortunately, there has been no book of comparable quality dealing with American-Chinese relations. A partial exception is K. C. Liu, *Americans and Chinese: A Historical Essay and a Bibliography* (Cambridge, Mass., 1963), which contains a short but judicious interpretation of the two peoples' historical contact. Harold Isaacs, *Scratches on Our Minds, American Images of China and India* (New York, 1958), while concentrating on postwar images, is a good guide to historical literature. These books, however, have much more to say on the American side than on China and Japan.

THE INITIAL ENCOUNTER

A number of excellent monographs on nineteenth-century American history serve to put American-Asian relations in their proper perspective. Felix Gilbert, *To the Farewell Address, Ideas of Early American Foreign Policy* (Princeton, 1961) relates early American diplomacy to European thinking in the eighteenth century. Ideas of continental and trans-oceanic expansionism are ably traced by R. W.

Van Alstyne, *The Rising American Empire* (Oxford, 1960), Albert K. Weinberg, *Manifest Destiny* (Baltimore, 1935), Frederick Merk, *Manifest Destiny and Mission in American History, A New Interpretation* (New York, 1963), and Henry Nash Smith, *Virgin Land, The American West as Symbol and Myth* (Cambridge, Mass., 1950). Norman A. Graebner, *Empire on the Pacific, A Study in American Continental Expansion* (New York, 1955), and Dexter Perkins, *The Monroe Doctrine, 1823–1826* (Cambridge, Mass., 1927), among others, are particularly useful for the study of interrelationship among American policy, the Pacific coast, and trade in Asia. Among numerous writings on American intellectual history, I have found most relevant the two books by Louis Hartz: *The Liberal Tradition in America* (New York, 1955), and *The Founding of New Societies* (New York, 1964).

Several studies, products of recent scholarship, deal with the Western impact, direct and indirect, on China and Japan in the nineteenth century. For China, the point of departure is John K. Fairbank's *Trade and Diplomacy on the China Coast, The Opening of the Treaty Ports, 1842–1854* (Cambridge, Mass., 1964). This pioneering study is now complemented by two first-rate monographs: Hsing-pao Chang, *Commissioner Lin and the Opium War* (Cambridge, Mass., 1964), and Frederick Wakeman, *Strangers at the Gate, Social Disorders in South China, 1839–1861* (Berkeley, 1966). For Ch'ing foreign policy after 1858, see Immanuel C. Y. Hsü, *China's Entrance into the Family of Nations, The Diplomatic Phase, 1858–1880* (Cambridge, Mass., 1960), and Masataka Banno, *China and the West, 1858–1861, The Origins of the Tsungli Yamen* (Cambridge, Mass., 1964). The way China's gentry reacted to increased foreign contact of the 1860's is analyzed authoritatively by Mary C. Wright, *The Last Stand of Chinese Conservatism, The T'ung-Chih Restoration, 1862–1874* (Stanford, 1957), and Paul A. Cohen, *China and Christianity, The Missionary Movement and the Growth of Chinese Antiforeignism, 1860–1870* (Cambridge, Mass., 1963).

For Japan, Marius B. Jansen, ed., *Changing Japanese Attitudes towards Modernization* (Princeton, 1965) contains excellent studies of late Tokugawa and early Meiji thought. For a broader outline, see George Sansom, *The Western World and Japan* (New York, 1950). More recent scholarship is reflected in Bernard S. Silberman and Harry D. Harootunian, eds., *Modern Japanese Leadership, Transition and Change* (Tucson, 1966). Also useful are Delmer M. Brown, *Nationalism in Japan* (Berkeley, 1955), and W. G. Beasley, *Select Documents on Japanese Foreign Policy, 1853–1868* (London, 1955). Albert M. Craig, *Chōshū in the Meiji Restoration* (Cambridge, Mass., 1961) is notable for its careful study of the impact of Western contact upon Japanese politics.

There are many works that deal specifically with the initial contact between the United States and East Asia. Still the best account is Tyler Dennett, *Americans in Eastern Asia* (New York, 1922), which has not been surpassed as a detailed but readable survey of American policies and activities in East Asia in the nineteenth century. For the early contact between China and America, see also Samuel Eliot Morison, *The Maritime History of Massachusetts, 1783–1860* (Boston, 1921), Kenneth Scott Latourette, *The History of Early Relations between the United States and China, 1784–1844* (New Haven, 1917), and Eldon Griffin, *Clippers and Consuls, American Consular and Commercial Relations with Eastern Asia, 1845–1860* (Ann Arbor, 1938). Chinese sources are fully utilized in Earl Swisher, ed., *China's Management of the American Barbarians, 1841–1861* (New Haven, 1953), and Te-kong Tong, *United States Diplomacy in China, 1844–1860* (Seattle, 1964). Also informative is Earl Swisher, *Chinese Representation in the United States* (University of Colorado Studies, Series in History, No. 5, 1967). For American-Chinese relations in California, I have found most useful Gunther Barth, *Bitter Strength, A History of the Chinese in the United States, 1850–1870* (Cambridge, Mass., 1964).

The list is also long for accounts of early Japanese-American relations. The most solid diplomatic history is Payson J. Treat, *Diplomatic Relations between the United States and Japan,* 3 vols. (Stanford, 1932–1938). Some colorful details are given in Neumann's *America Encounters Japan,* cited above, and such other volumes as Foster Rhea Dulles, *Yankees and Samurai, America's Role in the Emergence of Modern Japan* (New York, 1965), Shunzo Sakamaki, *Japan and the United States, 1790–1835* (Tokyo, 1939), and Arthur Walworth, *Black Ships Off Japan, The Story of Commodore Perry's Expedition* (New York, 1946). There is still need for less conventional and bolder approaches. Instead of repeating well-known episodes, historians will have to ask fresh questions and examine new evidence. Arthur H. Christy, *The Asian Legacy in American Life* (New York, 1945) was a step in the right direction, and we need more books like it.

IMPERIALISM, NATIONALISM, RACISM

The literature on imperialism is enormous. My understanding of the changes in international and domestic life in the 1880's and the 1890's has been particularly helped by such books as Richard Koebner and Helmut Dan Schmidt, *Imperialism, The Story and Significance of a Political Word, 1840–1960* (Cambridge, 1964), A. P. Thornton, *The Imperial Idea and Its Enemies* (London, 1963), the same author's *Doctrines of Imperialism* (New York, 1965), O. Mannoni, *Prospero and Caliban, The Psychology of Colonialism* (New York, 1956), H. Stuart Hughes, *Consciousness and Society, The Reorientation of European Social Thought, 1890–1930* (New York, 1958), and Edward Mead Earle, ed., *Makers of Modern Strategy, Military Thought from Machiavelli to Hitler* (Princeton, 1941). Among the more recent interpretations of imperialism the most stimulating are Raymond Aron, *Peace and War, A Theory of International Relations* (New York, 1966), and relevant chapters in W. W. Rostow, *Stages of Economic Growth* (Cambridge, 1960), and C. E. Black, *Dynamics of Modernization, A Study in Comparative History* (New York, 1966). The last two offer different non-Marxist ways to relate domestic development to imperialistic foreign policy.

For diplomatic history in the age of imperialism, William L. Langer, *The Diplomacy of Imperialism, 1890–1902,* 2nd ed. (New York, 1951) is still basic and indispensable. The opening of Foreign Office documents, however, has resulted in significant additions. Notable for this reason are Nathan A. Pelcovits, *Old China Hands and the Foreign Office* (New York, 1948), George Monger, *The End of Isolation, British Foreign Policy, 1900–1907* (London, 1963), and Edmund S. Wehrle, *Britain, China, and the Antimissionary Riots, 1891–1900* (Minneapolis, 1966). Also important is George Lensen, *Korea and Manchuria between Russia and Japan, 1895–1904* (Tallahassee, 1966), which reprints, with an excellent introduction, the diary kept by Sir Ernest Satow. Among the works utilizing Russian sources, the most valuable is A. A. Malozemoff, *Russian Far Eastern Policy, 1881–1904* (Berkeley, 1958). The process of decision making in late Ch'ing China is brilliantly described in Lloyd E. Eastman, *Throne and Mandarins, China's Search for a Policy during the Sino-French Controversy, 1880–1885* (Cambridge, Mass., 1967). See also Chester Tan, *The Boxer Catastrophe* (New York, 1955) and E-Tzu Zen Sun, *Chinese Railways and British Interests, 1898–1911* (New York, 1954). Hilary Conroy, *The Japanese Seizure of Korea, 1868–1910* (Philadelphia, 1960) is an ambitious, pioneering study, attempting to find patterns of realism and idealism in Meiji foreign policy. Ian H. Nish, *The Anglo-Japanese Alliance, The Diplomacy of Two Island Empires, 1894–1907* (London, 1966) is solidly based on a correlation of British and Japanese sources.

Of the host of writings on America's emergence as a world power, the most stimulating general interpretations are Howard K. Beale, *Theodore Roosevelt and the Rise of America to World Power* (Baltimore, 1956), and Walter LaFeber, *The New Empire, An Interpretation of American Expansionism, 1860–1898* (Ithaca, 1963). Also relevant are Foster Rhea Dulles, *The Imperial Years* (New York, 1956), Robert E. Osgood, *Ideas and Self-Interest in American Foreign Relations* (New York, 1953), Louis J. Halle, *Dream and Reality, Aspects of American Foreign Policy* (New York, 1959), William A. Williams, *The Tragedy of American Diplomacy* (New York, 1959), and Richard Hofstadter, *Social Darwinism in American Thought* (Philadelphia, 1945). For American naval and military expansion, see Harold and Margaret Sprout, *The Rise of American Naval Power, 1776–1918* (Princeton, 1946), Walter Millis, *Arms and Men* (New York, 1956), and William R. Braisted, *The American Navy in the Pacific, 1897–1907* (Austin, Texas, 1958).

America's involvement in East Asia and the Pacific in the 1890's are subjects of good monographs. Fred H. Harrington, *God, Mammon, and the Japanese, Dr. Horace N. Allen and Korean-American Relations, 1884–1905* (Madison, Wis., 1944) is still useful. Alfred Vagts, *Deutschland und die Vereinigten Staaten in der Weltpolitik, 1890–1906,* 2 vols. (New York, 1935), and Otto Graf zu Stolberg-Wernigerode, *Deutschland und die Vereinigten Staaten von Amerika im Zeitalter Bismarks* (Berlin and Leipzig, 1933) contain pertinent chapters dealing with American policy in Asia and the Pacific. For the Spanish-American War, Ernest R. May, *Imperial Democracy, The Emergence of America as a Great Power* (New York, 1961) is standard. See also Julius W. Pratt, *Expansionists of 1898* (Baltimore, 1936), Hilary Conroy, *The Japanese Frontier in Hawaii, 1868–1898* (Berkeley, 1953), Charles S. Campbell, *Anglo-American Understanding, 1898–1903* (Baltimore, 1957), and Merze Tate, *The United States and the Hawaiian Kingdom* (New Haven, 1965). Various interpretations of Hay's Open Door policy, its meaning and origin, are given in George F. Kennan, *American Diplomacy, 1900–1950* (New York, 1951), Tyler Dennett, *John Hay, From Poetry to Politics* (New York, 1933), Paul A. Varg, *Open Door Diplomat, The Life of W. W. Rockhill* (Urbana, Ill., 1952), Charles S. Campbell, *Special Business Interests and the Open Door* (New Haven, 1951), and Raymond A. Esthus, "The Changing Concept of the Open Door, 1899–1910," in *Mississippi Valley Historical Review,* XLVI (1959).

For American policy in East Asia in the age of Theodore Roosevelt the best monographs, in addition to that by Beale noted earlier, are: Edward H. Zabriskie, *American-Russian Rivalry in the Far East* (Philadelphia, 1946), Tyler Dennett, *Roosevelt and the Russo-Japanese War* (New York, 1925), John A. White, *The Diplomacy of the Russo-Japanese War* (Princeton, 1964), Raymond A. Esthus, *Theodore Roosevelt and Japan* (Seattle, 1966), and Robert A. Hart, *The Great*

White Fleet, Its Voyage Around the World, 1907–1909 (Boston, 1965). White and Esthus utilize some Japanese sources and bring Dennett's classic account of Rooseveltian diplomacy up to date. Esthus's book also deals with Japanese-American exchanges on the immigration question and thus complements the authoritative book by Thomas A. Bailey, *Theodore Roosevelt and the Japanese-American Crises* (Stanford, 1934). Japanese-American estrangement after the Russo-Japanese War is also dealt with in such volumes as Roger Daniels, *The Politics of Prejudice, The Anti-Japanese Movement in California and the Struggle for Japanese Exclusion* (Berkeley, 1962), Charles Vevier, *The United States and China, 1906–1913, A Study of Finance and Diplomacy* (New Brunswick, 1955), Herbert Croly, *Willard Straight* (New York, 1924), George Kennan, *E. H. Harriman,* 2 vols. (New York, 1922), and Outten J. Clinard, *Japan's Influence on American Naval Power, 1897–1917* (Berkeley, 1947). See also Carey McWilliams, *Prejudice, Japanese-Americans, Symbol of Racial Intolerance* (Boston, 1944), and E. Tupper and G. McReynolds, *Japan in American Public Opinion* (New York, 1937).

The Wilsonian era has been a genre in itself in historical writing. Especially relevant to the present study are: Tien-yi Li, *Woodrow Wilson's China Policy, 1913–1917* (New York, 1952), Roy W. Curry, *Woodrow Wilson and Far Eastern Policy, 1913–1921* (New York, 1957), Russell H. Fifield, *Woodrow Wilson and the Far East, The Diplomacy of the Shantung Question* (New York, 1952), Burton F. Beers, *Vain Endeavor, Robert Lansing's Attempt to End the American-Japanese Rivalry* (Durham, N.C., 1962), Arno Mayer, *Political Origins of the New Diplomacy, 1917–1918* (New Haven, 1959), Daniel Smith, *The Great Departure, The United States and World War I, 1914–1920* (New York, 1965), and Edward H. Buehrig, *Woodrow Wilson and the Balance of Power* (Bloomington, Ind., 1955). The best account in English of the Twenty-One Demands episode is in Arthur S. Link, *Wilson: The Struggle for Neutrality, 1914–1915* (Princeton, 1960). For the Siberian expedition, earlier writings have been superseded by James W. Morley, *The Japanese Thrust into Siberia 1918* (New York, 1957), George F. Kennan, *Russia Leaves the War* (Princeton, 1956), his *The Decision to Intervene* (Princeton, 1958), and Richard H. Ullman, *Intervention and the War* (Princeton, 1961).

For the Washington Conference, one would have to wait for the soon-to-be-published works by Ernest R. May and Sadao Asada. Theirs will be the first monographs that adequately examine Japanese sources. Among the existing volumes, some light is shed by Harold and Margaret Sprout, *Toward a New Order of Sea Power* (Princeton, 1946), and John C. Vinson, *The Parchment Peace* (Athens, Ga., 1956), a study of Congressional viewpoints. The naval question in the 1920's is taken up in an interesting monograph by Gerald E. Wheeler, *Prelude to Pearl Harbor, The United States Navy and the Far East, 1921–1931* (Columbia, Mo., 1963). For the mid-1920's, see Dorothy Borg, *American Policy and the Chinese Revolution, 1925–1928* (New York, 1947), and L. Ethan Ellis, *Frank B. Kellogg and American Foreign Relations, 1925–1929* (New Brunswick, 1961). America's role in the Sino-Soviet clash of 1929 is traced in Pauline Tompkins, *American-Russian Relations in the Far East* (New York, 1949), Peter S. H. Tang, *Russian and Soviet Policy in Manchuria and Outer Mongolia, 1911–1931* (Durham, N.C., 1959), and Robert H. Ferrell, *American Diplomacy in the Great Depression, Hoover-Stimson Foreign Policy, 1929–1933* (New Haven, 1957). Also valuable for the special topics they discuss are Wesley R.

Fishel, *The End of Extraterritoriality in China* (Berkeley, 1952), and Paul A. Varg, *Missionaries, Chinese, and Diplomats, The American Missionary Movement in China, 1890–1952* (Princeton, 1958). Although these books cover a longer time span, they are especially informative on the 1920's. My own *After Imperialism, The Search for a New Order in the Far East, 1921–1931* (Cambridge, Mass., 1965) discusses American policy in relation to those of other countries, in particular the Soviet Union, China, and Japan. Selig Adler, *The Isolationist Impulse* (New York, 1957) is still the best account on the subject and is full of pertinent data. After all that has been written on the interwar years, however, the wisest comments are still included in a book written in 1939, E. H. Carr, *The Twenty Years' Crisis, 1919–1939* (London, 1939).

There are still very few studies in Western languages of Chinese and Japanese attitudes toward the West in general and the United States in particular. Some excellent beginnings have been made by such works as Chow Tse-tsung, *The May Fourth Movement, Intellectual Revolution in Modern China* (Cambridge, Mass., 1960), and Y. C. Wang, *Chinese Intellectuals and the West, 1872–1949* (Chapel Hill, 1966). The latter has important statistics for Chinese students in the United States. Otherwise the most valuable studies remain biographical case histories. For instance, two prominent Ch'ing intellectuals have been analyzed in Joseph R. Levenson, *Liang Ch'i-ch'ao and the Mind of Modern China* (Cambridge, Mass., 1953) and Benjamin Schwartz, *In Search of Wealth and Power, Yen Fu and the West* (Cambridge, Mass., 1964). Although there is no study that specifically examines the Chinese Communists' attitude toward the United States before the war, much insight is gained by the reading of such books as Stuart Schram, *The Political Thought of Mao Tse-tung* (New York, 1963), Donald M. Lowe, *The Function of "China" in Marx, Lenin, and Mao* (Berkeley, 1966), and Maurice Meisner, *Li Ta-chao and the Origins of Chinese Marxism* (Cambridge, Mass., 1967). Two Japanese intellectuals who spent their formative years in the United States are portrayed in Hyman Kublin, *Asian Revolutionary, The Life of Sen Katayama* (Princeton, 1964), and Edward Seidensticker, *Kafū the Scribbler, The Life and Letters of Nagai Kafū, 1879–1959* (Stanford, 1965).

SINO-AMERICAN CO-OPERATION AGAINST JAPAN

The Manchurian incident has been a subject of intensive study almost from its inception. Here it will be sufficient to cite only the most recent and reliable works. The best account of the events in Manchuria, evolving around the Kwantung Army, is Sadako N. Ogata, *Defiance in Manchuria, The Making of Japanese Foreign Policy, 1931–1932* (Berkeley, 1964). See also Takehiko Yoshihashi, *Conspiracy at Mukden, The Rise of the Japanese Military* (New Haven, 1963). A provocative reinterpretation, based on solid research, is given by James B. Crowley, *Japan's Quest for Autonomy, National Security and Foreign Policy, 1930–1938* (Princeton, 1966). The author tries to combat the "conspiracy" theory of Japanese militarism and aggression and relate the Manchurian and other incidents to an overriding concern for security. For American response, the best work is Armin Rappaport, *Henry L. Stimson and Japan* (Chicago, 1963). See also Richard N. Current, *Secretary Stimson, A Study in Statecraft* (New Brunswick, 1954), and Elting E. Morison, *Turmoil and Tradition, A Study of the*

Life and Times of Henry L. Stimson (Boston, 1960). The naval aspect of the Japanese-American crisis is detailed in Thaddeus V. Tuleja, *Statesmen and Admirals, Quest for Far Eastern Naval Policy* (New York, 1963). The international context of the Manchurian crisis is well developed in F. P. Walters, *A History of the League of Nations* (Oxford, 1952), and R. Bassett, *Democracy and Foreign Policy, A Case History, The Sino-Japanese Dispute, 1931–1933* (London, 1952).

For Japanese policy after the Manchurian episode, the best accounts, in addition to Crowley's book noted above, are F. C. Jones, *Japan's New Order in Eastern Asia* (New York, 1954) and Robert J. C. Butow, *Tojo and the Coming of the War* (Princeton, 1961). See also David J. Lu, *From the Marco Polo Bridge to Pearl Harbor* (Washington, 1962), Frank W. Iklé, *German-Japanese Relations, 1936–1940* (New York, 1956), and Nobutaka Ike, *Japan's Decision for War, Records of the 1941 Policy Conferences* (Stanford, 1967). This last translates certain key documents reflecting the decision for an American war. The psychology of Japanese military thinking is best analyzed in Masao Maruyama, *Thought and Behavior in Modern Japanese Politics* (New York, 1963). Also to be noted is Richard Storry, *The Double Patriots, A Study of Japanese Nationalism* (New York, 1958). An intellectual history of Japan in the 1930's is just beginning to be written. The atmosphere of the period, however, is well conveyed by Chalmers Johnson, *An Instance of Treason, Ozaki Hotsumi and the Sorge Spy Ring* (Stanford, 1964).

American attitudes in the 1930's in general are ably sketched by Manfred Jonas, *Isolationism in America, 1935–1941* (Ithaca, 1966) and Robert A. Divine, *The Illusion of Neutrality* (Chicago, 1962). Also suggestive is Lloyd Gardner, *Economic Aspects of New Deal Diplomacy* (Madison, Wis., 1964). For America's over-all foreign affairs during the period 1937–1941, no work has yet come close to challenging the depth and documentation of the two standard volumes by William L. Langer and S. E. Gleason, *The Challenge to Isolation* (New York, 1952) and *The Undeclared War* (New York, 1953). American policy in East Asia, however, has been a subject of extensive study by a generation of historians. For the mid-1930's Dorothy Borg's *The United States and the Far Eastern Crisis of 1933–1938* (Cambridge, Mass., 1964) supersedes all earlier works and will remain the most authoritative book for years to come. The economic aspects of American-Chinese relations are traced by A. S. Everest, *Morgenthau, the New Deal and Silver, A Study of Pressure Politics* (New York, 1950), and Arthur N. Young, *China and the Helping Hand, 1937–1945* (Cambridge, Mass., 1963). For the Japanese-American crisis leading up to Pearl Harbor, Herbert Feis, *The Road to Pearl Harbor* (Princeton, 1950) remains standard. But its mildly affirmative tone has been criticized by more openly critical writings, among which the best is Paul W. Schroeder, *The Axis Alliance and Japanese-American Relations* (Ithaca, 1958). More frankly partisan in approach and presentation, but containing useful quotes, are Charles A. Beard, *President Roosevelt and the Coming of the War* (New Haven, 1948), Charles C. Tansill, *Back Door to War* (Chicago, 1952), and Anthony Kubek, *How the Far East Was Lost, American Policy and the Creation of Communist China, 1941–1949* (Chicago, 1963). An entirely fresh approach is offered by Waldo H. Heinrichs, *American Ambassador, Joseph C. Grew and the Development of the United States Diplomatic Tradition* (Boston, 1966). It focuses on an American ambassador's role in the crisis and assesses his evaluations of Japanese policy against the reality of Japanese policy. Another useful biographical study is Forrest C. Pogue, *George C. Marshall, Ordeal and Hope, 1939–1942* (New York, 1966). Some colorful details are given in such journalistic books as A. A. Hoehling, *The Week before Pearl Harbor* (New York, 1963), and Ladislas Farago, *The Broken Seal* (New York, 1967), a study of American and Japanese intelligence activities. The best scholarly work on this subject, however, is Roberta Wohlstetter, *Pearl Harbor, Warning and Decisions* (Stanford, 1962). Finally, extra dimensions are added by two recent monographs: Raymond A. Esthus, *From Enmity to Alliance, United States-Australian Relations, 1931–1941* (Seattle, 1964), and Nicolas R. Clifford, *Retreat from China, British Policy in the Far East, 1937–1941* (Seattle, 1967).

For the military aspect of the Pacific war, I only mention the key volumes in the official series, *United States Army in World War II:* M. Matloff and E. M. Snell, *Strategic Planning for Coalition Warfare, 1941–1942* (Washington, 1953) and Matloff's volume for 1943–1944 under the same title (Washington, 1960). For the navy, there is Louis Morton, *Strategy and Command, The First Two Years* (Washington, 1962). A good summary for the entire war is Samuel Eliot Morison, *The Two-Ocean War, A Short History of the United States Navy in the Second World War* (Boston, 1963). The diplomacy of the Pacific war may be studied in Herbert Feis, *Churchill, Roosevelt, Stalin, The War They Waged and the Peace They Sought* (Princeton, 1957), Gaddis Smith, *American Diplomacy during the Second World War* (New York, 1965), and Willard Range, *Franklin D. Roosevelt's World Order* (Athens, Ga., 1959). The end of the Japanese war, including the decision to drop the atomic bomb, is dealt with in the three standard works: Herbert Feis, *Between War and Peace, The Potsdam Conference* (Princeton, 1960), his *The Atomic Bomb and the End of World War II* (Princeton, 1966), a revision of *Japan Subdued, The Atomic Bomb and the End of the War in the Pacific* (Princeton, 1961), and Robert J. C. Butow, *Japan's Decision to Surrender* (Stanford, 1954). The atomic bomb decision has been a subject of renewed debate and writing recently. The most provocative revisionist essay is Gar Alperovitz, *Atomic Diplomacy, Hiroshima and Potsdam* (New York, 1965), which tries to link the use of the bomb to calculations of an assertive policy in Eastern Europe.

The complex developments in Sino-American relations in wartime are given massive documentation and perceptive analysis by Herbert Feis, *The China Tangle, The American Effort in China from Pearl Harbor to the Marshall Mission* (Princeton, 1953), and Tang Tsou, *America's Failure in China, 1941–1950* (Chicago, 1963). For more details, especially in connection with the Stilwell mission, one has to turn to the three-volume official army history written by Charles F. Romanus and Riley Sunderland: *Stilwell's Mission to China* (1953), *Stilwell's Command Problems* (1956), and *Time Runs Out in CBI* (1960). Of the host of personal accounts of the subject, mostly partisan, particularly informative are: Albert C. Wedemeyer, *Wedemeyer Reports!* (New York, 1958), *The Stilwell Papers,* edited by Theodore White (New York, 1948), and Claire Lee Chennault, *Way of a Fighter* (New York, 1949).

American-Asian relations in the immediate postwar years are ably summarized by Kenneth Scott Latourette, *The American Record in the Far East, 1945–1951* (New York, 1952), and Harold Vinacke, *Far Eastern Politics in the Postwar World* (New York, 1956). The best scholarly work on Sino-American relations is Tang Tsou's book mentioned earlier, and the most partisan is Kubek's, also noted above. For the American occupation of Japan, see Kazuo Kawai, *Japan's*

American Interlude (New York, 1960). The first editions of Fairbank's *The United States and China* (1948) and Reischauer's *The United States and Japan* (1948) are also good sources.

THE SINO-AMERICAN CRISIS

The literature on recent and current affairs involving the United States and East Asia is staggering and ceaselessly expanding. The period is not yet susceptible to scholarly treatment, and most of the writings are useful more as primary sources than as secondary works. No attempt is here made to be exhaustive; instead I shall list the items that were particularly helpful in writing this book.

The impact of the Communist take-over of China upon American policy, politics, and public opinion is skillfully delineated by Norman A. Graebner, *The New Isolationism, A Study in Politics and Foreign Policy since 1950* (New York, 1956). Extremely valuable is Isaacs's *Scratches on Our Minds,* noted earlier, which reports on the author's survey among 181 Americans, who were interviewed intensively about their thinking on China and India. A similar and more recent account, but relying heavily on anonymous public opinion polls, is A. T. Steele, *The American People and China* (New York, 1966). A rather one-sided comment on American attitudes toward Communist China is provided by Felix Greene, *A Curtain of Ignorance* (New York, 1964), an attack on distortions by the press. More valuable is John Hohenberg, *Between Two Worlds, Policy, Press and Public Opinion in Asian-American Relations* (New York, 1967). American opinion on certain specific issues is surveyed by Robert P. Newman, *Recognition of Communist China?* (New York, 1961), and Sheldon Appleton, *The Eternal Triangle?* (East Lansing, 1961). See also the informative book by Alfred O. Hero, *The Southerner and World Affairs* (Baton Rouge, 1965). Problems for American policy and future alternatives are outlined in such books as Edwin O. Reischauer, *Wanted: An Asian Policy* (New York, 1954), A. Doak Barnett, *Communist China and Asia, Challenge to American Policy* (New York, 1960), Morton H. Halperin, *China and the Bomb* (New York, 1965), and Robert Blum, *The United States and China in World Affairs* (New York, 1966). This last, edited by A. Doak Barnett after the author's untimely death, offers a sane but rather colorless summary of trends and possibilities. John K. Fairbank, *China, The People's Middle Kingdom and the U.S.A.* (Cambridge, Mass., 1967) includes several articles written in 1966, all alike reflective of the author's historical discipline and insight. All these books must be put in proper perspective by the reading of other aspects of postwar international relations. Among the best studies of the cold war are: Hugh Seton-Watson, *Neither War nor Peace, The Struggle for Power in the Postwar World* (New York, 1960), and John Lukacs, *A History of the Cold War* (New York, 1961). Secretary Dulles' thinking, in particular, is well presented in Andrew H. Berding, *Dulles on Diplomacy* (New York, 1965).

The Chinese side of the picture is treated competently by such works as Harold C. Hinton, *Communist China in World Politics* (New York, 1966), and Benjamin I. Schwartz, "The Maoist Image of World Order," in *Journal of International Affairs,* XXI (1967). A very good idea of Chinese Communist thinking on the past is given by Hu Sheng, *Imperialism and Chinese Politics* (Peking, 1956). The hate-America movement is graphically depicted in a psychological study, Robert

Lifton, *Thought Reform and the Psychology of Totalism* (New York, 1961). China's decision to enter the Korean War is authoritatively described by Allen S. Whiting, *China Crosses the Yalu, The Decision to Enter the Korean War* (New York, 1960). For further studies of the Korean War, primarily from the American side, see T. R. Fehrenbach, *This Kind of War* (New York, 1963), David Rees, *Korea, the Limited War* (New York, 1963), John W. Spanier, *The Truman-MacArthur Controversy and the Korean War* (Cambridge, Mass., 1959), and Henry A. Kissinger, *Nuclear Weapons and Foreign Policy* (New York, 1957).

Concerning Japanese-American relations, the best treatments of the peace treaty are given by Frederick S. Dunn, *Peace Making and the Settlement with Japan* (Princeton, 1963), and Bernard C. Cohen, *The Political Process and Foreign Policy, The Making of the Japanese Peace Settlement* (Princeton, 1957). The more recent phase of the two countries' relations is examined by such books as Herbert Passin, ed., *The United States and Japan* (New York, 1965), Douglas Mendel, *The Japanese People and Foreign Policy* (Berkeley, 1961), George R. Packard, *Protest in Tokyo, The Security Treaty Crisis of 1960* (Princeton, 1966), and Robert A. Scalapino, *The Japanese Communist Movement, 1920–1966* (Berkeley, 1967).

BOOKS IN CHINESE AND JAPANESE

Various factors have combined to retard the progress of Chinese and Japanese scholarship in diplomatic history, compared with American scholarship. Before the war only a fraction of archival materials was published. While some promising beginnings were made by historians in the 1930's, soon the exigencies of war and revolution put an end to free inquiry. The situation still persists in mainland China and Taiwan. While Japanese scholars enjoy unprecedented freedom from political interference, they are not always free from outworn dogmas. Both China (including Taiwan) and Japan, however, have been printing countless volumes of documentary material. Not only official diplomatic documents but also private papers, old newspapers, and even old books have been reprinted. I have based my account of Chinese and Japanese images of America primarily on these sources. Particularly useful, apart from the standard *Nihon gaikō bunsho* [*Japanese diplomatic documents*] and *Ch'ing-chi wai-chiao shih-liao* [*Diplomatic documents of the Ch'ing dynasty*], have been: *Chin-tai-shih tzu-liao* [*Documents on modern history*] (Peking, 1954–   ), *Hsin-hai ko-ming ch'ien shih-nien chien shih-lun hsüan-chi* [*Collection of essays on current affairs published during 1900–1911*] (Peking, 1960–   ), *Gendai-shi shiryō* [*Documents on contemporary history*] (Tokyo, 1963–   ), and *Shin Chūgoku shiryō shūsei* [*Documents of the new China*] (Tokyo, 1963–   ). For Chinese Communist writings during the 1940's and the 1950's, one must turn to the numerous pamphlets which almost invariably contain excerpts from party newspapers and directives. Postwar Japanese writings are easily accessible; the monthly magazines *Sekai* and *Chūōkōron,* among others, are good sources.

There are comparatively few monographs written in China and Japan that are directly relevant to the study of American–East Asian relations. The most extensive study by a mainland writer is Ch'ing Ju-chi, *Mei-kuo ch'in-Hua-shih* [*History of American aggression in China*], 2 vols. (Peking, 1952, 1956), which, however, covers only the nineteenth century. Two good studies of late Ch'ing diplomacy have been published by the Institute of Modern History of Academia Sinica (Taipei): Li En-han, *Wan-Ch'ing te shou-hui kung-ch'üan yün-tung* [*The movement to recover mining rights in late Ch'ing China*] (1963) and Chang Tsun-wu, *Kuang-hsü san-shih-i-nien Chung-Mei kung-yüeh feng-ch'ao* [*The Chinese-American dispute of 1905 concerning the immigration of laborers*] (1965). For more general background, see Liu Yen, *Chung-kuo wai-chiao-shih* [*Diplomatic history of China*], revised and expanded by Li Fang-ch'en (Taipei, 1962), Fu Ch'i-hsüeh, *Chung-kuo wai-chiao-shih* [*Diplomatic history of China*] (Taipei, 1957), and Hsiao I-san, *Ch'ing-tai t'ung-shih* [*History of the Ch'ing dynasty*], 5 vols., new ed. (Taipei, 1963). Among the surveys of early Chinese-American relations, factually the more useful are Li Pao-hung, *Chung-Mei wai-chiao kuan-hsi* [*Sino-American diplomatic relations*] (Changsha, 1940) and Li Ting-i, *Chung-Mei kuan-hsi-shih* [*History of Chinese-American relations*] (Taipei, 1960).

For the study of Japanese policies and attitudes, the ever-increasing volume of biographical writings is of particular help. I have especially benefited from the memoirs or autobiographies of Yoshida Shigeru (1957), Shigemitsu Mamoru (1953), Nishi Haruhiko (1965), and Yamamoto Gombei (1966), and from the "official" biographies of Yamagata Aritomo (1929), Saitō Makoto (1941–1942), Komura Jutarō (1953), Okada Keisuke (1956), Shidehara Kijūrō (1955), Tanaka Giichi (2 vols., 1958, 1960), and Hirota Kōki (1966). These and other materials are fully utilized in the two recent multi-volume histories of modern Japan: *Nihon no hyakunen* [*A hundred years of modern Japan*] by Tsurumi Shunsuke and others (Tokyo, 1961–1964), and Volumes XIX to XXVI of *Nihon no rekishi* [*A history of Japan*], published by Chūōkōron-sha (1965–1967). For a survey of modern Japanese foreign relations, see, among others, Kajima Morinosuke, *Nihon gaikō seisaku no shiteki kōsatsu* [*A historical interpretation of Japanese foreign policy*] (Tokyo, 1951). I have tried a brief interpretation of ideas and assumptions underlying Japanese policy in *Nihon no gaikō* [*Japanese diplomacy*] (Tokyo, 1966).

The initial encounter between the United States and Japan is ably traced in the six volumes of *Nichi-Bei bunka kōshō-shi* [*History of Japanese-American cultural relations*] (Tokyo, 1956). For more official relations, see Kajima Morinosuke, *Nichi-Bei gaikō-shi* [*Diplomatic relations between Japan and the United States*] (Tokyo, 1958). Especially pertinent for the study of images are the studies dealing with Meiji leaders that are contained in *Sekai no naka no Nihon* [*Japan in the world*], a volume in the series *Kindai Nihon shisō-shi kōza* [*Studies in modern Japanese intellectual history*] (Tokyo, 1961), and Kamishima Jirō, ed., *Kenryoku no shisō* [*Ideologies of power*] (Tokyo, 1965). See also studies on Hara Kei, Kawaji Toshiakira and others in Shinohara Hajime and Mitani Taichirō, eds., *Kindai Nihon no seiji shidō* [*Political leadership in modern Japan*] (Tokyo, 1965).

Among monographs dealing with specific periods or incidents, particularly relevant are: Ishii Takashi, *Meiji ishin no kokusai teki kankyō* [*The international environment of the Meiji Restoration*] (Tokyo, 1957), Kurihara Ken, *Man-Mō seisaku-shi no ichi-men* [*Aspects of Japanese policy toward Manchuria and Mongolia*] (Tokyo, 1966), Horikawa Takeo, *Kyokutō kokusai seiji-shi josetsu, ni-jū-ikka-jō yōkyū no kenkyū* [*Introduction to East Asian international relations, A study of the Twenty-One Demands*] (Tokyo, 1958), Hosoya Chihiro, *Siberia shuppei no shiteki kenkyū* [*A historical study of the Siberian expedition*] (Tokyo, 1955), Shimada Toshihiko, *Kantōgun* [*The Kwantung Army*] (Tokyo, 1965),

Tsunoda Jun, ed., *Taiheiyō sensō e no michi* [*Road to the Pacific War*], 8 vols. (Tokyo, 1962–1963), Usui Katsumi, *Nit-Chū sensō* [*The Sino-Japanese War*] (Tokyo, 1967), Irie Keishirō, *Nihon kōwa jyōyaku no kenkyū* [*A study of the Japanese peace treaty*] (Tokyo, 1951), Kuno Osamu and others, *Sengo Nihon no shisō* [*Postwar Japanese thought*] (Tokyo, 1966), and Tanaka Naokichi, *Kaku jidai no Nihon no anzen hoshō* [*Japanese national security in the age of nuclear weapons*] (Tokyo, 1966). For the Pacific war, there are, among others, Hattori Takushirō, *Dai-Tōa sensō zenshi* [*Complete history of the Great East Asian War*] (Tokyo, 1953), and Kojima Noboru, *Taiheiyō sensō* [*The Pacific War*], 2 vols. (Tokyo, 1965–1966). See also the Foreign Ministry–edited *Shūsen shiroku* [*Record of the ending of the war*] (Tokyo, 1948). An interpretation of postwar and current international affairs, representing the scholarship and thinking of the postwar generation, is offered by Kōsaka Masataka, *Kokusai seiji* [*International politics*] (Tokyo, 1966).

China's international relations have been studied by generations of Japanese historians. Noteworthy for their treatment of Sino-American relations are: Ueda Toshio, ed., *Gendai Chūgoku o meguru sekai no gaikō* [*World diplomacy and China*] (Tokyo, 1951); also Ueda-edited, *Kindai Nihon gaikō-shi no kenkyū* [*Studies in modern Japanese diplomatic history*] (Tokyo, 1956), which includes chapters on the Sino-Japanese War, the 1911 revolution, and Manchuria; Tamura Kōsaku, *Saikin Shina gaikō-shi* [*History of modern Chinese diplomacy*] (Tokyo, 1938–1939); and some essays in *Gaikō-shi oyobi kokusai seiji no shomondai* [*Problems in diplomatic history and international politics*] (Tokyo, 1962). Finally, my own *Bei-Chū kankei no imeiji* [*American-Chinese relations, A study in images*] (Tokyo, 1965) offers a brief history of mutual images between the two countries.

DEVELOPMENTS SINCE THE 1960'S

In the last twenty-five years, since this book's first publication, an enormous amount of scholarly literature has appeared on many aspects of United States–East Asian relations, past and present. The scholarly output itself attests to the significant transformation of these relations, which are no longer a quaint subject of research by a small number of specialists but constitute a vital part of an educated person's understanding of history. This is not the place to review this scholarly literature, but the reader is referred, for a succinct review of some of the important recent works in the field, to Warren I. Cohen's useful essay, "The History of American–East Asian Relations: Cutting Edge of the Historical Profession" in *Diplomatic History,* Vol. 9 (Spring 1985). I should also note the launching, in the spring of 1992, of a new publication, *The Journal of American–East Asian Relations,* which will serve as a focus of scholarly activities in American-Asian relations, broadly defined.

In writing Chapters 13 and 14, I have consulted many works dealing with U.S.-Asian relations since the 1960's. There are some important studies of mutual images, of which two stand out: David L. Shambaugh, *Beautiful Imperialist: China Perceives America, 1972–1990* (Princeton, 1991), and Allen S. Whiting, *China Eyes Japan* (Berkeley, 1989). Both are thorough studies of contemporary Chinese images of the United States and of Japan, respectively, based on wide-ranging sources and interviews. See also R. David Arkush and Leo O. Lee, trans. and eds., *Land without Ghosts: Chinese Impressions of America from the Mid-Nineteenth Century to the Present* (Berkeley, 1989); Michel Oksenberg and Robert B. Oxnam, eds.,

Dragon and Eagle: United States–China Relations, Past and Present (New York, 1978); and John K. Fairbank, *China Watch* (Cambridge, Mass., 1987). This last, a collection of the leading China specialist's book reviews, offers an excellent introduction to contemporary American scholarly perspectives on the People's Republic of China. Among the many studies of the U.S.-Chinese rapprochement of the early 1970's, one of the most useful is a collection of essays edited by Gene T. Hsiao and Michael Witunski, *Sino-American Normalization and Its Policy Implications* (New York, 1983).

While nothing on U.S.-Japanese relations that compares with the studies by Shambaugh and Whiting has been published, Sheila K. Johnson's *The Japanese Through American Eyes* (Stanford, 1988) offers an interesting analysis of American best-sellers that deal with Japanese themes. Moreover, there is in a sense an embarrassment of riches of raw materials concerning the ways in which Americans and Japanese have viewed each other in the last quarter century. *The Pacific Rivals* (Tokyo, 1972), written by *Asahi* newspaper correspondents, was one of the first attempts at examining American-Japanese mutual images in transition. Since then, volumes have been published on the subject, but it still awaits a comprehensive scholarly analysis. Many have analyzed the U.S.-Japanese trade dispute that became serious in the 1970's. I. M. Destler, Haruhiko Fukui, and Hideo Sato, *The Textile Wrangle: Conflict in Japanese-American Relations, 1969–1971* (Ithaca, 1979) is useful because it carefully traces the first of such disputes, that concerning Japanese textile exports to the United States.

One important feature of recent U.S.-Japanese relations has been the holding of frequent meetings not only by the two countries' officials but by their businessmen, journalists, scholars, labor leaders, artists, and many others. Sometimes their deliberations as well as papers presented at such gatherings have been published, and they serve as fascinating primary sources. See, for instance, Herbert Passin and Akira Iriye, eds., *Encounter at Shimoda: Search for a New Pacific Partnership* (Boulder, 1979). To balance the too often emotional language used on both sides of the Pacific, one may well turn to a book like Edwin O. Reischauer, *My Life between Japan and America* (New York, 1986), a fascinating memoir by a man who was deeply involved in the history of U.S.-Japanese relations in all their vicissitudes. For some pertinent information concerning Japanese perspectives, the best guide is John Welfield, *An Empire in Eclipse: Japan in the Postwar American Alliance System* (London, 1988). Also useful are the essays contained in William J. Barnds, ed., *Japan and the United States: Challenges and Opportunities* (New York, 1979); and Akira Iriye and Warren I. Cohen, eds., *The United States and Japan in the Postwar World* (Lexington, Ky., 1989). I have explored my own views on recent Japanese foreign relations in *China and Japan in the Global Setting* (Cambridge, Mass., 1992); *Shin Nihon no gaikō* [*Japanese diplomacy since the Second World War*] (Tokyo, 1991); and *Nichi-Bei kankei no gojūnen* [*Fifty years of Japanese-American relations*] (Tokyo, 1991).

For a more extensive discussion of the implications of the Vietnam War on U.S.–East Asian relations than I have been able to give in this book, see, among others, George M. Kahin, *Intervention: How America Became Involved in Vietnam* (New York, 1986); George C. Herring, *America's Longest War: The United States and Vietnam, 1950–1975* (New York, 1979); Gabriel Kolko, *Anatomy of a War: Vietnam, the United States, and the Modern Historical Experience* (New York, 1985); and Gary R. Hess, *Vietnam and the United States: Origins and Legacy of War* (Boston, 1990).

Index

Abbott, James F., 135
Abe Isoo, 72
Abeel, David, 38
Acheson, Dean: peace treaty with Japan, 294; speech of Jan. 12, 1950, 283–84; view of China, 265, 283, 291
Adams, Brooks, 62, 77
Africa, 391
Aguinaldo, Emilio, 74
Alaska, 13
Amau doctrine: 176; Chinese reactions to, 189
American Board of Commissioners for Foreign Missions, 19
American China Development Company, 75, 76, 80, 95–96
American educators, in Japan, 37, 71, 72
American Historical Association, 345
American Indians, Chinese view of, 90–91
American merchants: in Asia, 33–34; in China, 3, 10, 16, 36
American missionaries: in Asia, 18–20, 33–34; in China, 20–21, 36, 94, 130, 160; Chinese Communist view of, 301; in Japan, 19, 37, 72
American officials, in China, 15
American scholars on China, postwar training of, 375–76
American schools, in Japan, 38, 72
American visitors, in China (since Korean War), 375
American writings on China, before and after 1972, 376
Americanization, of China and Japan, 18
Amoy-Hankow railway, 100
Anglo-Chinese War (1856–60), 35, 42
Anglo-Japanese alliance: 97; abrogation of, 143; and Taft-Knox policy, 123–24
Anti-American boycott, in China (1905), 93–95; American policy toward, 109
Anti-American demonstrations, in Japan (1905), 102
Anti-Chinese movement, in U.S., 29–30, 43, 62, 89
Anti-Imperialism: (Pacific war), 233; in Asia, 85; in China, 71, 84, 85, 145, 146–47, 154; in Europe, 84–85; in U.S., 85; in West, 70
Anti-Japanese agitation, on West Coast, 104–5, 106, 114, 116, 131, 151
Anti-Japanese boycott, in China: (1908) 116; (1919) 142

ANZUS, 335
Arita, Hachirō, 208
Arms embargo, in 1930's, 187
Asanuma, Inejirō, 310
Ashida Hitoshi, 177
Asia: American view of, 4, 5, 7, 14, 19, 27–28, 62, 76; Japanese view of, 230
Asia-Pacific region: 351, 355, 356, 362; integration of, 391–92
Asian economic miracle (1980's): Asian-Americans and, 382; causes of, 380–81
Asian isolation, ending of, 17
Asian market, idea of, 14
Asian Monroe Doctrine: 110; Chinese view of, 193. *See also* Pan-Asianism
Asiatic fleet, augmentation of, 89
Association of Southeast Asian Nations (ASEAN), 372, 381
Atkinson, J. L., 19
Atomic bomb, 232, 248
Australia, 335
Austria, 380
"Awakening" of Asia, 326; of Japan, 26
Axis Alliance: Matsuoka's view of, 209–10; and pan-Asianism, 211; U.S. policy toward, 205, 206

Baba Tatsui, 49, 71
Bandung Conference, 304, 355
"Barbarian experts," 41
Barnds, William, 376
Belgian syndicate, in China, 75, 80, 95–96
Benedict, Ruth, 243
Bentham, Jeremy, 48
Berlin crisis, 284
Berlin, Isaiah, 392
Beveridge, A. J., 77
Bisson, T. A., 246
Boat people, 382
Bolshevik revolution, 135, 143
Boxer incident: 70; American public interest in, 89; implications for U.S. policy, 87; indemnity, remission of, 118, 124; Japanese participation in, 86; U.S. participation in, 83
"Boxer indemnity scholars," 124
Bradley, Omar N., 289
Bretton Woods system, 363, 364, 365, 368
Brezhnev doctrine, 352
Bridgman, Elijah, 34, 38
Brussels Conference (1937), 196–97
Bryan, W. J., 119, 129
Buck, Pearl, 155, 171, 184, 241
Bureaucracy, in Japan, 71
Burgevine, Henry A., 34
Burlingame, Anson, 15, 28–30, 34
Burlingame mission, 29
Burlingame Treaty, 29, 30
Burma: and Great East Asian Conference, 230; independence called for by Mao, 238; and Japanese aid, 372; postwar, 256
Burma Road, British closing of, 221
Byres, James, 255

Cairo Conference, 234
California, 4, 13, 30; anti-Japanese sentiment in, 105; Asian immigrants in, 382
Cambodia, 371, 382
Canada, 342, 372
Canton: conquered by Japan, 203; Customs episode (1923), 148; trade at, 3, 10
Canton Christian College, 148
Canton-Hankow railway, 95, 108–9
Carter, Jimmy, 369, 370
Casablanca Conference, 234
Castle, William J., 180, 181, 186
Chamberlain, Joseph, 54
Chang Chih-tung, 55, 70, 76, 95–96
Chang Hsüeh-liang, 183
Chang Tso-lin, 149, 154, 158, 165
Chekiang, Japanese expansion in, 67
Ch'en, Eugene, 159
Ch'en Kung-po, 129
Chiang Kai-shek: and abolition of extraterritoriality, 234; and Chinese Communists, 159, 183, 188, 235; and civil war, 271; and Japan, 155, 190; marriage, 161; predicts world war, 162; and Sian incident, 183; and U.S.: (1920's) 155, 158–59, (1930's) 211, 212, (Pacific war) 235–36, (postwar) 263, 336; view of Soviet Union, 271
Chiang Kai-shek, Madame, 235, 247
Chiang Kung-shen, 162
Chin Chung-hua, 215
China: assessment of domestic and foreign affairs in 1960's, 353–54; crisis with Japan, 166, 171–72, 193; and Cultural Revolution, 333; democratic movements (1980's), 378; and Eastern Europe, 353; economic problems since 1960's, 346; and Europe, 353; end of isolation, 12; and ending of diplomatic isolation, 352; exchange programs with Japan, 390; and human rights, 389–90; and IMF, 363; and Japan's war guilt question, 361; in Japanese-American talks (1941), 220, 224; middle class, development of, 390; nationalism in, 130, 138, 145, 150; and Pacific war, 228, 233, 235, 250; as potential superpower, 386; rapprochement

with Soviet Union, 378; and Russo-Japanese War, 91; and Sino-Japanese War (1894–95), 75; and Soviet aids, 352; and trade with Japan, 353; treaty with Soviet Union (1945), 259, 370–71; and Tsinan incident, 156; and Versailles peace, 142; and Vietnam War, 354, 371, 378; view of American society, 376–77; view of Belgium, 75–76; view of Britain, 42, 75, 193–94, 198; view of Christianity (1920's), 146; view of France, 42, 75, 198; view of Germany, 75, 198; view of its role in Vietnam, 341; view of Japan, 43, 83, 86, 90, 91, 92, 137, 142, 162, 172, 189; view of Japan in detente with U.S. 360–61; view of Japan's wartime aggression, 389–90; view of postwar world, 233, 238; view of Russia, 35, 42, 75, 90, 93; view of Soviet Union, 190, 193, 198, 211–12, 259, 334, 335–36; view of trade with U.S., 353–54; view of trade with the West, 353–54; view of (and/or policy toward) U.S.: (pre-1840) 10, (1840–80) 33, 34, 35–36, 38, 39, 41–42, 43, 44, (1880–1900) 54, 75, 82, 83, (1900–12) 86, 90, 91, 93–94, 96, 97, 124, (1912–18) 125, 129, 130, 136, 137, 138, (1918–31) 143, 147, 154, 155–56, 162, (1931–41) 172, 188–90, 191–92, 193–94, 198–99, 211, 214, 215, 222–24, (Pacific war) 232–33, 234, 235, (1945–50) 258–64; view of the West, 9, 69–71, 76, 91, 110, 146; view of the world, 8; and Washington Conference, 144, 145; and World War I, 136; and Yalta Conference, 243, 273. *See also* Chinese Communists; Chinese Nationalists; Chiang Kai-shek; Sino-Soviet dispute

China White Paper, 265–66, 272

China-Burma-India theater, 228–43

Chinese academic visitors in U.S., 375

Chinese Communists: in 1920's, 147; and abolition of extraterritoriality, 236; and China White Paper, 274, 275–76; debate over policy direction since 1960's, 377; at end of Pacific war, 253; foreign policy after 1949, 275, 303–5; and Korean War, 288; and Marshall mission, 254, 261; and Nationalists (1945–50), 260; nuclear tests, 321–22; and Soviet Union, 213, 223, 274; and Taiwan, 307–8; view of Acheson, 275; view of Britain, 213, 223; view of Byrnes, 261; view of France, 213; view of Franklin Roosevelt, 261, 262; view of Hurley, 261, 262; view of imperialism, 274–75; view of Japan, 162, 223, 277–78, 300, 310; view of Japanese-Soviet neutrality pact, 223; view of Manchurian crisis, 188; view of Open Door, 276; view of past American-Chinese relations, 302–3; view of Stuart, 275; view of Truman, 260, 262, 275; view of U.S.: (1931–41) 162, 188, 212–13, 214–16, (Pacific war) 222–24, 236, 237, (1945–50) 256–63, 273–74, 275, 276–77, 284, (Korean War) 288, 300–301, (after Korean War) 304, 306, (since 1960's) 321, 324, 325, 358–59; view of Wedemeyer, 261, 262, 275; view of World War II, 213

Chinese Eastern Railway, 101

Chinese in America: American view of, 28–31; immigration dispute, 29–30, 43, 93; students, 28, 129, 130

Chinese in Japan: revolutionaries, 129; students, 92, 129

Chinese Nationalists: after Sun's death, 153–54; alliance with Soviet Union, 148; and anti-imperialism, 147, 148; break with Communists (1927), 155; and end of Pacific war, 253; first united front, 148–49; and Marshall mission, 254; struggle with Communists (after 1939), 212, 253; view of Soviet-Japanese neutrality pact, 224; and Wedemeyer, 248

Chinese writings on America after 1972, 377

Chinese-American relations, post-1972 on, 375–76

Chinese-Japanese communiquè, 361

Ch'ing dynasty, 40, 85, 116

Ch'ing Ju-ch'i, 302, 303

Chou Chi-ch'üan, 214

Chou En-lai: 262, 354, 355, 371; view of Soviet policy, 352

Chou Fu, 95

Christianity: in America, 18; in Asia, 6; in China, 21, 36, 126, 146; in Japan, 37, 72

Chu Teh, 236, 277

Churchill, Winston, 220

Civil service reform, 28

Civil War (in U.S.), 13, 22

Civilization, American view of, 22–23, 57–58

Clark, William, 37

Clyde, Paul W., 205–6

Committee on American–East Asian Relations, 346

Committee on Scholarly Cooperation with the People's Republic of China, 375

Conference on Security and Cooperation in Europe (CSCE), 371, 372, 373

Confucianism, 7–8, 10, 41
Conger, Edwin, 88
Conlon report, 309
Consumers, Japanese and Americans compared, 384
Containment policy, 264, 265
Coolidge, Calvin, 151, 156
Crichton, Michael: on U.S.-Japanese relations, 388
Crow, Carl, 134
Cultural initiatives, in international relations (1970's), 375
Cultural issues: growth of (1970's), 372–73; in U.S.-Chinese relations, 377–78
Cultural Revolution, *see* Great Proletarian Cultural Revolution
Cushing, Caleb, 14

Davies, John P., 247
Davis, Norman, 196–97
Defense perimeter, 284
DeGaulle, Charles, 354
Democratic League, 263–64
Democratic Party Convention (1968), 345
Dennett, Tyler, 184–85
Despotism, in Asia, described by Americans, 5
Dewey, John, 142
Diem, Ngo Dinh, 338
Diplomacy of imperialism: 56, 57; China as an arena of, 69, 75; Japanese participation in, 87
"Dollar diplomacy," 123
"Domino theory," 337
Doolittle, Justus, 20, 21
Dreadnought, 115
Dulles, John F.: foreign policy characterized, 295; on Japanese export, 366; and Khrushchev, 297; and Laos, 314; and peace treaty with Japan, 294; and peaceful co-existence policy, 296; policy toward China, 295, 298; and Sino-Soviet dispute, 308
Dutch East Indies: independence of, visualized by Chinese, 233, 238; Japanese attack on, 201, 208
Dutch merchants, in Japan, 11

East, European idea of, (1920's), 145–46
Eastern Europe: and human rights, 373; reformist movements in, 378
East Asia, American view of (1840–80), 16
East Asian crisis, American view of, 181–83, 185, 202, 203
East-West relations: American view of, 59–64, 82, 105–18; Chinese view of, 146; Japanese view of 113, 114, 115, 116. *See also* Pan-Asianism
Eisenhower, Dwight D.: commander of NATO, 290; foreign policy orientation, 295; policy toward China, 294; trip to Japan cancelled, 312; view of Southeast Asia, 337
Emerson, Ralph Waldo, 18–19, 28
Environmental issues, as cultural phenomenon in 1970's, 373
Europe: American view of, 5, 9; "decline" of, 145; as center of economic power, 391
European Economic Community, 365, 391
Extraterritoriality, abolition of, 154, 234, 236

Fairbank, John K., 345, 376, 389
Fallows, James, 384, 387
Far Eastern crisis, *see* East Asian crisis
Fenollosa, Ernest, 64, 72
Field, Henry M., 26
Fillmore, Millard, 14
Fiske, John, 60
Forbes, W. Cameron, ambassador to Japan, 166, 167, 171
Foreign loans, to China, 75, 124, 132, 142, 150, 151
Formosa, *see* Taiwan
"Four Big Policemen," 243–44
France: 385; Chinese view of, 35; entente with Japan (1907), 114; loans to China, 75, 124; and Sino-Japanese War, 66, 73
France, Anatole, 145
Franklin, Benjamin, 48
Free China, idea of, 221
Freedom, concept of, lacking in Japan, 12
French Revolution, 9
Fukien: American interest in, 87; Japanese expansionism in, 67, 100
Fukuda Takeo, 374
"Fukuda doctrine," 374
Fukuzawa Yukichi, 65, 87
Fulbright programs, and China, 375

"Gang of four," 355
Gardels, Nathan, 391
Gauss, Clarence E., 159, 221
General Agreement on Tariffs and Trade (GATT), 369
Gentlemen's agreements, 115–16
Geopolitics: 362; in U.S. redefinition of China policy, 349–51; in U.S.-Chinese relations, 375
George III, 9

Germany: 385; aggression in 1930's, 202–3; American view of, 205; end of imperialism in Asia, 138; invasion of Soviet Union, 213, 224; loans to China, 124; non-aggression pact with Soviet Union, 213; and Sino-Japanese War, 66, 73; and World War I, 131
Global economy: (1960's) 362–63; crises of 1930's and 1970's compared, 368; crisis in early 1970's, 362; summit of principal industrial nations, 369
Goodnow, Frank J., 136–37
Gorbachev, Mikhail, 378
Grant, Madison, 134
Grant, U. S., 27, 43–44
Great Britain: 386; Chinese view of, 35; leading role played in China, 17; loans to China, 124; loans to Japan, 99; and Opium War, 12; policy toward China: (1890's) 80, (1930's) 190, (1941) 220; war with China (1856–60), 35, 42
Great East Asian Conference, 230
Great East Asian Co-prosperity Sphere, theory of, 210
Great East Asian War, 230
"Great leap forward," 339, 340
Great Proletarian Cultural Revolution, 324, 339, 342, 345, 346, 349, 352, 353, 358, 360, 361
Greece, 266
Grew, Joseph C.: ambassador to Japan, 196; American-Japanese Society speech (1939), 204; "green light message," 207; and Japan's Emperor system 239–40; view of East Asian crisis, 181–82; view of Japan, 217–18, 221
Griffis, William E., 21–22
Grimke, Frederick, 22
Griswold, A. Whitney, 205–6
Guam: annexed to U.S., 74
"Guam doctrine," 351

Haiti, 128
Hakone conference (1969) on Pacific war, 348
Han loyalty, 10–11
Hankow, conquered by Japan, 203
Hankow-Canton railway, 76
Hara Kei: policy toward U.S., 111, 141–42; visits U.S., 111
Harding, Warren G., 143, 147, 151
Hardy, Thomas, 145
Hardy, Thomas Lake, 31
Harris, Townsend, 15, 21, 36–37
Harvard University, 31
Hate-America campaigns, 300
Hawaii: annexed to U.S., 74; defense of, 107, 135. *See also* Pearl Harbor
Hay, John: basic policy toward China, 88–89, 102; Dennett's view of, 185; and first Open Door notes, 80, 81; and Kaneko, 99; second Open Door notes, 88
Hayashi Tadasu, 114–15
Hearn, Lafcadio, 72
"Heart-to-heart" diplomacy, 374
Hesse, Herman, 145
Heusken, Henry, 21, 37
Hilsman, Roger, 316
Hippisley, A. E., 80
Hirota Kōki, 175–76
History: American view of, 6, 60; Chinese view of, 8; Japanese view of, 11
Hobson, R. P., 118
Hong Kong: in American vision of postwar Asia, 241; and boat people, 382; economic growth in 1980's, 380; loan to China, 96
Honolulu, proposed leader's conference, 218
Hoover, Herbert, 166, 167, 180
House, E. H., 22
House, Edward M., 133
Hsieh Ch'ing-kao, 10
Hsü Chi-yü, 38
Hsüeh Fu-ch'eng, 55, 70
Hu Shih, 129, 146
Huang Hsing, 125, 130, 136
Huang Yao-mien, 223
Hughes, Charles Evans, 148, 149
Hukuang loan, 124–25
Hull, Cordell: handling of November 26 note, 219, 225; negotiations with Japan (1941), 218–19; view of Japan, 195; view of Pacific war, 239; view of world crisis, 203; vision of postwar world, 242
Human rights concern as cultural phenomenon in 1970's, 373
Hundreds Days' Reform, 69
Hungary, 295
Hurley, Patrick J.: ambassador to China, 236, 237; Chinese Community view of, 237, 301; "Hurley strategy," 237, 253

Ickes, Harold, 222
Ii Naosuke, 24–25
Ikeda Hayato, 312, 318, 336
Immigration: Act of 1924, 151, 163; of Asians (since 1960's), 382; dispute with China, 108; dispute with Japan, 114–15, 151–52; laws revised (1943), 234
Imperialism: (late 1800's) 54–55; (after 1880) 57; American, 53, 55; Chinese

Communist view of, 236, 260, 329; Chinese view of, 85; concept introduced to Japan and China, 70; factors underlying, 54; Marxist-Leninist interpretation of, 56–57
India: border dispute with China (1962), 336; independence called for by Mao, 238; independence of, visualized by Chinese, 233; and Soviet Union, 336; and U.S., 336; war with Pakistan (1965), 339
Indochina: independence called for by Mao, 238; Japanese invasion of, 201, 208, 217; in Japanese-U.S. negotiation (1941), 220; postwar, 286
Indonesia, and Japanese aid, 372
Industrial revolution, 9
Industrialization, in America, 4, 13
Informal empire, 57
Inner Mongolia, Japanese policy toward, (World War I), 132
Inoue Kaoru, 65
Intellectuals, in China, around 1900, 84
International Banking Consortium: organized to finance China, 123; and President Wilson, 129
International events, 1980 and 1990 compared, 378
International Monetary Fund (IMF), 363, 369
Iraq, invasion of Kuwait, 379
Ishihara Kanji, 163, 231
Ishii Kikujirō, 133. *See also* Lansing-Ishii agreement
Isthmian canal, 78, 107
Italy, 202–3, 380
Itō Hirobumi, 46, 48, 65, 114
Iwakura mission, 46, 47

Jacoby, Annalee, 257
Janes, L. L., 37
Japan: (1960's) 315, 318–19; aggression in north China, 190; American security treaty, 311; army and Soviet Union, 175; army's view of U.S., 153, 163, 194, 195, 207–8; and boat people, 382; cultural diplomacy and China, 374; and Cultural Revolution, 347; economic growth, postwar, 336, 346; economic reconstruction, 265; economic ties to Southeast Asia (1970's), 372; emergence as a power, 67; entente with Russia, 114; expansion in Manchuria, 100–101, 114, 123, 132; expansionism in 1890's, 82; foreign policy after Russo-Japanese War, 114; as future superpower, 386; and Inner Mongolia, 174; and International Monetary Fund, 363; Liberal Democratic Party, 336; middle class, development of, 390; model of economic growth, 381; navy's view of China, 131; navy's view of U.S., 115, 131, 153, 163, 175, 194, 195, 207–8, 218; neutrality pact with Soviet Union, 209, 213, 222; Official Developmental Aid (ODA), 372; and Pacific Basin concept, 372; Pacific war, 229–30; and peace treaty of 1951, 334; peace treaty with Taiwan, 294; policy of isolation, 11–12; policy toward China: (1921–31) 151, 164, (1931–41) 174, 177, (Pacific war) 232, (postwar) 311, 325; policy toward Korea, 66; policy toward Soviet Union, 177, 229, 232; rapprochement with China, 359–62, 366; and Russo-Japanese War, 98–102; and Sino-Japanese War (1894–95), 73; surrender, 228–29, 232; textbook reference to wartime aggression in China, 389; trade with China, 164, 360; trade with U.S., 163, 164, 218, 381; and U.N., 335; and Vietnam War, 333, 347, 348; view of American war of independence, 11; view of Asia, 68; view of China, 65, (since 1960's) 333, 334; view of Britain, 50, 73, 114, 177, 208; view of East-West relations, 113, 114, 115, 116; view of France, 97; view of itself, 10, 73–74, 86, 112, 113, 318–19; view of perception gaps with U.S., 374; view of Russia, 50, 66, 86, 87, 97; view of (and/or policy toward) U.S.: (pre-1850) 12, 33, (1850–80) 36–37, 38, 45, 46–47, 48, 49, (1880–1900) 54, 72, 73, 74, 82, (1900–1905) 87, 98–99, 100, 101, 102, 110, (1905–21) 111–12, 114, 115, 117, 131, 132–33, 139, 142, (1921–31) 144, 152–53, 163, 164, (1931–41) 174, 177, 195, 202, 207, 219, 225, (Pacific war) 230–31, (postwar) 281–82, 311, (since 1960's) 312–13, 318–20, 325, 328–29, 365–66; view of the West, 45, 46, 68, 139, 174, 229–30; view of the world, 11, 68, 139, 311; and Washington Conference, 144; withdrawal from League of Nations, 174, 175, 176–77; and World War I, 131, 132–33, 138, 142
Japan bashing (late 1980's), 384–85
Japan Foundation, 373–74
Japanese businesses, funding of Japanese studies abroad, 374
Japanese Communist Party, 310
Japanese embassy of 1860, 31, 45–46

Japanese in America, 39, 48–49; American view of, 31; embassy of 1860, 31, 45–46; laborers, 71, 74; students, 31, 45
Japanese Socialist Party, 310
Jefferson, Thomas, 4, 14
Joffe, Adolfe, 148
Johnson, Lyndon B., 338, 346, 350, 352
Johnson, Nelson T., 159, 160, 166–67, 181–82, 196
Judd, Walter, 269

Kalgan incident, 149
Kaneko Kentarō, 99, 101
Kasson, John A., 32
Katayama Sen, 72, 100
Katō Takaaki, 87
Katō Tomosaburō, 131, 144
Kawaji Toshiakira, 36
Kearny, Lawrence, 35
Kellogg, Frank B., 157–58
Kemmerer, Edwin W., 165
Kennan, George F., 264, 286, 350
Kennedy, John F.: assassination of, 316, 338; Chinese Communist view of, 307; foreign policy orientation, 313, 315; and peaceful coexistence policy, 313; policy in Asia, 313–14; and Vietnam War, 337, 350; view of Communist China, 314; view of Southeast Asia, 337
Kennedy, Paul: on America in decline, 386, 387
"Kennedy round," 363
Khrushchev, Nikita, 297
Kiangsi soviets, 188
Kinoshita Naoe, 100
Kishi Nobusuke: and Communist China, 310; resignation, 312; and revision of security treaty, 311–12
Kissinger, Henry: 354, 359, 365, 368, 370, 371; China policy, 349–50; on Chou En-lai, 352
Knowland, William, 268
Knox, Philander, 120, 122–23
Koo, Wellington, 129, 156, 159
Korea: independence recognized by U.S., 44; Japanese army in, 173; Japanese expansionism in, 66, 97, 104; opening of, 44; postwar independence visualized by Chinese, 233, 238; and shared experience in Asia-Pacific, 390
Korean War: 338, 356, 364; causes of, 285; and Chinese-American relations, 281, 288
Kuei-liang, 35, 42
Kung, H. H., 190
Kung, Prince, 34
Kuo Mo-jo, 278
Kurino Shin'ichirō, 65
Kwantung Army: and death of Chang Tso-lin, 165; and Manchurian crisis, 172–73; view of U.S., 174

Lamont, Thomas W., 160–61
Lansing, Robert: view of China, 133; view of Japan, 133, 136; and Shantung question, 141
Lansing-Ishii agreement: 133; Chinese view of, 136
Laos, 314
Latin America, 391
Lattimore, Owen, 221, 282
League of Nations: Japanese participation in, 141; and Manchurian crisis, 179; and U.N. charter, 334–35
LeGendre, Charles, 22, 43
Lenin, V. I.: impact on China, 147; and new diplomacy, 135; theory of imperialism, 147, 188; view of the state, 212
Li Hung-chang, 44
Liang Ch'i-ch'ao: 84; view of Russo-Japanese War, 92; view of the West, 85–86; view of U.S., 86, 90
Liaotung peninsula: Japanese leasehold in, 101; during Sino-Japanese War, 66, 73, 75
Liberal Democratic Party, 312
Lin Piao: fall from power, 353, 355; strategy of global conflict, 341, 352, 353
Lin Tse-hsü, 34, 38
Lindbergh, Charles, 167
Liu Shao-ch'i, 275
Liuchiu Islands, 43
Lodge, Henry Cabot, 99
London Naval Conference, 164, 166, 167
London Naval Treaty, 175
Long March, 184
"Loss of China," debated in U.S., 269
Lowell, Percival, 63
Lu Ting-i, 263
Luzon Island, American base at, 89, 107
Lyautey, Louis Hubert Gonzalve, 54

MacArthur, Douglas: calls for extension of war to China, 289–90; and North Korea, 286; and Taiwan, 292; view of Mao, 287–88; and Wake Island Conference, 287
McCarthy, Joseph R., 269; hearings conducted by, 298
Macartney, Lord, 10
McClatchy, Valentine S., 139–40
McKinley, President William, 86

MacMurray, John V. A.: and Japanese immigration dispute, 152; memo of 1935, 186–87; and Shanghai coup, 159; view of China, 141; view of Japan, 140–41; view of Nationalist split, 159
Mahan, A.T., 55, 60–61, 78, 89
Makino Shinken, 142
Malaya: independence called for by Mao, 238; postwar, 256
Malaysia, 372, 380
Manchukuo, 173, 207, 230
Manchuria: Japan ready to give up, 232; Japanese expansionism in (1930's), 173; Russian penetration of, 90, 97
Manchurian crisis: causes of, 172–73; as an ideological phenomenon, 173
Mao Tse-tung: and Cultural Revolution, 340–41; denounces Chiang Kai-shek and U.S. (1947), 274; "On Coalition Government," 237; policy of "leaning to one side," 274; view of U.S., 237–38, 259–60, 263; vision of postwar world, 238
Maoism: in 1930's, 188; people's new democracy, 212–13; in U.S., 342, 344
Marco Polo Bridge incident, 194
Maritime Customs Administration, 41
Marshall, George C., *see* Marshall mission
Marshall, Humphrey, 15, 16
Marshall mission: characteristics of, 254; and Chiang Kai-shek, 259; and China, 255; Chinese Communist view of, 260, 275, 301–2; Congressional support for, 267; failure of, 263; origins of 253; supported by American public, 256–57
Matsuoka Yōsuke, 209–10
May Fourth movement, 143
Meiji Restoration, 25, 27, 37
Metternich, Prince, 9
Mexicans in California, 382
Mexico, and President Wilson, 128
Middle East, 362, 378
Miki Takeshi, 370
Mill, J. S., 48
Mission, idea of, 7, 8–9, 17–18, 30
Missionaries, *see* American missionaries
Modernization: of China, 90, 146; in Europe, 9; of Japan, 23, 36, 45, 46, 48, 56; Japanese view of, 231–32
Monroe Doctrine for Asia, 110
Morgan, J. P., 96, 109
Morgenthau, Hans, 350
Morgenthau, Henry, 220–21
Morley, James W., 328
Most-favored-nation principle: 15; in Chinese-U.S. treaty (1928), 157
Mukden incident, 172–73
Munich crisis, 203
Mutsu Munemitsu, 73
Myers, Myrl, 165

Nagoya, 354
Nakae Chōmin, 49–50, 67
Nanking government, *see* Chinese Nationalists
Nanking incident: and Japan, 155; settlement of, 156, 159, 160; and U.S., 154–55
Napoleon, 12
Napoleonic wars, 9, 11
National Science Foundation, and China, 375
National security:
Japanese view of, 11, 56, 173, 325; redefined in late 1800's, 54
National Security Council, 337
Nationalism, in postwar Asia, 297
Nationalist, *see* Chinese Nationalists
Nationalist unification (1928), 154, 156
Neeshima, Joseph, *see* Niijima Shimeta
Nehru, Jawaharlal, 355
Neutralism in Asia, U.S. policy toward, 298, 313–14
Neville, Edwin, 165, 171, 182–83
Nevius, John L., 20
"New diplomacy": traced from Taft, 127; U.S. as champion of, 135
New life movement, 190
New Mexico, 13
New order in East Asia: as an idea, 208, 210–11; proclaimed, 203; U.S. reaction to, 204
New York Chamber of Commerce, 77–78
New Zealand, 335
Newsmen, exchange of, between U.S. and China, 308
Niijima Shimeta, 39, 40, 45
Nine Power Treaty: 144; Chinese Communist view of, 301
Nishihara loans, 132
Nitti, Francesco Saverio, 145
Nixon, Richard: 354, 355, 356, 357, 358, 361, 365, 370; and geopolitics in China policy, 349, 350; and Guam doctrine, 351
"Nixon shock," 349, 359–60
Nomura Kichisaburō, 219
Non-recognition policy: (1915) 134; (1930's) Chinese Communist view of, 301
Norman, Robert S., 160
North Atlantic Treaty Organization, 267, 290, 335, 371

North Korea, U.S. invasion of, 286
North Vietnam, 338, 354
Northern Expedition, 154, 155, 156
Norton, Charles Eliot, 58
Nuclear test-ban treaty, Chinese opposition to, 307
Nuclear weapons, Chinese development of, 306
Nye, Joseph: refutation of Paul Kennedy's views, 386–87

Ōhira Masayoshi: and Pacific Basin idea, 372; view of comprehensive security, 373
Oil shock, second (1979), 378
Okawa Shumei, 231
Okinawa: reversion from U.S. to Japan, 348
Ōkubo Toshimichi, 46, 47
Open Door, 358
Open Door policy: 80–81; Chinese response to, 82; Chinese view of, 172, 192, 199, 214, 303; expansion in meaning of, 119; Japanese response to, 82; nature of, 81; under Taft and Knox, 123
"Opening," of China and Japan, 7, 13, 16, 17
Opium War, 4, 12, 34
"Orange" war, 165, 204
Organization for Economic Cooperation and Development (OECD), 369
Organization of Petroleum Exporting Countries (OPEC), 364, 368
Oriental Development Company, 150, 151
Oxenberg, Michel, 376
Ozaki Hotsumi, 210

Pacific Basin, idea of, 372
Pacific war: and American–East Asian relations, 227; Chinese Communist view of, 301; Chinese view of, 232–33; consequences of, 250; interpretations of, 202; summary of military developments, 228
Pan-Asianism: (after Russo-Japanese War) 116, 117; (World War I) 132; (1920's) 153; (1930's) 173, 208–9; Chinese view of, 189, 193; and Japanese attack on U.S., 226; of Japanese navy, 131; rise of, in Japan, 50, 68
Panay incident, 194–95
Park, Chung Hee, 336, 370
Parker, Peter, 15, 34
Particularism, in Japan, 11
Peaceful coexistence: Chinese Communist view of, 306; and Kennedy, 313; Soviet policy of, 296; U.S. response, 296
Pearl Harbor: American reaction to Japanese attack, 239; construction of naval base at, 120; Japanese attack on, 202, 216, 226; Japanese view of attack on, 229–30; U.S. fleet at (1940–41), 217
Peck, Graham, 269
Peiping, Nationalist term for Peking, 291
Peking-Hankow railway, 75, 80
"Pentagon Papers," 354
People's diplomacy, 327
People's Liberation Army, 341
People's new democracy, 212–13
Perry, Matthew C.: expedition to Japan, 11, 12, 14, 16; in Japan, 15; Japanese response to, 23, 36, 45
Pescadores Islands, 299
Philippines: acquired by U.S., 67, 74, 78; American suppression of rebels, 85, 91; Chinese view of acquisition by U.S., 86; concern with security of, 78, 80, 81, 87, 89, 103, 107, 135; cooperation with Chinese Nationalists, 272; economic growth, 380; and Great East Asian Conference, 230; independence of, 182, 233; and Japanese aid, 372; Japanese ambitions in, 67, 74; and Lansing, 133
Phouma, Prince Souvanna, 314
Ping-pong players, Chinese and American, 354
Plan Dog, 216
Pnom Penh, 371
Pol Pot, 371
Poland, 295
Polycentrism, 308
Popular rights movement, in Japan, 48, 49
Portsmouth Peace Conference, 101; Japanese reaction to peace terms, 102
Portugal, 380
Potsdam Conference, 232
Powell, John B., 160
Protestantism, in America (19th century), 18
Public opinion, emergence of: in China, 84, 93, 94–95; in the West, 9
Pye, Lucian, 345

Quarantine speech, 197

Rainbow plans, 204, 216
Rambouillet, 369
Rankin, Karl Lott, 283
"Rape of Nanking" (1937), 389
Rapidan, 166, 171
Raymond, Andrew, 60
Reagan, Ronald, low-tax policy of, 379

Reform movements, in Ch'ing China, 41, 68–69, 76, 90, 93; in Communist China, 388–89
Reinsch, Paul S., 129, 133–34, 137
Reischauer, Edwin O., 318
Religious movements, as cultural phenomenon in 1970's, 373
Republican revolution: anti-Manchu revolutionaries, 85; course of events, 116, 125; and Hukuang loan, 125; turmoil of early years, 126–27; and U.S., 125
Reston, James, 354
Rhee, Syngman, 198, 336
Rights recovery movement, 96, 116
Rockhill, W. W., 80, 95
Roosevelt, Franklin Delano, 181; Chinese Communist view of, 275; and "four big policemen," 242, 243; and Germany and Italy, 187; naval construction programs, 182, 189; view of China during Pacific war, 243; view of East Asian crisis, 187–88; view of Japan, 197, 218; view of Pacific war, 238–39; and Yalta Conference, 243
Roosevelt, Theodore: and anti-Japanese agitation on west coast, 106; and Canton-Hankow railway dispute, 109; general policy in Asia, 122; naval expansion under, 120; policy on immigration, 120; policy toward China, 89, 103, 108, 121; policy toward Korea, 108; policy toward Manchuria, 108, 120, 123; and Russo-Japanese War, 99, 101; view of Chinese-Japanese relations, 119–20; view of East-West relations, 105–6; view of Japan, 107–8, 120, 123; view of Philippines, 107
Root-Takahira agreement, 115, 120–21
Rousseau, Jean-Jacques, 48
Rusk, Dean, 291, 315
Russia: expansion in Manchuria, 90; Japan's most likely enemy, 117; loans to China, 75; policy toward Japan, 66, 73, 90, 98; policy toward Korea, 98. *See also* Soviet Union
Russo-Japanese War: anti-Japanese sentiment in U.S. at end of, 83; Chinese response, 90; implications for U.S., 103; outbreak, 90, 98; peace settlement, 101; Straight's view, 122; and Yalta Conference, 243
Rutgers, the State University, New Jersey, 31
Ryūkyū Islands, 43, 294

Sakhalin Island, 101–2, 232
SALT II, 378
Samurai: response to Christianity, 37; view of the West, 37–38
San Francisco peace treaty (1951), 334, 335, 348
San Francisco system: 335, 336, 349, 351, 352, 355, 356, 371, 372
Santo Domingo, 128
Satō Eisaku, 347, 359–60, 361, 370
Satō Tetsutarō, 115
Scalapino, Robert A., 309, 345
Schlieffen, Count Alfred von, 54
Scholar-gentry class, in China, 37, 68
Schurman, Jacob G., minister to China, 149
Second Anglo-Chinese war, 35, 42
Security, *see* National security
Seeley, John R., 54
Self-strengthening, 41, 55–56
Senate Foreign Relations Committee, hearing on China, 323–24
Senate hearings (1966) on China, 344–45
Sendai, 72
Seward, William, 13, 29
Shambaugh, David, 377
Shanghai communiqué (Feb. 2, 1972), 355–57, 361–62
Shanghai coup (1927), 155, 159
Shanghai incident (1932), 174
Shanghai *Takungpao*, 199
Shantung: expeditions, 163; transfer of German rights in, to Japan, 132
Shantung question: in Japanese-American relations, 141; and President Wilson, 141; settlement of, 144
Sheng Hsüan-huai, 75
Shidehara Kijūrō: Japanese foreign minister after 1929, 166; and Manchurian incident, 175; policy toward Britain, 164; policy toward China, 164; policy toward U.S., 164, 175
Shufeldt, Robert W., 44
Sian incident: 183, 188, 190, 193; U.S. view of, 183
Siberian expedition: Japanese troops cut down, 142; U.S. policy toward Japan during, 136; urged by Japanese navy, 131; and Wilson, 135
Silver, U.S. sale of, to China, 167
Silver Purchase Act, 190, 197
Simpson, Jerry, 77
Singapore: 201; economic growth in 1980's, 380
Sino-Japanese War: (1894–95) 66, 69, 73; (1937–45) military actions, 194, 196; develops into Pacific war, 201–2

Sino-Soviet dispute: 335; border clashes, 352; impact on American-Chinese relations, 305–6; implications for Japanese-American relations, 310; Kennedy's policy toward, 313; U.S. view of, 308–9
Smith, Adam, 7
Smith, Arthur H., 79, 118–19
Snow, Edgar, 354
Social Darwinism, 59
Social gospel, 79
Socialism: in America, 72; in Japan, 72
Sojourners, 30
Sokolsky, George, 293
Soong, T. V., 190, 242, 245
South Asia, 391
South Korea: (after 1961) 315; cooperation with Nationalists, 272; export to U.S., 381; postwar economic growth, 336, 380
South Manchuria, transfer of Russian rights to Japan, 101
South Manchuria Railway: proposed U.S. loan to, 155; U.S. competition with 123
South Vietnam, 337, 338
Southeast Asia: economic growth in 1980's, 380; in Japanese-American relations, 201; U.S. involvement in, 347, 350, 352, 357, 371; U.S. view of Chinese ambitions in, 342; viewed as part of San Francisco system, 337
Southeast Asia Treaty Organization (SEATO): and ASEAN, 372; as collective security system for Indochina, 371, 335; dissolution (1977), 371; organized, 295
Southern advance: and American response, 201, 216; and German victories, 201 Japanese plans for, 175, 201, 207–8
Soviet Union: after Pacific war, 250–51; entrance into war against Japan, 228; forces in Siberia, 175; in geopolitical logic in U.S. China policy, 350; and human rights, 373; invasion of Afghanistan, 369, 370, 378; invasion of Czechoslovakia, 352; and Korean War, 285; and Manchurian incident, 173; new diplomacy, 138; peaceful coexistence policy, 303, 306; policy in Eastern Europe, 252, 253; policy of dealing with Chungking, 237; policy toward China: (1918–21) 143, (1933–37) 190, (1945) 252–53; policy toward Japan (1950's), 310–11 postwar aids to China, 339
Spain, 193
Spanish-American War, 69, 71
Spykman, Nicholas J.: 242–43; Chinese view of, 234
Stalin, Joseph, at Yalta Conference, 243
Stark, Harold R., 216
Stilwell, Joseph: 236; condemns China's inefficiency, 248; recalled, 237, 301; and vision of postwar world, 242
Stimson, Henry L.: and Manchurian incident, 171, 178–79; non-recognition doctrine, 174; view of China, 166; view of Japan, 166, 179; and world economic crisis, 167, 206
Stoddard, T. Lothrop, 140
Straight, Michael, 245
Straight, Willard: against Japanese control of Manchuria, 121; proposal for a stronger policy in Asia, 122; and Taft-Knox policy, 122; view of China, 122; view of Japan, 103–5
Strong, Anna Louise, 263
Stuart, John L., 272
Subic Bay (Luzon), 107
Suez Canal, 14
Sun Ch'uan-fang, 154
Sun Fo, 224–25, 232–33, 234
Sun Yat-sen: death of, 153; and Germany, 148; and Japan, 148; and pan-Asianism, 193; and Russia, 148; view of U.S., 147–48; and Yüan, 125, 126
Sung Chiao-jen, 129
Switzerland, 367

Taft, William Howard: 327; and the China market, 109, 121; moralistic diplomacy in East Asia, 122–24; view of Japan, 123
Taiping rebellion, 16, 34, 40
Taiwan: 15; Chinese Communist view, 302; defense of, by U.S., 291, 299, 308, 345; export to U.S., 381; Formosan expedition (1874), 43; Japanese acquisition of, 66–67, 78; Japanese expansionism in, 66; postwar economic growth, 336, 380; and U.N., 355, 360
Taiwan question, in Sino-U.S. accommodation, 356–57, 358
Taiwan Straits, 351, 357
Takahashi Korekiyo, 152
Takahira Kogorō, 87, 98, 101
Takamura Kōtarō, 229
Takano Fusatarō, 72
Tanaka Giichi: on continentalism, 116; policy toward China, 163–64; view of U.S., 116–17
Tanaka Kakuei: 361; and cultural diplomacy, 373–74
T'ang Shao-yi, 124
Tariff, autonomy: 48; revision, 154
Taylor, Bayard, 23

Teng Hsiao-ping: U.N. address (1974), 371
Terrill, Ross, 376
Texas, 13
Thailand, and Japanese aid, 372
Three people's principles, 154
Tiananmen Square, 388
Tientsin, Sino-American treaty of (1858), 42
Tokutomi Roka, 112–13
Tokutomi Sohō, 115
Tonkin Gulf resolution, repeal of, 354
Trans-Siberian Railroad, 66
Treasury Department, and China, 190, 197
Treaty revision: China's effort at (1920's), 154, 156–57; Japan's effort at, 47, 50, 73; U.S. Policy toward, 165
Tripartite intervention, 66, 73, 75
"Triple deficits," in U.S., 379, 385
Truman, Harry S.: and China, 255; decision to intervene in Korea, 286, 287; MacArthur, controversy with, 288–89; policy criticized, 269; policy toward Asia assayed, 268; view of China, 288, 291; and Wake Island Conference, 287
Tseng Kuo-fan, 34–35
Tseng Shao-ch'ing, 95
Tsinan incident, 156, 163
Tsungli Yamen, 42
Tsushima Islands, 66
T'ung-chih restoration, 34
Twenty-One Demands: 132; Chinese policy during, 136
Two-Chinas policy: under Eisenhower, 295–96; under Kennedy, 307; origins of, 299
Tyler, John, 14

Uchimura Kanzō, 72, 100
Unconditional surrender, formula of 240
Unequal treaties, 14, 49
United Front (1930's), 183, 188
United Nations: 334–35; admittance of PRC, 354–55; and principles of human rights, 373; question of Chinese representation in, 283, 308, 317
United States: accessibility of markets by Asia, 381; and Asian economic miracle (1980's), 380–81; Asian-Pacific strategy, 335; attitude toward Nationalist-Communist struggle, 247–48; and boat people, 382; and China: confrontation, 341, cultural exchanges, 375, exchange programs, 390, rapprochement, 334, 354–57, 359, 362, 371, 373, rapprochement, underlying causes of, 350–51; collaboration with Britain in Asia, 17; consumer preference of Japanese goods, 383–84; cultural revolution in, 343–44; declinist argument, 385–86; defense spending (1980's), compared, 380; economic problems since 1960's, 346; economic supremacy challenged, 334; economy (early 1970's), 363–64; emergence as a Pacific power, 74, 82; fiscal deficits (since 1970's), 379; fleet in Pacific, 174, 217; foreign investments and loans in (since 1970's), 379; imports from Asia (1980's), 381; investments in China, 165; and Japan: economic relations, 364–66, peace treaty (1960), 336, security treaty, 359, 360, self-perceptions (1960's and 1970's) compared, 348–49, trade, 117, 152, trade friction since 1980's, 382–83, 385, 390; and Korea, 335, 370; and Korean War, 281, 284, 285–87, 290–92; loans to China, 150; loans to Japan, 150, 152; military planning (1939–41), 204, 216–17; and Nationalists, 157, 158, 160, 161, 165, 246–48, 256; navy's view of China, 78–79, 88; navy's view of Japan, 78, 165, 182, 196; openness of society, 382; peace treaty with Japan, 294; and Philippines, 335; policy during Boxer uprising, 87–88, 89; policy during Sino-Japanese War (1937–45), 195–97, 199–200; policy regarding Chinese representation in U.N., 308, 317; policy toward India, 314; policy toward Laos, 314; policy toward Manchuria, 102; policy toward Manchurian crisis, 178, 180; policy toward Okinawa, 284; policy toward Philippines, 284; policy toward Republican China, 126, 127, 129; policy toward Southeast Asia, 284; policy toward Taiwan, 284, 292, 295, 316–17; postwar policy toward Eastern Europe, 254, 292; postwar policy toward Soviet Union, 253, 255, 264, 287, 290; purchase of silver from China, 190; and recognition of PRC, 334; response to Japan's southern advance, 217; revisionist view of foreign policy, 344; and Russo-Japanese War, 99, 101, 102, 104–5; and SEATO, 335; and security in Asia, 372; and Sino-Japanese War (1894–95), 73, 80; and South Korea, 295; and Soviet Union: 188, 191, 243, 247, 252, 337, arms negotiation, 334, 339, 373, 378, condemnation of Iraqi invasion of Kuwait, 379, detente, 378; as spokesman of principles of rights and freedom, 390;

stereotypes of Japan and China, 391; as supplier of capital, 117; and Taiwan, 335, 364, 370; as target of Chinese nationalism, 93; trade with Asia, 4, 13, 14, 16, 77; trade with China, 77, 110, 121, 165, 364; and U.N. admittance of PRC, 354–55; and Vietnam: 333, 334, anti-war ideology, 342–43, anti-war protests, 342, military withdrawal, 351, Paris peace talks (1968), 352, view of its role in, 341, *see also* Vietnam War; view of Asia, 13, 17, 182, 185, 240, 265, 298, 315; view of (and/or policy toward) China: (pre-1840) 5, 10, (1840–80) 13, 16, 17, 22, 23–24, 28, (1880–1900) 62, 89, (1900–1912) 103, 109, 110, 112, 188, 119, 123, 124, 127, (1912–18) 135, 136–37, 141, (1921–31) 144–45, 149, (1931–41) 179–80, 181, 182, 183, 184, 198, 205, 222, (Pacific war) 240, 241–42, 243, 244, 246, 247, 248–49, 251, (1945–50) 154, 155–58, 251, 265, 267, 268, 269, 271, 282, 283, (1950's) 292–94, 295, 298–99, (since 1960's) 312, 315–18, 321, 323, 329, 333–34, 335, 337, 338, 358–59; view of Chinese Communists, 183–84, 246–48, 265–66, 287, 290–92, 309, 314, 317–18; view of Chinese-Japanese crisis, 166; view of Communism, 258, 267, 268; view of East-West relations, 59–64, 82, 105, 118; view of itself, 6, 7, 58, 59; view of (and/or policy toward) Japan: (1840–80) 13, 17, 22, 23–24, 25, 26, 27, 31–32, 47, (1880–1900) 62, 77, 78, (1900–1905) 98, 104–5, 110, 112, (1905–21) 117–18, 119, 127, 134, 139, 140, (1921–31) 145, 151, 165–66, (1931–41) 181, 197, 205, 207, 217, 219–20, 222, (Pacific war) 239, (postwar) 254, 265, 284, 294–95, (since 1960's) 318, 328, 359, 365–66; view of Japanese trade practices, 383–85; view of postwar world, 240, 252; view of Russia, 89; view of Sun Yat-sen, 126; view of Yüan Shih-k'ai, 126, 129, 136–37; and Washington Conference , 144–45; and World War II, 228, 238–39, 241, 244, 250
University of Michigan, 31

Versailles treaty, U.S. opposition to, 141
Vietcong, 338
Vietnam: 372; conflict with Cambodia, 382; independence of, visualized by Chinese, 233; unification of, 371
Vietnam War: 292, 321–22, 333, 339, 345, 346, 347, 348, 349, 351, 357, 371, 382; effects on U.S. economy, 364; and Korean War compared, 338; and U.S.-China confrontation, 341–42, 337
Vietnamese, 338, 349, 390
Vogel, Ezra: on U.S.-Japan relations, 387
Vrijheid, 12

Wake Island, annexed to U.S., 74
Wake Island Conference, 287
Wallace, Henry A., 235
Wang, C. T., 149
Wang Ching-wei, 211
War Plan Orange, 120
War scares, between U.S. and Japan, 118
Ward, Frederick Townsend, 34
Warlords, and nationalism, 149, 154
"Wars of liberation," 306
Warsaw, meetings between U.S. and Chinese representatives, 308
Warsaw Pact, 371
Washington, George, 38, 126
Washington Conference: and American-East Asian relations, 143; Chinese Communist view of, 301
Washington Naval Treaty, 175
Washington powers, co-operation among, 151
Wedemeyer, Albert C.: Chinese Communist view of, 301; and Nationalists, 248; succeeds Stilwell, 236
West: American view of, 58–60, 85; Chinese view of, 9, 69–70, 71, 76, 91, 110, 146; Japanese view of, 45, 46, 139, 174, 229, 230
West coast: anti-Japanese agitation, 151; Japanese view of, 152
Westernization: in China, 68, 70, 79, 82; in Japan, 25, 38, 64–65, 67, 326
Westward movement, 4, 13
White, Harry Dexter, 220
White, Theodore H., 257
Whiting, Allen, 345
Whitman, Walt, 31
Williams, E. T.: head of Far Eastern division of State Department, 129; view of China, 134; view of Japan, 134, 140
Williams, Samuel Wells, 20
Willkie, Wendell, 240–41, 248
Wilson, Woodrow: basic policy orientation, 127–28, 138; and Lansing-Ishii agreement, 133; "new diplomacy," 128, 135, 327; and Shantung, 141; view of China, 128; and Yüan's imperial ambitions, 137

Wilsonianism, 358
World cruise, by U.S. navy, 115
World economic crisis (1929), 167
World War II, in Europe, 202
Wu, C. C., 156, 159
Wu Ting-fang, 156

Yale University, 39
Yalta Conference, 243, 251, 273, 356
Yamagata Aritomo, 56, 65, 66
Yang Fang, 35
Yang Shu, 92
Yano Ryūkei, 100
Yarnell, Harry E., 196
Yeh Ming-ch'en, 34
Yellow peril, 90, 99, 104
Yen Fu, 69–70, 76
Yen Hsi-shan, 272–73
Yenan, 237, 301
Yoshida Shigeru, 277, 294, 336
Young, John Russell, 27, 62
Young America, 5
Young China, 129, 138
Yüan Shih-k'ai: death of, 137; imperial ambitions, 136–37; and republican revolution, 125, 126–27; view of Japan, 92, 124; view of U.S., 124, 136
Yung Hung, *see* Yung Wing
Yung Wing, 39–40

Zaibatsu, dissolution of, 239